HITLER'S BRANDENBURGERS

Brandenburger troops searching for Greek guerrillas in the Balkans in 1944

HITLER'S BRANDENBURGERS

The Third Reich's Elite Special Forces

Lawrence Paterson

Foreword by David R. Higgins

Greenhill Books

Naval Institute Press
Annapolis, Maryland

Hitler's Brandenburgers: The Third Reich's Elite Special Forces

Greenhill Books

Greenhill Books, c/o Pen & Sword Books Ltd,
47 Church Street, Barnsley, S. Yorkshire, S70 2AS
For more information on our books, please visit
www.greenhillbooks.com, email contact@greenhillbooks.com
or write to us at the above address.

Published and distributed in the United States of America and Canada by the
Naval Institute Press, 291 Wood Road, Annapolis, Maryland 21402-5043
www.nip.org

Text copyright © Lawrence Paterson, 2018
Foreword copyright © David R. Higgins, 2018

The right of Lawrence Paterson to be identified as the author of this work has been asserted in accordance with Section 77 of the Copyrights Designs and Patents Act 1988.

CIP data records for this title are available from the British Library
Library of Congress Cataloging Number: 2018932808

Greenhill Books ISBN 978-1-78438-228-5
Naval Institute Press ISBN 978-1-68247-372-6

Typeset and designed in 10.5pt Minion Pro
by JCS Publishing Services Ltd
Printed and bound in England by TJ International Ltd, Padstow, Cornwall

Contents

List of Plates		vii
Foreword by David R. Higgins		ix
Introduction		xv
Glossary and Abbreviations		xix
Comparative Rank Table		xxiii
Prelude	The Concept Behind the Brandenburger Regiment	1
1	Baptism of Fire	15
2	Operation '*Weserübung*' and 'Case Yellow': Scandinavia and the West	33
3	The Regiment Brandenburg	56
4	Declared and Undeclared War in the Balkans	73
5	Hitler Turns East: The Invasion of the Soviet Union	86
6	War in the Desert	111
7	Rebuilding	145
8	'Case Blue'/Operation '*Braunschweig*': The 1942 Summer Offensive in the Soviet Union	158
9	Regeneration, 1943	184
10	Partisan Warfare in the Balkans	228
11	Metamorphosis, 1944–1945	256
Appendix	Major Decorations Awarded	287
Notes		291
Bibliography		302
Index		305

Plates

1. *Kampforganisation Jablunka* photographed before the attack on Poland
2. A second photo taken at the same time
3. Theodor von Hippel
4. Officers of the *Deutsche Kompanie* in their Slovakian base at Sliač, August 1939
5. *Hauptmann* Hans-Jürgen Rudloff inspecting his men of the *3rd Baulehr Kompanie z.b.V. 800*
6. A bridge over the Juliana Canal, captured by *Leutnant* Hermann Kürschner's West Platoon
7. The Gennep railway bridge after its capture by *Oberleutnant* Uwe-Wilhelm Walther's *4th Baulehr Kompanie z.b.V. 800*
8. The Nieuport bridge after its capture by *Leutnant* Siegfried Grabert's assault group on the night of 27 May 1940
9. Grabert's original drawing of the new regiment's insignia
10. Siegfried Grabert
11. Deputy Führer Rudolf Hess greeting Knight's Cross holders
12. Not all bridges were captured intact; this one over the Drava River was successfully destroyed by retreating Yugoslavian troops, 1941
13. Uwe-Wilhelm Walther
14. The raising of the flag over the Acropolis in Athens by Brandenburgers
15. *Oberstleutnant* Paul Haehling von Lanzenauer and *Major* Friedrich Wilhelm Heinz
16. Ukrainian troops of the Nachtigall Battalion in training at Neuhammer
17. A destroyed Brandenburger vehicle next to a disabled Soviet BT7 light tank
18. Brandenburger troops in Soviet uniform during the opening day of Operation '*Barbarossa*'
19. The sheer volume of Soviet prisoners taken during '*Barbarossa*' was staggering

20 *Feldwebel* Willi Hein and *Leutnant* Oskar Schatz in full Soviet disguise
21 Casualties within the regiment were relatively heavy
22 A *Fallschirmjäger* wearing an early pattern army belt buckle
23 The grave *Leutnant* Hermann Lütke and his fellow *Fallschirmjäger*
24 *Oberleutnant* Hans-Wolfram Knaak
25 The grave of Knaak and four of his men
26 Nachtigall troops on the streets of Lviv at the end of June
27 Checking a dusty Russian road for mines
28 An officer of the '*Azad Hid Fauj*' (Free India Army) at *Regenwurmlager*
29 The Free India Army was raised in Germany and trained as part of the Brandenburgers
30 Friedrich 'Fritz' von Koenen
31 Brandenburgers of the 13th Company using captured Allied vehicles
32 *Rittmeister* Conrad von Leipzig
33 Brandenburger troops in North Africa
34 An LWSI of the Tropical Company during rehearsals with *Kampfgruppe Hecker*
35 Tobruk finally fell to Rommel's forces in June 1942
36 *Hauptmann* Count László Almásy and *Major* Nikolaus Ritter
37 Ritter and Almásy brief Luftwaffe pilots for the disastrous flight into Egypt during June 1941
38 Brandenburger troops returning to German lines
39 Odo Wilscher
40 Light vehicle of the 13th (Tropical) Company, equipped with a single 20mm flak cannon
41 Car emblazoned with the emblem of *Sonderkommando Blaich*
42 A soldier of the 'Free Arabia Legion'
43 Brandenburger recruits for the *Kustenjäger Abteilung*
44 Identity card of a Soviet prisoner of war recruited into the Brandenburger Regiment
45 *Admiral* Wilhelm Canaris on a visit to Brandenburg units at the front lines in Russian, October 1941
46 *Leutnant* Trommsdorf and Finnish troops
47 Brandenburgers kayaking towards the Murmansk railway line, August 1942
48 Adjusting the small outboard motor aboard one of the Brandenburgers' kayaks

49 Brandenburgers in Finland used a mixture of German, Soviet and Finnish uniform and equipment
50 Fritz Babuke
51 Chief instructor *Leutnant zur See* Alfred von Wurzian and *Gebirgsjäger Hauptmann* Fritz Neitzert (middle) was the Abteilung's first commander
52 The Brandenburger *Meeresjäger Abteilung* on parade in Piazza Dante, Valdagno, 1944
53 'Case Blue', the advance into the Caucasus in pursuit of oil, spearheaded by Brandenburger units
54 Alexander von Pfuhlstein with *Generalmajor* Karl von Graffen
55 *Admiral* Canaris inspecting Brandenburger troops with Friedrich Wilhelm Heinz and Alexander von Pfuhlstein
56 An NCO briefing during the advance of 'Case Blue'
57 Cooperation between Brandenburg and Romanian forces had begun before the invasion of the Soviet Union
58 Siegfried Grabert's death in action announced in the newspaper *Die Bewegung*
59 Adrian Baron von Fölkersam
60 Fighting for the oil transport depots in the Caucasus, 1942
61 The bridge over the Bjelaja named after *Leutnant d.R.* Ernst Prochaska
62 *Oberleutnant* Karl-Heinz Oesterwitz
63 Kurt Konrad Steidl
64 The huge stone eagle that guarded the entrance gate to the Regenwurm training camp
65 Personnel in training at *Regenwurmlager*
66 The brutality of anti-partisan warfare became an increasingly common theatre of action for the Brandenburgers
67 Brandenburgers were used in the inhospitable forests and marshes that surrounded the Prip'yat' River to fight Soviet partisans in 1944
68 *Jäger* of the Brandenburger Division receiving fresh winter clothing
69 Men of the *Kustenjäger Abteilung* at sea on the Adriatic aboard a heavy *Sturmboot*
70 *Leutnant* Helmut Demetrio and his French men of the 8th Company, II Battalion
71 An Italian soldier of the Blackshirt III 'M' Assault Battalion '9 September (Pontida)'
72 Brandenburger troops were committed to searching for and fighting Greek guerrillas

73 Brandenburgers and Chetniks, uneasy allies of convenience – most of the time
74 Brandenburgers question captured Yugoslavian Partisans
75 Well armed, disciplined and well organised, the communist Partisans that followed Marshal Josip Broz Tito were formidable adversaries
76 Brandenburgers in action in Yugoslavia, 1943
77 Brandenburger *Fallschirmjäger* rowing ashore on Levitha
78 Brandenburger troops during the fighting for Leros, November 1943
79 Troops of the 1st Company, *Kustenjäger Abteilung* on Monte Racchi, Leros
80 Relaxing once the fighting had ended on Leros
81 Brandenburgers displaying an interesting mix of uniforms, Leros, 1943
82 Wilhelm Walther with *Oberleutnant* Max Wandrey and *General der Flieger* Helmuth Felmy
83 Brandenburger troops boarding a *Marinefahrprähme* in the Dodecanese, 1943
84 *Oberleutnant* Werner Lau, II Battalion, 4th Regiment 'Brandenburg'
85 *Major* Karl-Heinz Oesterwitz
86 Friedrich 'Fritz' Kühlwein
87 Brandenburger PaK40 of the 2nd Regiment in action against Yugoslavian Partisans
88 Otto Skorzeny in Budapest, 1944
89 Dawn on the Eastern Front.
90 The Brandenburg cuff title

Photos 27, 47, 48, 49, 51, 52, 58, 69, 73, 83, 84, 90: Author's collection
Photo 70: ECPA Paris
Photo 9: John Edward DeMicoli
Photo 43: U-Boot Archiv, Altenbruch
All other photos: Bundesarchiv

Foreword by David R. Higgins

For all the attention production numbers, vehicle firepower and tactics receive as factors in achieving battlefield success, such results were often contingent on the covert, unconventional actions of small teams of specially selected, highly-trained and motivated, and largely unsung warriors. Whatever quality of arms and quantity of material a modern army possesses, its reliance on a host of arguably unglamorous necessities – such as logistics and manufacturing, or less tangible assets like security, morale and sleep – to function effectively can become targeted as a vulnerability or liability. For all the effort allocated to protecting these valuable resources and services, the need for human beings in the mix, with all their insecurities, fears, greed, obedience to authority, and a host of other potentially exploitable attributes, can represent a military's greatest weakness given the right circumstances and psychological incentives. With the right combination of leadership, planning, audacity, creativity and cunning, a determined adversary conducting effective covert missions involving long-range reconnaissance, sabotage, assassination, propaganda, infiltration and other similar tasks can cumulatively disrupt an enemy's ability to sustain itself in the field, impede its command and control, and undermine resolve. If implemented correctly, such behind-the-lines actions can produce decisive outcomes out of all proportion to initial expenditures.

Considering that 'All warfare is based on deception,' Sun Tzu's further postulation that 'The supreme art of war is to subdue the enemy without fighting' encapsulates the potential of the indirect, unanticipated attack as the foundation upon which victory is achieved. Typically, asymmetrical warfare has been associated with insurgency or guerrilla forces. Due to their comparative inferiority to a conventional, established adversary, the use of hit-and-run strikes and attacking targets of opportunity offer a cost-effective way to sow confusion, achieve a degree of battlefield parity, and generally wage war – provided sufficient time and resolve exist to achieve a positive political solution. Although irregular actions have always been a combat fixture, during the Second World War several nations established what were collectively called commandos, a designation derived from the teams of Dutch Afrikaner fighters that fought the British during the Boer Wars. Historically, militaries have contained an often considerable number of internal elements resistant to deviation from established, conventional solutions to contemporary battlefield problems, whether due to their unproven potential, inherent risks, or simply an aversion to bending or breaking recognised laws of combat or what may be seen as 'unsportsmanlike' actions. Officially integrating unconventional assets into the ranks, and keeping numbers relatively small to maintain high-quality personnel and peak combat effectiveness, offered a considerable combat asset. While the First World War's victorious nations were free to develop post-war unconventional forces unhindered, their collective branding of Germany as the conflict's aggressor resulted in a host of punitive measures designed to leave the country militarily and economically prostrate. Forced to rebuild its military in secret, what became Germany's first special forces group originated within the Ministry of Defence's Abwehr section responsible for sabotage.

The force was at first under the experienced and creative leadership of men like Theodor von Hippel and Helmuth Groscurth, who were both as committed to defending Germany as they were to the fight against Communism and Hitler's regime. Initially established in company strength just after the 1939 Polish campaign, the Brandenburgers were incrementally expanded in size to manage additional roles and responsibilities, as they operated not only within the battlezones of conventional ground forces, but well beyond, in areas including Afghanistan, Iraq and South Africa. Many Brandenburger operations proved unsuccessful, due either to their own actions or orders from men outside the organisation, including Hitler. Those who achieved their goals greatly facilitated friendly efforts in several major campaigns, especially in France and the Soviet Union. For such undertakings only volunteers were suitable, as fear, pain and coercion were poor incentivisers to get soldiers to achieve the impossible on the battlefield. With many members having come from regions subjected to the brutalities of Soviet occupation, vengeance and payback were frequently key motivators in the east.

Considering the secretive nature of the Brandenburgers and their operations – not to mention that so many documents and other related primary material were destroyed by Allied strategic bombing or regime personnel attempting to eradicate incriminating evidence, or were simply lost – the production of such an authoritative work is remarkable. This book goes a long way towards clarifying a complex, often murky, subject, and treats the reader to in-depth coverage of the formation's origins, organisation and actions. Too often the victors write the history books, resulting in varying degrees of bias and a desire to highlight the positive and minimise the negative. To history's benefit Lawrence Paterson avoids any such disservice and provides a very informative, enlightening, and balanced account of what is an early example of a modern special forces organisation that provided a framework from which future such formations would benefit, especially during wartime. As an early example of a modern special forces organisation, the Brandenburgers provided a framework from which subsequent formations would benefit, especially during wartime.

Ever since I was a kid I've had a great interest in military history, an itch I scratched by reading books from the weekly neighbourhood bookmobile, building and painting model tanks, ships and aircraft, and family vacations that regularly included visits to American Civil War battlefields. Over the years something that bothered me was that many books seemed to slant in favour of one particular side, to the exclusion of pertinent facts. While it is understandable that the victors would desire to present their adversaries as two-dimensional characterisations, such a complex subject as warfare is never black and white. With the passage of time old resentments and attitudes tend to mellow, which, in combination with the uncovering of new source material, can present a revised, more accurate assessment of the subject. A case in point was the access to Soviet archives in the years following the USSR's collapse – an unfortunately limited window of opportunity.

As a student of military history and technology, in particular the Second World War in Europe, I found the literature authoritative and insightful, but also effectively disseminated, crafted, polished and presented. I know how difficult it can be to reach the truth of a matter, particularly when it involves the chaotic, complex nature of combat. A non-fiction book's narrative should fit the facts, and not the other way around; every effort must be made to get to as close to the truth of a matter as possible, and any attempt to cherry-pick and selectively present information should naturally be treated as suspect. The process of tracking down pertinent primary material on esoteric subjects, especially that which can be verified by other reliable sources, is time-consuming and often tedious, but when real gems are uncovered and a quality product such as *Hitler's Brandenburgers* results, such considerable efforts are eminently worthwhile for both author and reader. As an author of military history and technology books and articles and a television contributor on armoured vehicles, what matters most to me is that I have been given an opportunity to preserve and present the deeds of men who have confronted the horrors of war and for a variety of reasons and motivations continued to perform their duties. Having written about the Brandenburgers and their audacious 1942 mission into the Northern Caucasus that infiltrated the front line to secure valuable Soviet oil resources and undermine resistance ahead of the German advance into the area, I feel I have particular insight into both subjects.

Perhaps best known for his engaging books on often under-reported U-Boat, Kriegsmarine, and Luftwaffe maritime subjects, and the insightful coverage of related technologies, Lawrence Paterson has more recently directed his detective talents towards early modern special forces. In addition to covering the fledgling British SAS and their participation in the Second World War's first commando operation (Colossus), his work on Germany's Brandenburgers brings the same high standards and balanced coverage to an all-too-neglected subject. Examining the organisation from its rather ad hoc beginnings as Battalion Ebbinghaus, through the much more professional, effective and determined Brandenburg iteration to its transition to a conventional fighting formation, the book represents a fitting tribute to Germany's clandestine warriors, and a guarantee that their extraordinary efforts have not been relegated to comparative obscurity or entirely forgotten.

David R. Higgins
Columbus, Ohio, US

Introduction

The history of the 'Brandenburgers' is a complex interweave of Wehrmacht, Abwehr and Waffen SS operations. There are some previously published works that examine this most unusual unit; some of them truly excellent, others less so. There can be an undeniable tendency to exaggerate events that did happen, invent some that didn't and appropriate yet others that may have occurred but were not actually undertaken by the 'Brandenburgers' themselves. I have attempted to stay away from the hyperbole that the unit attracts and to verify stories from as many different sources as possible, using original documentation, if available, first-hand accounts, scholarly articles and research papers and, of course, other reliable secondary sources.

Please note that I have anglicised much of the German terminology within this book. Included in this is the fact that in German, both the singular and plural for Brandenburger are the same. However, I have used the plural form 'Brandenburgers' for the benefit of English readers. I would also like to point out that, unless otherwise stated, all translations from German are my own.

To fully explore the story of this unit, it is essential to look at some of the characters that provided its genesis. It is important to understand the original motivation behind the 'Brandenburgers' as it then becomes apparent how far from its original purpose it strayed as it grew in stature to a degree that was almost directly in inverse proportion to its diminishing usefulness as a true commando unit. While some people figure throughout the entire story, most have a more finite influence on events, especially those involved from the very beginning. However, it can be difficult to trace what happened to some of these men as the records relating to their service history are frequently missing. Perhaps the perfect example is that of Theodor von Hippel, the man who first created the original commando unit after lobbying his superiors. His tenure with the Brandenburgers is well documented, but his subsequent career less so, until it reaches the point that the date of his death is difficult to ascertain, a published work of 1974 quoting a letter from him dated 30 October 1968. Perhaps to fully examine this one man's history would require a book of its own. Other people are mentioned briefly and sometimes only by surname, before disappearing from the story. This can sometimes be unavoidable with incomplete Wehrmacht service records of the unit itself and is not helped by the occasional use of cover names. However, I hope that the reader can look past that and see the general picture of events.

Some written accounts have tried to 'novelise' the events in this book. I do not like that and have avoided it at all costs. This isn't a novel; I don't know if the ground that they were lying on was wet, I don't know if the taste of fear was in their mouths and I don't know if they chatted about home before going into action. While I appreciate that this approach can sometimes bring events to life, I don't believe it is the correct approach for a book of this type. If possible – and relevant – I've included direct quotes that can be attributed to people, either from their own memoirs, letters or verifiable quotations from books such as that written by Helmuth Spaeter, a wartime officer in the *Grossdeutschland* Division, historical archivist of that formation and related units and leader of the *Grossdeutschland* Veterans' Association. His major work on the Brandenburgers includes many first-hand accounts from letters and diaries that provide much information.

Another complexity is the frequent overlap between operations mounted by the SS, SD, Abwehr, Wehrmacht and Brandenburgers. Germany's intelligence apparatus, of which the Brandenburgers were originally a component, was a labyrinthine mess of competing organisations, each with its own agenda, bias and opportunistic goals. This was extremely common within the Third Reich and appears to be a hallmark of such totalitarian leaders as they pit their subordinates against one another in a bid to remain unassailable themselves. Many operations mounted by the Abwehr (German military intelligence) have been attributed to the Brandenburgers. Unfortunately, this is frequently not accurate. Often there are individual Brandenburger-trained men involved in such operations, but they are not *specifically* Brandenburger missions. This confusion arises from the fact that the unit was used as a 'catch-all' pot in which to place potential agents and saboteurs for training and even to provide a 'home unit' while they acted independently outside of Brandenburger control. These I have tried to avoid in this book as they lead off in directions away from the core study that this is supposed to be. Similarly, there were missions mounted by the SS security services that borrowed heavily from Brandenburger methods and, sometimes, personnel. These are also outside of the central narrative.

Individual Brandenburger men were found in virtually every theatre of war that Germany fought in during the Second World War. As the term 'Brandenburger' (justifiably) summons up an image of daring commando operations, it is often overused if even the most tenuous link can be found. I have tried to move past that and concentrate solely on the unit that started as a small group of volunteers and eventually reached divisional status.

From 1943 onward, the 'Brandenburg' Division was largely used as a traditional light infantry unit. There was still some measure of special operations throughout 1943, but these lessened considerably in the year that followed. Indeed, during April 1944 it became the Panzergrenadier Division 'Brandenburg' and was involved in fierce fighting against Tito's Partisans and then on the Eastern Front where it ended its last days of combat. This period I have not covered as I have chosen to focus upon the 'special operations' nature of the Brandenburgers' story. However, I have included a little more information about an SS unit to which many Brandenburgers transferred at the point when they realised they were to be converted into 'ordinary' soldiers. That formation was Otto Skorzeny's SS *Jagdverbände* that originated from a direct Waffen SS/SD attempt to rival the Abwehr's 'Brandenburg' Regiment. While the study of *Jagdverbände* activity included here is certainly not exhaustive, it flows from the narrative point of view directly from events preceding it and involves some of the central characters of the story up to that point.

The Brandenburgers were a unique part of the Wehrmacht. This is their history.

Acknowledgements

I'd like to take the opportunity to thank a few people who have helped with this project. Firstly, my wife Anna and children Megan and James who put up with the tribulations of being around an obsessive author. Thanks to Audrey 'Mumbles' Paterson for constant support from the other side of the world. Also, thanks to Michael Leventhal, my esteemed publisher. Greenhill is back! Countless friends have also helped me along in more ways than I can list and I'd like to thank them all for that. I'd also like to single out some people who directly assisted with aspects of this manuscript: Sakis Nikas in Greece for an illuminating discussion about events there during the war; John Edward DeMicoli and his son Leighton John in Malta, for a glimpse at the treasure trove of Siegfried Grabert's letters (see: https://youtu.be/u5FLrUtYCXE); Karin and Ted von Hippel; Don Pawsey for coming to the rescue with Finnish translation.

Over the course of several years I have had the good fortune to communicate with many veterans of the Second World War. Sadly, most of them are no longer with us. Nonetheless, the time I spent in their company continues to inspire me not only to write these books, but to also try and get them as accurate as I can to what actually happened. I would like to mention a few of these people once again here and thank them and their families for the time they spent teaching me about events that took place so many decades ago. My eternal gratitude to: Jürgen Oesten; Hans-Rudolf Rösing; Erich Topp; Gerhard Buske; Georg Seitz; Manfred Fischer; Hans-Joachim Krug; Ernst Gothling; Horst Bredow; Wolfgang Hirschfeld; Bernard Geissman; Fritz Weinrich; Volmaar König; Ludwig Stoll. Thanks to Frau Hanne Suhren and Gesa Suhren for memorable evenings in Hamburg. Plus, a special thanks to Jürgen Weber and the München U-bootskameradschaft of which I was honoured to be a member.

I'd like to dedicate this book, once more, to Lemmy and to Bruce West, one of New Zealand's finest.

Glossary and Abbreviations

Abwehr – German military intelligence. Divided into three sections:
   Abteilung I: Military and economic espionage ('Abwehr I').
   Abteilung II: Sabotage and insurgency ('Abwehr II').
   Abteilung III: Counter-espionage and Wehrmacht security ('Abwehr III').
der Reserve – Suffix to officer rank denoting 'of the Reserve'. Normally indicates assignment to a *Wehrkreis* headquarters.
EK I – *Eisen Kreuz I* (Iron Cross First Class).
EK II – *Eisen Kreuz II* (Iron Cross Second Class).
FAK – *Frontaufklärungskommando*; mobile reconnaissance units.
FFI – *Forces françaises de l'intérieur*; French Resistance fighters.
GFP – *Geheime Feldpolizei*; Secret Field Police. Plain-clothes military secret police whose primary tasks were counter-espionage, counter-sabotage, detection of treasonable activities, counter-propaganda, protecting military installations and assistance in Wehrmacht courts-martial investigations. They also became responsible for the detection of Resistance activity in Germany and occupied France. Under Wehrmacht control between 1939 and early 1942, they were absorbed into the spreading umbrella of the RSHA (*qv*) during 1942.
Halbtarnung – 'Half camouflage', i.e. an enemy greatcoat and headgear worn over a German uniform.
Heer – Germany Army.
Ia – Operations officer.
Ib – Quartermaster.
Ic – Intelligence officer.
Kampfdolmetscher – Combat interpreter.
Linsen – Explosive motor boat. Normally operated in threes; two piloted towards the target, the pilot bailing out when close and the boat guided on its final run to target by the third 'control *Linsen*' using remote control.
Luftwaffe – German air force.
LVF – *Légion des volontaires français contre le bolchevisme*; French volunteers for the Wehrmacht.

KvK – *Kleinkampfverbände der Kriegsmarine*; German naval small battle units (*Linsen*, human torpedoes, midget submarines etc).

Kriegsmarine – German Navy.

MAS – Italian motor torpedo boats of the *Decima Flottiglia Mezzi d'Assalto*.

MFP – *Marinefahrprähme*; landing craft.

Milice – French fascist militia.

Neger – Original one-man 'human torpedo' design used by the KvK.

NKVD – The People's Commissariat for Internal Affairs; Soviet secret police from 1934 to 1946 which also fielded armed units in combat.

NOVJ – National Liberation Army and Partisan Detachments of Yugoslavia.

NSDAP – National Socialist German Workers' Party (*Nationalsozialistische Deutsche Arbeiterpartei*), abbreviated to 'Nazi'.

OKH – *Oberkommando des Heeres*; Army high command.

OKL – *Oberkommando der Luftwaffe*; Air Force high command.

OKW – *Oberkommando der Wehrmacht*; supreme military command.

OSS – Office of Strategic Services; wartime intelligence agency of the United States and predecessor of the Central Intelligence Agency.

PaK – *Panzerabwehrkanone*; German anti-tank gun.

Pionier – Engineer; 'Sapper' in British parlance.

PPF – *Parti Populaire Français* (French Popular Party); French fascist and anti-Semitic political party.

RSHA – *Reichssicherheitshauptamt*; Reich Main Security Office, subordinate to Heinrich Himmler as both head of the SS and *Chef der Deutschen Polizei* (Chief of German Police).

SA – *Sturmabteilung*; Stormtroopers. Known as 'Brownshirts', the SA were the Nazi Party's paramilitary unit formed to protect Nazi rallies and meetings and fight with opposing paramilitary militia as well as attempting to enforce Nazi directives such as the boycott of Jewish businesses.

SD – *Sicherheitsdienst des Reichsführers-SS*; Security Service of the *Reichsführer SS*, the intelligence agency of the SS.

SOE – Special Operations Executive; British organisation created to conduct espionage, sabotage and reconnaissance in occupied Europe.

Sonderführer – literally 'specialist leader'. Typically a specialist in a particular field given temporary command in the Wehrmacht, Waffen SS and other organisations such as the Organisation Todt. Frequently given to men without military training, the rank of *Sonderführer* allowed the military to exploit the expertise of civilians who were paid at a military rank deemed equivalent to their role.

Glossary and Abbreviations

SS – *Schutzstaffel*; paramilitary organisation of the Nazi Party founded in 1925 as security for Adolf Hitler. Grew into a multi-faceted sprawling organisation that included a military branch known as the Waffen SS.

STO – *Service du travail obligatoire*; forced enlistment and deportation of French workers to Germany.

V-Leute – Informants or spies.

Volltarnung – Full camouflage, i.e. an entire foreign uniform worn over a German one.

Volksdeutsche – Ethnic Germans who resided outside of Germany.

Wehrkreis – German military district centred around a major city. There were fifteen in Germany: I Königsberg, II Stettin, III Berlin, IV Dresden, V Stuttgart, VI Münster, VII Munich, VIII Breslau, IX Kassel, X Hamburg, XI Hanover, XII Wiesbaden, XIII Nuremberg, XIV Magdeburg and XV Jena. Two in Austria: XVII Vienna and XVIII Salzburg. One each in territory annexed to Poland after 1918 and later retaken: XX Danzig and XXI Posen. Two others were established in Poland and Czechoslovakia after invasion: *Wehrkreis* General Government and *Wehrkreis* Böhmen-Mähren, respectively.

z.b.V. – *zur besonderen Verwendung*; for special use.

Comparative Rank Table

Heer	Waffen SS	British/US Army
Generalfeldmarschall	*Reichsführer SS*	Field Marshal/General of the Army
Generaloberst	*Oberstgruppenführer*	General
General der . . . (Infanterie, Artillerie etc)	*Obergruppenführer*	Lieutenant General
Generalleutnant	*Gruppenführer*	Major General
Generalmajor	*Brigadeführer*	Brigadier/Brigadier General
	Oberführer	
Oberst	*Standartenführer*	Colonel
Oberstleutnant	*Obersturmbannführer*	Lieutenant Colonel
Major	*Sturmbannführer*	Major
Hauptmann/Rittmeister	*Hauptsturmführer*	Captain
Oberleutnant	*Obersturmführer*	Lieutenant/1st Lieutenant
Leutnant	*Untersturmführer*	2nd Lieutenant
Stabsfeldwebel/ Obermeister	*Sturmscharführer*	Warrant Officer I Class/ Sergeant Major
Oberfähnrich	*Standarten Oberjunker*	Senior Ensign
Hauptfeldwebel/ Hauptwachtmeister		
Oberfeldwebel/ Oberwachtmeister	*Hauptscharführer*	Warrant Officer II Class/ Master Sergeant
Feldwebel/Wachtmeister	*Oberscharführer*	Staff Sergeant/Technical Sergeant
Fähnrich	*Standartenjunker*	Officer Candidate/Ensign
. . . der Reserve (d.R.)		. . . of the Reserve
Unterfeldwebel/ Unterwachtmeister	*Scharführer*	Sergeant/Staff Sergeant
Unteroffizier	*Unterscharführer*	Corporal/Sergeant
Stabsgefreiter		Senior Lance Corporal

Heer	Waffen SS	British/US Army
Obergefreiter		Senior Lance Corporal
Gefreiter	*Rottenführer*	Lance Corporal
Oberschütze/Oberpionier/ Oberjäger	*Sturmmann*	Senior Private/Private First Class
Schütze/Pionier/Jäger	*Schütze*	Private

PRELUDE

The Concept Behind the Brandenburger Regiment

'The conventional army loses if it does not win. The guerrilla wins if he does not lose.'

Henry Kissinger

The Brandenburgers were amongst the first of the world's military 'special forces'. This pioneering work by the Wehrmacht has been variously under- and overestimated by historians and the layman alike. Their actual military successes have garnered little accurate attention, while their legend appears to have spread far and wide, Brandenburgers frequently being attributed with military operations in which they actually played no part. Their relationship to the wider sphere of Abwehr work often leads to connection with various military intelligence missions that were not part of the Brandenburgers' operational history, not helped by intelligence operatives frequently being attached to the unit for administrative or training purposes.

This book focuses on the unit that began life as the *Baulehr Kompanie z.b.V. 800* and ended as 'Division Brandenburg' four years later. We won't be going down the rabbit hole of Germany's far-flung – and frequently unsuccessful – intelligence missions that did not involve the unit as a whole. Connected though they may be by certain individuals, they are not germane to the study of the Brandenburgers themselves. Nevertheless, to fully understand the genesis of this remarkable formation it is necessary to trace its lineage back to the previous world war and then through the tangled web of conflicting loyalties that complicated much of the Wehrmacht's ambition from before the war had begun. Though a formation of soldiers, the Brandenburgers were created from the murky world of intelligence and espionage as Germany teetered upon the brink of national catastrophe in 1939. Initially, however, we must begin in 1914 during the first of the century's worldwide conflicts.

Histories of the First World War are understandably dominated by the landscapes of the Western Front and years of virtually static trench warfare that decimated the armies involved. The storied 'sideshow' of the Dardanelles campaign has also achieved a prominence in historical literature, nowhere more so than in my home country of New Zealand, for Gallipoli and the blooding of the ANZACs is seen as a defining moment in forging Australian and New Zealand national identity. Perhaps less well documented are the Allied campaigns fought on the African continent against Ottoman and German forces. Germany, having only recently achieved statehood, had joined the European scramble for African colonies during the 1880s, seizing Cameroon, Togoland (now Togo and part of Ghana), German East Africa (Rwanda, Burundi and Tanzania) and German South-West Africa (Namibia). With the outbreak of war in 1914, Allied troops moved to occupy all the German African territories, despite a marked lack of enthusiasm in the colonial outposts themselves; an editorial in the Kenyan *East African Standard* on 22 August 1914 going as far as to advocate the collaboration of all white European colonists in Africa to continue the suppression of the numerically superior indigenous peoples.

In German East Africa, *Oberstleutnant* Paul Emil von Lettow-Vorbeck proceeded to wage a highly successful guerrilla war against British forces. Unusually in an era that had been dominated by extreme colonial brutality by European powers in Africa – particularly the savage suppression of the Herero rebellion in German South-West Africa and subsequent genocide committed by German forces – Lettow-Vorbeck was both trusted and respected by the black troops (Askaris) that he commanded and who comprised the bulk of his force. Lettow-Vorbeck spoke Swahili fluently and promoted black soldiers to at least non-commissioned officer rank, once proclaiming that he believed 'we are all Africans here'. Of course, while this appears an admirable trait of this German officer, the four-year campaign that he and his men waged contributed to the devastation of the region and the malnutrition and starvation of the local population that ensued. Nonetheless, from a military standpoint Lettow-Vorbeck fought a remarkable campaign against superior enemy troop numbers that ended in 1918 with the surrender of his undefeated force; the survivors numbering thirty German officers, 125 German non-commissioned officers and enlisted men, 1,168 Askaris and approximately 3,500 porters.

Amongst the non-commissioned officers that had served under Lettow-Vorbeck was Theodor von Hippel. The 24-year-old from Toruń on the Vistula River volunteered for service with the *Schutztruppe* in German East Africa on 18 October 1914, earning the Iron Cross Second Class (EK II) that year. By August 1915 he had been promoted to *Unteroffizier*, designated an officer-aspirant on 17 February 1916 and promoted again to *Feldwebel* on the first day of April. However, just five days later he was wounded and taken prisoner during the fighting that followed an offensive launched by the South African General

J.C. Smuts at the head of 45,000 men. Hippel remained a prisoner of war until December 1920 whereupon he returned to Germany, having been discharged from the military with the rank of *Leutnant der Reserve*.

Following his return to civilian life, Hippel achieved a doctorate in Political Science (*Doktor der Staatswissenschaft*) before reenlisting in the Wehrmacht in 1935. He served as an *Oberleutnant* in the *Pionier-Bataillon 43* stationed at Brandenburg an der Havel and was promoted to *Hauptmann* later that year. Hippel was later described by Erwin von Lahousen as 'a somewhat confused, very atavistic adventurer. An old South-West African, [he was] no Nazi.'[1] A powerfully built man of medium height with grey hair, he frequently resembled the very essence of a foreigner's picture of a Prussian officer, complete with officer's breeches, monocle and 1916 pattern steel helmet. On 1 November 1937, he joined the Abwehr – German military intelligence – reporting to a third-floor office marked with 'II N/W' on the door in Abwehr headquarters at 76–78 Tirpitzufer, Berlin. He had been subordinated to the sabotage section headed by *Oberstleutnant* Helmuth Groscurth.

The Abwehr was only one of six different intelligence services in Hitler's Third Reich, though its chief rival was the SS security service, the *Sicherheitsdienst des Reichsführer-SS* (SD – Security Service of the *Reichsführer SS*). The energetic head of the Abwehr, *Admiral* Wilhelm Canaris, had been born in 1887 in Alperbeck, Westphalia. He joined the Imperial German Navy at the age of 17 in 1905 and served during the First World War aboard the cruiser SMS *Dresden* as Intelligence Officer. Canaris demonstrated a genius for his work as he guided the ship's escape following the disastrous Battle of the Falkland Islands during which all but two of the German East Asia Squadron (six cruisers and some auxiliaries that comprised Germany's only 'blue water' squadron of the war independent of German home ports) were sunk by the Royal Navy. *Dresden* was the sole cruiser to escape, evading the enemy for three months thanks to Canaris' skilful intelligence work until cornered in Cumberland Bay on Chile's Robinson Crusoe Island. Faced with destruction by gunfire or capture, *Dresden* was scuttled on 14 March 1915 and the crew interned in neutral Chile.

With his captain's permission Canaris escaped internment and travelled back to Germany, his fluency in six languages including English and Spanish no doubt aiding his convoluted journey. His path crossed the Andes to Buenos Aires from where he travelled aboard the Dutch Lloyd steamer *Frisia* to Plymouth, posing as Chilean widower Reed Rosas and sufficiently plausible in his disguise to go as far as assisting a group of Royal Navy officers that were making enquiries about fellow passengers. From there the ship sailed to Rotterdam from where Canaris was able to make the final leg of his journey over the German border.

The young officer's successful return made him something of a minor celebrity in naval circles and he quickly came to the attention of *Oberst* Walter Nicolai, head of the Imperial German Army's '*Abteilung IIIb*' that was concerned with military intelligence. Enlisted into Nicolai's service, *Kapitänleutnant* Canaris was soon posted to Madrid, Spain, where he continued his previous cover as Señor Reed Rosas and took a small flat while he began reporting Allied shipping movements for the benefit of Germany's U-boats. Codenamed 'Kika', Canaris was extremely successful, U-boat victories in the Mediterranean rising and covert refuelling facilities in neutral Spanish harbours established that allowed longer combat patrols. However, he requested a return to active service and on 21 February 1917 left Madrid to return overland to Germany, arrested by Italian troops in Genoa after a tip-off that Señor Rosas was in fact a German spy. The uncontainable Canaris was not incarcerated for long and after exploiting connections that potentially led as far as the Vatican, he was released, though strong protests by French and British officials saw him placed on a ship bound for Marseilles. Undeterred, Canaris convinced the ship's Spanish captain to do otherwise and he was landed at Cartagena, arriving back in Madrid by 15 March. However, after a further six months of intelligence work and constant requests to transfer to active service, he was taken aboard *U-35* to the Austrian base at Cattaro and thence to Germany.

Awarded the Iron Cross First Class (EK I) for the 'extraordinary skill with which he carried out his mission', Canaris transferred to the U-boat arm and was given command of the minelayer *UC-27* on 28 November 1917 before transferring to the post of First Officer aboard *U-34*, the larger Type B boat offering more aggressive action with its torpedo patrols. Serving in the Mediterranean, Canaris earned command of *U-128* before Cattaro was evacuated in October 1918 and he returned to Kiel, bringing his boat into a harbour filled with ships flying the red flag of mutiny as revolution overwhelmed the Imperial German Navy and the country's last vestiges of order disintegrated.

Caught up in the revolutionary violence in Germany following the 1918 armistice, Canaris became involved in the *Freikorps Noske* of ex-officers who fought to resist the virulent strains of communism that had taken root within the navy. Gradually, some form of order was restored, though Canaris had developed a loathing of all things communist, despite his relatively liberal views on most matters. He helped restore military discipline to Kiel's naval base, using his intelligence experience to instigate numerous black market deals and obtain the money required to establish a reserve of trustworthy and reliable officers which would remain invisible to the Allied Naval Control Commission enforcing the severe terms of the Versailles Treaty.

A dull posting to a junior post aboard the training ship *Berlin* followed, during which time he established a rapport and friendship with an arrogant, though intellectually gifted, naval cadet by the name of Reinhard Heydrich. Nonetheless, bored at his new post, Canaris considered resigning his commission, until the world of subterfuge beckoned once more and he was posted to Osaka to oversee the secret construction of a U-boat design in Japanese yards, circumventing the terms of the Versailles Treaty and paving the way for clandestine German rearmament. Though his mission was repudiated by the newly arrived naval chief *Vizeadmiral* Adolf Zenker under pressure from a suspicious Royal Navy, Canaris' thirst for secretive work had been reawakened.

He subsequently became involved with *Kapitän zur See* Walter Lohmann, son of a Bremen shipping magnate and fellow disciple of clandestinity and shadowy business deals. Despite Zenker, many naval officers were committed to a path of military rearmament hidden behind dummy civilian corporate fronts. Lohmann, Chief of the Reichsmarine's Transportation Division and a man of experience in international business, was charged with administering whatever money was available through various 'off the books' dealings that Germany's naval administration had made. The accumulated 'black fund' allowed armament development to be carried out in secret under the noses of the Allied Armistice Control Commission. In this he was assisted by Canaris and the officer who would go on to head Germany's minesweeping service, *Oberleutnant zur See* Friedrich Ruge. Together they established, amongst other things, TRAYAG (*Travemünder Yachthafen A.G.*) in 1924 as a base and shipyard for the covert development and trial activities for fast motor torpedo boats (S-boats). The following year they created the 'High Sea Sports Association' (HANSA) for the training of personnel in basic seamanship, small motor and sailing boat usage as well as radio communication. The Neustädter Slip GmbH was formed as a repair and training plant for sport boats (and S-boats) in 1925 and the following year 60,000RM was given from the Reichsmarine's 'black fund' to the Motor-Yacht Club of Germany for the testing of the motor boats developed by TRAYAG. The subterfuge proved successful – not only for S-boat development, but also U-boat and aircraft projects.

Somewhat ironically, Lohmann was forced to resign in 1928 by pressure from within Germany after it became publicly known that he had also poured money into various non-military ventures – either to increase the dwindling amount available in the secret fund through the generation of profits or to gradually accumulate a network of trustworthy agents through foreign investment. Using Canaris' Spanish connections, German investment broke the stranglehold exerted by the Bank of England over Spanish naval construction, earning the gratitude of the Spanish King and further laurels for Canaris. However, investment in foreign and diverse firms was where Lohmann finally came unstuck. His ventures ranged from the Berliner Bacon Company (attempting to wrest the lucrative British bacon market from Danish firms) to a firm attempting to raise sunken ships by encasing them in ice.

His fatal weakness was involvement with the Phoebus Film Company which collapsed financially in August 1927. Lohmann's stake in the company was revealed by the journalist Kurd Wenkel who had investigated the source of the film company's hidden revenue that had allowed it to function for years despite dwindling sales. Paradoxically, it was not Lohmann's real rearmament mission that caused the ensuing scandal, but rather the fact that German pacifists correctly claimed that he had been influencing the film company to make increasingly nationalistic features which could strengthen the burgeoning right-wing political parties.[2] However, Lohmann's subsequent exit forced only a brief delay in the establishment of new business fronts behind which the military could continue its secret work.

Nonetheless, Lohmann's fall resulted in Canaris' return to Germany, posted by the new chief of the navy *Admiral* Erich Raeder to command of the obsolete battleship *Schliesen*. Two years showing the flag at sea followed, during which time Adolf Hitler had become the new Chancellor of Germany. Canaris was, at first, enthusiastic about the Nazis; their pathological hatred of communism, the return to a centralised authoritarian government after the ramshackle and confused Weimar Republic and their promise to abrogate the emasculating terms of the Versailles Treaty were all tenets that struck a strong chord with him. However, Canaris and his penchant for shady dealings and conspiracy had fallen out of favour with his immediate naval superiors, including the strictly conventional Raeder, and he was posted to command the fortress of Swinemünde in 1934, the equivalent of military exile.

Events in Berlin that would shape the future of Canaris, the Abwehr and the Brandenburgers were meanwhile in motion. The head of the Abwehr, *Oberst* Ferdinand von Bredow, was promoted to a senior position in the Reichswehr and recommended that a naval officer take control of the Abwehr for the first time since its creation. *Kapitän zur See* Conrad Patzig was appointed head of the intelligence service, a capable officer who had earned the trust of his subordinates and established solid relationships with the Baltic states by exchanging information about the USSR. However, Patzig frequently clashed with the head of the SD, which was surreptitiously absorbing other police agencies in its drive to become the centralised state police and intelligence network. The SD's young head was none other than Reinhard Heydrich who had joined the SS after being cashiered from the navy in 1931 for 'dishonourable conduct'. Heydrich's clinically precise application of brutality and cunning had extended his reach into all corners of German life. During 1934, he was a prime mover in the crushing of the *Sturmabteilung* (SA) that had fought in the streets during Hitler's revolutionary rise to power but now threatened the stability of the Nazi state as their loyalty was divided between their own leadership and that of the party. The subsequent 'Night of the Long Knives' and the murder of Ernst Röhm and the SA leadership at the end of June deeply shocked Patzig and other members of the Abwehr. Amongst the victims was none other than Ferdinand von Bredow, opportunistically murdered during two days of bloodletting, due to his previous opposition to Adolf Hitler when he had served as deputy defence minister in Kurt von Schleicher's Weimar Republic cabinet. Hitler had used the purge of the SA as an opportunity to rid himself of bitter enemies unconnected to the SA.

Patzig was appalled, as was his deputy, cavalry *Major* Hans Oster, who decided at that moment to devote himself to unseating the Nazis from power. Patzig's tenure as head of the Abwehr was curtailed, through both his own desire to seek the safer waters of an active service posting and the machinations of his unfettered rival Reinhard Heydrich. It was Canaris' name that was subsequently put forward to replace him and on 1 January 1935 Canaris became the head of the Abwehr.

Promoted to *Konteradmiral*, Canaris threw himself into the role he was destined for. Canaris enlarged the Abwehr staff from 150 to approximately 1,000 by 1937 and clarified the domains of the three main offices and two satellite posts as well as their respective spheres of employment. *Abteilung I* ('Abwehr I'), initially commanded by *Oberst* Hans Piekenbrock, was responsible for espionage abroad, subdivided into Army, Navy and Air Force sections and other branches encompassing industrial and economic espionage. *Abteilung II* ('Abwehr II'), commanded by Groscurth, was responsible for sabotage, fostering insurgency and, later, commando activity behind enemy lines. *Abteilung III* ('Abwehr III') under Major Rudolf Bamler was tasked with counter-espionage, this being the department that worked closest with Heydrich's SD due to its domestic security remit. There also existed the 'Foreign Section' under *Admiral* Leopold Birkner that evaluated foreign military intelligence and dealt with military and naval attaches and 'Section Z' under *Generalmajor* Hans Oster that was responsible for Abwehr administration and organisation. This placed the committed anti-Nazi Oster in perhaps the most vital junction point of all Abwehr activity and enabled him to place personnel sympathetic to his beliefs in key positions while removing those who could provide ideological obstacles and pose a danger to future conspiracies against the Führer.

Canaris and Heydrich established defined areas of responsibility between the Abwehr and the SD, though they would continue to joust with one another throughout the years that followed. Their unusual bond of friendship endured until Heydrich's death, tempered by Canaris' knowledge that Heydrich was a 'brutal fanatic' and Heydrich distrusting his former superior as a 'wily old fox'. Nonetheless, in the early stages of his Abwehr command, Canaris advocated 'comradely cooperation with the Gestapo' and remained an adherent to the Nazi regime's path, benefitting from unfettered access to Hitler and frequent private meetings with the Führer in the Reich Chancellery. It is widely believed that it was Canaris that put forward the idea of identifying Jewish citizens by the attachment of a yellow star to their clothing, probably proffered in an air of simplistic intellectual solution to the 'Jewish problem' rather than rooted in inherent anti-Semitism. Canaris himself appears to have not been particularly anti-Semitic in his views, though he clearly had no major issue with the treatment of Jewish Germans as second-class citizens, at best.

Canaris was fully involved in German operations that took place during the Spanish Civil War, negotiating the use of the Condor Legion with Franco by use of his already well-established connections that extended back to the previous world war. However, during June 1937, he became disillusioned with at least some aspects of the application of Nazi power outside of Germany's borders. Canaris became aware of Stalin's brutal purge of Soviet officers and the peripheral role that the SD had played in the violent murder of so many by the planting of false evidence against Soviet officers with whom a joint German–Soviet military training alliance had been agreed during 1926. This and other SD operations shocked and appalled Canaris, who was equally stunned by Heydrich's ambivalence to complicity in the bloodbath Stalin had unleashed. By now fully aware that Hitler's desire had been for the Soviet high command to decimate itself, Canaris began to understand that the path that Germany had embarked upon was unbound by any recognisable humanitarian principles and would almost certainly lead once again to war. His subordinate, Erwin von Lahousen, would later characterise Canaris during testimony at the Nuremberg Trials as 'a pure intellect, an interesting, highly individual and complicated personality, who hated violence as such and therefore hated and abominated war, Hitler, his system and particularly his methods'.[3]

His previous identification with National Socialism rapidly deserted Canaris and he began to develop his own agenda, aided by Oster, in which he would undermine the nation's leadership in order to prevent another conflict. His first attempt included the staging of deception operations that clearly showed Germany mobilising troops to invade neighbouring Austria. However, the demonstration went unremarked and on 13 March 1938, the unprepared Austria was successfully absorbed into the Greater German Reich.

Following the *Anschluss*, the aristocratic *Oberstleutnant* Erwin Heinrich René von Lahousen was transferred to the Abwehr; his enlistment by OKW's

Generaloberst Beck made at the prompting of Canaris who vouched for the Austrian's 'political attitude'. Born in 1897 in Vienna, Lahousen served as an officer in the 14th Infantry Regiment on the Italian front during the First World War. Wounded in action, he survived the war and remained an active infantry officer in the Austrian Army's 2nd Division in Vienna, later completing his *Höheren Offizierskurse* (Higher Officer's Course) and promoted to *Major*.[4]

Following the 1918 collapse of the Austro-Hungarian monarchy, a Federal government was established with an associated Federal Army. Though this army had no military intelligence establishment, the former head of the wartime *Kaiserliche und Königliche Evidenzbüro*, *Generalmajor* Max Ronge, served as an 'honorary' adviser to the State Police on all internal security matters, primarily monitoring the various left- and right-wing paramilitary groups, as well as engaging in counter-espionage. Vienna at that time was a hotbed of international undercover activities and into this fevered atmosphere Lahousen was indoctrinated, graduating with top marks from his Officer's Course. Lahousen was transferred to the newly established Austrian Defence Ministry in 1933 at the behest of Ronge himself, to be trained as Chief Intelligence Officer for the Austrian Army and its newly established Intelligence Section. Between 1933 and 1937 the emphasis for Austrian Intelligence was gathering information on Czechoslovakia (which was engaging in anti-Austrian intelligence work of its own, somewhat ironically using Austrian officers dismissed from the military due to pro-Nazi activities) and Yugoslavia as well as monitoring events along the Austro-German border for the illegal activities of Austrian Nazis, though there was no intelligence work officially carried out *against* those nations with which Austria exchanged information: Italy, Hungary and Germany. Lahousen was promoted to *Oberstleutnant* and transferred to the General Staff in 1936. During the following year, Lahousen was present at a meeting between Austrian military and intelligence leaders with the head of *Abwehr Amt. Ausland*, Wilhelm Canaris, to discuss information to be exchanged regarding Czechoslovakia. It was the first time that he had met directly with the head of the Abwehr, a meeting that would have fateful consequences.

Following his transfer to the Abwehr after the *Anschluss*, Lahousen was made deputy head of Abwehr I (responsible for espionage) and soon taken into Canaris' confidence, who appealed to his 'anti-Nazi attitude, with which he was familiar'. Lahousen, though a loyal and dedicated soldier, was primarily an Austrian nationalist and he firmly believed that his country would only be returned to its former greatness with the elimination of the Nazis and separation from the German state. Canaris knew that following the relatively effortless annexation of Austria, Hitler's next objective was the absorption of Czechoslovakia, to be achieved by agitating the Sudeten-German issues that had been left in the wake of the First World War. Canaris was certain that this would mean war, as he judged it inconceivable that both Great Britain and the USSR would remain silent after yet another bold strike by the German Chancellor. Canaris instructed Lahousen to help prevent the annexation of Czechoslovakia by deliberate overestimation of Czech military force and preparedness while also assisting in the enlistment of other anti-Nazi Austrian officers into the Abwehr. At the end of 1938 Prussian *Oberstleutnant* Helmuth Groscurth left Abwehr II for OKW and subsequent field commands, *Oberstleutnant* Erwin von Lahousen being transferred to replace him at the beginning of 1939.

Meanwhile, the 'atavistic adventurer' Hippel had been hard at work outlining his ideas for a new Wehrmacht formation. Inspired by the known success of the German East African campaign that he had been a part of and his study of pioneering work with indigenous irregulars by T.E. Lawrence during the British Middle Eastern campaigns, Hippel desired to create the first German 'special forces'. He maintained that small elite units of men could achieve exceptional results, particularly those skilled in demolition and small arms combat and able to speak relevant foreign languages fluently. Hippel's proposals for the formation of such a unit for employment behind enemy lines in psychological warfare were rejected by his military superiors, who remained rooted in military orthodoxy. Even once the idea reached Canaris' ears, they were rejected. Though Canaris was far from orthodox in his approach to warfare, he viewed Hippel with suspicion, believing him and his unique proposal to be pro-Bolshevik. Canaris informed Hippel that he believed that such activities as psychological and ideological warfare were the prerogative of the ruling political party, not the military.

Unswervingly committed to his idea, Hippel turned to his former commander Groscurth who had long advocated the formation of ethnic German sabotage units in the Sudetenland and Poland. Groscurth brought pressure to bear at OKW and strongly backed Hippel's suggestion. With this added impetus, authorisation was soon received to create his unit which was to be placed under Abwehr command. Once Canaris was reconciled to this decision, he changed his stance and instead saw the new unit as potentially enhancing secret instructions that he had recently given to Lahousen.

Following his appointment as head of Abwehr II, Lahousen had held lengthy discussions with Canaris, who gave him explicit instructions on how he was to run his section, both in public and secret. Publicly, Lahousen was instructed to: limit his tasks to military matters only and not become involved in 'political actions'; reject all methods that were employed by the SD and Gestapo; and absolutely refuse collaboration with either the SD or Gestapo. These instructions were unequivocal and repeated by both Canaris and Lahousen at all discussions and meetings involving Abwehr II, particularly for the benefit of officers that were judged sympathetic or fully indoctrinated by the Nazi ethos.

These 'covert' instructions were to form a dedicated anti-Nazi cadre in Abwehr II, prepared to commit illegal acts by which the Nazi state could be sabotaged from within. It was to this end that Canaris believed Hippel's new unit could be used. A gradual but systematic removal of National Socialist officers from Hippel's command was begun by Lahousen and the unit was strictly forbidden to engage in 'kidnapping, assassination and poisoning, or similar actions related to the methods of the SD'. Lahousen was also secretly instructed to passively resist by under-employing his resources while making a show of great activity, avoiding any operations entirely that could be justifiably abandoned. These latter instructions were greatly relaxed following Operation '*Barbarossa*' and intended more in relation to the Western Allies than the USSR. Canaris' rationale remained a final attempt to prevent the war that he knew was sure to come if Hitler continued his territorial ambitions in Eastern Europe.

> Beginning with his very detailed conversations with me relative to my taking over Abt. II of the Abwehr (beginning of 1939) up until my departure from the *Amt./Ausland*, Abwehr (middle of 1943), Canaris had spoken constantly – whether by paraphrases and hints or quite openly – of the necessity of doing away with Hitler, Himmler and Heydrich (the '3-Hs') and of deposing the whole criminal gang. He also explained therewith my appointment as head of Abwehr II and the real reason for forming the Brandenburg Regiment ... The role that he had destined for my Abteilung, specifically for me and the Brandenburger Regiment, was as follows; I was to prepare myself at a given time for the acquisition of material (explosives and time fuses) for the accomplishment of the 'action'.
>
> On the other hand, the Brandenburg Regiment was, to a degree, to be set up as Special Troops at the disposal of that first, powerful occupation by certain 'key units' of the National Socialist juggernaut (the RSHA, radio network, Intelligence branch of the OKW etc.)[5]

Lahousen was assisted in his tasks by his adjutant *Kapitän der Reserve* Hans-Joachim Wolfgang Abshagen. This 41-year-old native of Stralsund had been a pre-war member of the NSDAP and SS, but had joined solely in order to remain in Germany's cinema business, which had become increasingly dominated by Joseph Goebbels and his approved output. A foreign correspondent of some repute, he was called up for military service as a member of the Wehrmacht reserve at the outbreak of war. It was Abshagen who assisted Lahousen in his gradual removal of Nazi officers with 'great cleverness and with characteristic intelligence'.[6] Amongst those men that Abshagen and Lahousen chose to remove was eventually Hippel himself, though not due to any political motivation, but rather his dedication to the Wehrmacht. However, that lay some years in the future as Hippel, with the assistance of his adjutant, Luftwaffe Flak artillery *Wachtmeister* Wilhelm Johannes, began to create the first of his special units. Johannes was the perfect foil for Hippel's sometimes vague theoretical notions. Where Hippel embraced the concept of forming small specialised units, it was frequently Johannes' gift for organisation and his ability for managing people that allowed the wish to become reality. They were further supported at the outset by *Leutnant der Reserve* Verbeek, Bavarian *Hauptmann* Putz, leader of the Abwehr II in Vienna, and Austrian *Hauptmann* Fleck of the Breslau Abwehr.

Recruited primarily from volunteers from the '*Sudetendeutsches Freikorps*' that comprised mainly First World War veterans and local SA men drafted into the Wehrmacht, Hippel's men were not spies. Even though the use of disguise using captured or manufactured enemy uniforms was a fundamental tool for Hippel's service, he instructed that each man wear his Wehrmacht uniform underneath, able to discard the disguise before engaging in combat and therefore arguably not contravening the articles of the Hague Convention. *Oberleutnant* Lazarek became the small force's second in command and training began under the supervision of Verbeek and his chief instructors *Leutnant* Dr Gottfried Kniesche and *Leutnant* Siegfried Grabert. The formation's codename '*Baulehr Kompanie (Deutsche Kompanie) z.b.V.*' (Training and Construction Company (German Company) Special Purpose) was first used on 15 August 1939 when it had moved to the Slovakian base at Sliač north-west of Bratislava in preparation for the invasion of Poland. These members of the Wehrmacht would soon become merged with another unorthodox formation; the Ebbinghaus Organisation.

The origins of this paramilitary grouping can be traced back to the violence surrounding the plebiscite for the self-determination of Upper Silesia that had been guaranteed by the conditions of the Versailles Treaty. The Prussian province of Silesia had been divided into Upper and Lower at the end of the First World War. The region not only contained an enormous quantity of coalmines and heavy industry but was ethnically split between Polish- and German-speaking inhabitants. British, French and Italian troops occupied the region on behalf of the Supreme Allied Council as both the Polish and German governments began to campaign in the months leading up to the ballot. Two Polish uprisings took place a year apart during the campaign, in August 1919 and August 1920, both of which were quelled by League of Nations forces but both of which led to violent clashes between German and Polish paramilitary forces; the former comprised primarily of *Freikorps* troops. Following a German majority in the overall plebiscite vote, Britain suggested the region split in a way that would provide only a fraction of the industrial capacity to Poland, triggering a third Polish uprising that took place during April 1921. Once again, the insurrectionists clashed with German paramilitary volunteers in large-scale fighting that culminated in the Battle of the Annaberg.

Unable to determine or control the partitioning process, the Supreme Allied Council passed the matter over to the League of Nations who partitioned Upper Silesia along lines that followed plebiscite voting, with most of the industrial and mining regions going to Poland. Though the fighting was finished, resentment over this decision would simmer until the outbreak of war in 1939. German paramilitary units continued to exist within the occupied area, including the *Industrieschutzes Oberschlesien* (Industrial Protection Upper Silesia) that had tasked itself with safeguarding transport and industrial installations now under Polish control. However, as tensions gradually eased, the small group slowly became dormant.

During 1935 and the remilitarisation of the Reich, the *Industrieschutzes Oberschlesien* was reactivated and expanded, subsumed into Canaris' *Abwehrstelle VIII* (Breslau) and renamed the 'Ebbinghaus Organisation', such units traditionally taking the name of their leader, in this case purported to be Ernst Ebbinghaus. The formation remained paramilitary by nature and it is difficult to ascertain exactly how many members it comprised, though the most reliable figures appear to be between 500 and 600 men.[7] So too is there confusion over exactly what the organisation was titled as various secondary accounts name '*Freikorps Ebbinghaus*', 'Ebbinghaus Battalion', '*Sonderformation Ebbinghaus*' and '*Kampfgruppe Ebbinghaus*'. It appears likely that these are the same, officially listed as '*Organisation Ebbinghaus*' (subsequently anglicised for the sake of this text as 'Ebbinghaus Organisation'). They were far from the sole paramilitary unit to take part in the invasion of Poland, but remain the focus of this study due to their subsequent role as a building block for the Brandenburgers.

The actual identity of Ebbinghaus himself remains something of a mystery, a common explanation given is that this was simply a cover name for Hippel. However, biographical details have been provided by Polish researcher Grzegorza Bębnik that cite Ebbinghaus as a genuine character, born in 1889 in Westphalia, schooled in Kassel and later attending the Mining Academy in Berlin before wartime service as an officer in the Engineers. Later, working for the Prussian Ministry of Economy and Labour, he is cited as covertly heading the paramilitary group that bore his name while employed during 1939 in the Prussian Main Mining Office in Wrocław, scheduled to become Director of the Silesian Central Mine Rescue Station in Bytom.[8]

The Ebbinghaus Organisation undertook training in Oels, Glatz and Lamsdorf, members wearing civilian clothes with the addition of a swastika armband when on active service. Armed with automatic pistols, rifles, machine guns, hand grenades and batons, the men infiltrated through the so-called 'Green' Polish border of occupied Upper Silesia – an area used for clandestine crossings of the Polish frontier – as the start date of the German invasion approached. While his men moved forward, Ebbinghaus, his deputy *Oberleutnant* Lazarek and their small headquarters occupied the Promenade Restaurant in Bytom as a makeshift headquarters. The Ebbinghaus Organisation featured several section commanders that had taken part in the *Freikorps* battles between 1919 and 1921 and who subsequently had become local lights in the Silesian NSDAP, including *SA-Standartenführer* Hans Ramdohr from Gliwice, *SA-Hauptsturmführer* Wilhelm Pisarski from Bytom, *SA-Sturmführer* Karl Rolle from Gliwice and *SA-Sturmbannführer* Josef Piontek also from Bytom.

The Abwehr had also supplied extra men with military training for the Ebbinghaus Organisation, including Siegfried Grabert, an ex-*Leutnant* of the Reichswehr's 5th *Kraftfahr-Abteilung* (Motorised Battalion), 5th Infantry Division, who had retired from the military following a sports injury. Enlisted into the Abwehr by Canaris while studying medicine in Tübingen, Grabert was responsible for the establishment of the *Deutsche Kompanie* (German Company) that was subsequently attached to Ebbinghaus, comprised of Polish-speaking *Volksdeutsche* from both the *Industrieschutz Oberschlesien* and the *Sudetendeutsches Freikorps*. Grabert's men trained in standard Slovakian Army uniforms with an armband bearing the legend '*Deutsches Kompanie*' and later donned various disguises for their part in the forthcoming invasion.

The term *Volksdeutsche* may not have originated with Nazi Germany, but it was most certainly used as a common theme by Hitler in his approach to racial matters. In a 1938 Reich Chancellery memorandum, the term is defined as indicating 'races whose language and culture had German origins but who did not hold German citizenship'. *Volksdeutsche* were those who were considered of Germanic culture but who lived outside the borders of German-speaking nations such as Germany, Austria and Switzerland. It did not refer to 'recent' German migrants who lived elsewhere, rather it encompassed those who considered their identity and culture to be of German origin, generally due to past migration or inhabitants of territory lost through war. An equivalent English term would be 'ethnic Germans' though that does not fully cover the racial overtones of the Nazi application, espousing the idea that Germany was a 'cultural nation' whose inhabitants were part of a 'race' as opposed to a 'nation state'. Those who were considered Jewish Germans were excluded from the category of *Volksdeutsche* no matter what their claimed ethnicity.

CHAPTER 1

Baptism of Fire

'If you win, you need not explain . . . If you lose, you should not be there to explain.'

Adolf Hitler

Hitler's original planned date for the invasion of Poland was 26 August 1939. However, an 'Agreement of Mutual Assistance' signed between Great Britain and Poland at noon the previous day which guaranteed military assistance to either party should another 'European country' attack them prompted a nervous Hitler to postpone until the morning of 1 September. Unfortunately, notice of this rescheduling came too late for one of the new covert Abwehr units led by *Leutnant der Reserve* Dr Hans-Albrecht Herzner.

Herzner was a reserve officer of the 9th Infantry Regiment and had also acted as a *Wissenschaftlicher Mitarbeiter* (civilian scientific assistant) to the Wehrmacht's regional command in Breslau. He had also become involved in a plot to force Hitler's resignation during the Sudetenland crisis of 1938, formulated by several high-ranking officers and police officials. *Generaloberst* Erwin von Witzleben had been an ardent anti-Nazi since the 'Night of the Long Knives' and the death of Ferdinand von Bredow. Part of Oster's circle of conspirators, he had determined to enter the Reich Chancellery escorted by reliable officers of his headquarters staff, gain access to Hitler and demand his resignation and subsequent trial. Painstaking chronicles of the excesses committed by the SS and Gestapo were to be used as evidence against him, while psychiatrist Karl Bonhoeffer was prepared to provide a professional opinion of Hitler's mental health. Canaris was amongst these high-level conspirators and, while he himself argued for Hitler to be arrested, an escorting 'raiding party' had gone as far as to plan a provocation of the Führer that could justify his being shot lest the SS manage to stage a counter-coup.[1] This 'raiding party' was led by officers who included Herzner as well as Friedrich Wilhelm Heinz – who had argued forcefully for the assassination of Hitler – and Hans-Wolfram Knaak, also of the Abwehr. The group assembled in Berlin during September in preparation for their attempted coup before British acceptance of Hitler's Sudeten gamble threw the conspirators into enough confusion to cancel their attempt, justifying it by presuming an Anglo-French declaration was imminent that they would stage military intervention should Hitler move to invade the remainder of Czechoslovakia.

On 24 August 1939 Herzner crossed the German–Slovakian border from Breslau by car, under the assumed identity of businessman Heinrich Herzog. He was headed to a rendezvous with his men, twenty-four members of '*Abwehrstelle Breslau*' designated *Kampforganisation Jablunka*. The Abwehr operated three types of organisation during 1939:

- *Kampforganisation*: tasked with capturing and protecting important strategic objectives such as bridges, railway stations, tunnels and the like to enable a German military advance;
- *Sabotageorganisation*: tasked with destroying objectives behind the enemy's front line to sever reinforcement links;
- *Fallschirmorganisation*; involving air-dropped saboteurs to carry out operations behind the front lines.

Herzner's command was a *Kampforganisation* tasked with the capture and safeguarding of the 300m-long railway tunnel at the Jablunka Pass through the Beskids mountains, as well as the Mosty railway station in the pass itself. Defensive demolition of the tunnel that sat on the main single-track Vienna–Warsaw railway line would severely impede German invaders attempting to enter southern Poland. The Poles, fully aware of the strategic significance of this western Carpathian pass, had mined the tunnel during June and, every day after the final train had passed through, the fuses were made live and ready for firing.

Dressed in civilian clothes, *Kampforganisation Jablunka* proceeded from Čadca northwards across the Slovakian border, accompanied by a hundred men of the Slovakian fascist militia, the Hlinka Guard. Passing over the Polish frontier just after midnight, they travelled through densely wooded country where, due to faulty navigation and difficult topography poorly illuminated by the waxing moon, Herzner's men had become scattered into small groups, he himself arriving west of the train station with *Gefreiter* Jung and twelve men slightly behind schedule at 0245hrs.

Herzner determined that Polish machine-gun positions and a defensive trench were unmanned though he could see that the tunnel's northern end was guarded by a pair of sentries, the opposite end also patrolled by four riflemen of the 21st Mountain Division. At 0300hrs gunfire from another assault group was heard from the direction of the tunnel and Herzner attacked the train station shortly afterwards, the building being successfully taken along with a group of

Polish steel workers inside. Unfortunately for Herzner and unbeknown to the attackers, there was a military communications centre in the station basement and a female Polish telegraphist alerted local troops who immediately took up defensive positions. As these Polish troops foiled the initial German attempt on the tunnel itself, a small group of Herzner's men endeavoured to take control of the situation in the tunnel using a stolen locomotive but were defeated by Polish machine-gun fire. Herzner was painfully aware that the attempted operation had failed and he then discovered that the entire invasion had been postponed following a message from *Major* Paul Reichelt, Chief of Staff of the Wehrmacht's 7th Infantry Division that manned that portion of the Polish border. Herzner's small group prepared to retreat, though they remained pinned down until midday the following day, after which they managed to break away and retrace their path into Slovakia with two wounded men. The commander of the 7th Infantry Division, *Generalmajor* Eugen Ott, apologised to his opposite Polish number *General* Józef Rudolf Kustroń of the 21st Mountain Division for the attack, blaming a single 'insane individual' for the action. Herzner was recommended for the EK II by Canaris but Wilhelm Keitel blocked the award as the action had occurred during peacetime and Herzner only belatedly received the decoration on 29 October 1939.[2]

While Herzner's premature private invasion had been foiled, the Ebbinghaus Organisation began subsequent operations on schedule upon receipt of the code word 'Falcon'. At 0300hrs on 1 September they attacked and seized several vital industrial and mining complexes as well as the railway transport hub at Katowice. The latter was taken and held by Grabert's eighty men of the *Deutsche Kompanie* who came under heavy Polish attack throughout the day. Speaking fluent Polish, Grabert and his troops had crossed over the border during the last day of August, assisted by local volunteer guides who led them to the road to Chorzhow. The men were disguised as Polish railway workers and carried concealed small arms and explosives. By midnight they had reached the freight station of the Katowice railway yards which they successfully occupied, though the *Deutsche Kompanie* was thinly spread as it attempted to hold several key buildings. The arrival of Polish troops by train to counter-attack ten Germans in the main warehouse was observed at some distance by Grabert, who ordered a handful of his men to stage a diversionary attack on a nearby bridge. With Polish attention elsewhere, Grabert, assisted by a man named Schmittainsky, managed to creep aboard the locomotive that had brought the Polish troop train into the station and incapacitate the two drivers. Shouting to attract the attention of the enemy troops assaulting the warehouse, Grabert convinced their officer that German forces were now attempting to destroy the bridge, the Poles reboarding the train that headed at speed towards the new conflagration. Grabert and

Schmittainsky subsequently took the train from the station and headed west, handing over the nearly 800 men aboard to advancing Wehrmacht troops. The Poles that had been left to contain the *Deutsche Kompanie* troops in the warehouse were too few to dislodge the invaders and subsequently Wehrmacht spearheads captured the railway station and its yards intact later that day.

Elsewhere the Ebbinghaus units suffered greater losses. While attempting to capture the 'Max' mine at Michałkowice, fierce Polish defence that involved pitched battles throughout the mining complex killed twenty-eight men including '*Kampfgruppe Pisarski*' leader SA-*Hauptsturmführer* Wilhelm Pisarski and wounded a further twelve. Sixty-four others were subsequently taken prisoner while only a small number, including Pisarski's deputy Hargut, managed to escape. Those captured were, of course, later released by the advancing Wehrmacht. Polish losses during the battle were also significant and ultimately the German aim was accomplished as the mine was captured intact. Elsewhere, Ebbinghaus units and men from *Abwehrstelle XVII* (Vienna) that attacked the Huta Hubertus Steelworks, Chorzów power station and Orzeł Biały mines were defeated with heavy casualties, though Polish defenders were unable to sabotage any of the valuable objectives, which were likewise captured intact by the Wehrmacht. To the north near Danzig the two parallel bridges over the Vistula at Dirschau were successfully demolished by Polish troops, despite a combined attack by Luftwaffe, Wehrmacht, SS and Abwehr troops from *Abwehrstelle I* (Königsberg). In total the Ebbinghaus Organisation lost 174 men killed and 133 wounded on the first day of the invasion of Poland; nine others were killed by 4 September and a further two wounded.

On 2 September 1939 Ebbinghaus troops were subordinated to *Grenzschutz-Ahschnitts-Kommando 3* in Gliwice, combining with SS *Standarte* 'Germania' and troops of the 239th Infantry Division the following day. That same morning, Ebbinghaus ordered the surviving men under his command to 'cleanse' the area of Orzesze of Silesian insurgents while also safeguarding the flank of the Wehrmacht advance. At 1645hrs Ebbinghaus men seized and held the Katowice radio station, the remainder of their involvement in the Polish campaign seeming to be the occupation and pacification of Katowice and the surrounding area.

Engaged in paramilitary combat in which racial identity and its incumbent deeply ingrained hatreds were to the fore, the men also appear to have been involved in the massacre of Poles including seventeen defenders of Pszczyna (including Boy Scouts from the Pszczyna secondary schools), twenty-nine citizens of Orzesze and six more in Siemanowice on 8 September. On 1 October, they shot eighteen people in Nowy Bytom and larger atrocities are believed to have been carried out in and around Katowice. SA *Sturmführer* Karl Rolle and others were also known to have been involved in the torture and murder of Polish captives in Bytom. The SS *Einsatzgruppen* were already active immediately behind the front lines, rounding up Jews and Poles that fitted their target demographics. Though also tasked with intelligence work involving the recovery of documents, they, alongside the Ebbinghaus Organisation and other paramilitary units, provided a clear vision of Poland's immediate future.

The Ebbinghaus Organisation was disbanded following its role in the Polish campaign, some of the more meritorious survivors being absorbed into *1. Baulehr Kompanie z.b.V.* which was formed at the existing base of the *Deutsche Kompanie* in Sliač. *Hauptmann* Putz gave the new unit its first orders; the men were to assemble in their base without attracting the attention of Slovakian border guards, the country's new government having sealed the borders with military units, police and customs men. Travelling in small groups, once successfully in Sliač they again donned Slovakian Army uniforms with the '*Deutsche Kompanie*' armbands. The company commander was the recently promoted *Hauptmann* Verbeek, with his chief instructors the now battle-experienced *Leutnants* Siegfried Grabert and Dr Gottfried Kniesche assisted by NCOs *Feldwebel* O.A. Süss and *Gefreiters* Fritz Buchholz and Pasche Klüver. Their intensive training included techniques for the taking and holding of bridges and other strategic objectives, as well as demolition and sabotage methods.

Meanwhile, on 27 September 1939, Adolf Hitler summoned his military chiefs to the Reich Chancellery. He ordered plans prepared for invasion of The Netherlands, Belgium and France during October in a knockout blow before Britain could fully mobilise its military. Though an impossible task, given the fact that the Wehrmacht had already expended vast energy subjugating Poland – the country surrendering on that day but the final battle at Kock not concluding until 6 October – the campaign strategy was slowly drawn up, while Army heads attempted to persuade their Führer to postpone the attack. Amidst the planning for war were instructions issued by Canaris to Hippel for the creation of a company of sabotage troops for commitment in the West. Hippel ordered the transfer of the Abwehr's 320-man strong *1. Baulehr Kompanie z.b.V.* from Slovakia to Germany, now officially redesignated '*Baulehr Kompanie z.b.V. 800*' (800th Special Purpose Construction Training Company) on 25 October. He had even secured the ideal training ground for his sabotage troops.

In the Prussian province of Brandenburg, west of Berlin, the small town of Brandenburg an der Havel was chosen as the headquarters of Hippel's troops, he himself having been quartered there during his time as an officer in the 43rd Engineer Battalion until 1937 and his transfer to the Abwehr. There, on the eastern shore of the Quenzsee, on an estate crowned by a three-winged manor house, the Abwehr established a 'Training and Sabotage School', known as

'*Quenzgut*', under the command of *Hauptmann* Seeliger.[3] The rural estate was surrounded by a high wall and the grounds would eventually boast weapons ranges, a laboratory for the development of explosives, an explosives testing bunker (*Sprengbunker*), a locksmith's workshop, models and mock-up bridges and traffic installations, a gymnasium, lakeside quay and various sports fields. All three branches of the Abwehr would send men to the school, ranging from specialised training for *Hauptmann* Verbeek's soldiers to agents and spies ('*V-Mann*' – *Vertrauens* man – a paid informer whose task it was to infiltrate political movements, or a spy). Explosives specialist *Major* Hans Maguerre, a First World War veteran of 2nd Engineer Battalion – and who had been engaged in work that had included potential biological sabotage – was responsible for procuring and maintaining equipment for the school, including enemy uniforms, arms, radio gear and explosives. He had played a major role in the establishment of the training centre despite 'numerous difficulties' put in his way by Wehrmacht administrative staff.[4] Those piqued administrators subsequently spread the rumour that Maguerre had misappropriated state funds provided for establishing the school to construct his own house in the country, though this failed to impede Maguerre's progress. 'Technical Inspector' Kutschke was on hand to instruct the recruits in engineering matters and the techniques employed by combat Engineers while Grabert and Kniesche would also act as military instructors.

Nearby, on Magdeburger Strasse, the barracks that had accommodated the *Feldartillerie-Regiment 'Generalfeldzeugmeister' (1. Brandenburgisches) Nr. 3* of the Imperial German Army's 6th Infantry Division served as the main quarters for Hippel's *Baulehr Kompanie z.b.V. 800*. Brandenburg an der Havel was no stranger to the military; cavalry and infantry regiments of the same Imperial Army division had occupied barracks in the town and the Wehrmacht's 68th Infantry Regiment (23rd Infantry Division), 59th Artillery Regiment, 22nd Flak Regiment and an engineer battalion were stationed there.[5] The *Generalfeldzeugmeister Kaserne* was an impressive multi-storey brick building with high-ceilinged rooms and narrow corridors which became home to Hippel's recruits.

The small town also boasted some important military manufacturing that would ultimately attract the attention of Allied bombers in later years. During 1934 Arado Werke opened an aircraft factory that edged the shoreline of the Quenzsee to the south of the Abwehr school at the end of the freight railway spur. In 1935 Adam Opel A.G. opened a factory inland towards the town itself, producing Opel 'Blitz' trucks and employing 6,000 men by 1939. Further heavy industry was also established in the town, the industrial conglomerate 'Reichswerke Hermann Göring' creating steel and weapons manufacturing plants.

The initial troops assigned to the new barracks were from the ranks of the Abwehr and various other military units; many *Volksdeutsche* of the border guard units in Spiš, north-west Slovakia (*Grenzwach-Regiments 'Zips'*), forty German mountain troops (*Gebirgsjäger*) who had formerly been part of the Czech Army and engineers from the Berlin military district, coming together to constitute the original complement of *Baulehr Kompanie z.b.V. 800* under Hippel's direct command.

Canaris also enlisted the aid of Kurt Jahnke, a highly successful saboteur and intelligence agent during the First World War. A naturalised American citizen, he had served under the command of the German Consul-General Franz Bopp at the behest of the German Admiralty from his San Francisco base, transferring to Mexico following the American declaration of war in 1917. After returning to Germany and following Hitler's accession to power, Jahnke established the 'Diplomatic Information Office '*Büro I*', also known as the '*Abteilung Von Pfeffer*' after SA *Obergruppenführer* Pfeffer von Salomon. Although Jahnke was in control, Pfeffer was nominally in command of what was a private intelligence agency, granted independence from OKW and reporting directly to Rudolf Hess despite partial funding by the Abwehr. However, pressure from Martin Bormann, Himmler and Heydrich encouraged Hitler to shut down *Büro I* on 26 April 1940. From the moment that Hippel had been ordered to create the *Baulehr-Bataillon z.b.V. 800*, Jahnke and his secretary Carl Marcus had been attached as intelligence officers (the Wehrmacht designation being 'Ic'); Marcus enlisted into the battalion after being called up for Wehrmacht service. He trained for four weeks and was despatched on an intelligence-gathering mission into Belgium and The Netherlands, before both he and Jahnke were moved away from the battalion by Heydrich and into *Amt VI* of the SD upon the dissolution of *Büro I*. Marcus was subsequently classified as 'unfit for military duties' in order that he could continue his work with Jahnke, now at the behest of the SD.[6]

Meanwhile with the existing timetable of an attack on the West still not postponed by Hitler, an experienced combat engineer and expert in radio deception, Berliner *Hauptmann* Hans-Jürgen Rudloff, arrived in Hippel's company as a platoon commander. Rudloff, an engineer by trade and veteran of the First World War as *Fahnenjunker* (Officer-Aspirant) in the 17th Engineer Battalion, had spent nine years in the Argentine before returning to Germany intending to enlist in the Army early in 1939. Initially rejected due to his age (39), he was finally commissioned as a *Leutnant* in the 3rd Engineer Battalion during July. However, he saw no service at all with the battalion as he was almost immediately transferred onwards to the Abwehr in Hamburg where his engineering expertise was solicited. His primary task was keeping records on so-called 'cultural' buildings in Denmark and England judged as targets of possible military importance, and Rudloff was frequently consulted for his expert opinion on the potential demolition of various foreign objectives. Following the end of the Polish campaign, Rudloff was promoted and transferred to *Baulehr Kompanie z.b.V. 800*.

He was under direct orders from Abwehr II to take up to a dozen men from his platoon (*3rd Zug der Baulehr Kompanie z.b.V. 800*) to Bad Münstereifel where he began immediate preparations to lead *Fall Gelb* ('Case Yellow'), the planned attack on the West. Rudloff's small contingent was reinforced by 100 men transferred by *Hauptmann* Fleck from Breslau to Jülich, less than 20km from the Belgian border.[7] From there they travelled to nearby Bad Münstereifel and trained under the auspices of the Fourth Army; *Oberleutnant* Moll and *Leutnant* Hütten of the Fourth Army and *Leutnant* Kutschera, formerly of the Czech military, enlisted to assist Rudloff in his training regime.

Rudloff was briefed on his coming tasks by the Army's Chief Intelligence Officer *Major* Joachim Schwatlo-Gesterding. He and his men were to cross the Belgian frontier before the main attack, primarily concerned with the seizure of important bridges in the Eupen-Malmedy region before the enemy could destroy them. Fortunately for an unprepared Wehrmacht, however, delays began to mount until 'Case Yellow' was finally postponed to 1940 due to weather considerations. Remaining in their forward base, Rudloff's group now formed the nucleus of a company-sized unit under Hippel's command, comprised primarily of Romanian and Sudeten *Volksdeutsche*.

Leutnant Grabert and his first eleven Sudeten *Volksdeutsche* men arrived in Brandenburg an der Havel from Sliač in November 1939 and joined Hippel's company, soon joined by further volunteers from Grabert's *Deutsche Kompanie*. The numbers of Hippel's force were beginning to swell, volunteers from the Banat and Transylvania regions, the Baltic states and Palestine joining the ranks so that he soon had enough men to reorganise into three separate companies and a manpower reserve.

Hippel's original *Baulehr Kompanie z.b.V. 800* was serving as a collection point for troops wishing to enlist in the special force. Berlin had authorised Hippel to appeal for volunteers from existing Wehrmacht formations, each separate company designating a recruiting officer who would travel from garrison to garrison combing the ranks for willing recruits. Maintaining his rationale of enlisting foreign-speaking men, Hippel was then able to distribute them into a platoon (*Zug*) grouped loosely by ethnicity and cultural heritage. His approach was, in many ways, the antithesis of that taken by the Waffen SS who were also attempting to plunder the manpower pool provided by *Volksdeutsche* recruits. The SS had been constrained in its ambition to expand due to strict recruitment limits imposed by the Wehrmacht in Germany. However, Heinrich Himmler's extremely efficient head of recruitment, SS *Brigadeführer* Gottlob Berger, had circumvented these restrictions by opening enlistment to suitable 'Nordic' recruits and *Volksdeutsche* from outside Germany's borders. Fortunately, Hippel was unconstrained by delusions of racial purity, the ability of a man to assimilate in potential foreign operational areas being of greater value to him than his heritage. Recruiting by individual officers yielded large numbers of men willing to join Hippel's force and by 15 December there were enough troops gathered to reorganise as a battalion:

- *Baulehr-Bataillon z.b.V. 800* (*Hauptmann* von Hippel);
- *Stabskompanie* (*Oberleutnant* Kutschke);
- *1st Baulehr Kompanie z.b.V.* (*Oberleutnant* Dr Kniesche);
- *2nd Baulehr Kompanie z.b.V.* (*Hauptmann* Fabian);
- *3rd Baulehr Kompanie z.b.V.* (*Hauptmann* Rudloff).

In fact, the rapid expansion of the Brandenburgers had begun to cause problems at the *Generalfeldzeugmeister Kaserne* as space became a serious issue. By their very nature Brandenburger units were loose organisations that experienced frequent reshuffles and changes, therefore it was decided that small constituent parts could be accommodated in pockets in villages neighbouring Brandenburg an der Havel. Kutschke's headquarters company moved to Plaue while others moved to Kranepul, north on the bank of the Havel River. The various companies then began to be stationed away from Brandenburg itself as a matter of operational routine, located near to their expected combat areas.

While Fabian's 2nd Company remained in Brandenburg an der Havel, *Oberleutnant* Dr Gottfried Kniesche's *1st Baulehr Kompanie z.b.V.* had begun training east of Vienna in Neustift-Innermanzing in the Wienerwald. Kniesche had received orders from Abwehr III (counter-espionage) to gather as many men from the *Deutsche Kompanie* with relevant linguistic abilities to relocate to the Wienerwald. From there they would be tasked with Operation 'Sportverein Wiking', a mission to ensure the security of the Romanian railway route which transported oil from the oilfields at Ploieşti to Germany. Rudloff, meanwhile, continued training for the upcoming invasion of the West stationed in Bad Münstereifel. Over the winter of 1939/40 volunteers continued to arrive as Hippel's formation received an unofficial soubriquet on Christmas Eve during celebrations at the *Generalfeldzeugmeister Kaserne*. According to the written account by the semi-official historian of the Brandenburgers (and later Quartermaster Officer of the Brandenburg Panzergrenadier Division) Helmuth Spaeter, during these raucous celebrations, in which Siegfried Grabert appeared in costume as the Devil, a nickname was given to the unit during a speech that soon stuck and was subsequently officially adopted: 'Brandenburgers'.

Men were not necessarily posted to the Brandenburgers, but claims that they remained strictly a volunteer unit are slightly misleading. Sepp De Giampietro enlisted in the Wehrmacht during 1940 and was assigned to the 8th Company. There he trained as a *Gebirgsjäger* and appears to have been perplexed after becoming aware of the fact that he was part of a unit that bore the designation 'z.b.V.' – for special purpose – fearing that it meant potentially risky operations. Not until immediately before deployment in Romania were he and his comrades informed by Siegfried Grabert of the specialised nature of their unit. Warned to remain silent about what they were being told on pain of court martial, it was at that point that they learned their commander-in-chief was not a *Gebirgsjäger* general, but *Admiral* Wilhelm Canaris of the Abwehr.

However, once aware of their status as part of a specialist force, theoretically each man could decline an operation, particularly those that required the wearing of a disguise and thus had the potential for execution as a spy if captured. The ideal Brandenburg recruit was a long way from many of those who had comprised the bulk of the Ebbinghaus Organisation who had been more militia than soldier. They were required to possess a degree of maturity and self-reliance that would enable them to carry out their allotted missions either as part of a small team or individually. They needed to be fleet-footed and quick-thinking; one exercise in initiative that was carried out involved recruits being tasked with obtaining the fingerprints of the Brandenburg an der Havel police officials without their targets being aware of what was happening. Dietrich von Witzel, an early recruit, later characterised the calibre of Hippel's new unit:

> What sort of men did this new force require and where did they come from? The first precondition was that they should be volunteers, then versatility, quick reactions, the gift of improvisation, a high degree of individual initiative, even to the last man, coupled with a strong team spirit; and besides these things, a sense of adventure, albeit restrained, tact when dealing with foreigners and of course physical stamina. Other priority requirements were a high level of linguistic expertise and cultural awareness to such a degree that a man could pass himself off as a British officer or a Soviet soldier . . . Ultimately, the men should have a solid military training and should know how to remove or plant explosive charges (to protect or destroy installations).[8]

The familiar drills that all Wehrmacht soldiers mastered were included, but taken a step further for the Brandenburgers. Training at Quanzsee included more theoretical components such as language instruction, messaging in secret, radio operation and recognition of enemy uniforms and ranks. Basic fieldcraft was expanded to give recruits the ability to move silently and undetected through undergrowth and forests while perfecting infiltration and camouflage techniques. Physically demanding skills such as swimming, small boat and kayak handling, long-distance running and the like raised them to peak condition while lessons were also held in both German and foreign weapons and vehicles, the manufacture and use of explosives, hand-to-hand combat, silent killing techniques using the knife or garrotte, and the customs, traditions and lifestyle associated with target regions. Lectures also focussed on the required sabotage – and 'small sabotage', i.e. without explosives – techniques for different targets such as bridges, power stations, industrial and railway installations, ships, cables and wireless stations. The nearby Arado works and the railway workshops at Kirchmöser were toured and used by Brandenburger instructors to demonstrate the theory and different requirements for railway and industrial sabotage.

There were two general forms of disguise employed by the Brandenburgers: *Halbtarnung* (literally, 'half camouflage') which essentially comprised an enemy greatcoat over a German uniform with corresponding headgear that could confuse an enemy in poor visibility, and *Volltarnung* (full camouflage) which was an entire enemy uniform worn over the German one. The latter was obviously more convincing, but also limited both the wearer's freedom of movement and ability to remove the uniform before opening fire. It would not be uncommon in the heat of action for the Brandenburgers to begin combat before they had removed their disguises, thereby running the risk of being legally considered as spies.

Brandenburger units were typically small and autonomy was as essential as the ability to integrate as a team. A sense of camaraderie was fostered, not dissimilar to that in the early Waffen SS, with officers and men encouraged to greet one another with handshakes rather than salutes. This of course further alienated Hippel's force from the orthodoxy of the traditional Wehrmacht who likened the techniques being perfected in Brandenburg an der Havel as those used by 'renegades and bandits'. It could have been the shadow cast by the excesses committed by elements of the Sudeten paramilitaries during the Polish campaign that influenced many Wehrmacht officers' views of the Brandenburgers and it would take fresh military success to vindicate Hippel and his troops.

In combat Brandenburgers were answerable only to their own commanders and the Ic (Intelligence Officer) of the Army Corps in whose area they were operating. However, in practice they frequently continued to receive and act only upon orders issued by their own headquarters. German military staffs were, as a rule, smaller than their Allied counterparts. In general, there were Intelligence Officers attached at Division, Corps, Army and Army Group level.

However, they were always rated as subordinate to the Operations Officers (Ia). The German Army Handbook of 1938 states:

- The Ic is subordinated to the Ia and is his helper in working up the enemy picture.
- Estimating the enemy picture is a matter for the commander in cooperation with the Chief of Staff or the Ia.
- The judgement of the enemy situation always proceeds from the command authorities, not from the Ic alone.

This 'action before brain' approach rendered an intelligence officer's judgement as constantly rated secondary to the will of his military commander. Therefore, the effect of accurate intelligence was entirely dependent upon the degree to which individual commanders appreciated its value. In many ways, this tendency was seen throughout German military hierarchy all the way to the supreme commander himself, Hitler frequently dismissing intelligence reports if they failed to fit the narrative that he desired to see.

While on operations, Brandenburg men were issued with that standard identity document of the Wehrmacht soldier – the *Soldbuch* – that showed them belonging to an ordinary military formation. Generally, a Brandenburger liaison officer was supplied to the umbrella Army Corps to allow such a free-wheeling unit to function within what was a highly methodical and fixed Wehrmacht command structure. These liaison officers' tasks included defining the method of employment for the Brandenburgers: full or partial camouflage, dates, times and places. The troops needed to be clearly identified to other Wehrmacht units and supporting troops that stood ready to exploit their success, while also allowing the rapid extraction of the commandos once their mission was complete. They were not designed to be used as traditional 'line troops' in any but the most extraordinary circumstances, their armament remaining light with mobility and deception their primary means of waging war. They also fully embraced the concept of *Auftragstaktik*; the issuing of an order for the accomplishment of an objective but with broad parameters that allowed subordinates to fulfil the stated objective using their own initiative.

The multinational makeup of the Brandenburgers was beginning to achieve some form of cohesive separation within the battalion. By this stage of the Brandenburgers' development, Kniesche's 1st Company in Austria was formed around men that could be described as ethnic Russians – sometimes Finns – or those from the Baltic states of Lithuania, Latvia and Estonia; Fabian's 2nd Company (based in Brandenburg an der Havel) would come to comprise primarily English-speaking North Africans or South Africans as well as those from Palestine and

Portugal. At least one recruit, *Gefreiter* Siemens, had been born in Melbourne, Australia.[9] In general, they were men who had returned from Germany's former colonies. The Palestinian *Volksdeutsche* were from Haifa's German colony, descendants of Templers – a southern German Protestant sect – that had emigrated to the Holy Land in 1868. By 1937, 34 per cent of those Palestinian *Volksdeutsche* were registered members of the NSDAP and many younger members returned to Germany, those remaining that retained German citizenship being interned by the British at the start of the Second World War. It was recorded that 232 such young men eligible for military service returned to Germany on the eve of war, primarily from ex-members of the Palestinian Hitler Youth and predominantly ending up in the Brandenburgers.[10] Rudloff's 3rd Company in the western base at Bad Münstereifel was made up of Sudeten Germans who spoke Czech, Slovak and Ruthenian, with an added platoon of men able to speak Dutch, Flemish and French, required for the impending invasion in the West.

During the first weeks of 1940 *Oberleutnant* Uwe-Wilhelm Walther was appointed commander of a newly established 4th Company in Brandenburg an der Havel, comprised primarily of *Volksdeutsche* from Poland, Belorussia and the Ukraine. A native of Dresden, Walther, who celebrated his thirtieth birthday on 27 January, had joined the Reichswehr in 1934, his face marked with a duelling scar on his left cheek, which was popular as a mark of honour amongst German university students. While in higher education studying to become an architect, Walther had been a member of the *Nationalsozialistischer Deutscher Studentenbund* (National Socialist Student League) that had been founded to attempt to integrate university-level education with National Socialist principles. He had served as an officer in reconnaissance units before being recruited for the Brandenburgers. Hippel also established smaller semi-autonomous elements, including a Brandenburger *Fallschirmjäger* (paratrooper) unit to be commanded by Upper Silesian *Leutnant* Dlab. Dlab was charged with selecting a small group of suitable candidates who were transferred to Oranienburg by *Feldwebel* Erich Blöhme to begin parachute training. There, a 40-year-old veteran of the last war's naval air arm, *Oberleutnant* Karl-Edmund Gartenfeld, instructed them. Following the 1918 armistice, Gartenfeld had flown for Lufthansa before enlisting in the Luftwaffe during 1936, transferred to the *Versuchsstelle für Höhenflüge* (Test Centre for High-Altitude Flights) upon the outbreak of war and subsequently to parachute training in Oranienburg during March 1940.[11]

Unsurprisingly in a military that was riven with inter-service rivalry and competition, the training of Army troops for a role reserved for Luftwaffe paratroopers caused initial problems between the Abwehr and OKL. The Army had already formed a *Fallschirmjäger* company during 1937, expanded to a battalion the following year, though then transferred en-masse to the

Luftwaffe on 1 January 1939. The vainglorious Hermann Göring jealously guarded 'ownership' of all of Germany's military airborne assets, his previous authority over police units already having been undermined by the SS. However, the Abwehr could circumvent Luftwaffe apprehension regarding new Army parachute units as the Brandenburg men were clearly a small, highly specialised unit to whom parachute training would provide a method by which to infiltrate enemy lines.

After graduation, the Brandenburgers received their Luftwaffe *Fallschirmschützenabzeichen* (Parachutists' Badges), as opposed to the specially commissioned version that had been briefly issued to Army men during 1937. It wouldn't be until the expansion of the Brandenburgers' *Fallschirmjäger* unit to company strength in 1943 that the Army badge would be reissued. The qualified airborne troops formed a platoon in Walther's 4th Company under the command of *Leutnant* Hermann Lütke, though based at Stendal where the Luftwaffe maintained an airfield and two squadrons of Ju 52 transport aircraft.

During early January 1940, 22-year old *Feldwebel* (Officer-Aspirant) Hermann Kürschner, formerly of the 12th Battalion, 115th Infantry Regiment, was enlisted by Hippel to form a small shock troop for service in the upcoming 'Case Yellow' invasion in the West. Kürschner was placed in command of his own minor unit, named '*Baulehr-Zug z.b.V.*' or '*Westzug*' (West Platoon), into which he enlisted many men from the coalmining area of Kerkrade-Herzogenrath, notably Srass. This village near Aachen straddles the German–Dutch border and his new recruits were fluent in both languages, many having served in the border guard formation *Grenzwacht-Abschnitt 46*.

The invasion of the Low Countries and France would comprise two phases: 'Case Yellow' in which the Channel would be reached and the British Expeditionary Force and swathes of other Allied troops isolated in Belgium, and *Fall Rot* ('Case Red'), the final subjugation of France. The Wehrmacht applied one of its major advantages to 'Case Yellow' – the ability of officers such as Manstein and Guderian to consider operational possibilities not rooted in military orthodoxy. The decision had been taken that rather than crashing against the buttresses of the Maginot Line that trailed virtually the entire length of the Franco-German border, troops of Army Group A and B would advance through The Netherlands and Belgium into France. However, this broad front advance was reminiscent of that used by the Imperial German Army in 1914 and stood every chance of ending in the same impasse. Manstein's modification involved German armour and troops breaking through the heavily wooded Ardennes region, sparsely defended by the Allies as it was considered unsuitable terrain for such an advance. Hitler, who had already proposed a similar idea to OKH, enthusiastically endorsed the plan and the original plans for 'Case Yellow' were altered accordingly. Key to the successful rapid advance through the southern provinces of The Netherlands and into Belgium would be the taking and holding of bridges that spanned the formidable waterways which provided natural defensive barriers.

On 15 February Kürschner was ordered to report to Lahousen at the Abwehr's Tirpitzufer offices in Berlin. Once there, he was presented with reconnaissance photos and a map on which four Dutch bridges across the Juliana Canal at Obbicht, Berg, Urmond and Stein were highlighted. The West Platoon was tasked with the capture of all four of these bridges west of Sittard that would need to be taken and held until the main invasion force of the 7th Infantry Division arrived to make the crossing. The Abwehr would place at Kürschner's disposal whatever camouflage and specialist equipment he would require, including fabricated Dutch uniforms to be worn over their German ones. Intensive training began, the West Platoon moving into the Erkelenz area and concentrating on night manoeuvres, orienteering and hand-to-hand combat. Intelligence reports of explosives rigged to at least one of the bridges also placed emphasis on speed of movement and the rapid defusing of sabotage equipment. During April, Kürschner was promoted to the rank of *Leutnant*.

The defence of The Netherlands hinged primarily on establishing water obstacles. The Dutch military was relatively small and the eastern and southern area that required guarding stretched for 700km. Neutrality had protected The Netherlands during the previous war, though the army had mobilised as a precaution, but the threat posed by Nazi hostility was judged to be perceptibly greater than that of twenty-six years before. Moreover, Dutch interpretation of 'strict neutrality' prevented any form of potential high-level defensive coordination with the Allied powers or neighbouring Belgium before 1939. The Dutch Prime Minister, Hendrikus Colijn, believed that any potential German invasion could be halted by 'opening the floodgates' and judicial flooding of the polder alongside rapid demolition of bridges. While it would not defeat an invasion, it was hoped that it would delay an attacking force long enough for complete mobilisation and for defensive lines to be established to the west.

The Netherlands finally acknowledged the threat of European war against the Axis powers following the Italian invasion of Abyssinia, but last-minute attempts at purchasing advanced weaponry were too late to significantly alter the composition of the Dutch Army. Immediately before the outbreak of war and despite assurances from the German ambassador that Dutch neutrality was 'inviolate' on 27 August, the country fully mobilised its forces. The hurried German military build-up near the border that had presaged Hitler's initial invasion plans during November 1939 had already raised alarm levels, but the failure of the invasion to take place fatally denigrated the standing of Dutch intelligence officers who had forecast the attack.

While Kürschner's men continued to mount exercises in preparation for seizing their assigned bridges, further small Brandenburg units were formed for the Western offensive. Two platoons belonging to Walther's 4th Company were also moved to forward bases in preparation for 'Case Yellow'. During the middle of February *Leutnant* Witzel and *Feldwebel* Stöhr took approximately sixty men (1st Platoon) into a camp in the Reichswald near Asperden to operate against four bridges in the Dutch province of Brabant. Witzel's force was subordinated to XXVI Army Corps and company commander Walther attached himself to the attack on the Gennep railway bridge. Canaris visited Witzel's men near Asperden at the beginning of May and was apparently impressed, though Witzel later recalled that he had been less enthusiastic about demonstrations of killing with knife and garrotte.[12]

Siegfried Grabert took another forty men of 2nd Platoon further south, operating adjacent to Kürschner's West Platoon and stationed in a small camp in the woods near Arsbeck, subordinated to XI Army Corps. Grabert's targets were four more bridges over the Maas between Roermond and Maaseik. Over the weeks that followed, various Brandenburgers slipped across the border to reconnoitre the layout of the enemy's defences. Moving in pairs or singly they took the opportunity to prepare a full picture of the terrain they would be traversing once the invasion day arrived. Weekend passes for the troops in training were limited to controlled visits to nearby towns, the destinations themselves rotated to prevent any kind of relationships forming between the men and the locals.

Rudloff's 3rd Company in Bad Münstereifel numbered three officers and 154 NCOs and men and was assigned Belgian targets. *Leutnant* Hütten and his section would attack objectives in the area between Eupen and Malmedy while *Leutnant* Kutschera and his troops operated to the south in the region surrounding St Vith. Rudloff exercised overall command, dividing his men into small parties of between three and fifteen men armed with small arms, hand grenades and explosives. Attached to IV Army Corps, the 3rd Company was to clear the path for the panzers that would provide the vital edge in the invasion, passing through the weakly defended Ardennes. They were not the only commando-type troops engaged; several hundred men of the elite *Grossdeutschland* Division were to be air-landed in Luxembourg and Belgium by shuttles of Fieseler Fi 156 Storch aircraft to hinder the movement of French and Belgian reinforcements.

During March two platoons of Fabian's 2nd Company were moved to forward staging areas from where they too would move into Luxembourg. *Leutnant* Schöller commanded a small detachment based at Trier while *Feldwebel* Eggers took his men to Sankt Thomas, moving into advanced positions amongst the bunkers of the West Wall around Ammeldingen bei Neuerburg after first returning home to fetch suitable civilian clothes for the purpose of disguise.

The Brandenburgers were divided into small teams that rarely numbered more than twelve for 'Case Yellow'. While many of the chosen Brandenburgers could speak fluent Dutch, volunteer Dutch nationals were attached for the missions. Many members of Anton Mussert's *Nationaal-Socialistische Beweging* (NSB – Dutch Nazi Party) had been jailed as The Netherlands declared the country to be in a state of siege during April, others fleeing over the border to Germany to join those who had already relocated and been surreptitiously enlisted by the Abwehr. The Dutch Nazis were therefore members of the *Nationaal-Socialistische Bond van Nederlanders in Duitsland* (NSBND), their leader Julius Herdt Mann attending a meeting with Lahousen in Berlin on 14 November 1939. Though minutes do not remain of the meeting, it is assumed that Herdt Mann was informed of plans for the occupation of The Netherlands as he offered a significant number of NSBND members for the task outlined to him. At least forty of these expatriates were taken on as *Kampfdolmetscher* (combat interpreters). While linguistics was an integral part of Brandenburg training, the edge provided by genuine native speakers was worth the inclusion of additional men. This subsequently proved so successful that it would become a frequent feature of future Brandenburg actions in all theatres, augmenting those who could pass as indigenous to the theatre of operation.

A separate Abwehr formation was also created for 'Case Yellow'. The Austrian *Hauptmann* Fleck, late of *Abwehrstelle Breslau*, was placed in command of *Bataillon z.b.V. 100*, charged with taking and holding the bridges in and around Maastricht in support of the army advance towards Fort Eben Emael. Fleck's battalion was made up of 550 Abwehr men with fifty seconded from the Brandenburgers. Fleck's unit remained separate to Hippel's battalion and was a combination of orthodox Wehrmacht troops and special forces employing the same methodology. Fleck's command was comprised of a headquarters company with attached bicycle and motorcycle units, one Engineer company, one combined engineer and infantry company, a battery of four 88mm Flak guns and two armoured vehicles. A special formation was created internally, led by Fleck's adjutant *Leutnant* Hans-Joachim Hocke, designated *Sonderverbänd Hocke*. It was to this special unit that the task of capturing the bridges over the Maas near Maastricht would fall.

At OKH in Berlin it had become apparent that the burgeoning *Baulehr-Bataillon z.b.V. 800* had reached the point where it required a more expansive regimental command structure to achieve the variety of tasks now being demanded of it in widely dispersed geographical locations. Those men not assembled for impending action in any theatre were grouped in Brandenburg an der Havel as battalion headquarters, forming a reserve pool ready for transfer wherever required. However, with the likely upgrading of *Baulehr-Bataillon z.b.V. 800* to regimental status, a new forward operations staff was created under the command of *Major* Hubert Kewisch. Kewisch had been the pre-war commander of the armoured cars of 1st Squadron (*Panzerspäh*) of Potsdam's *Aufklarungsabteilung 8* (8th Reconnaissance Battalion) in the rank of *Rittmeister*. Then, his unit had been incorporated in the 5th Panzer Division, primarily made up of Silesians or Sudeten *Volksdeutsche*. Promoted to *Major* after the Polish campaign, Kewisch was subsequently transferred by OKH to *Baulehr-Bataillon z.b.V. 800* in anticipation of its expansion to regimental size.

Meanwhile, despite the loss of fifty men to Fleck's battalion, the Brandenburgers were now combat-ready for the impending invasion of the West but events in Scandinavia overtook them and all eyes were momentarily diverted to the north.

CHAPTER 2

Operation 'Weserübung' and 'Case Yellow': Scandinavia and the West

'If you find yourself in a fair fight, you didn't plan your mission properly.'
David Hackworth

Germany's industrial war machine relied heavily on raw materials imported from Scandinavia, particularly iron ore extracted from Sweden's Gällivare mines and shipped through neutral Norwegian coastal waters to Germany in accordance with international agreements. Hitler had long feared Allied interference with these crucial imports through an invasion of Norway and not without justification. Winston Churchill advocated seizure of Norway or, at the very least, the vital mines under a pretext of military assistance to Finland, which had been under attack by the Soviet Union since November 1939. The cessation of those hostilities removed the potential for such subterfuge, but British, French and Polish troops were nonetheless made ready for an attack on Norway.

The Wehrmacht had in the meantime begun preparation for the same strategic move. With 'Case Yellow' delayed from Hitler's initial November timetable, his misgivings about Allied intentions in Scandinavia grew. On 15 February 1940, the Royal Navy ignored Norway's neutrality and attacked the German supply ship *Altmark* that had moored in Norwegian territorial waters. British prisoners taken by the 'pocket battleship' *Admiral Graf Spee* were aboard, being transferred to German captivity, and were freed by the Royal Navy, seven German sailors being killed in the action. This removed the last of Hitler's restraint towards the region and an invasion of Norway and Denmark was ordered prepared under the command of *Generaloberst der Infanterie* Nikolaus von Falkenhorst. The new operation took precedence over all previous instructions and France and the Low Countries were to be dealt with shortly thereafter.

Denmark was to be occupied in Operation '*Weserübung Süd*', Norway invaded with the more extensive '*Weserübung Nord*' that required huge commitment from all three branches of the Wehrmacht. The attack on Denmark has often been presented as a bloodless coup, a footnote in the history of '*Weserübung*'.

However, although resistance was relatively futile and brief, the Wehrmacht suffered casualties almost disproportionate to the amount of actual fighting. Denmark itself was not of major interest to Germany: the small country was destined for invasion to secure the southern flank of Scandinavian operations and provide the forward airfield at Aalborg for use by the Luftwaffe against Norway. Though Denmark had reliable intelligence that invasion was at hand, its government refused to allow military defensive deployments lest they provoke Germany.

The Brandenburger commitment to '*Weserübung*' was quite small, their first operation against Denmark codenamed '*Sanssouci*'. A small unit led by 28-year-old Latvian *Feldwebel* Robert Sorgenfrey crossed over the border near Flensburg during the night of 8 April, dressed in civilian clothes. Sorgenfrey's task was to ensure the swift capture of the railway station at Tinglev, securing the line for German use during the following day. Undefended, the station was quickly taken and German troops breached the border at Kruså at 0415hrs, skirmishing with Danish guards and losing two armoured cars and three motorcycles. The defenders were quickly forced to retreat with one man killed and another injured, and the German advance continued, shortly linking with Sorgenfrey's Brandenburgers, whereupon the small team returned to Germany.[1]

Skirmishes between the Kriegsmarine and Norwegian warships around Oslo began on the night of 8 April and at 0500hrs the German Ambassador informed the Norwegian government both verbally and in writing that they were 'requested' to place themselves under German military protection, citing the imminence of Allied occupation as the cause. A similar note had been delivered to the Danish government. The latter acquiesced under protest, the former refused. Landings by *Fallschirmjäger* and amphibious troops in Denmark proceeded as planned, meeting little resistance. '*Weserübung Süd*' progressed smoothly with troops landed in the capital Copenhagen from the ship *Hansestadt Danzig*. Other amphibious landings were made near Middelfahrt to protect the bridge over the Little Belt and at Gjedser, Nyborg and Korsoer. The brief but sharp skirmishes that had been fought near the German border were finished within six hours when Denmark formally capitulated, but left at least 203 German troops dead, twelve armoured cars destroyed or damaged and four tanks damaged. The Danes lost sixteen men killed and twenty wounded.

In Norway, the battle would last considerably longer, particularly in and around Narvik and Trondheim, with German troops consolidating their initial landing positions to differing degrees, but the main beachhead at Oslo failed to break out to the north and link up the German pockets. Falkenhorst's intelligence assessment of Norwegian strength before the beginning of '*Weserübung*' had overestimated the size of the Norwegian military, but underestimated its willingness and ability to fight. Although the Allied expeditionary force that had also landed in Norway was badly coordinated and chaotic, it managed to severely blunt the German offensive in the north. Hippel's men were not utilised in the first wave of troops of '*Weserübung Nord*', but as the advance rapidly stalled with heavy Norwegian resistance and British, French and Polish reinforcements, the Brandenburgers were called into action.

A new *Nordzug* (North Platoon) – actually more like company size – was created in Brandenburg an der Havel for potential service in Norway. Leipzig-born *Leutnant* Johann Karl Fürchtegott Zülch, only recently turned 27, was placed in command of the platoon, which was subdivided into separate components. The first, comprised primarily of men from Upper Silesia, was intended to operate against four Polish battalions that had landed near Narvik on 9 April under French command, soon formed into the Polish Independent Highland Brigade. A second platoon, mainly made up of Palestinian Germans led by *Feldwebel* Lange, combined with the so-called *Bergzug* (Mountain Platoon) of predominantly South Tyrolian mountaineers, gathered under the command of *Leutnant* Fritz Benesch.

A forward operational headquarters under the command of *Major* Kewisch (*Einsatzstab Kewisch*) was flown to Oslo on 20 April by Ju 52 aircraft, all four of which were destroyed that night by British bombing while still on the newly captured aerodrome. Kewisch received his briefing from *Oberst* Erich Buschenhagen, Chief of Staff to Falkenhorst. The orders for the Brandenburg troops were relatively broad in their scope. Codenamed Operation '*Carolus*', Kewisch's men were to mostly wear civilian clothes and secure bridges and other river crossings, clear or mark approach roads of mines, disable Norwegian Army communications centres and disrupt troop movements wherever possible. Supply centres for both the Norwegian and Allied troops were to be attacked and destroyed and Kewisch's men to infiltrate behind enemy lines to harass the Allied supply routes.

As the first men of the North Platoon arrived in Oslo at the end of April, Kewisch immediately began moving into action, leading the spearhead of his men north from Oslo on 1 May, flown by Ju 52 aircraft towards the front line of the 181st Infantry Division at Trondheim. Benesch's Mountain Platoon was shortly thereafter detached from Kewisch's command and ordered to accompany the 2nd Mountain Division as it headed towards Narvik. The division was attempting to reinforce the hard-pressed German invasion force which had been pushed on to the defensive and would soon be forced to abandon the town and move east.

During the advance, the Mountain Platoon went into action during the attack towards Mo i Rana. A frontal assault along the main road that ran alongside

Ranfjorden by mountain troops was halted at the Dalselva River by fierce defence that comprised 1st Scots Guards (less C Company, which was detached at Bodø), No. 1 Independent Company, a troop of 203 Battery, 51st Field Regiment, Royal Artillery, with four 25-pounder guns, a troop of 40mm Bofors anti-aircraft guns of the 55th Light Anti-Aircraft Regiment, Royal Artillery and other attached smaller contingents that included a Norwegian troop (the entire Allied force named 'Trappescol' as a whole). Thwarted by the strong defence, the Mountain Platoon marched east with a company of mountain troops to begin an outflanking manoeuvre that traversed the river and reached the lake of Andfiskvatnet before swinging west and attacking the defensive lines from the rear. The speed with which they moved prompted the British commander of the North-Western Expeditionary Force, Lieutenant General Claude Auchinleck, to complain in a letter to General John Dill, Vice Chief of the Imperial General Staff, regarding the rather precipitate retreat from Mo: 'Why our soldiers cannot be as mobile as the Germans I don't know, but they aren't apparently.'[2]

Benesch's men assisted in the capture of the mines and smelting works at Mo i Rana though they were unable to prevent the destruction of the bridge over the Renaelva River, demolished by retreating British troops on 18 May. However, the bulk of 'Trappescol's' supplies plus all the Royal Artillery 25-pounder guns, cabling and signals equipment were left behind and captured by the Germans. The Mountain Platoon continued to harry the retreating Allied forces alongside the 2nd *Gebirgs* Division, Benesch's men using commandeered bicycles to advance towards Skjerstadfjorden and open fire with small arms at Allied troops while they boarded a large ferry and ten trawlers at Rognan as the evacuation from Norway began. The same pattern was repeated as the advance continued through Fauske, devastated by Luftwaffe air raids, and the last Allied troops were evacuated by sea from Bodø.

The troops of North Platoon operated in their familiar small groups – eleven in total – one five-man party led by *Unteroffizier* Friedrich Deininger travelling by truck from Trondheim to Kongsmoen, destroying Norwegian telephone communications en-route. From Kongsmoen they voyaged by small motor cutter to Foldereid and then overland towards Terråk. Their convoluted path took them to Vik near Bindalsfjorden on the last day of May, where they encountered resistance. Deininger was hit a glancing blow on his steel helmet and rendered unconscious for twenty-four hours while 23-year-old Austrian *Pionier* Günther Ernst Bergmann was killed. The small group attempted to avoid being encircled by the enemy, but in the early hours of the morning they were captured. The prisoners, including Deininger, were taken north to the camp on Skorpa Island near Tromsø. They were held there until the capitulation of Norway secured their release.

The Wehrmacht had begun the oft-postponed 'Case Yellow' on 10 May against France and the Low Countries, leading to the Allied decision to evacuate Norway. Despite localised success in Narvik, the Allied Norwegian expedition had been chaotic, with little coordination between it and Norwegian forces, for whom they mistakenly had little regard. With little choice, the Norwegian government bowed to the inevitable and capitulated on 12 June, by which time disaster had also overtaken Allied forces in mainland Europe. Deininger and his men arrived in Oslo to rejoin the remainder of the North Platoon on 19 June. Kewisch's small force had lost two men killed and another severely wounded during the fighting in Norway. *Generaloberst* von Falkenhorst went as far as to issue a letter to the '*Carolus*' men from Trondheim on 12 June, praising their 'dedication, their courage and their good achievements'. From Oslo, the Brandenburgers travelled back to their German headquarters while other units of the battalion had already entered combat in the west.

'Case Yellow' – the Invasion of the Low Countries and France

It is almost surprising that 'Case Yellow' succeeded as well as it did. There had been enough security breaches in the Wehrmacht to completely reveal German intentions, let alone the fact that German military forces visibly massed along the Dutch and Belgian borders, while the Luftwaffe mounted an increasing tempo of reconnaissance flights along the entire frontier.[3] Ironically, the Dutch still failed to fully grasp the scale of the impending attack despite specific information having been passed to the Dutch military attaché in Berlin, Major Gijsbertus J. Sas. In direct language, the scope of Hitler's plans in western Europe were provided by none other than the Abwehr's *Oberst* Hans Oster. Oster felt that if 'Case Yellow' met with disaster for Germany then the commanders of the Wehrmacht as well as the German population would rise up against the Nazis and expel them from power. A new government could then negotiate peace with the Allies. Though there is no evidence to prove Canaris was connected to this, there is equally nothing to prove that he was not. It is known that a visit to the Polish battlefield had left him, as German diplomat Ulrich von Hassell remembered, 'completely broken after he had seen the results of our brutal conduct of the war'.[4] Furthermore, despite Canaris' best efforts and instructions, the *Geheime Feldpolizei* (GFP – Secret Field Police), under Abwehr command, had been frequently compelled to work alongside the SD in the rounding up of Polish intellectuals for execution. Treason appeared the only resource available to derail Hitler's war of conquest.

The Dutch also benefitted from observing the modus operandi of the Wehrmacht in Scandinavia, noting the effectiveness of parachute landings and sabotage work undertaken by the so-called 'fifth column' as well as an apparent disdain for declared neutrality. Martial law was expanded in the provinces of The Netherlands which culminated in the 19 April declaration by the Dutch government that The Netherlands were officially in a state of siege. On 9 May Sas sent a final message from Berlin to The Hague: 'Tomorrow at dawn. Hold tight.'[5] That same evening the Brandenburgers began to move, their part in the invasion codenamed Operation '*Morgenrot*'.

In the south, *Leutnant* Kürschner's West Platoon moved forward from their base at Erkelenz to Millen on the Dutch–German border during the night of 9 May. A small battalion command post had been established under the control of *Oberfeldwebel* Töpelmann – formerly of the 115th Infantry Regiment, the 'oldest regiment in Christendom' – which would accompany the strike force over the border. There they would halt while the remainder forged onward to their targets; four constituent groups, each with a bridge over the Juliana Canal to take. Reconnaissance had shown that hastily improvised demolition charges for all four bridges were triggered by fuses located along the spans themselves, rather than in cover on the eastern bank. The Brandenburgers would use this vulnerability to their advantage, having only to reach the centre of each bridge to control the firing mechanism.

After donning a *Volltarnung* disguise of complete Dutch uniforms over their Wehrmacht ones, the West Platoon men prepared to cross the frontier on foot at about 0130hrs, each carrying a black Dutch bicycle. Guided by a local sympathiser, their route took them over the narrow Geleenbeek River by flimsy footbridge and through countryside between the conurbations of Oberhoven and Nieuwstadt until they reached an orchard that had been designated the point of dispersion for the four combat groups. Setting off at intervals of five to ten minutes, the groups made good time towards their allotted targets, each man riding with main weapon slung and pockets filled with pistols and grenades.

Kürschner led the attack on the bridge at Berg himself, riding his bicycle between two concrete sewer sections placed upright and filled with sand that provided an improvised anti-tank obstacle. Dismounting, Kürschner approached a group of Dutch soldiers gathered in the middle of the bridge who immediately began nervously backing away from their unexpected visitors. Using his command of the Dutch language, Kürschner called out, 'Halt! Where is the commander of the guard?' This commanding gambit gave him valuable seconds of uncertainty during which time he and his men had reached the Dutch soldiers. 'Boys, put down your weapons', Kürschner quietly ordered them and the guards were swiftly disarmed. A single man made a sudden dash for the demolition controls at the bridge railing and was shot in the leg by *Unteroffizier* Bergner with his pistol. The remainder implored the Germans not to shoot and

Kürschner swiftly cut the wires leading to the ignition panel as his men began to remove the inert TNT charges. A sudden burst of Dutch machine-gun fire laced through the darkness, aimed at both the German troops and the explosives in an attempt to blow the bridge. Kürschner was hit in both thighs and the right foot and as *Gefreiter* Frey dragged the wounded officer to shelter, he too was hit as the final bundle of TNT was removed and thrown into the river. The first bridge was in German hands and above them Luftwaffe aircraft began passing overhead to targets inland. The two wounded Brandenburg men were later taken to hospital in Sittard for medical treatment.

Unteroffizier Klein led the attack on the Stein bridge while *Unteroffizier* Klausmeier handled that at Urmond. Both were taken rapidly with minimal fighting and the explosive charges swiftly defused and removed. To the north, the strongest resistance was encountered by *Unteroffizier* Landvogt at the Obbicht bridge. There too, the Dutch had upended concrete sewer pipe sections and filled them with sand, Landvogt and his men passing between them in Dutch Gendarme uniforms before being challenged by sentries. The Dutch guard commander, a young Reserve Lieutenant, approached the group and requested identification, whereupon he received the reply: '*Hände hoch!*' Shouting for his men to open fire, the Dutch officer, Lieutenant Hendrik Gerrit Nijland, was the first to be fatally shot, Corporal Mindert Epema also being hit while attempting to reach the fuses, though the fierce defensive fire also forced the German attackers back and into cover.

The small Brandenburg unit was pinned down by machine-gun fire from a bunker on the east bank as they removed their Dutch disguises and returned fire, identifying the demolition fuse's ignition point midway across the bridge. Landvogt kept Dutch troops away from it with accurate submachine-gun fire until advance troops from the 7th Infantry Division brought up a 37mm PaK and silenced the Dutch machine gun, allowing Landvogt to race onto the bridge and remove the charges.

The West Platoon had successfully taken each objective, suffering two seriously wounded men and twelve lightly injured during the process. In return they had captured 175 Dutch prisoners, including five officers. While the men of the West Platoon returned to Erkelenz, the 7th Infantry Division raced west through Dutch territory into Belgium.

Immediately north of West Platoon's zone, *Leutnant* Grabert's 2nd Platoon encountered significant obstacles during their missions. Like Kürschner's men they had donned disguises that ranged from full Dutch uniforms, the *Halbtarnung* of greatcoats and helmets (sometimes Abwehr-created copies of greatcoats with paper-mâché helmets only good enough to be convincing in darkness) to civilian metalworkers' clothes. Their most southerly target was the bridge at Masseik that crossed the Maas River at a point at which the river delineated The Netherlands from Belgium (in which country the river is named the 'Meuse'). First the Juliana Canal needed to be crossed via the concrete sluice bridge near Roosteren, unable to be rigged for demolition due to its composition and important sluice function. Likewise, the bridge over the canal just over 5km to the south at Born which would be taken later by an advanced unit of 82nd Infantry Regiment despite strong Dutch resistance that inflicted casualties.

Grabert's men approached the Roosteren bridge disguised as Dutch Gendarmes, the defending troops totalling approximately forty men distributed between three bunkers plus a 57mm light infantry gun. The Germans passed by one squad of infantry despite using a password that was twenty-four hours old before being halted at the eastern end of the bridge by a Dutch police corporal. The commander of the watch was summoned as Corporal Van der Velde had detected distinct anomalies with the newcomers' uniforms. As he attempted to interrogate the disguised Germans, a chaotic firefight erupted after the arriving Dutch Reserve Captain, Petrus Maria Braun, was shot and killed at point-blank range. The defenders abandoned their position with several others killed and the bridge taken while the Brandenburgers hurried on, led by Grabert himself. However, their next target would not fall so easily. Though they managed to bluff their way close enough to the Dutch guards on the eastern end of the Masseik bridge, they were stopped by the Belgians that held the western end.

> At 4.00am a young officer, Lieutenant Fernand de Vinck, who oversaw watching the large bridge over the river Meuse or Maas between Belgium and Holland and Germany a few miles away. Fernand rang my father: 'Major: I can detect some Grey or Green uniforms on the bridge, what must I do?' (half of the bridge was Belgian and the other half Dutch). 'Hold on,' answered my father, 'I am coming.' Imagine blowing the bridge up with Dutch soldiers on it! What a diplomatic incident!! As my father arrived and approached the bridge, the Germans fired at his car and he received two bullets; one in the shoulder and the other deeply into the groin. Of course, the young Lieutenant knew they had to be Germans and immediately blew the bridge up. Later, we heard through the Belgian military attaché in Berlin what the papers said, 'Those ghastly Belgians waited until we had 300 soldiers on the bridge to blow it up . . .' the true story tells you another side . . .[6]

Grabert's men had been reinforced by members of the *Aufklärungs Abteilung 31* (31st Infantry Division's Reconnaissance Battalion) and the blast killed three German engineers and an infantryman who had rushed onto the bridge to defuse the explosives.

Three kilometres to the south, another of Grabert's detachments approached the bridge over the Juliana Canal near the hamlet of Illikhoven, lightly defended by only thirty-five men stretched along a front of 2km in three small bunkers. The Brandenburgers were disguised as Dutch bicycle troops, but the care and attention to their disguise had been incomplete and suspicious Dutch troops spotted 'irregularities' with the cyclists and quickly opened fire. The Germans immediately took cover and removed their disguises to return fire but within seconds the bridge was demolished before their eyes. Wehrmacht troops of the 31st Infantry Division would later pound the defenders and their bunkers to rubble with 88mm guns and force a river crossing at 0900hrs.

A further passage over the Juliana Canal was to be taken by a small five-man group under the command of *Unteroffizier* Hegel, but they were thwarted by alert defenders who also quickly penetrated their disguise. Pinned down and soon encircled, Hegel and his men surrendered. As they were led across the bridge towards the Dutch rear, Hegel pulled out a concealed stick grenade and threw it. Dutch and Germans alike dived to the ground, the Brandenburgers recovering first and escaping to recover their discarded weapons and resume the fight. This time they swiftly gained the upper hand in close combat, subduing the defenders and able to defuse the demolition charges before they were detonated. The grenade blast severely wounded Hegel, and the remaining Brandenburgers held the bridge against some half-hearted counter-attacks until relieved by approaching German armour that fortunately arrived as the Brandenburgers fired the last of their ammunition. Hegel was taken to hospital shortly afterwards. It was a rare success for 2nd Platoon.

The Maas crossings at Roermond were of crucial importance to the planned advance of the 19th Infantry Division and two vital bridges were assigned to Grabert's platoon. The first was a large road bridge in the outskirts of the city itself that was to be taken by eleven men under the command of *Feldwebel* Weber and led by a guide from the borderland, all disguised in Dutch military uniforms though carrying German weapons. The second was nearly 2km north; a railway bridge at Buggenum that was targeted by six Brandenburgers dressed as metal workers led by *Unteroffizier* Hilmer. Behind the German border an armoured train armed with light weapons (*Eisenbahn Panzerzug* No. 5) was scheduled to leave immediately the bridge was taken, followed by a troop train holding the 2nd Battalion, 59th Regiment that was waiting to cross the Buggenum bridge and breach the Peel–Raam defensive line of at Weert. The armoured trains used in 'Case Yellow' were National Railroad locomotives, painted field grey with white aircraft identification. They sported an open carriage each with two 60cm side boards separated by a 35cm sand-filled gap designed to act as gunfire and splinter protection. Each carriage mounted a MG34 medium machine gun on a tripod and carried armed infantry; 130 men aboard in total with between six and ten heavy machine guns and four MG34 twin mounts. In front of the train an empty wagon acted as a mine-destruction device.

The advance to the Roermond road bridge took the disguised Germans through the town itself before a Dutch patrol stopped them only a few hundred metres from their target. Weber watched as their guide, dressed as an army lieutenant, presented forged Abwehr papers for inspection by the Dutch patrol leader. However, what the Abwehr had failed to realise was that the guard detachment that held Roermond's bridges had been stationed in the town for nearly two years and therefore any strange troops were automatically suspect. Their opposite numbers remained unconvinced and Weber decided to seize the initiative and order the startled patrol to surrender at the top of his voice. However, their reflexes were as good as the Germans' and they scattered in seconds, Weber and his men taking cover while discarding their disguises. Before any shots had been fired, the bridge exploded at 0355hrs; the exact moment set for the main invasion force to begin crossing the border. Though they subsequently escaped capture, Weber's men had failed completely.

At the Buggenum railway bridge, Dutch police stood guard before an iron gate that was always closed and locked during the hours of darkness when there was no scheduled railway traffic. Such crossings this close to the German border had been so secured since the announcement of national siege conditions in The Netherlands. An extra iron barrier blocked the track on the eastern bank while the western bank also boasted an equivalent iron gate, covered by two 50mm artillery pieces and a heavy machine gun in thick riverside bunkers.

At 0300hrs nearby troops notified the guards of the presence of an unidentified group of six men coming on foot down the railway line from Leeuwen. Gunfire from Roermond had already raised the Dutch alert level and once Hilmer's disguised Brandenburgers reached the eastern checkpoint they were stopped by four guards who almost immediately requested an infantry squad to arrest the Germans. At that moment, the Brandenburgers opened fire, hitting Corporal Petrus Dirk Touw in the face and killing him instantly as well as severely wounding Police Sergeant de Vries. As the remaining lightly injured corporals dragged de Vries towards the western bank, the Germans pursued them closely in their bid to reach the demolition fuses, but to no avail as the defending troops detonated explosives that destroyed the bridge, killing three of the attackers and severely injuring the remainder.[7]

Twenty minutes after the successful demolition, the armoured train appeared, coming to a stop 500m from the ruined bridge and immediately being shelled by Dutch artillery that crippled the locomotive by fracturing her brake line, killing seven of the seventy-five Wehrmacht troops aboard. The German armoured train returned fire as the troop train arrived and disgorged its infantry passengers, the combined artillery and machine-gun fire killing several of the new arrivals. Nonetheless, by 0930hrs the Wehrmacht had forced a crossing of the river and taken the west bank. However, the loss of both bridges would remain a major logistical problem for the German advance until engineers could provide makeshift pontoons.

Fifty kilometres to the north the 4th Company had mixed results from their operations. *Oberleutnant* Walther's company had been given five main bridges to deal with: the railway bridge at Gennep; the railway bridge across the Maas near Mook; the road bridge at Malden; the lifting lock on the Maas at Heumen; and the road bridge at Hattert. Walther himself led the attack on the Gennep bridge, using three Dutch *Kampfdolmetscher* disguised as Gendarmes of the *Marechaussee* whose duties included that of military police for the Dutch Army. These men would infiltrate the defences by masquerading as the escort of six German 'deserters', each carrying concealed weapons.

At 2200hrs on 9 May the company moved from their camp in the Reichswald towards the border to prepare for their crossing during the early hours of the morning. The six Germans wore their standard Wehrmacht uniform while the Dutchmen received their disguises and weapons at the forward staging area. Walther's 'deserters' had perfected their weapon concealment and each wore an unbuttoned greatcoat without a belt, a machine pistol carried under the armpit, a pistol and wire cutters each stuffed in the back of their trouser waistband and pockets full of egg and stick grenades.

At 0230hrs the small column of men crossed the border and began their journey towards the Gennep bridge. One of the Dutchmen experienced a change of heart once over the border and Walther quickly detailed one of his men to escort him back to the staging area in Germany, where he was to be kept under lock and key to prevent any potential security breach. The remainder pressed on and in time they reached the bridge, stopping 800m short for a final briefing. The group then emerged into full view and walked slowly towards their target. Walther's immediate subordinate, Bavarian *Feldwebel* Hermann Stöhr, later recalled the attack:

> The bridge itself, an imposing iron construction, was about 150 metres long and had a Dutch defence system with bunkers and a permanent guard of platoon strength if not more. I think everybody in our 'commando' got a little queasy when they saw it. But impudence wins; something we proved later.
>
> An open road to the bridge and the Dutch have already seen us. At the entrance to the bridge, four Dutchmen intercepted us. Now it was time for acting! Did they still think that we were prisoners and if so, was there any

danger from this handful of German soldiers, were there still any more German troops yet to see? Who knows! *Oberleutnant* Walther and I suddenly put our pistols against the guards' chests, the action invisible from the other end of the bridge. Walther kept the sentries at bay, while I took the two steps to the guardhouse, with a deep breath, pulled out my knife and cut all the wires that could be reached. I did not see what was going on around me, since I only had eyes and ears for this wire. Meanwhile it appears that a Dutchman had become suspicious and fired a shot and we had our first badly wounded man. It's still a mystery to me today how this went unnoticed.[8]

Indeed, somewhat miraculously, the men holding the other end of the bridge displayed no reaction to the gunshot. Walther and Stöhr, along with another Brandenburger and a single Dutch interpreter, Martin van Haalen, continued along the length of the bridge, maintaining their disguise while the remainder of Walther's group took cover on the west bank. The four men passed a guard stationed midway without hindrance and reached the far end whereupon they were confronted by raised weapons from the remaining guards. Walther improvised as the sound of German aircraft could be heard overhead, shouting, '*Fliegerdeckung!*' ('Aircraft, get down!') at the top of his voice. As all men present dived for cover the Brandenburgers pulled free their hidden weapons and rapidly disarmed the startled guards. Three bunkers were taken by a combination of 'weapons and cunning' and approximately forty Dutch troops captured, though some defenders remained at large and began shooting at the small Brandenburg group. With the eastern end of the bridge secured, Walther fired a signal flare that summoned the armoured train (*Eisenbahn Panzerzug* No. 1) that was waiting on the German border, arriving shortly thereafter and silencing a single bunkered Dutch artillery piece that had begun firing. Minutes later a second train carrying a battalion of troops from the 256th Infantry Division passed by as elements of the 7th Panzer Division also flowed west over the major crossing point.[9]

Walther and his troops returned to Germany, the young officer subsequently being recommended for the Knight's Cross, which was awarded on 24 June 1940. Commander of XXVI Army Corps, *General der Artillerie* Albert Wodrig, wrote Walther a personal letter eight days after the operation:

After the directive to occupy Holland, I would like to recall once more the fighting which you have carried out for the task of the Corps. It is only now that we can fully appreciate the importance for the whole operation of your bravery and your circumspection on the campaign's first day of combat.[10]

Wodrig's Army Corps made up the left flank of the Wehrmacht's Eighteenth Army and relied heavily on the capture of the northern bridges. However, despite Walther's success, attacks on the three remaining targets were mostly failures. At Hatert, *Stabsfeldwebel* Babuke's group approached the bridge in civilian clothes, but were quickly unmasked by observant Dutch guards who opened fire, driving the attackers to ground and allowing the Dutch to withdraw to the west bank and blow the demolition charges. However, due to improper positioning of the explosives, the structure did not completely collapse and despite one man in a 'black suit' being killed by defending gunfire, Babuke's men continued the battle until reinforced by armoured cars of the SS *Verfügungstruppe* reconnaissance battalion. With most of the bridge decking still intact, SS armoured cars began crossing the bridge, the Dutch quickly surrendering despite not suffering a single casualty. Opposing them, every single member of the SS assault group had either been killed or wounded, *Untersturmführer* Vogt capturing the bridge with only four active men of his unit left. However, the bridgehead obtained on the far bank was, somewhat bizarrely, not exploited to its full potential. The SS unit was denied permission to continue west as the Wehrmacht officer in command of the spearhead formation – *Major* Einstmann – put no trust in the bridge's structural integrity.[11] The SS raged at being held back, their ultimate target the bridge at Grave, less than 7km away.

A group of Brandenburgers in civilian clothing attacked the bridge at Malden. Four men approached the bridge's guards from the 26th Infantry Regiment and demanded authorisation to cross at approximately 0400hrs but were denied by the suspicious sentries. The Brandenburgers retreated into the early morning gloom along the approach road, only to return in a larger group of nine men who immediately spread out and opened fire. Bluff appeared to have failed so now they applied force. Storming forward, they reached the eastern bank and immediately attempted to consolidate their hold after taking most of the surprised guards prisoner. However, the corporal commanding the bridge defences had summoned help, which arrived in the shape of ten men armed with a light machine gun and small arms. Led by a Captain Peeters, they silently took up position before opening fire on the Germans. Four of the attackers were killed instantly – *Gefreiters* Kurt Kleebauer, Hans Krön and Erhardt Neuhöfer – as well as their Dutch interpreter. The remaining five men surrendered and, being still in civilian clothes, were briefly interrogated before Peeters ordered them shot as spies. Fortunately for them, this order was soon cancelled and the five taken to the rear while the bridge was successfully destroyed. Moments later SS armoured cars commanded by *Obersturmführer* Pötschke arrived at the far bank and, after a brief exchange of fire that saw two SS men killed, moved off to find an alternative crossing.

Leutnant Dietrich Witzel led probably the largest group of the entire attack against the sluice gates at Heuman. Using four disguised Dutchmen as Gendarmes, they escorted nearly thirty Brandenburgers dressed in civilian clothes. The bridge was raised during the hours of darkness and guards from the 26th Infantry Regiment challenged the disguised 'Gendarmes'. German intelligence had provided the correct recognition codes and the entire party was soon authorised to cross once the bridge was lowered into place. The midway point passed over a small island upon which were heavy bunkers and the bridge controls; it was here that the Germans sprang into action with machine guns and grenades, taking three of the five bunkers before the remaining defenders opened fire.

On the western bank, the guard commander, Captain Dr Postma, raced to the scene and rallied the defence despite being hit by a stray bullet. The Dutch managed to raise the bridge once more, temporarily isolating the attackers who eventually managed to force a captured civilian operator to lower it from their end, operating it by hand as gunfire had destroyed the electric controls. Dutch mortar fire began landing amongst the German raiders though the first elements of the SS reconnaissance battalion soon arrived in the shape of four Sdkfz 231 armoured cars, after having intercepted a Dutch force attempting to attack the Brandenburgers from the rear from the direction of Groesbeek.

Both sides continued to reinforce the battle, with German artillery fire also being directed against the defending casemates. An initial SS assault across the bridge was repulsed, with their commander *Untersturmführer* Gerhard Letz killed, and repeated attempts defeated by accurate Dutch fire. However, efforts by the defenders to retake lost ground also stalled amidst heavy German artillery fire directed by reconnaissance aircraft that had arrived with the dawn light. Finally, the tide of battle turned irrevocably in the attackers' favour and at 1700hrs the final defending machine gun was silenced and the bridge taken. In total the Dutch had lost sixteen men killed and fifty wounded while the Germans suffered twelve dead. Amongst those were Brandenburgers *Pionier* Josef Jelinek, *Gefreiter* Franz Koudele and Dutch interpreter Anton Lukessen from Didam. While ultimately the bridge was taken intact, Witzel's surprise attack had failed to achieve its objective, the protracted battle that dragged into the late afternoon already putting the German offensive behind schedule.

During the final moments of early morning darkness, *Unteroffizier* Ziesold's small group failed to take the 400m railway bridge at Mook which was destroyed by its guard unit at the first sign of the approaching Germans. The task fell to the 474th Infantry Regiment to storm the river using conventional methods during the day with the help of heavy artillery support.

The Brandenburgers had lost more bridges than they had taken, but their combination of daring, subterfuge, bravery and ruthlessness had captured enough crossings to warrant their commitment to action. While these were the most significant units committed along the northern river line leading into Belgium and The Netherlands, it appears that smaller units or even individuals were committed elsewhere, as evidenced by at least two deaths of men attributed to the strength of *Baulehr-Bataillon z.b.V. 800*. In Nijmegen, 23-year old *Pionier* Theodor van den Hurk – a German from Kleve – was caught in civilian clothes at Neerbosch, apparently scouting the bridge approaches. Interrogated by Captain F.J.A. Boers, he was then shot and his body hastily buried by the roadside. *Stabsfeldwebel* Josef Hempelmann, formerly of the 1st Battalion Grenzwacht-Regiment 36 (border guards) but attached to the Brandenburgers, was wounded in Arnhem and later died in a German field hospital. Further west, *Pionier* Leopold Habicher was killed at Grave, the objective of the German spearhead forces once over the initial river and canal line.

A separate Abwehr unit had also been committed to action. At Maastricht three main bridges crossed the Maas River and *Bataillon z.b.V. 100* had been raised specifically to deal with these. A special assault group of Luftwaffe *Fallschirmjäger* undertook a daring attack on the formidable Belgian Fort Eben Emael to neutralise this cornerstone of Belgium's border defence. Maastricht provided the key to ground support reaching the heavily outnumbered *Fallschirmjäger* and a special subsection of the battalion, designated *Sonderverbänd Hocke* after its commander *Leutnant* Hans-Joachim Hocke, was tasked with seizing the bridges in the same manner as the Brandenburgers had employed. Hocke's assault group included motorised regular infantry units, Flak troops and a small number of armoured vehicles as well as bicycle and motorcycle infantry, signalmen and engineers, superseded by disguised infiltrators using the same methods as the Brandenburgers.

The battalion was subdivided into three sections for the operation at Maastricht:

- A small commando unit consisting of seven men – one German and six Dutch collaborators – dressed in civilian clothes were met in the Maastricht suburb of Wijk on the day preceding the attack. They were to attack the guards of the Wilhelmina Bridge at dawn the following day to secure the crossing.
- A second commando of thirty men in civilian disguise crossed the border at Herzogenrath and took possession of bicycles stored at Bleierheide and Kerkrade before heading to Maastricht to tackle the Servaas and railway bridges.
- A third unit that comprised much of the bicycle infantry – approximately forty men – were also to cross the border south-east of Sittard wearing

Dutch Gendarme uniforms. The motorcycle detachment would follow them, similarly clothed. This heavier force would assist the vanguard units and help secure the bridges against counter-attack while the remainder of the battalion crossed the border at 0430hrs on 10 May.

However, efforts to secure every assigned target failed and losses were heavy, including Hocke himself killed as he attempted to cross Maastricht's railway bridge and defuse explosives at the exact moment they were detonated. The first group of seven men were ironically not defeated in combat, but by heavy drinking the night before which rendered all but the German and a single Dutchman unable to conduct their mission in the morning darkness. The two that attempted their task were so dishevelled and awkward that they immediately aroused guards' suspicions and were arrested, the Dutchman attempting to flee and shot dead. The group of thirty men on bicycles was stopped shortly before reaching Maastricht and arrested en-masse, while those disguised as Gendarmes were found to be wearing incorrect uniform and forced to fight their way towards their targets. At 0645hrs the Servaas Bridge was destroyed, at 0652hrs the Wilhelmina Bridge and at 0700hrs the railway bridge was also demolished. At 0720hrs, the remains of *Bataillon z.b.V. 100* informed the vanguard of the 4th Panzer Division that all Maastricht bridges had been lost, though they had managed to secure a small lodgement on the western bank after storming across in rubber boats. They then finally reached the Albert Canal bridge at Vroenhoven which had been taken by the *Fallschirmjäger* group 'Concrete'.

Nonetheless, the attack on Eben Emael itself was a stunning success; a total *Fallschirmjäger* force of force of eleven officers and 427 NCOs and men divided into four separate assault groups (codenamed 'Iron', 'Steel', 'Concrete' and 'Granite') had captured the imposing fort and three bridges over the Albert Canal. Indeed, the 'Granite' group of eighty-five *Fallschirmjäger* neutralised the entire fort, capturing its 750-man garrison. Though the loss of the Maastricht bridges delayed the relieving ground forces, they eventually reached the *Fallschirmjäger* during early morning on 11 May.

Meanwhile, further to the south, Rudloff's 3rd Company went into action across the Belgian and Luxembourg borders. Rudloff's men had been assigned twenty-four objectives that included bridges to be taken intact, communication centres either destroyed or captured, anti-tank obstacles removed and Gendarme stations neutralised. They would be operating in the Ardennes forest through which the Wehrmacht was attempting to make its crucial armoured attack, their role being to facilitate the initial passage of heavy troops through an area considered naturally unsuitable for such troops.

Rudloff's men divided into small groups of six to nine men and infiltrated the borderlands with the *Halbtarnung* of civilian outer garments over their army uniforms. Once on enemy soil the company regrouped somewhat into three combat groups deployed in different areas: *Leutnant* Hütten (an instructor from Quenzgut) took approximately thirty men to the zone around Sourbrodt; *Leutnant* Kutschera led another forty-five to the region of Bütgenbac; Rudloff the remaining seventy-five men towards St Vith.

Hütten and his group moved by truck from Münstereifel towards the border during the afternoon of 9 May, reaching Kalterherberg by 2300hrs. His primary task was to prevent the reporting of the imminent German invasion by Belgian reconnaissance troops that were stationed at points along the border. Five separate units were formed, their objectives being the railway bridge at Küchelscheid and protection of the tracks by occupation of the small monastery at Am Grünen Kloster; the Sourbrodt railway station; the crossroads and telephone exchange at Elsenborn; and the transport hub of Baugnez near Malmedy. Hütten was assisted by *Unteroffizier* Peter Hardy (who hailed from the Belgian area they were to operate in) and Zeipel and Austrian *Feldwebel* Johann Tanzer, who had already served in the Sudetenland and Poland after having enlisted in the Abwehr in 1938.

Passing over the frontier near border-marker number 640, Hütten's men immediately cut telephone lines and isolated the military exchange at Elsenborn Camp, largely empty after Belgian troops and civilians that had been stationed there had moved to their mobilisation regions. Three telephone operators from the camp were captured near Küchelscheid, the Brandenburgers engaging in a brief firefight with a trio of Belgian soldiers in Leykau at 0400hrs, wounding two. The remaining man raced from the scene by bicycle – his front tyre hit by a bullet – and reached a second Belgian outpost (Post 25), immediately ordering the Küchelscheid railway bridge destroyed using the pre-prepared charges before Hütten's troops could secure it. A Belgian engineer hurried onto the exposed bridge and successfully lit the fuses under fire from the approaching Brandenburgers. With the bridge blown, the Gendarmes and soldiers retreated to Elsenborn Camp where they were later captured; a Belgian corporal being hit in the back during their hurried escape and later dying in hospital in Butgenbach.

Rudloff had moved his men south to a forward staging post near the Rhineland village of Winterscheid in preparation for his southernmost penetration of the border. The ease with which they passed over the guarded border and began their advance on St Vith exceeded his expectations. With civilian outer garments, his men moved unobserved and made the 6km trek to St Vith in good time. The main target was the town's railway station, though *Unteroffizier* Ille led a small detachment to take and hold the 285m-long 'Freiherr-von-Korff' Viaduct at the entrance to the village of Born. They encountered fierce resistance from a

Belgian motorcycle detachment and suffered several dead and wounded during the protracted fight, after which Belgian engineers successfully demolished the viaduct, a second viaduct at Hermanmont also being blown up at the other end of that section of railway.

In St Vith itself the Germans' arrival clashed unfortunately with that of an elite unit of Belgian mountain troops boarding a troop train destined for the west. The attackers opened fire and the panicked driver got underway prematurely, passing over a railway bridge that was already in Brandenburger hands and taking heavy small-arms fire. The sound of the fighting urged Belgian engineers to destroy a road bridge that was also on Rudloff's objective list, but the remainder of his targets were successfully taken and held despite strong resistance from Belgian troops and Gendarmes. The success of the German assault was aided enormously by local *Volksdeutsche* residents also joining the battle, bolstering the relatively weak strength of the Brandenburgers until reinforcements arrived.

To the east, near the border, the bridge over the Our River at Schönberg had been successfully taken by a small team led by Sudeten *Gefreiter* Peichel, allowing the tanks of the 5th Panzer Division to roll straight across towards Rudloff. The Our was also bridged at Steinebrück, taken and held by four Belgians and three Sudeten Brandenburgers and Burg-Reuland, taken by *Feldwebel* Heumann and a small group of men.[12] The panzers rolled west, as did an armoured train of 2nd Company making for St Vith, crossing the border near the village of Lommersweiler. The train moved slowly and carried a unit of Engineers, stopping short of each unoccupied railway station en-route to allow the troops to disembark and secure any crossings or junctions. The train reached St Vith before it was halted by the demolished viaduct, the Engineers helping Rudloff's Brandenburgers to break Belgian resistance before the spearhead troops of the 5th Panzer Division reached them around 0700hrs that morning. Of the twenty-four targets assigned to the 3rd Company, nineteen were successfully taken and Rudloff's men received eight EK Is and eighty-four EK IIs as a result, Rudloff receiving his '*Spang*' (clasp, i.e. bar) to his EK I earned during the previous war. By midday Rudloff's surviving troops were transported back to Münstereifel, travelling by train a day later to the training ground at Düren where they would form the nucleus of the 3rd Battalion of *Lehrregiment 'Brandenburg' z.b.V. 800.*

Collectively the efforts of the Brandenburger troops were judged as highly successful during Operation '*Morgenrot*' and allowed the Blitzkrieg to proceed at a pace that would go on to shortly stun the Western Allies. Luxembourg fell on the first day of the invasion and within four more days the armed forces of The Netherlands – except for troops fighting in Zealand – also surrendered. By 17 May, Zealand had also fallen to German forces and eleven days later Belgium surrendered and, with German troops on the Channel coast, the Allied armies in Flanders were penned into a pocket centred between Calais and Ostend. To the south, the remaining half of the French Army lay behind the Somme River, but they could wait as elimination of the Allied pocket around Dunkirk was the Germans' initial priority. The British launched Operation 'Dynamo' to evacuate the defenders of the Allied enclave while German forces halted, seemingly content to allow the Luftwaffe to mount the only opposition to the British evacuation craft. It was into this chaotic battle that a small unit of Brandenburgers returned towards the end of May.

During the First World War the Belgian Army had held the left flank of the Allied front line at the coastal town of Nieuport during October 1914, under severe pressure from a relentless German Army.

> It was then that the Belgians, in this pitiless conflict, summoned to their aid a terrible and invincible assistant, the inundation of low-lying lands. The canals in the valley of the Yser spilled their water into the fields. The water rose and streamed along the German trenches; while on the left bank, where the level of the soil was higher, the Belgians heroically defended their positions.
>
> The Germans, threatened with death by drowning, rushed forward in a terrible offensive, seeking to break our lines, to conquer the dry land. In this unprecedented attempt, they succeeded, on the 30th of October, in capturing one of our points of support, the village of Ramscappelle; but this essential position was immediately recaptured by two Belgian divisions and a few French battalions. This was the coup de grace.
>
> On the 31st, decimated, dejected, defeated, the Germans abandoned their project of crossing the Yser; they retreated, abandoning guns and mortars engulfed in mire, enormous quantities of weapons, thousands of corpses and many wounded.[13]

With the opening and closing of the sluice gates at the mouth of the Yser River at Nieuport over the course of three consecutive nights, the canals quickly overflowed, though the Yser River itself never actually burst its banks. Nonetheless, the Wehrmacht feared a repeat attempt by the Allies which would limit their ability to cross the Belgian polderland and ultimately provide extra protection for the Dunkirk pocket. With the Brandenburger men having returned to Germany during the reorganisation and expansion of the unit, Siegfried Grabert was recalled from leave to Brandenburg an der Havel around 24 May and ordered to gather a small unit for immediate transfer to Ghent. Grabert, his adjutant *Leutnant* Johannes and eleven other men arrived in the Belgian city and were accommodated in a hotel where they met with members of the 'Hercules Group', Belgian collaborators who were in the pay of the Abwehr. Grabert was briefed at the hotel by *Oberleutnant* Wilhelm Hollmann, who not only commanded the 'Hercules Group' through the liaison man *Sonderführer* Johannes Carl, but also had formed his own small formation named *Sonderstab Hollmann*. The slightly stooped, middle-aged Hollmann had been the pre-war owner of a porcelain factory in eastern Germany. He had previously also served in the military; an old *'Baltenkampfer'*, he had won the Baltic Cross, awarded to men of the *Landeswehr* and various *Freikorps* who had fought against Bolsheviks in the Baltic states for at least three months during the years 1918 and 1919. Hollmann had been on the staff of the Jahnke bureau until its dissolution in April 1940 whereupon he enlisted in the Abwehr and began to establish his own '*Sonderstab Hollmann*', collecting men who were predominantly ex-colleagues of the Jahnke bureau. Hollmann was brought into the Brandenburgers and had taken part in the operations in Luxembourg before transferring to Belgium and taking control of local Abwehr combat missions. Part of his remit was to coordinate the Belgian 'Hercules Group' which had been formed by right-wing militants to provide actual sabotage as well as information and guidance for German forces. American intelligence later described Hollmann as '45 years old, but looks at least 50' with a gold right incisor tooth and 'very little hair; what hair he has is clear blond'. Though he walked with rounded shoulders, he had 'long arms, very thin legs and blue eyes'.

Grabert was tasked by Hollmann with taking and holding the Nieuport *Ganzepoot*, a lock and sluice complex that linked six waterways via the Ijzermonding with the North Sea. The Nieuport road bridge (*Langebrug*) marked the centre of the complex, and controls for the six adjacent canal sluice gates were situated in a building on the southern canal bank alongside fuses for all prepared demolitions. The mission was codenamed Operation '*Martin*' and Grabert's men would wear Belgian Army uniforms over their own, using a commandeered local hotel bus to transport them through enemy lines and towards Nieuport. It is believed that at least six of the 'Hercules' men accompanied them, including Antoon Schalkans and Edmond de Batist, the latter born in Antwerp in 1914 and graduating through the Flanders militia to the *Verdinaso*, a fascistic Belgian/Dutch political movement of the 1930s in which Batiste was known as 'The Eagle'. Batist and five of the 'Hercules Group' would later formally enlist in the Brandenburgers in June 1940.

Grabert's assault group successfully mingled with streams of retreating Belgian troops during their advance to Nieuport on 27 May, travelling via Ostend, the front line being extremely porous, having collapsed in many places as the country teetered on the verge of surrender. Once within the outskirts of Nieuport itself, they encountered an eerie silence that had descended over the

Operation 'Weserübung' and 'Case Yellow': Scandinavia and the West 53

battlefield. This marked the eastern edge of the Dunkirk perimeter as Operation 'Dynamo' had finally got underway and the British Expeditionary Force began to be evacuated to escape destruction. Pockets of troops from a melange of formations controlled the town of Nieuport and its environs: cavalry of the French 2nd Light Mechanised Division, British troops of the 12th Lancers, 53rd Medium, 2nd Medium and 1st Heavy Anti-Aircraft Regiments of the Royal Artillery and 7th Field Company, Royal Engineers, all fighting as infantry. Meanwhile engineers of the 101st Army Field Company, Royal Engineers, worked frantically to destroy all bridges between Dixmude and Nieuport.

Grabert's bus was unmolested until it approached to within 150m of the target bridge, a single dead German soldier lying on the roadway next to his motorcycle – the remains of a brief clash between a motorcycle patrol and armoured cars of the 12th Lancers. The man had attempted to get close enough to fire his pistol through an armoured car's gun port, but had obviously failed. It was at that point that Grabert's men finally came under fire, their disguises no longer viable in the face of British and French troops. Light machine-gun fire smashed the bus's front window and the men rapidly disembarked into cover as the bus skidded to a halt broadside on to the bridge. It was still early evening, approximately 1900hrs and light enough to discern the enemy positions and terrain features near the bridge. A shallow dip of dead ground was visible near the bridge and Grabert's men crawled forward to regroup in the defilade and establish a plan of attack. They had discarded their Belgian *Halbtarnung* and crouched awaiting nightfall as bursts of machine-gun fire whistled impotently overhead.

Their strategy was simple. Under cover of darkness Grabert and *Gefreiter* Werner Alfred Janowski approached the *Langebrug* on their stomachs, crawling slowly forward to feel for any wires that could lead to explosive charges. Grabert took the left side of the bridge while Janowski handled the right, both keeping as flat as they could beneath periodic bursts of suppressing fire and freezing when white Very lights ignited above their heads and bathed the battlefield in their harsh magnesium glow. Each man carried wire cutters and a submachine gun, but neither could find any wires along the edge of the roadway. They were forced to crawl slightly higher along the pavement edges of the bridge itself with bullets passing only centimetres above them. Wires were eventually found and cut one-by-one, the defenders apparently unaware of their presence while the charges, which had been built into the bridge rather than simply attached, were gradually dealt with. The bridge itself was constructed with a slight hump and once past the incline that reached its apex in the centre of the span, the two men would be plainly visible to any observant gunner on the far side. However, both Germans remained apparently undiscovered as they inched forward, cutting a total of three leads each. The young officer was also convinced that there would be a second firing system and located electric wires that were attached to a nearby telegraph pole, the two men rolling down the far bank onto a towpath where they traced the electrical circuit and cut it while sheltering from view.

Grabert and Janowski had reached the far bank, whereupon they began phase two of the plan. Using the meagre cover provided by the low bridge approach structure, they opened fire at the defending positions and threw several grenades in quick succession. Hoping to both suppress and confuse the enemy, the sudden firing was the signal for the remainder of Grabert's men to storm across the bridge and within seconds they were across and began firing all weapons while staying as mobile as possible, confusing the enemy gunners and providing the illusion of greater numbers. The British gunners' positions were taken one-by-one, by small teams of Brandenburgers using grenades and automatic weapons. Finally, the sluice controls were reached and the *Ganzepoot* secured, though both the bridge and lockkeeper's house had taken damage.

At 1100hrs the following morning, Wehrmacht troops reached Nieuport, taking heavy losses in combat against men of the 12th Lancers, but successfully reinforcing Grabert's bridgehead before moving into the town itself. Though most of Nieuport remained in Allied hands, the sluices were secure and German armour able to continue its advance without the threat of inundation. Grabert and his men were relieved of their bridge and began the return to Ostend, fortunate enough to find some abandoned British transport that they commandeered for their journey.

Wehrmacht officers feted the small group upon their return, Janowski receiving a promotion to *Feldwebel* and the EK I, while Grabert was promoted to *Oberleutnant*, though he was also admonished for his failure to remove the explosive charges rather than simply cut their fuses. Nonetheless, his success was complete. Later he would write to his brother Gerhard on 2 June: 'I held the houses and bridge at Nieuport with my few men and am now in a magnificent castle . . . I was lucky to survive since I was one of the men who removed the explosive charges . . . now in this castle there are some mercenaries celebrating with my men. I wish you were here with me too, celebrating this victorious moment in a magnificent castle surrounded by 1,000 bottles of wine.' He also proudly recounted a new development for the Brandenburgers now that they were a regiment: 'Our insignia is a sword, a question mark and an Iron Cross and it will be found on every truck and car in the future.' Somewhat curiously, the image he drew to accompany his words replaced the *Eiserne Kreuz* with the *Hakenkreuz*.

Oberleutnant Siegfried Grabert and his platoon returned to Brandenburg an der Havel where they would provide the nucleus of 8th Company of the *Lehrregiment 'Brandenburg' z.b.V. 800*. It was a time of great upheaval and change in the ranks of the formation that had begun as an idea by the maverick engineer officer Theodor von Hippel; the sudden twist that his subsequent career took would almost act as a symbol of an impending fundamental shift in the formation's employment by the Wehrmacht.

CHAPTER 3

The Regiment Brandenburg

'What counts is not necessarily the size of the dog in the fight – it's the size of the fight in the dog.'

General Dwight D. Eisenhower

On 15 May 1940, the order *Geheime Kommandosache* 1450/40 had been issued to expand the battalion to a regiment, *Lehrregiment 'Brandenburg' z.b.V. 800* officially coming into being on 1 June 1940. They had proved themselves in combat both in Scandinavia and the West and already the men of the original battalion had accrued one Knight's Cross and at least 120 EK I and EK II. Brandenburger training was improving and becoming more expansive, the sabotage school at *Quenzgut* continuing to be utilised as well as the establishment of a Brandenburger training centre at the *Regenwurmlager*, a military training camp of large barracks amidst the pine forests of eastern Germany. Located near the village of Nipter south-west of Meseritz, the camp was named after the nearby creek, Regenwurm, and in later years would grow into a labyrinthine complex of tunnels and fortifications above and below ground that marked part of the so-called '*Ostwall*'.

The first two campaigns of 1940 had been an auspicious combat debut for the Brandenburgers as a unified command and, with further operations planned in geographically diverse regions, the regiment was divided between four primary locations. In Berlin, *Major* Hubert Kewisch maintained the regimental headquarters at Number 5, Mathäikirch Platz, south of the Tiergarten and only a few hundred metres from the Tirpitzufer head office of the Abwehr and the Army's Bendler Block. In Kewisch's building he maintained his liaison staff (which included *Oberleutnant* Zülch from the North Platoon as his Regimental Adjutant and *Oberleutnant* Pinkert as his Chief of Staff) and a newly established signals unit. In Brandenburg an der Havel, as well as the continued use of *Quenzgut* for training, the Regiment's 1st Battalion – intended for use overseas – was stationed at the *Generalfeldzeugmeister Kaserne* under the command of Theodor von Hippel. The 2nd Battalion, under the command of *Oberleutnant* Walther, was quartered in Baden Unterwaltersdorf near Vienna ready for deployment in eastern and south-eastern Europe. *Hauptmann* Rudloff commanded the 3rd Battalion, which was based at the *Theodor-Körner-Kaserne* in Aachen, later moved to Düren and prepared for operations in western, northern and southern Europe.

The 1st Battalion had kept most of its original members intact at that time, while the others were forced to form from much smaller constituent parts. The 3rd Battalion at least received most of the men who had made up the original 3rd Company as a nucleus, while the 2nd Battalion took considerably longer to form virtually from scratch. It is, however, important to note that while the composition of the Brandenburger Regiment appeared to coalesce over a familiar skeleton of Wehrmacht organisational hierarchy, each battalion was essentially independent, which meant that those battalion commanders had the disciplinary authority of an equivalent regimental commanding officer in orthodox units.

During mid-June 1940, an overstrength platoon of between forty to sixty men of Rudloff's company, which included at least six ex-Belgian Army deserters, had been attached to the Wehrmacht's Seventh Army for their planned offensive through the formidable Maginot Line. Due to the speed of the German advance, however, the various proposed assignments for this Brandenburger unit were never realised, regular line troops reaching all special objectives before the Brandenburgers were deployed. He and his men returned to Aachen following the French armistice on 18 June, though on 25 June Rudloff received an urgent phone call from Lahousen's deputy at Abwehr II in Berlin, *Major* Erwin Stolze. Rudloff was to receive specific instructions from a courier, *Leutnant* Peter Kreuziger, during the following day for an operation codenamed '*Wespennest I*' that entailed the destruction of the only rail link between what would become Vichy France and Switzerland. Secret documents that had been recovered from an abandoned French military train near Dijon had revealed definite plans for joint Franco-Swiss resistance to any German attack, fuelling the Wehrmacht's ire towards their southern neighbour.

However, Rudloff's was not the first Brandenburger mission to target Switzerland. In June 1940, Swiss Bf 109 fighters – ironically procured from Germany in an arms deal – had shot down some Luftwaffe aircraft provocatively invading their airspace. An enraged Göring demanded a sabotage mission be mounted to destroy the Swiss fighters on the ground at their airfield and eight men were assembled for Operation '*Adler*' (later renamed to Operation '*Wartegau*'). Two of the men sent on this mission were Swiss nationals living in Germany and at least some of the remaining six were Brandenburgers. The eight were kitted out in identical and conspicuous civilian clothes; knickerbockers, capes, black berets and, somewhat ridiculously, parachutists' backpacks. They crossed the border on the night of 12 June in two small groups with the aid of German customs agents and later rendezvoused and boarded a train bound for Zurich at Kreuzlinger Station. Their somewhat absurd disguises attracted unwelcome attention as they divided into four identical pairs, the first handing the conductor two invalid train tickets before attempting to buy new ones with a crisp new 100-franc note. Before the train had passed two more stations the Bupo (*Bundespolizei* – Federal Police) picked the men up, discovering their Czech pistols and explosives. It is, in fact, highly likely that Oster or Canaris deliberately mounted the mission in such a foolhardy and slapdash manner to provoke a foreign reaction against Hitler's government. The eight men subsequently languished in a Swiss jail for the remainder of the war.

Hitler detested the Swiss and seriously contemplated a surprise invasion. At the very least he was determined to 'encircle' those who he called in 1943 'the most despicable and wretched people, mortal enemies of the new Germany'. There was also validity to his concern about the free passage of Swiss goods through unoccupied France and into Allied hands, exports for Britain and the United States being consigned via Spain and Portugal.

> The political leadership wanted to make sure that the rail connection between Switzerland and France is cut off. For this reason a corresponding order has been given to List to destroy the rail line La Roche–Annecy. Given the course the war has taken, this order could no longer be executed. The Supreme Command of the Army demands therefore that now, after the armistice has taken effect, a patrol task force of the army should execute this destruction. I object. After a cease-fire has been permitted to occur, such a military order is impossible. At best it could be executed by Canaris ... After consultation with General Keitel, I give the respective orders to Canaris ...[1]

Rudloff and his adjutant *Oberfeldwebel* Heumann immediately relocated to Freiburg and personally reconnoitred the ground over which they would operate. The decision was made to bring three teams, each of nine men – one non-commissioned officer and eight enlisted men – from Aachen to Freiburg and attack the 260m-long railway tunnel north-west of the village of Les Aires, between Groisy and Evires. However, his mission appears to have been a failure, some question remaining over whether it was ever actually launched as there is no documented evidence of it. Operation '*Wespennest II*' later achieved greater success, but it was not handled by the Brandenburgers. Instead, four Rexists of the 'Hercules Group' acting as informers and spies (known to the Germans as *V-Leute*) for the Abwehr approached the Lavillat viaduct between La Roche and Annecy on 4 September 1940 under cover of darkness in two cars and two trucks. In civilian clothes the men faked a mechanical breakdown underneath the viaduct. Four hours after the 'disabled' vehicle finally departed, the explosion of several hundred kilograms of Melinit explosive destroyed the two central supporting pillars of the viaduct. Rumours were then circulated that successfully pinned the blame on British intelligence agents.

During July, Rudloff was granted leave in Berlin where he married Elisabeth Kordes before returning to his unit, which had been expanded to the strength of a battalion – approximately 500 men. After four weeks of intensive training they were redeployed to the West as part of the build-up for Operation '*Seelöwe*' ('Sealion'); the planned invasion of England. The lead elements of the 3rd Battalion arrived in Normandy and were located near the mouth of the Seine River, north of Caen, subordinated to Sixth Army, while Hippel's 1st Battalion (which still numbered only two companies with a third under formation) was also transferred for '*Seelöwe*' to Nieuport, Belgium, and placed under the control of Sixteenth Army. An element of the 1st Battalion, plus the 10th Company which had recently relocated from Aachen to the *Riemann Kaserne*, Düren, both travelled to the island of Heligoland to begin training.

Hippel's men were factored into the '*Seelöwe*' invasion plan as an air-landing unit, forging ahead of the main invasion force into the area between Folkestone and Dungeness. Once on the ground, the locks of the southern port of Folkestone were to be destroyed by one part of the battalion while the second part would land on the pebble beach at Dungeness and seize the sluices and hydroelectric power stations as well as defensive bunkers, coastal guns and a railway battery that could obstruct the main beachheads. After they were secure, the Brandenburgers were to signal to Luftwaffe aircraft that the main invasion force could land. Rudloff's companies were to disembark from a flotilla of small motor vessels and seize Weymouth which lay at the boundary between the westernmost landings of Sixth Army and Ninth Army. Once the harbour and town were secure, Rudloff's companies were to separate and swing both west and east and make for the harbours of Plymouth and Portsmouth in support of the main troop landings. Ninth Army would also benefit from a 100-man English-speaking Brandenburger force wearing *Volltarnung* of British Army uniforms landing ahead of the main force to infiltrate coastal defences and neutralise artillery batteries at Dover. Their mission plan, which included Janowski and Grabert and their respective units, was to land ashore and proceed along the White Cliffs to a point outside Dover where steps led down to the beach. From this point, they would continue along the pebble beach in order to avoid a military encampment located on a head of land behind Dover and regain the cliff top by a second set of stairs closer to the town. Once off the beach, their planned route passed alongside the railway station whereupon they would take control of three docks on which were mounted gun emplacements as a second reinforcing Brandenburg unit would soon follow. Success was to be signalled to Luftwaffe aircraft and consequent disembarkation carried out using the captured piers. The invasion was scheduled for the latter half of September.

Like most of 'Seelöwe', it was a dangerously ambitious plan with little of the necessary support available to enable any real chance of success. The entire invasion was being planned in the manner of a major river crossing, which failed to consider not only the geographical problems but also the fearsome prospect of strong defence by the Royal Navy against a Kriegsmarine that had suffered grievous losses during the invasion of Norway. Likewise, for Hippel and other traditional *Fallschirmjäger* landings that were planned, the Luftwaffe were suffering a severe shortage of Ju 52 aircraft after heavy losses caused by accurate Dutch anti-aircraft fire during the airborne operations against The Netherlands.

Nonetheless, training continued apace, the 11th Company now being stationed at St Honoré south of Dieppe and the 10th having returned from Heligoland to Bayeux. The newly formed 12th Company moved from Aachen to Büsum where they practised disembarkation techniques before also moving to Normandy. Rudloff's 3rd Battalion continued its training along strictly infantry lines and although the plan was to commit them to an amphibious landing at Weymouth the unit never received the shallow-draught landing craft necessary for such an operation. The enigmatic *Oberleutnant* Wilhelm Hollmann and his self-titled *Sonderstab* was also involved in plans to spearhead the invasion force, though he was reprimanded once his actions became known as they had never been officially sanctioned by his superiors. Though initiative and independent thought were crucial attributes within the Brandenburgers, the chain of command still existed for a purpose, and correspondingly Hollmann's tenure with the regiment was not only apparently turbulent, but relatively brief.

Hollmann organised a projected agent drop in Ireland to assist with 'Seelöwe'. Despite Canaris' strict instructions to all Abwehr departments to cease attempts at infiltrating Britain through Ireland, Hollmann acted independently, claiming authority from Army Group Northern France. Operation '*Möwe*' ('Seagull', originally codenamed '*Hummel*' ('Lobster') *II*), involved the landing of two Brandenburgers on the Irish coast at Sligo. Once there, they were to establish contact with the IRA who might, presumably, assist them in travelling to England where they were to enlist guides that could act as pathfinders for projected Brandenburger landings at Dover. The pair – *Obergefreiter* Bruno Reiger (formerly of Abwehr I and a skilled radio operator) and another NCO, Helmut Clissmann – were put aboard a Breton fishing boat captained by Christian Nissen, an experienced sailor who had served during the previous war and now worked for the Abwehr. They departed France bound for Ireland, but events conspired to foil their mission. At sea, the boat's bilge pump failed in heavy weather and the Danish mechanic was thrown off balance and knocked unconscious. With no alternative, Nissen turned about and returned to Brest, the mission never to be attempted again. After the war's end Lahousen painted an unflattering portrait of Hollmann to Allied interrogators.

> According to Lahousen, Hollmann and his colleagues of the Brandenburg Regiment were fanatical Nazis, who in the summer of '40 were preparing a spate of daredevil stunts in conjunction with the invasion of England. Hollmann did not take the CO of his regiment into his confidence on the pretence that he was working directly for Abwehr II HQ in Berlin. Inquiries in Berlin elicited the reply that Hollmann was not employed on special duties. Undismayed by this and following rebuffs, Hollmann continued to prepare his own schemes; neither Lahousen nor his CO exercised more than a nominal control or were aware what he was doing. Rumours began to reach Lahousen that Hollmann was working for the SS and this coincided with a new complaint from the CO of the Regiment. Lahousen was forced to take action and had Hollmann transferred from the Brandenburg Regiment.[2]

Hollmann left the Wehrmacht in 1941 and returned to his factory, though he would be recalled to the Brandenburg Division two years later. Meanwhile, his existing *Sonderstab* elements were broken up and distributed piecemeal throughout the regiment.

Fortunately for the Wehrmacht, '*Seelöwe*' was postponed during a meeting on 17 September between Hitler, Göring and *Generalfeldmarschall* Gerd von Rundstedt. The single prerequisite for the invasion to be launched was Luftwaffe dominance of the skies over Britain and after weeks of fighting in what is now known as the Battle of Britain, this condition had not been met. On 12 October, the Führer finally issued a directive releasing forces for other fronts, while maintaining at least the appearance of continued invasion preparations to maintain political pressure on Britain to surrender. Rudloff himself later remembered that it had been common talk amongst the staff officers of Sixth Army that the invasion had been called off in order 'not to antagonise the British too much'. At that time, many Germans believed that the British would soon be ready to contract a compromise peace with the Germans when they saw that their situation was truly dire with little hope of recovery. Upon receipt of their release, the 1st Battalion returned to Brandenburg while the 3rd travelled to Düren.

While the '*Seelöwe*' training had been underway, a minor crisis appeared to have overtaken the regiment. When originally developed, the battalion's purpose had been to gather together a pool of linguist volunteers – preferably from the circles of *Auslandsdeutschen* – to be held in reserve for special assignments for the Abwehr and at the same time for a combat unit to be used on special operations. During summer 1940 at the end of the Western campaign, Abwehr II, in conjunction with OKW's *Kriegsgefangenenwesen* (Prisoner of War Directorate), began segregating prisoners that belonged to national minorities into special compounds. For example, Ukrainians would be separated from Poles, Flemings from Walloons, Bretons from French and Irish from British. Though largely unrealised, the ambition was to attempt to form pools from which to recruit saboteurs, agents or potential men for the Brandenburgers. Other German agencies that required access to these 'national pools', such as Abwehr I or the Propaganda Ministry, were only granted access through the office of Abwehr II.

In the 1st Company/1st Battalion, with the possible addition of the headquarters company, the attempt was made to recruit linguists who were then put through the *Quenzgut* special training courses in radio, coding and decoding, languages and local customs. That part of the regiment which was stationed in Brandenburg an der Havel was primarily responsible for the 'special assignments', the Regimental Headquarters Company – which largely functioned as a 'paper company' through which genuine Abwehr agents could receive their sabotage training at *Quenzgut* – plus the 1st Battalion.

By contrast the 2nd and 3rd Battalions were essentially combat units. Their commitment to action generally followed a request by field commanders for Brandenburg troops and their assignments normally of a similar nature; rapid dashes through enemy lines to take and hold important objectives and prevent their demolition. With most tasks of an engineering nature, the troops were classed as engineers, reflected in their general training and even the black *Waffenfarbe* (arm-of-service colours) that they sported on their uniform piping.

However, under Major Kewisch's command, the Brandenburgers were gradually diverted from their originally planned purpose and developed along more traditional infantry lines. Kewisch was perceived as having managed to transfer friends into the unit as officers and thus increase the scope of his control considerably, most his colleagues arriving as traditionally trained line officers without any form of specialist ability or experience and therefore only able to lead their units along infantry lines. Rudloff would later remark under post-war interrogation that 'their own personal bravery, coupled with an utter lack of understanding for the assignments, brought about high and bloody losses . . . his old 3rd Battalion, for example, wiped out completely on the Russian front.'[3] The officer corps in the regiment was in a constant state of flux, so that the commanders were barely able to establish efficient working relationships with their junior officers as the latter were frequently moved. This was advantageous neither for training nor for operations, but the personal ambitions of various officers and the special politics in the personnel sections of the regiment and the OKW appeared to be of greater importance to those in charge than the good of the regiment itself.

The issue came to a head during October 1940 and resulted in re-staffing of several positions in the regiment. Perhaps ironically, it was a failed mission by two South African Abwehr agents to Ireland that prompted the final confrontation between leading personalities in the Brandenburgers. The pair, who had trained as Brandenburgers before secondment to Abwehr III, had declined to undertake the planned parachute drop after all preparation had been completed. This was in accordance with Hippel's assertion that his men volunteered for each operation, the risk of capture and execution as a spy if using disguises in the field being a factor that each man could judge for himself. In Berlin, OKW had rescinded their earlier acceptance of this special circumstance of Brandenburger deployment and subsequently issued instructions that all men of the regiment were to swear an oath to carry out any and all operations assigned to them. Hippel, informed of the instructions by his adjutant *Leutnant* Johannes, flatly refused to comply with this new directive.

At the end of September Hippel attended an intelligence briefing that had been called at the headquarters of Rundstedt's Army Group A in the 'Pavillon Henri IV', Saint Germain-en-Laye, just west of Paris. Amongst those in attendance were regimental commander Kewisch and *Oberst* Stolze from Lahousen's Abwehr II office as well as *Oberst* Günther Blumentritt, Operations Officer of Army Group A and a major part of the planning staff for Operation 'Seelöwe'. Hippel later recalled the meeting:

> The two gentlemen [Kewisch and Stolze] had an order from *Admiral* Canaris that all Brandenburgers had to sign the following declaration: 'I have been informed of the duties of the *Lehrregiment Brandenburg*, will remain silent in this regard and obey all orders from the Abwehr as a soldier.'
>
> I was so upset when I heard this unreasonable demand that *Oberst* Blumentritt attempted to calm me down in his elegant manner as the gentlemen from OKW asked from whom the order came. I stated to them: I refuse to accept this directive as a responsible commander of the *Lehrregiment* and absolutely do not regard it as an order! When Stolze replied that it was given on the wishes of the Führer, I replied that the Führer had been given the wrong advice. As long as I was commander, this command was not going to be passed on to my people. I then approached *Oberst* Blumentritt and requested official [court martial] proceedings to be started against me and asked for

my transfer to *Seelöwe*. I did not provide any further objections and asked *Hauptmann* Hollmann and *Leutnant* Herzner, who had accompanied me, to pack up and take off at once. We no longer took part in the officers' dinner, but returned to Nieuport immediately after I had applied for the proceedings again in writing . . . The next morning I gathered some officers, who were lawyers, from the regiment. Two hours later, in an officers' meeting of the regiment, I announced the [forthcoming] operation. Soon, however, Operation '*Seelöwe*' was blown out. At the end of October I was still at the regiment, then came the long-awaited telegram, which ordered me to Berlin.[4]

Hippel was summoned to Tirpitzufer to discuss his 'case'. Arriving at the Abwehr office, a meeting was held with Canaris in the company of Oster, Lahousen, Kewisch and Stolze. Canaris was cordial in his manner as he gently rebuked his subordinate for refusing to obey a direct order. However, Hippel was not deflected from his convictions and explained his reasoning in the clearest terms he could, given free rein to state his case.

'*Herr Admiral*, I would only mention the following incident, which could easily occur. Picture the possibility of six men seized in English uniforms during an operation like *Seelöwe*. These men would almost certainly not be immediately shot or hanged, but paraded in their English uniforms in front of cameras and microphones. If only one man says that they have been ordered to do so, the entire world would soon be talking about it! Keep in mind that America is still neutral. All current and future operations would be called into question.

'The principle in the *Lehrregiment* is the voluntary commitment of each individual. The individual or the leader of a group, a platoon, or even the regimental commander can still refer to such stratagems, but there can be no "commander's orders".'

Canaris was impressed with Hippel's argument and rescinded his original directive. The voluntary nature of Brandenburger service, at least while the Abwehr had control, remained intact and Kewisch was instructed to issue an order of the day to the regiment with the corresponding declaration. The charges against Hippel of disobeying an order were dropped, though his tenure in the regiment had ended. Canaris was aware that some form of reaction would be required and so Hippel was transferred back to Africa per a longstanding wish that he had previously discussed with his commander. He had been promoted to *Major* on 1 October 1940, his departure from the regiment possibly seen as a brief sideways step back to the Wehrmacht Engineer Corps (his original service branch) before returning to the Abwehr. After service with an Abwehr mission in

Casablanca, he emerged in North Africa as an officer in the *Deutsche Arabische Lehr Abteilung* (DAL – German-Arab Legion), promoted to *Oberstleutnant* on 1 June 1942 and taking command of *Kommando Deutsch-Arabischer Truppen* (KODAT, a restructured DAL) after the death of its previous commander Hermann Meyer-Ricks in an air raid on 24 February 1943.

Hippel's KODAT command was attached to Fifth Panzer Army and was divided into companies of 150 Arabs with five Germans each. Additionally, each battalion was formed along the national lines: 1st and 2nd Tunisian Battalions, the Algerian Battalion, the Moroccan Battalion and the *Kampfbataillon* (Combat Battalion) *der DAL* with Palestinian volunteers, Iraqis, Syrians, Transjordanians, Saudis, Lebanese, Egyptians, Bedouins, Sanussi tribesmen and the like. While recruitment was handled in Tunisia, KODAT's headquarters – *Ersatz Abteilung der DAL* – was in Sicily near the *Aussentelle des OKW für Arabische Frage* (Wehrmacht Office of Arab Affairs) in Palermo. It was at the head of KODAT in combat against American troops in May 1943 that Hippel was captured.

Meanwhile, Kewisch had gradually been moving the regiment away from its commando-style origins during the previous months, which had had a discernible destabilising effect within the ranks. Correspondingly, at the same time that Hippel was transferred, Kewisch too was removed from the regiment and posted elsewhere, rising to the rank of *Oberst* on 1 June 1944. *Major* Hubertus von Aulock, a veteran of the First World War and current Quartermaster of III Army Corps was placed temporarily as acting commander until the more permanent appointment of *Oberstleutnant* Paul Haehling von Lanzenauer on 30 November 1940.[5]

Born in February 1896 in Berlin-Charlottenburg, the son of a *Generalmajor*, Lanzenauer had served during the previous war as an officer of the *1st Badischen Leib-Grenadier-Regiment Nr. 109* from 1915, ending his wartime service a *Leutnant* decorated with the Iron Cross, Wound Badge and the Order of the Zähringen Lion (a Baden decoration). At the end of hostilities, he began a career as a police officer in Karlsruhe, made *Polizei Hauptmann* in the Baden Interior Ministry during 1924 and acted as adjutant to police chief Erich Blankenhorn. During October 1935, he rejoined the Army as a *Hauptmann*, appointed company commander in the 13th Infantry Regiment. By November 1940 he had risen to *Oberstleutnant* and been a battalion commander in the 11th Infantry Regiment before transferring to the *Lehrregiment 'Brandenburg' z.b.V. 800*.

A general reshuffling of the regiment's officers was undertaken to bring a welcome period of stability, while also serving as an opportunity for Canaris to take what he hoped was a firmer ideological hold of the regiment. Through personnel reassignment by Lahousen as head of Abwehr II, Canaris desired the regiment to maintain a core of officers and men who were loyal to Germany the historical nation state rather than the political entity of the Third Reich. His aversion to Hitler's government remained undiminished and the Brandenburg Regiment was still hoped to be a weapon that could be turned against the Reich government at the moment of insurrection. However, it was an unrealistic view. The machinations of power within the Third Reich was a veritable minefield for all those involved, as remembered by Lahousen:

> My deputy, General Stolze had been active in the Abwehr for thirteen years. He is a born Prussian (typical Berlin philistine). In the counteractivity, I could use him only with limitations and even then, only with the greatest care. At times, he was a serious drawback for me. Stolze was a moderate Nazi, with links to Prussian reactionaries. Within the narrow limits of his Prussian mentality he intrigued against me as the Austrian who had been advanced ahead of him.
>
> The role that [Canaris] had destined for my *Abteilung*, specifically, for me and the Brandenburg Regiment was as follows: I was to prepare myself at a given time for the acquisition of materiel (explosives and time fuses) for the accomplishment of the 'action.' On the other hand, the Brandenburg Regiment was to a degree to be set up as Special Troops at the disposal of that first, powerful occupation by certain 'key units' of the National Socialist juggernaut (the RSHA radio network, Intelligence branch of OKW etc.).
>
> These two assignments – variously adapted over the course of time – remained the 'leitmotif' of the conversations that Canaris had with me on this subject. His and Oster's particular confidant in the '20th of July' affair was Hauptmann [Friedrich Wilhelm] Heinz, at that time (1938–39) still assigned to Abwehr, *Abteilung III*.
>
> With the establishment of the *Lehrregiment 'Brandenburg'* – 1940/1941 – Heinz at the particular request of Canaris and Oster was 'smuggled' by me into the outfit as Battalion CO, in order thereupon to assemble around him a core of reliable officers. Heinz commanded the battalion that was based in Brandenburg. Heinz's confidant was Leutnant Herzner. Whether Heinz had initiated others, I don't know since, generally speaking, I was rather poorly up on the 'goings-on' within the Brandenburg Regiment, both 'official' as well as secret.'
>
> The great majority of those in this special outfit, comprised of *Volks* and *Ausland* Germans – some ignorant idealists, others fanatical adherents of Hitler – had reported voluntarily for an especially hazardous undertaking (the so-called 'Ascension Day Commandos').
>
> These people – particularly the young officers – at the slightest suspicion that something inimical to the system was being undertaken, would at once have taken a stand against Heinz and those few, mostly the more elderly officers

of the circle, to wit, would have shot them out of hand. This was recognised by Oster also, who in my opinion acquiesced completely. Canaris, on the other hand, clung to the point of view that Heinz would make it work. Heinz himself, however, may well have recognised the difficulties of a mission with such a topsy-turvy order of battle' ('*Verkehrter Front*'), since from 1942 on, the Brandenburg Battalion was manned very strongly by Russian – particularly Mohammedan, I believe – volunteers from the Caucasus whom Heinz had levied with the secret thought of their utilisation in something like a '20th of July'.[6]

Even the former Brandenburg commander Hippel – who had remained ignorant of Canaris' intention of keeping the regiment as a blunt weapon of potential revolt – later expressed surprise that it was even thought a possibility: 'I consider this line of reasoning mistaken. The Brandenburgers certainly accepted a large number of ardent Nazis after 1940 and their fighting spirit made them unfit for being part of a popular insurrection.'[7]

Nonetheless, amongst Canaris' conspirators was Friedrich Wilhelm Heinz, a veteran of the First World War, during which he had won the EK I and II and been severely wounded. He had been part of the '*Marinebrigade Erhardt*' *Freikorps* in the revolutionary fighting in 1919, being wounded again in action in Upper Silesia during the Polish uprising. Heinz was a conundrum to some who knew him, capable of gentle sentimentality at times while also fierce in combat, a crack shot and able to create explosives from the simplest of ingredients. Until 1935 he was part of the *Stahlhelm, Bund der Frontsoldaten*, an anti-republican paramilitary nationalist organisation that was monarchist in its philosophy and attempted to resist National Socialism until the organisation was officially dissolved in 1935 by Führer decree. Heinz, who had written a semi-autobiographical novel *Sprengstoff* and numerous articles for the *Stahlhelm* magazine, had long been critical of Hitler and his Party, even after joining the SA for a brief period, perhaps inspired by his own nationalism more than an affinity with Nazism. Eventually, his writing was placed on the subversive list by the Gestapo.

In 1936 he joined the Wehrmacht as *Leutnant der Reserve* with the 26th Infantry Regiment before transferring as *Hauptmann* to Abwehr III. It was here, while engaged in scripting an anti-espionage film for the UFA (*Universum Film AG*) studios that he came into the orbit of Oster and other National Socialist sceptics, taking part in the abortive plot to arrest Hitler during the Sudetenland crisis that had also involved Dr Hans-Albrecht Herzner. On 26 August 1939, he assumed command of Abwehr IIIC, still concerned with propaganda, but also using the position to accumulate documentary evidence of Nazi excesses in occupied Poland. However, the opportunity to educate an unsuspecting German population with such material and attempt to bring about the overthrow of Hitler's government never transpired as the Wehrmacht's military success only increased Hitler's popular appeal. Though Heinz and Lahousen were not on particularly good terms, on 1 December 1940 the latter appointed Heinz commander of the Brandenburger Regiment's 1st Battalion at Oster's request. Lahousen regarded him as 'a decidedly conspiratory type . . . I frequently had differences with him in official matters. Personally I, as an Austrian, did not like his character, mixed together from his *Stahlhelm* and *Freikorps* past and with a strong Potsdam imprint.'

Lahousen also continued his reshuffling of men in the Brandenburg Regiment. Despite his obvious qualities as both a purely military and an intelligence officer, amongst those that were transferred out was Hans-Joachim Rudloff, relieved of his command on 1 November 1940 after a brief period of illness. Lahousen later described him to Allied interrogators as an 'overbearing Prussian' but it is clear throughout his recorded testimony that he was a staunch Austrian nationalist with a declared aversion to any trace of 'Prussian officer mentality' such as one was likely to find in the Wehrmacht. Rudloff was promoted to *Major* and transferred to Abwehr I, dealing specifically with Spain and Portugal. One of his final activities before leaving the regiment had involved liaising between Canaris and Spanish Army officers regarding the potential seizure of Gibraltar. During July, Rudloff travelled to Madrid to investigate the feasibility of the plan.

Encouraged by senior officers, Hitler had ordered the preparation of Operation '*Felix*', the planned capture of Gibraltar. *General* Heinz Guderian went as far as to urge postponement of the French armistice in June 1940 so that he could race through Spain to take Gibraltar with two panzer divisions and then invade French North Africa. Canaris and his small group of officers met with the Spanish dictator General Francisco Franco and his Minister of War General Juan Vigón. Militarily, one of the primary logistical obstacles was the transfer the necessary troops – at least two infantry regiments, three engineer battalions and twelve artillery regiments – through neutral Spain without attracting international attention. With Vichy France neutral at that time it was proposed to transfer them by sea into Spain, where they would be concentrated in camps, disguised as *Feldpolizei* while training for the assault. To spearhead the attack, the bulk of Rudloff's 3rd Battalion were to travel overland by truck, using minor roads and disguised as civilians.

The plan was ambitious to the point of being ridiculous and, though the objective of Gibraltar's capture was worthy, the entire proposal was shelved, but only temporarily. Officially, it appeared to Rudloff that security difficulties created by a large concentration of Spanish-speaking Brandenburg troops in southern France were the deciding factor as they would have aroused intense suspicion at the very least. Plus, he reported to Canaris that even with the use of unfrequented roads and camps in the wild, the likelihood of successfully sneaking a battalion of Brandenburgers – not matter how they were disguised – undetected through a country swarming with British spies was virtually zero. The final obstacle to the attack was the complete absence of cranes in Ceuta harbour to unload the heavy weapons of the seaborne invasion force.

Following his departure from the regiment, Rudloff was returned to Spain where he met with Canaris and *Oberst* Hans Piekenbrock, head of Abwehr I, responsible for espionage abroad. Rudloff was now known as 'Rodrigo' and later tasked once more with planning an operation against Gibraltar. One hundred and fifty Brandenburgers were readied for the mission, fifty transported to the south of France and the remainder held on standby for an attack on the steel fence that delineated Spanish and Gibraltarian territory. Designated Operation '*Basta*', the Brandenburger attack would precede the same invasion plan as before, the covert troops disguised as Spanish Foreign Legionnaires and carrying Spanish weapons infiltrating the Rock itself to carry out sabotage missions and demoralise any defence. However, '*Basta*' was also indefinitely put on hold as Canaris could plainly see there was little Spanish enthusiasm to undertake such a risky operation.

Spain had little genuine appetite to join the fighting; the country was still licking its wounds from its own costly civil war and cooperation with Germany would drag it into this new world conflagration, thereby also rendering its island possessions vulnerable to British attack. Franco feared German invasion should he decline to help but Canaris confidently reassured him that Hitler harboured no desire to open a Spanish campaign, fixated as he already was on the Soviet Union. Over time, Franco's obstructive prevarication about joining the Axis during subsequent meetings with the Führer – emboldened by Canaris' assurances – brought an absolute end to Operation '*Felix*' and any Brandenburger mission in Spain.[8]

Canaris also clashed with OKW over orders for the Abwehr – and possibly a small Brandenburger unit – to assassinate the French General Maxime Weygand. Though the directive stemmed from Hitler himself, Canaris refused to countenance the idea of his men acting with the 'methods of the SD'.[9] Weygand had been appointed Delegate General to Vichy's North African colonies and, although responsible for a harshly repressive regime that included imprisonment of Jews and opponents of the Vichy regime, he also remained an outspoken critic of Nazi Germany. In Berlin, Hitler worried that he could become a focal point for French opposition to either Nazi collaboration or rule and ordered his murder by an assassination squad. Canaris received instructions from Keitel to carry out the killing. All three heads of the Abwehr's services colluded with Canaris and refused to either plan or pass on the order. As Lahousen recalled, the Abwehr officers were deeply angered and he refused (as the head of Abwehr II) to 'force my subordinates, whose job was fighting, to become treacherous assassins'.[10] Somewhat remarkably, there were no repercussions from their decision, helped by obfuscation on the part of Canaris when later cornered into discussing the matter with Keitel.[11]

By the beginning of 1941, the *Lehrregiment 'Brandenburg' z.b.V. 800* was comprised of three battalions of four companies each, with additional regimental components soon added in the form of special purpose units:

Regimental Commander: (Headquarters in Berlin) *Oberstleutnant* Paul Haehling von Lanzenauer.
Regimental Adjutant: *Oberleutnant* Johann Zülch.
Regimental Operations Officer: *Oberleutnant* Helmut Pinkert.
1st Battalion (Headquarters in Brandenburg an der Havel): Major Friedrich Wilhelm Heinz.
   Battalion Adjutant: *Leutnant* Johannes.
   1st Company: *Hauptmann* Wilhelm Walther.
   2nd Company: *Hauptmann* Fabian (Dr Hartmann or G. Pinkert?).
   3rd Company: *Oberleutnant* Werner John.
   4th Company (light engineer unit plus *Fallschirmjäger* platoon): *Oberleutnant* Herman Kürschner.
2nd Battalion (Headquarters in Baden Unterwaltersdorf): *Rittmeister* Dr Paul Jacobi.
   Battalion Adjutant: *Leutnant* Ullmann.
   5th Company (*Gebirgsjäger*; formed in June 1940 by absorbing two platoons of Palestinian and African *Volksdeutsche* who were training in the Austrian Alps. With additional recruits from south Tyrol, the unit moved to Brandenburg before returning to Austria in August): *Oberleutnant* Dr Gottfried Kniesche.
   6th Company (reconnaissance company): *Oberleutnant* Meissner (ex-Luftwaffe).
   7th Company (created from 1st Company, *Gebirgsjäger*): *Oberleutnant* Kutschke.
   8th Company (*Gebirgsjäger*): *Oberleutnant* Siegfried Grabert.
3rd Battalion (Headquarters in Düren): *Hauptmann* Franz Jacobi.
   9th Company: *Oberleutnant* Wülberg.
   10th Company: *Oberleutnant* Aretz.
   11th Company: *Oberleutnant* Schoeler (*Leutnant* Fendt after Balkan campaign).

12th Company: *Oberleutnant* Schäder.
Fallschirmjäger Platoon: *Leutnant* Hermann Lütke (incorporated in 4th Company, independently based at Stendal).
Motorcycle Platoon: *Oberleutnant* Erwin Graf Thun.
***V-Leute* Company**: *Hauptmann* Vatter (created in the spring of 1940, later merged with 1st Company in May 1941, based at the *Regenwurmlager*).
Interpreter Company (formed spring 1940 in Brandenburg an der Havel).
Signals Company (*Nachrichten Kompanie* – formed in January 1941 with components detached to other units as required): *Hauptmann* Eltester.
13th 'Special' Company (formed in Brandenburg in April 1941).
14th Replacement Company (formed in Düren in April 1941).
16th *Jäger* (Light Infantry) Company (formed in Düren in April 1941).
17th 'Special' Company: recently commissioned *Leutnant* Fritz Babuke (formed in Baden in April 1941).
'Trommsdorf Company' (formed at Zossen in April 1941; later the 15th Company).
Lehr und Ausbildungskompanie (training unit formed at Meseritz in April 1941).

During this period of relative calm, the regiment consolidated its constituent elements and new units began training. An autobiography written by South Tyrolean recruit Sepp De Giampietro provides insight into conditions in the expanding regiment at this time as he joined the 8th Company at its training ground in the Pfeiffermühle near Wertach in the Bavarian Alps.

> The French campaign had ended. Grabert and his people were all safe. Grabert seemed to us to personify the Nibelungen hero that was his namesake. All his men had the EK II and he the EK I. We all admired them.
>
> They were almost all Sudeten Germans, though some were Baltic-Germans. These, unlike the Sudetens, were calm, prudent and approachable. They were all intellectuals: law students, assessors and the like. Grabert himself was 25 years old and a medical student in his sixth semester . . .
>
> We were divided into platoons and groups. Somehow, we managed to get five '*Hegelhaeuslers*' in the same platoon. As a superior, we received *Feldwebel* Hiller. Hiller was not very tall in stature, but very agile and fast-moving. The steel-rimmed spectacles he wore on his nose gave him the appearance of a librarian or a Latin professor. His eyes, however, had the sharpness and mistrust of a financial official. He was very ambitious and had only one goal: his platoon had to be the first, his people the best . . .

It was certainly no easy task for Hiller and his men to create from us simple and stubborn South Tyrolians soldiers that would fit the German pattern: after all, they themselves lacked the professional skill of a Prussian recruit. Through stubborn, relentless, back-breaking training we missed the essential atmosphere of the ice-cold barracks. We never got acquainted with it, thank God. We were always accommodated either in romantic and remote camps or in hotels, in which a barracks drill would not have been feasible.[12]

CHAPTER 4

Declared and Undeclared War in the Balkans

'Secret operations are essential in war; upon them the army relies to make its every move.'

Sun Tzu

While training continued, a small Brandenburger element also remained active in Romania. During November 1939 elements of *Oberleutnant* Dr Gottfried Kniesche's *1st Baulehr Kompanie z.b.V.* – most of them former members of the *Deutsche Kompanie* – had been involved in Operation '*Sportverein Wiking*' that protected Romanian rail transport of oil to Germany. Earlier that year, on 23 March 1939, the governments of Germany and Romania had signed a bilateral agreement for the fostering of economic relations between the two nations. Germany was essentially granted considerable control of major aspects of the Romanian economy guaranteeing the delivery of quantities of agricultural goods, timber and – perhaps most crucial to Germany's military machine – oil. In return, the Germans offered technical assistance and military equipment. Free trade zones for German companies were also established in Romania, much to the consternation of the British government who committed themselves publicly to the defence of Romania against potential German aggression during April 1939. Indeed, America's *Time* magazine reported on 3 April 1939:

> Under the 'heavy pressure of circumstances' the Kingdom of Romania last week signed a trade treaty with the Third Reich which, in effect, converted Romania from an independent nation to a German dependency. In no instance of modern times has one state made such humiliating, far-reaching economic concessions to another as Romania's King Carol II made in Bucharest last week to Dr Helmuth Wohlthat, Führer Hitler's travelling salesman.

There was also a pragmatism attached to Romania's acquiescence in Hitler's trade deal which drew the country closer to the Axis alliance. In the wake of the Russian Revolution of 1917 the region of Bessarabia had been unified with the Kingdom of Romania following intervention by Romanian troops to quell

Bolshevik uprisings. The Soviet Union subsequently refused to recognise this, and in Article Four of the secret Annex to the Molotov–Ribbentrop Non-Aggression Pact, Bessarabia fell within the recognised Soviet sphere of interest. In spring 1940 Stalin issued an ultimatum to King Carol II for the return of the region or face invasion. Although Carol submitted to the Soviet demand, brief and bitter fighting followed when Soviet troops entered Bessarabia before the withdrawal of Romanian troops, resulting in 356 officers and 42,876 Romanian soldiers dead or missing. Romania had mobilised and it took considerable diplomatic pressure from Berlin to prevent conflict. Hitler had long stated that he had no territorial ambitions in the Balkans and he subsequently brokered deals that settled outstanding territorial claims on Romania by both Hungary and Bulgaria. The Vienna Arbitration Award of 30 August forced Romania to yield one-third of Transylvania to Hungary, losing 16,600 square miles of territory and 2.4 million inhabitants, while southern Dobruja was ceded to Bulgaria in the Treaty of Craiova on 7 September. However, in return the Axis powers guaranteed to defend the territorial integrity of what remained of Romania.

King Carol II and his government had been ardent Francophiles and France's rapid defeat at the hands of the Wehrmacht served to alienate him from large portions of his people. The loss of swathes of territory sealed the matter and, once again under pressure from Berlin as well as his own populace, he abdicated on 5 September and yielded his dictatorial powers to the authoritarian Marshal Ion Victor Antonescu, bringing Romania further in line with Europe's fascist powers.

During the previous war, Anglo-French pressure to deny oil supplies to the Austro-Hungarian military had resulted in the destruction of 1,677 oil derricks, 26 refineries, storage tanks and the burning of 827,000 tons of oil derivatives. With Germany's favourable trade agreement now in place, similar ideas were raised once again in Whitehall. In spring 1940, British demolition parties of the 54th Royal Engineers Field Company set sail from Alexandria, Egypt, aboard the merchant vessel SS *Deebank* bound for Varna. The ship arrived off Kilia on the west side of the entrance to the Sea of Marmara on 28 May as the German Blitzkrieg shattered Allied defences in France and Belgium. Unnerved, King Carol II reconsidered the tacit agreement he had given to Allied plans and, following Italy's entry into the war on the Axis side, the British troops returned to North Africa as Romania declared itself of predominantly Axis alignment. An Allied attempt to block the Danube by sinking barges in the 'Iron Gates', a gorge through which the river runs that separates Romania from Serbia, to halt oil supply by fluvial transport was foiled during April 1940. The final British attempt at self-sabotage of the Tintea oilfield – owned by a British subsidiary company Astra Română – was also prevented at the end of June. Documents captured from the French General Staff on 19 June in a train at Charité-sur-Loire detailed the plan, its personnel and methods.[1] The captured papers also revealed the degree of King Carol II's somewhat duplicitous dealings between the Allied and Axis powers and allowed Germany to gain diplomatic leverage over the Romanian royalty.

Three men of the *Baulehr-Bataillon z.b.V. 800* had arrived in Bucharest at Christmas 1939: *Feldwebel* Gustl Süss and *Unteroffizieren* Walter Kriegisch and Leo Stöhr. The three had volunteered for the assignment and were supplied with large sums of money by the Abwehr as they stationed themselves in the Hotel Bucharest and began reconnoitring the oil installations of Ploiești, 60km to the north, paying particular attention to those of the Astra Română. Their activities had strayed into the realm of Abwehr III, concerned as they were with counter-espionage. Nonetheless, twelve more Brandenburgers (from the 2nd Battalion) arrived during January 1940, headed by *Leutnant* Dr Kurt Drögsler who had been a chemist with the Viennese Fire Department before being commissioned into the regiment and codenamed 'Victor Luptar' for the duration of the mission. Drögsler was not without previous military experience, having been a *Leutnant* in a Bosnian company of the Austro-Hungarian Army during the First World War. The sixteen men actively cooperated with the Romanian Secret Service to prevent Allied sabotage attempts in the entire oil-producing region.

Meanwhile a second detachment under the command of *Hauptmann* Heinrich Verbeek, of *Abwehrstelle Vienna*, was tasked with safeguarding oil-bearing vessels using the Danube River. Once again, the men he led were Brandenburgers in disguises that ranged from tourists and customs officers to sportsmen. With the tacit approval of the Bulgarian authorities and the active cooperation of the Romanians, Verbeek's men successfully prevented British attempts to block the river, leading to the planning of Operation '*Sigmaringen*' during April. This plan involved Verbeek's detachment destroying the Cernavodă bridge and blocking the Sulina Channel to delay any potential British advance into the Romanian heartlands. However, before the operation could be carried out, the complexion of the war in the West had changed dramatically and '*Sigmaringen*' was shelved.

Before the Brandenburgers' arrival the number of incidents of sabotage and 'accidental fires' recorded in the Ploiești oil refineries had been remarkably high and had resulted in a serious shortfall of exports to Germany, prompting a visit to Bucharest by Canaris himself during December before the arrival of Süss and his men. However, during the months that followed, oil production soared and transportation to Germany flowed virtually unhindered. Expulsions of British agents exposed by the Brandenburgers reached new heights between April and June and the discovery of the French military documents allowed Germany to demand the removal of British and French subjects still working in the oil industry in Romania. Small detachments of Brandenburgers would remain regionally as covert security, even after Romania officially joined the Axis on 23 November 1940.

Of course, the threat of Allied espionage was not the only issue facing German interests in Romania. There was considerable anti-German feeling in the country despite their apparent close alignment, the military junta being maintained largely by German backing. Nonetheless, Germany had managed to secure Romanian cooperation and during October 1940 three military missions were despatched to Bucharest representing the Wehrmacht service arms. The missions' tasks were threefold; security of oil production and delivery to Germany, reorganisation of the Romanian military and obtaining Romanian cooperation for the impending attack on the Soviet Union, already in its advanced planning stages. Germany insinuated itself into the communications and internal security of Romania and German–Soviet diplomatic relations soured as a result, Stalin's Foreign Minister Molotov journeying to Berlin for meetings with Ribbentrop and Hitler where he emphasised that, as a nation that bordered the Black Sea, the Soviet Union had an obvious and logical interest in the Balkan countries.

In the interim, during October 1940 Mussolini had launched an ill-considered war against Greece with the aim to establish a puppet vassal state while annexing several island chains in the Aegean. Advancing from the Italian protectorate of Albania, the offensive was a disastrous failure as Greek forces defeated the invading Italians and pushed them back beyond their starting points. Worse, the attack settled any question of Greece's obscure political alignment and it joined the Allies, providing a Balkan staging post for British and Commonwealth forces. Winston Churchill had long harboured a fascination with military possession of the Balkan region that dated back to the previous war, and Greece's accession to the Allied cause allowed him to transport forces from North Africa almost immediately, occupying Crete and Lemnos, much to the consternation of his overstretched commanders in Egypt.

With the Royal Air Force now within striking distance of the Ploiești oilfields, Hitler ordered additional Luftwaffe units to Romania and plans prepared for an invasion of Greece. Italian troops were failing on both the Greco-Albanian battlefield and against British forces in North Africa, so initial German objectives linked new operations in North Africa, Gibraltar and Greece to take control of the Mediterranean basin. Directive No. 18, issued on 12 November, outlined this ambitious concept. Vichy France was to be given the opportunity to defend its African possessions against the Allies or face occupation by Germany. Gibraltar was to be seized while Spain also defended against potential landings. German forces were to support an Italian offensive against Egypt while ten divisions seized northern Greece to permit the Luftwaffe to operate against British air bases in the eastern Mediterranean and correspondingly protect the Romanian oilfields. Neighbouring Yugoslavia would be coerced into either a pro-Axis stance or at the very least to remain neutral.

However, the failure to convince Franco to render aid for Operation '*Felix*' restricted the scope originally envisioned. Directive No. 20, issued by OKW on 13 December 1940, instead outlined an invasion of Greece codenamed Operation '*Marita*' and scheduled for May 1941 when weather conditions would permit the necessary logistics. Twenty-four German divisions were to be assembled gradually in southern Romania and made ready to enter Bulgaria in transit to the Greek frontier. The northern coast of the Aegean Sea and, if necessary, the entire Greek mainland were to be occupied. As the directive was being prepared Italy suffered further calamity in North Africa as a British offensive drove the Italian forces west in disarray deep into Libya, by January 1941 complete Italian defeat appearing almost inevitable. To prevent disaster, Luftwaffe units transferred to Sicily and the lead elements of the Afrika Korps were despatched to Tripoli during February 1941 (Operation '*Sonnenblume*') which marked the beginning of General Erwin Rommel's fabled career in the desert.

On 20 November Hitler secured Hungarian membership of the Tripartite Pact, Romania also joining three days later. Although Bulgaria at first refused to become a signatory – due predominantly to a fear of Soviet reaction – German access to the country through which it would reach Greece was granted and full cooperation extended. Inevitably, King Boris eventually bowed to German pressure and ultimately Prime Minister Bogdan Filov also signed the pact on behalf of Bulgaria on 1 March 1941. Of the countries bordering Greece, only Yugoslavia remained outside the influence of the Tripartite powers. Although Hitler's generals stressed the necessity of using Yugoslavia as a transit area for formations attacking Greece, the Führer secured Yugoslavian signature to the Axis pact on the condition that German troops did not enter the country. Hitler evidently valued their limited cooperation over any potential military advantages and the diplomatic situation was settled in preparation for '*Marita*'.

Hitler's satisfaction was, however, fleeting as a bloodless *coup d'état* led by General Dušan Simović, the former commander of the Yugoslav Air Force, deposed his country's existing government. Most of the nation, with the notable exception of Croatia, vehemently opposed any form of alliance with Nazi Germany, and Yugoslavia's borders were tightly sealed as anti-German nationalist demonstrators celebrated in the streets. German minority populations were evacuated from Croatia after Goebbels' newspapers reported subsequent 'outrages' which other Yugoslavian ethnicities had carried out against them, the vast majority of which had been grossly exaggerated. More significantly for

Germany, all freight traffic along the vital Danube waterway was brought to a complete standstill in Yugoslavian territory. Despite assurances from Simović's new administration that, though they would not ratify the signing of the Tripartite Pact, they wished to continue friendly relations with Germany, Hitler had decided to occupy Yugoslavia as well. At a meeting of his military chiefs on 27 March he demanded that Yugoslavia be destroyed as a 'military power and a sovereign state'. Directive No. 25 was hurriedly prepared and signed; Yugoslavia would be first to fall in '*Marita*' which had now become an attack on the last politically independent Balkan states. Berlin began laying the public groundwork for invasion by reporting in newspapers worldwide that intensive activity amongst Yugoslavian troops was being monitored along the Danube, all the while continuing to accuse the Yugoslavs of maltreating German minorities. The Brandenburgers had already begun preparations for the invasion of the Soviet Union, albeit unwittingly as the undertaking remained shrouded in the tightest security. Only elements of the 2nd Battalion – minus those troops already occupied in Romania – were hurriedly made available to support '*Marita*'.

The Brandenburgers covertly preceded the entry of German troop units into Bulgaria. The 8th Company had moved from Baden near Vienna to the region of Breaza in the foothills of the Transylvanian Alps, where they had been undergoing mountain troop training. An advanced detachment led by new company commander *Hauptmann* Buchler travelled in civilian clothes to the Bulgarian capital Sofia, meeting with *Oberst* Otto Wagner (alias Dr Delius) of the *Abwehrstelle* who issued final instructions to Buchler.[2] The Abwehr feared British sabotage of railway and road bridges as well as other crucial transportation hubs and Wagner claimed to have discovered explosives and plans in the British Embassy through reports from an implanted agent. The men of Buchler's company were to stand guard over important potential targets, dressed as Bulgarian soldiers or civilians as deemed appropriate to the location, their full military equipment being carried with them in boxes. Each small unit would be supplied with an interpreter, a graduate from the German school in Sofia. Shortly after the meeting, the 8th Company, with battalion commander *Rittmeister* Dr Paul Jacobi and *Hauptmann* Weiss, were en route to Bulgaria via the Danube, disguised as Romanian troops for their transit through that territory and Bulgarians after crossing the frontier.

The Brandenburgers subsequently occupied their allotted areas, alongside their interpreters and occasional accompanying *V-Leute* assigned by Wagner. There was not a single documented case of British sabotage and the operation was deemed a complete success by the time the leading Wehrmacht troops began entering the country on 9 March; eleven and a half divisions were *in situ* along the Greek border within eight days.

Wagner's fears had been almost completely groundless. The British Minister Plenipotentiary in Sofia, George Rendel, strongly opposed any covert sabotage operations in Bulgaria by SOE, or its forerunner Section D, while Bulgaria remained a neutral power. He was eventually persuaded to allow MI6 agents to contact various dissident organisations in the country and disseminate a small amount of anti-German propaganda, but by the time of Bulgaria's signing of the Tripartite Pact and subsequent arrival of the Wehrmacht, there had been no attempts at sabotage.

In the meantime, the Allies had been steadily reinforcing Greece, therefore the conquest of peripheral Yugoslavia required quick decisive strokes with the Brandenburgers leading the way. Approximately 58,000 Allied troops had been moved to mainland Greece by 2 April as part of Operation 'Lustre'. They comprised the British 1st Armoured Brigade, 2nd New Zealand Division and 6th Australian Division, followed shortly afterward by 7th Australian Division and the Polish Independent Carpathian Rifle Brigade.

By the time of the planned attack on Yugoslavia, the Brandenburger 2nd Battalion was spread relatively thinly. While Buchler's men had completed their Bulgarian assignments, *Oberleutnant* Kniesche's 5th Company was engaged in protection of the Danube waterway and its oil transports to Germany, and *Oberleutnant* Meissner's 6th Company continued to guard the refineries of Ploiești. A liaison officer from the Brandenburger Regiment attended an operational briefing during the afternoon of 29 March in Vienna during which the Deputy Chief of Staff for Operations, *Generalleutnant* Friedrich Paulus, outlined the final plans and timetable for '*Marita*'. *Generalfeldmarschall* Wilhelm List, commander of the Twelfth Army, was among those officers present and to him fell the task of conquering Yugoslavia. His troops had been assembled in Bulgaria for the invasion of Greece and List was compelled to hurriedly split his command, allowing Panzer Group 1 to launch a surprise three-pronged attack towards Niš, Kragujevac and Belgrade on 8 April, the capital timetabled for rapid capture and the three separate thrusts designed to hamper any orderly withdrawal of Yugoslavian troops. To the north, *Generaloberst* Maximilian von Weichs' Second Army was tasked with limited spoiling attacks over the Austrian border to probe defences and take control of tunnels and bridges, before launching its own offensive on 10 April towards Belgrade. Though the conventional Yugoslavian military was vastly inferior to the Wehrmacht, the geography itself posed daunting problems for a mechanised invasion. The country was mountainous with limited communications networks. Roads in both Greece and Yugoslavia were poor, with only a few exceptions of highway areas centred on major cities. For the invaders, the most important roads were those that travelled roughly parallel to the railway lines through northern Yugoslavia, along the Vardar River to Salonika and from there onwards to Athens, hugging the Aegean coastline. The roads that meandered through the northern half of the Peloponnesus, those along the Yugoslavian Adriatic coast, the few that penetrated the Dinaric Alps and some others in western Greece would also provide the Wehrmacht with invasion routes. However, only some were properly paved, the remainder constructed of crushed stone and unable to support the sustained heavy vehicle traffic without constant maintenance. Three major water obstacles also faced an invader, the Mura and Drava Rivers to the north and the Sava River to the east of Belgrade, all tributaries of the Danube which flowed through north-western Yugoslavia and all swollen with melted ice from the spring thaw.

The Brandenburgers were tasked with familiar missions: the capture of bridges immediately over the border, neutralising defensive border bunker networks, sowing disquiet and confusion amongst enemy frontier troops and cutting communication lines in Yugoslavian rear areas. They would begin their missions on 6 April at 0515hrs, geographically spread from Austria to Bulgaria. Two 'half-companies' of 5th Company, under the command of *Oberleutnant* Kniesche were stationed in the region of Kärnten, Austria, fifty of his men from the 2nd Half-Company flown to Mehadic in Romania from where they travelled by truck to reinforce *Oberleutnant* Kutschke's 7th Company. The latter were positioned near the 'Iron Gates' gorge. Yugoslavian border defences had been visibly strengthened in the area and trucks filled with sand and cement had been seen nearby, their presumed purpose to block or at least obstruct the narrow defile. The probability of Yugoslavian mining of the canalised area of the 'Iron Gates' also loomed large in Wehrmacht thinking. The 7th Company was to operate as conventional assault troops and became part of *Oberst* Richard Bazing's assault group alongside the 2nd Company of 651st Engineer Battalion. Equipped with five assault boats and six large *Flossäcke* (rubber rafts), Bazing's group were to cross the river south of Orsova – a kilometre wide at that point – and attack the Yugoslavian defences.[3]

Buchler's 8th Company was positioned with List's Army at the '*Dreiländereck*' – the meeting point of three countries, where the borders of Greece, Yugoslavia and Bulgaria intersect. Small reserves from the 2nd and 3rd Battalions were held in Baden, while expansion of the regiment was accelerated with *Oberleutnant* Fritz Babuke forming the 17th 'Special' Company at Baden Unterwaltersdorf and the regiment's Ia, *Oberleutnant* Helmut Pinkert, the 14th Replacement Company, created as a training unit for 2nd Battalion from predominantly Buchenland Germans and based in Düren.[4]

The Luftwaffe opened '*Marita*' with a heavy air attack on Belgrade (Operation '*Strafgericht*' – 'Punishment') and at dawn on 6 April the Brandenburgers went into action against Yugoslavian targets. Along the Austro-Yugoslavian frontier,

Leutnant Gebbers led a small eight-man group from 'Half-Company Hettinger' (5th Company, the half-company commanded by *Oberleutnant* Otto Hettinger) to Rosenbach to seize the railway tunnel that stretched for nearly 8km beneath the Karawanks mountain range. Linking Austria with Slovenia, the tunnel had been opened in 1906 by Archduke Franz Ferdinand to encourage Austro-Hungarian trade through their primary seaport of Trieste. Gebbers' unit comprised men who had received engineer training and were also linguists capable of speaking fluent Slovenian. Their operational instructions were simple: prevent destruction of the tunnel, remove any prepared charges and take control of the southern exit at Hrušica. It had been six days since the last train had passed through the passageway and Gebbers led his men slowly into the tunnel, reaching the presumed border at the approximate halfway mark without incident. Noticing no air movement, he surmised that at some point ahead, beyond their vision, the tunnel had been deliberately obstructed. The decision was made to leave the confined underground space and instead accompany troops of the 1st *Gebirgs* Division over the difficult terrain of the mountains above to take control of the tunnel from the other end.

By early morning the following day they were within striking distance of the southern tunnel entrance and after sighting lights in the presumed guardhouse, immediately stormed the position and took the surprised Yugoslavians prisoner. There was little defence and the tunnel was soon secured, the suspected obstruction found to have been created by partial demolition of the tunnel ceiling only a matter of 150m from the entrance, completely blocking the railway line. Nevertheless, Gebbers' men had achieved their objective and as German troops secured the area they marched towards Mojstrana, capturing a truck with Yugoslavian soldiers along the way. All eight men received the EK II on 9 April 1941. Other troops of the 5th Company would later form a small mobile reinforced platoon that advanced southwards into Croatia towards Karlovac before swinging west and linking up with advancing Italian troops at the Adriatic port of Fiume (now Rijeka).

At dawn on the first day Bazing's assault group that included the second half-company of the 5th crossed the Danube and attacked Yugoslavian positions on the western bank. In fierce though brief fighting the assault brushed the Yugoslavian defenders aside and the small beachhead was quickly reinforced. After the battle had ended, Kutschke's men remained temporarily in position comprising part of *Sicherungsgruppe Eisernes Tor* (Security Group Iron Gates) alongside the engineers and reinforcing light infantry troops, anti-tank units and men of the Luftwaffe's 'General Göring' Regiment.

The Brandenburgers led the way for List's Twelfth Army to advance from southern Bulgaria into Greece and Yugoslavia. Jacobi's men were launching what was codenamed '*Einsatz Alex*' and achieved great success as the Wehrmacht largely outflanked the formidable, though undermanned, Metaxas Line. While most Brandenburger targets were bridges, *Leutnant* Lange captured the Greek border guard post No. 150 at dawn, achieving almost complete surprise and allowing German troops to pass unhindered onto Greek soil. *Feldwebel* Kirchner captured a bridge near Kula on the border, enabling panzers to head rapidly west to sever communications links between Greece and Yugoslavia before pivoting south towards Monastir. *Unteroffizier* Hass seized the bridge 2km west of the Bulgarian border over the Sturmica River south of the Macedonian town of Novo Konjorevo, while *Feldwebel* Wagner's group took control of road and rail bridges near Dorjan Lake just over 22km to the south-west, permitting the 2nd Panzer Division to roll into action against a hastily shored-up Greek front line. *Hauptmann* Buchler and his small group penetrated far to the south and captured the bridge over the Gallikos River near Kristoni while *Leutnant* Hein led raiding parties disguised as Greek soldiers behind enemy lines to sow confusion and interfere with communications.

To Siegfried Grabert fell the task of taking and holding the strategically important bridge over the Vardar River between Axioupoli and Polikastro. Few bridges crossed this major waterway that flowed from Macedonia to discharge into the Aegean at Salonika. Greek and Allied forces had begun to retreat from the area east of the Vardar River, and the river would provide a natural barrier to the German advance, albeit a temporary one, unless the bridge could be taken. Grabert and his men of the 8th Company wore Yugoslavian greatcoats and helmets as they boarded two trucks which accompanied an armoured reconnaissance unit of the 2nd Panzer Division on the initial leg of the journey towards their objective. After parting company with the Wehrmacht vehicles, Grabert's men passed retreating Yugoslavian soldiers, asking directions to the crossing and even taking some aboard to act as guides. Reaching the wooden bridge, the two trucks slowed to a crawl as they became ensnarled in the traffic jam created by the flight of withdrawing enemy troops. They were finally brought to a complete standstill halfway across the 400m bridge, pulling to one side to make way for a truck travelling through the throngs of men from west to east. As the distant sound of German gunfire caused increasing levels of panic amongst the retreating Yugoslavian troops, through his binoculars, Grabert could clearly see at the far end of the bridge the unmistakeable sight of British Royal Engineers preparing the span for demolition. Grabert immediately leapt into action, taking some of his men and rushing on foot through the dejected Yugoslavs, scattering men with bursts from their submachine guns into the air. The Brandenburgers opened fire on the British engineers as soon as they were within range, driving them into cover and away from their task. With this bold attack, the western end of the bridge was taken and ninety minutes later the leading reconnaissance vehicles of the 2nd Panzer Division reached them and the German seizure of the Vardar River crossing was complete.

The capture of the bridge allowed German forces to quickly reach the Aegean coast at Saloniki, entering the town on 9 April, the same day that other Wehrmacht units reached the Monastir Gap in Macedonia to begin crossing into northern Greece to outflank the defences of the Metaxas and Aliakmon Lines. Though later the Royal Air Force would destroy some northern bridges over the Vardar by bombing, it was too little, too late to seriously impede the inexorable German advance. For his bold capture of the bridge, Grabert was recommended for the Knight's Cross, which he received on 10 June 1941, the second Brandenburger to be so decorated.

Meanwhile, the German advance continued. They ran headlong into New Zealand and Greek troops on 10 April at Klidi Pass in northern Greece, breaking through a stubborn defence in a fierce attack launched by men of the 1st SS Regiment *Leibstandarte SS Adolf Hitler*. On 14 April, the Wehrmacht made contact in the east with ANZAC troops of the 4th and 5th New Zealand Brigades and 16th Australian Brigade who had established a strong defensive line across the only road leading to Athens from Saloniki, passing between Mount Olympus and the Aegean coast. The defenders held three narrow defiles; the area of the Platamon railway tunnel, the Olympus Pass and the Servia Pass inland. German attempts to force the main route skirting the sea failed and before long German Engineers had been despatched to edge around the defensive lines by traversing the mountainous interior and attacking the enemy from the rear, timed to coincide with another frontal assault. Leading the flanking manoeuvre were men of the 8th Company in *Volltarnung*, using captured British equipment. Led by *Leutnant* Mohler, the English-speaking Brandenburgers – including *Unteroffizier* Siemens who had been born and raised in Melbourne, Australia – had outpaced most of the heavily encumbered engineers by the time they reached the defensive line. They were behind schedule and the main attack was already underway as they prepared to reconnoitre the enemy positions. Using their disguise, Mohler led his men through thick barbed-wire entanglements, mapping machine-gun bunkers and trench lines along the length of the Allied position. Before long they detected a New Zealand patrol at some distance, Siemens casually greeting them, fully confident in his disguise, only to be answered by bursts of fire that sent the Brandenburgers scuttling for cover. A ten-minute battle ensued, the engineers adding their weight to the skirmish before the Germans withdrew. Captured documents later revealed that Allied troops had been warned to expect German paratroopers disguised in British uniforms. To aid identification, all Allied patrols beyond their front line had been ordered to carry a small piece of tin plate cut from a ration tin on their left battledress pocket and an armband worn on the upper right arm; the Brandenburgers were obviously unaware of this and were quickly revealed to be Germans.

Though Mohler's mission appeared only partially successful, the men's presence alone was enough to force an Allied retreat as defensive lines in Albania collapsed under heavy German attack and the ANZACs were threatened with being outflanked and encircled. A general retreat of Allied forces was ordered from the Mount Olympus positions, leading to the capture of 20,000 Greek troops. On 17 April, after eleven days of fighting, Yugoslavia surrendered unconditionally and the Allied retreat in Greece had become a scramble for evacuation and a headlong German pursuit. Brandenburgers led an assault on the island of Euboea, travelling to the island from the captured port of Volos by boat on the morning of 14 April and encountering minimal resistance from demoralised defenders. Reinforced by motorcycle troops of the 2nd Panzer Division, they raced for the town of Chalcis from where they returned to the mainland to attempt to cut off the retreating New Zealand rearguard that had made a brief stand at Thermopylae.

On 27 April 1941, *Rittmeister* Dr Jacobi and a small unit of Brandenburgers hoisted the German flag at the Acropolis in Athens. The only flag that they had was not the familiar *Kriegsflage*, but rather a curious version of the national flag with an oversized swastika. Shortly thereafter the much-photographed raising of the *Kriegsflage* by men of the 2nd Panzer Division's motorcycle battalion would also take place and be reported around the world, but it was Jacobi's Brandenburgers who had reached the prize first. A small unit of Brandenburgers raced to secure the bridge over the Corinth Canal, meeting *Fallschirmjäger* dropped for the same purpose and initially successful in the capture of the crossing until stray British shellfire hit and destroyed the bridge. By the end of April the last Allied troops had been evacuated from Greece and the battle of Crete loomed – another campaign ultimately lost by the Allies though at severe cost to Germany's *Fallschirmjäger* forces.

Following the successful invasion of Greece, a Brandenburger platoon was used to guard Athens' water supply, the so-called Marathon Reservoir that had been created by the construction of a dam at the confluence of the Charadros and Varnavas Torrents near Marathon in 1931. Before long the constituent units of the 5th Company had returned to their barracks at Baden bei Wein, followed shortly by the 7th Company. Siegfried Grabert now commanded the 8th Company and, together with Jacobi and the headquarters of 2nd Battalion, they were the final troops to return to Austria from the Greek battleground. Only *Oberleutnant* Meissner's 6th Company remained on station in Romania, guarding the Ploiești oilfields.

It is interesting to note the experience of at least one recruit for the Brandenburgers during the Yugoslavian campaign. Thirty-year-old South Tyrolean Arthur Scheler had been drafted into the Wehrmacht on 3 December 1940. Enlisted into the *Stabsbatterie* of the Bavarian 82nd Artillery Regiment, he transferred to the Brandenburgers following the recruiting drive for experienced amateur Austrian mountaineers. Brought into the regiment, he took part in the Yugoslavian campaign, his wife recalling his passing through Zagreb and Celje before returning to the company depot at Bad Vöslau near Vienna, where they were housed in the Park Hotel. Arthur Scheler was only with the regiment until 30 June as he found it 'difficult as a man of 30 years old to keep up with the much younger *Gebirgsjäger* of his unit'. On 1 July 1941, he returned to his old Munich battery.[5]

The Brandenburgers' role in '*Marita*' had been highly successful and, in later years, they were to become very familiar with the Balkans region as they were increasingly committed to fighting the brutal and unrestrained partisan war that soon began to rage between disparate ethnic communities as well as against the occupying forces. However, before that time, the Brandenburgers would lead the way in the most decisive campaign fought by Hitler's Wehrmacht: Operation '*Barbarossa*', the invasion of the Soviet Union.

CHAPTER 5

Hitler Turns East: The Invasion of the Soviet Union

'If your sword is too short, take one step forward.'
                                    Admiral Marquis Heihachiro Togo

On 22 June 1941 Hitler took the most audacious gamble of his military and political life and launched a campaign into the cavernous expanse of the Soviet Union. The dreaded 'war on two fronts' had begun, though in reality the Wehrmacht was stretched across more than just two. While to the west Britain still obstinately refused to die, German troops were now active in North Africa to the south, the Kriegsmarine fought fiercely contested battles in the Atlantic and the attack against the Soviet Union would also open a northern front in the bitterly cold wastes of Finnmark. On all those battle lines, elements of the Brandenburgers would go to war.

The main continental invasion forces for Operation '*Barbarossa*' were divided into three large Army Groups: North, Centre and South. In the vanguard of each, the Brandenburgers assumed their now-familiar role as both shock troops and covert infiltration units, tasked primarily with the seizure of bridges, severing enemy communications, sabotage and sowing confusion behind enemy lines.

By the time of the German invasion, the Wehrmacht had established a very clear picture of the front-line Soviet military forces and their disposition thanks to Abwehr intelligence networks. While Hitler and OKW may have lacked the clear-sightedness to appreciate the enormous potential of mechanical production and manpower reserves that Stalin had at his command, they entered combat in June 1941 armed with knowledge accumulated since the Red Army had occupied half of Poland in 1939. During the beginning of 1941 the Abwehr had established the forward intelligence staff designated '*Abwehrbefehlsstab*' for reconnaissance duties in the east (*Frontaufklärungsleitstelle I Ost*). This new body was codenamed '*Walli*' and divided into three sections mirroring the purposes of the three Abwehr departments:

- *Walli I* (based at in Sulejowek, east of Warsaw) operated under the command of the 'short, thin, chain-smoking ex-infantryman' *Oberstleutnant* Hermann Baun and was responsible for military and economic intelligence on the Soviet-German front;[1]
- *Walli II* (situated in Suwalki, Poland, near the Lithuanian border) was commanded by *Major* Seeliger, late of the *Quenzgut* training school and was responsible for sabotage operations in the rear areas of the Red Army;
- *Walli III* (situated in Breslau, Lower Silesia), directed by *Oberstleutnant* Heinz Schmalschläger, concentrated on counter-espionage, predominantly collecting information about the Soviet NKVD.

It was with the staff of *Walli II* that the Brandenburgers would predominantly work; though, as with the Abwehr there was frequent cross-referencing between the three departments. Both *Walli I* and *III* would field groups ranging from a dozen to sixty men that cooperated with front-line Wehrmacht units, answerable to the Army Group's 'Ic' in the same manner as Brandenburg deployment. However, their primary missions were the collection of intelligence documents or hunting for enemy agents and operatives behind German lines. The Brandenburgers, on the other hand, continued their role as infiltrators and sabotage troops though their scope of responsibility had broadened significantly as the regiment had expanded. While still comprised of three battalions plus independent regimental units, a loose umbrella had also been thrown over separate formations, predominantly composed of various indigenous peoples and designed for operations in the Reich's new battlefields.

Before the invasion of the Soviet Union, the Abwehr had enlisted a unit of Ukrainian separatists under the control of Stepan Bandera, a 32-year-old political activist who had led the anti-Soviet and anti-Polish OUN (Organisation of Ukrainian Nationalists) national executive, dedicated to an independent Ukraine. The Abwehr had begun involvement with the OUN before the war when, on 13 June 1939, Lahousen had instructed an OUN representative named Roman Shusko to train a formidable force of 1,300 officers and 12,000 men for use in the impending attack on Poland. A separate 600-strong sabotage group, named the *Bergbauerhilfe*, was also envisioned, tasked with attempting sabotage in Polish territory and the fomenting of an anti-Polish uprising. However, the actual number of men gathered only reached 120 and though established on 15 August, they were disbanded in September and the Abwehr was subsequently ordered to cease all association with Ukrainian nationalists following the signing of the Molotov–Ribbentrop Pact.

Arrested during 1934 for coordinating the assassination of Polish Minister of Internal Affairs, Bronislaw Peratsky, Bandera had been sentenced to life and held in Wronki Prison until freed by the German invasion of 1939. He remained in occupied Poland and soon developed a close working relationship with the German General Government based in Kraków. Still of a revolutionary bent, he clashed with his replacement as leader of the OUN, Andriy Melnyk, and thus two factions were born: Bandera's aggressively nationalist OUN-B and Melnyk's more conservative and pro-German OUN-M.

Despite their contrasting approaches to nation-building, both were recruited into the Abwehr, Bandera soon pushing for the establishment of an armed 'Ukrainian Legion' to fight under the flag of the Wehrmacht. A productive meeting with Canaris resulted in permission to form the Legion being granted on 25 February 1941, approximately 800 men soon being assembled by Bandera's immediate subordinates Yaroslav Stetsko, Mykola Lebed and Roman Shukhevych, the latter named commander of this 'Ukrainian Legion', though primarily for political and ideological reasons as he lacked any military training.

During May 1941, the Legion was split into two battalions named 'Nachtigall' and 'Roland', the former training at Neuhammer (now Świętoszów in western Poland) and coming under Brandenburg command. There, the Imperial German Army had previously established a major training ground, with a nearby prisoner of war camp built for Russians captured during the First World War and by 1941 housing significant numbers of French and Polish prisoners (Stalag VIII-E).

Alongside the Ukrainian Shukhevych, the Abwehr installed their own Theodor Oberländer as a 'political officer' to the battalion at the nominative rank of *Oberleutnant*. Oberländer, a member of the Nazi Party since 1933, was a noted professor who advocated the principles of 'ethnic cleansing' in Germany and occupied territories, ultimately playing a significant role in laying the academic groundwork for what would later coalesce into the 'Final Solution' to the 'Jewish problem'. During 1939 he began working with the *Abwehrstelle Breslau*, moving to the University of Prague in 1940 from where he became active with the Nachtigall Battalion as an expert on 'ethnic psychology'. In contrast with Oberländer's obvious zeal for Party laws, in military command of the battalion was *Oberleutnant* Dr Hans-Albrecht Herzner who had mounted the first raid on Poland and long been part of the inner circle of Abwehr officers that opposed their own government. The men of Nachtigall were equipped with standard Wehrmacht uniforms and equipment, whereas the Roland Battalion – which was not placed under Brandenburg control – was outfitted with Czech uniforms adorned with a yellow armband upon which was printed '*Im Dienst der Deutschen Wehrmacht*' ('In the Service of the German Armed Forces'). With mixed Czech and German light weapons and First World War Austrian helmets, the battalion was attached to Army Group South and largely performed non-combatant roles.

During the final days preceding 'Barbarossa', the Nachtigall Battalion moved east to Zakopane from where it would cross the border at Przemyśl on the second night of the invasion. By the time that Nachtigall was moving into action, elements of the Brandenburgers had already been in action at various points along the line and to varying degrees of success. Though not all units would precede the first wave, nearly the entire strength of the regiment was committed to Operation 'Barbarossa', only a single company of each battalion being left out. Each of the regiment's constituent units was subdivided for operational purposes, sometimes into 'half-companies', or into smaller battlegroups dependent upon the mission requirements. This remained the nature of Brandenburger commitment, as the regiment as a whole was never designed to operate as a homogenous unit. The regiment was deployed as follows:

1st Battalion (*Major* Heinz), attached to Army Group South, headquartered in Kraków:
Liaison officer, *Oberleutnant* Dlab.
- **1st Company** (*Hauptmann* Vatter, with Headquarters unit and '*V-Leute*' Company that acted as a collection point for new recruits), remained in Brandenburg an der Havel.
- **2nd Company** (*Hauptmann* Dr Hartmann), stationed in the Tatra Mountains at Zakopane.
- **3rd Company** (*Oberleutnant* John), codenamed '*Sturm Kompanie Schulze*', advancing with III Panzer Corps.
- **4th Company** (*Oberleutnant* Kürschner), minus the *Fallschirmjäger* Platoon, stationed in the Tatra Mountains at Zakopane.
- **Fallschirmjäger Platoon** (*Leutnant* Lütke).
- **Nachtigall Battalion** (Herzner), temporarily attached and stationed in the Tatra Mountains at Zakopane.

2nd Battalion (Major Paul Jacobi):
- **5th Company**, elements engaged in guarding the Danube River while the rest was stationed in Baden bei Wien.
- **6th Company** (*Oberleutnant* Meissner), stationed in Romania guarding oilfields but scheduled to join German–Romanian forces attacking in the south-east under the command of the 22nd *Luftlande* (Air-Landing) Division.
- **7th Company** (*Leutnant* Pfannenstiels), stationed in East Prussia.
- **8th Company** (*Oberleutnant* Knaak), stationed in Tilsit, East Prussia (now Sovetsk, Russia).

3rd Battalion (*Rittmeister* Franz Jacobi):
- **9th Company**, in training and not ready for commitment to Russia until late summer 1941.

10th Company (*Oberleutnant* Aretz), stationed in the Schönewald near Płaska, East Prussia (now Szczęsne, Poland).

11th Company (*Oberleutnant* Fendt), designated as cadre for *Sonderverbänd Felmy (288)* in Potsdam destined for service in North Africa.

12th Company (*Oberleutnant* Schäder), transferred to Modlyn in preparation to advance to the border and seize bridges over the Bug River.

Regimental Units:

13th Company (*Oberleutnant* von Koenen), the 'Tropical Company' en-route to North Africa.

14th Company (*Oberleutnant* Berndt), 'Replacement Company' acting as training company for 2nd Battalion.

15th Company, 'Light Company' in Finland, redesignated 'Finland Company'.

16th Company (*Hauptmann* Benesch) 'Light Company' stationed in Düren but earmarked for amphibious/aerial assault on the Baltic island of Oesel;

17th Company (*Oberleutnant* Babuke) in training.

By the beginning of '*Barbarossa*', the regiment's 1st Company was still acting as a processing unit for fresh recruits, amalgamated with the headquarters company and the elderly Sudeten-German *Hauptmann* Fritz Vatter's *V-Leute* Company, that was engaged in training spies at *Quenzgut*. Vatter was in his sixties, a white-haired veteran of the Austro-Hungarian Army who sported a row of decorations from the 1914–18 war, including the Austrian *Tapferkeitsmedaille* (Medal for Bravery) in gold.

> He [Vatter] had a special way of celebrating the company's roll call. After the troops had been presented to him, he walked before them with slow heavy steps, looking deeply and seriously into the eye of every soldier. One of his usual phrases was: 'Men, when I look you in the eye . . .' Sometimes, however, he was not quite on top of the situation. At one roll call, he suddenly commanded: 'Attention! Shoulder rifles!' The *Leutnant* . . . who had presented the unit to him had to point out that everything was ready, except we had no rifles. Hauptmann Vatter apologised . . . but the order had to be finished . . . and so the next command came: 'Rifles down, stand at ease!'[2]

Major Heinz led the remainder of his 1st Battalion – plus the attached Nachtigall unit and minus the platoon of *Fallschirmjäger* – to assembly points near the Polish town of Zakopane which lies near the Slovakian border in the foothills of the Tatra Mountains. The picturesque town had already featured in

German–Soviet relations during March 1940 when representatives of the NKVD and Gestapo met for a week-long conference in Zakopane's Villa Tadeusz, coordinating the crushing of resistance in occupied Poland.[3] *Leutnant* Lütke had taken his detached *Fallschirmjäger* to Suwalki, quartered near the headquarters for Seeliger's *Walli II* and prepared to move east at short notice. Lütke's men would not make their first combat jump until 25 June after relocating to the captured airfield at Valena, Lithuania.

Attached to *Generalfeldmarschall* von Rundstedt's Army Group South, Heinz's troops were gathered and ready in southern Poland by 15 June, with *Oberleutnant* Dlab in Kraków as their liaison officer with the Army Group's Intelligence Officer. The 2nd and 4th Company and Nachtigall troops moved east to the border area opposite Przemyśl where they awaited orders to attack, subordinated locally to the 1st *Gebirgs* Division. *Oberleutnant* John's 3rd Company, renamed 'Sturmkompanie Schulze' for the invasion, was attached to *Generaloberst* Eberhard von Mackensen's III Army Corps (motorised), held in the staging area for the Sixth Army in preparations for operations against crossings over the Bug River.

Major Paul Jacobi's 2nd Battalion had left the 5th Company behind, spread between guarding the Danube waterways and reformation and training in Baden. *Oberleutnant* Meissner's 6th Company was moved from guard duty in the Ploieşti oilfields to attachment with the 22nd *Luftlande* Division. This division had been created after retraining of the 22nd Infantry Division for rapid deployment by air, particularly for the capture of enemy airbases for which it was used during the invasion of The Netherlands, albeit with heavy casualties and little success. *Generalleutnant* Hans Graf von Sponeck's division was part of Army Group South, advancing alongside Romanian forces into Bessarabia and the southern Ukraine, with the Brandenburgers in the vanguard as the division had to cross the Pruth and Dnestr Rivers before assaulting the formidable defences of the Stalin Line.

Both the 7th and 8th Companies were held ready for use with *Generalfeldmarschall* Ritter von Leeb's Army Group North advancing from East Prussia. *Hauptmann* Wilhelm Walther was in loose command of all the northern Brandenburger units, acting as liaison between them and Army Group North staff. Siegfried Grabert led his 8th Company by express train from Austria to Tilsit, East Prussia, on the Neman River that marked the frontier with Soviet-occupied Lithuania. On 19 June Grabert suffered a head injury in an accident that forced his temporary hospitalisation. *Oberleutnant* Hans-Wolfram Knaak was transferred by the Abwehr to take command until Grabert was fit for duty once more.

The two companies of *Rittmeister* Franz Jacobi's 3rd Battalion which were actively involved in *Barbarossa* also moved towards the frontier in preparation for the attack. *Oberleutnant* Schäder's 12th Company had travelled first from Baden to Düren, Germany, before moving east and preparing for action as part of Army Group Centre, being ordered to undertake 'night operations against the large road and rail bridges over the Bug River, prevent their destruction, take and hold them until infantry arrive'.

Oberleutnant Aretz's 10th Company was held at a camp in the in the dense woodland of the Schönewald near Płaska, East Prussia. Aretz's men were attached to the axis of advance taken by the 12th Panzer Division, Army Group Centre, two half-companies – one under the command of *Leutnant* Kriegsheim, the other under *Leutnant* Karl Kohlmeyer – tasked with taking control of the approaches to Grodno and ordered to 'take possession of all the road and railway bridges and to hold them until the infantry arrive'. In total eight different objectives were identified and the company divided into eight combat teams to fulfil their objectives. Timetables were set and agreed with local Wehrmacht commanders through their own intelligence officers, the password '*Vöcklabrück*' to be used to identify Brandenburg units to advancing troops.

Battles with Army Group Centre

The 26-year-old Prussian *Leutnant* Ernst Gerhard König of Aretz's company was the first Brandenburger to go into action in the Soviet Union as he led twelve men through the barbed wire that marked the frontier at 0130hrs on 22 June. König's men were in *Volltarnung*, ample Soviet uniforms having been supplied though they were often unrealistically 'new' and clean and the men were at pains to attempt to make them appear more 'lived in'. Though stocks of material, including uniforms, trucks and weapons, were available from Finland where they had been captured during the Winter War of 1939–40, the Brandenburgers still carried German weapons, trusting that darkness would hide that fact from their enemy. The border area was criss-crossed with streams, Soviet troops having removed planking from many small bridges to impede any progress through the marshy land, leaving only the upright pylons in place. König's men had come prepared, however, and laid boards over each skeletal bridge that they crossed for the benefit of troops to follow. The men paused once over the frontier, *Gefreiter* Rau, who spoke fluent Russian, crawling forward to scout the path ahead. Rau had volunteered for the mission and prearranged signals had been agreed upon that would bring König and the remaining ten men to Rau once the path ahead had been mapped out. Minutes dragged by with no sign until a sudden burst of noise followed by an ominous 'gurgling' noise was heard by König and his men. Without the signal and no sign of Rau, they could not advance with any certainty and the young *Leutnant* decided to await the opening of the German artillery barrage at 0305hrs to cover their advance. All the Brandenburger troops had been enjoined not to fire any weapons before the scheduled bombardment, the Wehrmacht running to a strictly timetabled plan of attack and counting upon the element of surprise and shock to their enemies.

The colossal bombardment began on schedule and masked the sound of König's resumed advance as he led his men across a small footbridge that Rau had obviously laid with planks. However, on the far side of the stream they found his body, still clad in its Soviet uniform, though with no obvious signs of violence. Pressing on into the gloom they were surprisingly able to pass unhindered through the Soviet lines which were already dissolving in a chaotic retreat. Mingling with the fleeing Soviet troops, their German weapons went unremarked and they successfully reached the railway bridge that had been their target. Though it was unguarded, demolition charges could be clearly seen and the Brandenburgers started to cut cables and throw the explosive charges over the railing when a sudden burst of gunfire erupted from a Maxim machine gun further along the east bank. König was the first to be hit and fell dead onto the bridge that he and his men had successfully taken. The Maxim was soon silenced and König's men held firm until Wehrmacht infantry arrived shortly before dawn. Ironically, alongside the advancing troops came photographers of the Propaganda Company, one of whom snapped a photo of a tired and dejected-looking Red Army soldier, later distributed in Germany as a photograph of the 'Soviet beast'. It was in fact one of König's men, Jurschewski, still wearing his Soviet disguise and awaiting orders to return to the rear.

Three of the teams from 10th Company headed south-east to attack bridges over the Bobr River which presented a major obstacle to the German advance. *Feldwebel* Rennkamp succeeded in taking his bridge near the village of Hołynka at the head of a ten-man detachment. However, despite successfully consolidating his position and holding the bridge against feeble counter-attacks, the demolition charges were not removed in time and were detonated remotely by Soviet engineers, the captured bridge being destroyed by the blast.

Unteroffizier Zöller led three men in the capture of a small bridge, approaching the target in *Halbtarnung* in a car captured from retreating Soviet soldiers. The bridge was lightly defended and, though successfully taken and held, both men accompanying Zöller were killed in the brief exchange of gunfire with retreating Soviet troops.

Leutnant Kriegsheim also travelled by car with two of his men and a Polish interpreter (*Kampfdolmetscher*) and guide. They were all clothed in *Halbtarnung*, Russian greatcoats over their German uniforms and side caps with the red star of the Soviet Army on the front in place of their familiar helmets. They had been furnished with the latest intelligence gleaned from deserters and listening posts, including what they hoped were current passwords if they were challenged. A German war correspondent later reported their advance into enemy territory:

> The Pole led the way as lead man. Kriegsheim controlled the direction of the march using his compass and they agreed. The three did not fully trust the Pole, he had appeared moody and nervous from the beginning. Suddenly two Russians were standing before them as if they had sprung from the ground, rifles clutched in their hands.
> '*Stoi! Parol!*' (Halt! Password!)
> '*Astrakhan!*'
> 'No! Stay Still!'
> The Germans were herded together without any chance to escape. The Russians gestured the direction in which to march, shouting sharply '*Dawai!*' (Come on!) and following at about three metres.[4]

Kriegsheim feverishly surveyed his options. They were being marched behind enemy lines and yet apparently their identities had not yet been established. Once they were properly searched the game would be up and they could expect little mercy. Even in this dire situation Kriegsheim reminded himself that he was under strict orders not to fire weapons before 0305hrs, but there seemed little alternative. Their captors were too distant to reach without shooting and he feared that the nervous Pole would soon betray everything. Even in the unlikely event that their identities remained undiscovered, they could be held as Soviet deserters.

As they approached a small building that showed light under its door, Kriegsheim's mind was made up. In one swift movement, he reached under his Red Army greatcoat and pulled his concealed pistol free, spinning around and showing the field grey Wehrmacht uniform while opening fire at the first surprised Russian. The bullet hit the man in the face and he dropped immediately, the second managing a single rifle shot that went low and hit the ground. Within seconds two bullets crashed into him, the first in his shoulder and the second a killing blow to his jaw.

Distant whistles blew and a flare arced into the sky as the Brandenburgers dived for cover into the scrub of a nearby stream. Their Polish interpreter complained vociferously that their chances were slim, as enemy reinforcements were sure to soon arrive with tracker dogs, but he was quickly told to keep quiet. The entire sector appeared to have been fully alerted and there was little chance of reaching the target bridge at Lipsk so Kriegsheim also decided to await the cover of the German artillery bombardment before attempting to complete their mission. At 0305hrs the heavens erupted as shellfire rained down on the Soviet front line, creeping forward ahead of troops advancing on the ground.

Exactly forty minutes later the first German infantry spearheads came into view. Even before the Brandenburgers could reveal their identities, their earth brown uniforms spelt doom. The first bursts of fire from the troops hit the Pole. Shortly thereafter *Gefreiter* Dietrichs was wounded. *Leutnant* Kriegsheim and *Gefreiter* Ebel screamed at the top of their voices: '*Vöcklabrück! Vöcklabrück!*'

The first man to approach was an infantry *Leutnant* and Kriegsheim rounded on him furiously: 'We are Brandenburgers! Do you know nothing of our special mission?!' The infantry platoon commander was completely distraught, the excitement and tension of the previous few days had probably confused him somewhat. 'Yes' was all he could reply, 'but when you see these uniforms you must consider all possibilities.' Medical personnel collected the two wounded men to take them to the rear while gunfire flickered along the front line. Once they had seen their two comrades taken away, *Leutnant* Kriegsheim and *Gefreiter* Ebel got moving in the direction of Lipsk.

With confusion engulfing the Soviet front line, the two men slipped through and contacted retreating enemy troops, merging amongst the disorganised stream of men headed east. Using his linguistic skills to the full, Ebel even asked two Red Army soldiers crouching behind a low wall for directions to Lipsk. They blended seamlessly amongst small groups of Soviet soldiers, nobody remarking on their German weapons, if they had been noticed at all, and before long they were in sight of the Bobr River and the wooden bridge that they had been tasked to seize. Kriegsheim and Ebel each followed an edge of the bridge railing, jostled and pushed across the narrow passage over the river by the mass of men funnelling to presumed safety on the eastern bank. Both had been searching for obvious demolition charges, though neither had seen any, nor any of the usual tell-tale wires.

As the two Germans waited beside the road on the eastern bank, the surge of Soviet troops thinned enough for them to venture back onto the bridge and ensure that it wasn't rigged for demolition. They found no trace though now Kriegsheim feared the arrival of Soviet engineers to prepare the bridge for destruction. As rifle fire echoed nearby his worries were vindicated by the sight of nearly forty Soviet troops approaching carrying fuel containers; unable to blow up the bridge they were going to burn it down.

Kriegsheim and Ebel were now alone on the bridge and stripped off their Soviet greatcoats, taking up defensive positions on the river bank and opening fire when the approaching enemy was within 70m. Several men went down and the remainder scattered, taking cover and returning fire in ragged volleys. Lightly armed, it didn't take long for Ebel to be down to his last MP40 magazine, shouting to Kriegsheim over the noise of battle, but was hit in the neck before the young officer could reply. Ebel's body slumped down the shallow bank and lay motionless.

Suddenly, Russian fire spread in a wider arc behind Kriegsheim, signalling the arrival of German infantry rushing forward to take the bridge. Kriegsheim took the opportunity to jump over to where Ebel lay in order to check his condition. As he tried to get his comrade to drink from his canteen he realised too late that three Russian soldiers had been hiding amongst the rushes in the water behind him. He barely had time to register their presence before a bayonet was thrust into his neck and he lost consciousness. Behind him the Wehrmacht spearhead charged across the bridge and routed the disorganised enemy, the crossing over the Bobr being captured intact and undamaged. Severely wounded, Kriegsheim was soon taken to a field hospital. Ebel did not survive. In total five of the eight bridges assigned to the 10th Company had been successfully taken, though the cost was relatively high for such small units. Kohlmeyer was awarded the EK I and Kriegsheim the EK II with simultaneous promotion to *Oberleutnant*.

The last ready company of the 3rd Battalion, *Oberleutnant* Schäder's 12th, advanced from its positions under cover of darkness, separated into two half-companies, one under Schäder's direct command. The troops were in *Volltarnung*, though as they made their way through the German lines they wore their *Zeltbahn* ponchos over the Soviet disguise. Under the cover of the ferocious artillery onslaught, as Stukas roared overhead, the two half-companies boarded Soviet trucks and raced through the lines, swiftly managing to mingle with retreating Soviet units, surrounded by men, trucks and tanks all headed east as German gunfire crashed behind them. Occasional rifle shots cracked around the Brandenburgers' heads, their disguise apparently not fooling all of the men that they passed. *Gefreiter* Vitus von der Lahr was hit in the stomach and badly wounded, but they raced onwards. The two units were to leapfrog each other as they raced to secure bridges over the Bug near Kodeń and its tributary Mukhavets River leading to Kobryn. At the first bridge, the Germans hurriedly dismounted to take control:

> A Russian tank terrified us, because we could not immediately make out whether the crew recognised us or whether it was unoccupied. While we recovered briefly, 'Gruppe Kraft' came into position at the still undamaged bridge. The first truck with the other group, including *Oberleutnant* Schäder and *Assistenarzt* [medical *Leutnant*] Arpo, continued past to reach the next bridge. Even before Gruppenführer Kraft had got clear of the truck he was in,

he was heavily bombarded. The machine-gunner jammed his MG into his hip, let loose a few bursts of fire and the group of Russians was down. Despite the wounded, injured in close combat with hand grenades, they held the position and the bridge until relief by Guderian's panzer spearhead.

Gruppe Schäder was already aware of a wide plume of smoke in the distance without knowing where it came from. A few metres further and it became clear that the bridge had already been burnt down to the supporting posts. Forgetting that we were all in Russian uniforms we leapt from the truck to quickly reach the other side of the river. The advancing German spearhead, however, knew nothing of German soldiers in Russian uniforms. Before we could think and drop our weapons, *Gefreiter* Wickede, a German from Romania, became our second wounded man. Our medic Dr Arp did his best, but he was no longer able to save Vitus von der Lahr.

While we were sheltered in roadside ditches, Guderian's tanks rolled past us all night long.

During the next morning, we looked at a housing complex, which we had passed the day before when it was full of Russians who hadn't recognised us. At the entrance a large stage with a picture of Stalin had been erected with lots of bags remaining in the back. Later, the Abwehr reported that Radio Moscow had broadcast the story that German soldiers in Russian uniform had tried to capture Stalin in the central zone . . . whether this is true is a little unlikely.

The decisive factor in the success of our initial use of the camouflage was due to the combat interpreter, our comrade E.v.H a Baltic German. He sat in the front passenger seat of the driver's cab and acted as a Russian officer. He always understood how to scare away any suspicion of us by using his language skills and his cold-bloodedness. Later, when he was so successful in further operations, he wanted to be and was supposed to become, an officer. But it was thought that he was a half-Jew. For us he was a solid comrade [*pfundskamerad*] and a real Brandenburger! The interpreter later assigned to us by the Abwehr, on the other hand, was scared stiff after the start of the operation.

As a young soldier, I was only the man who stood next to Schäder on the truck and passed the orders to E.v.H. in the driver's cabin.[5]

In total eight of Schäder's men were killed that day, though the 12th Company could not rest for long as they were thrown into the fighting for Minsk, Army Group Centre managing to encircle and destroy the Red Army's western front. The Brandenburger company was used as assault troops and by 24 July had lost thirty-nine men killed and two missing in action. They were eventually withdrawn back to Düren at the end of August.

Battles with Army Group North

The advance in the north involved two separate Armies and Panzer Group 4; a total of twenty-three infantry divisions, three motorised infantry divisions and three panzer divisions driving towards the ultimate prize of Leningrad, though the initial goal was to reach Dünaberg (now Daugavpils) in Latvia.

The 7th Company spearheaded the advance of 11th Infantry Regiment that crossed the frontier between Lithuania and East Prussia and moved to seize bridges over the Jūra River near the industrial centre of Tauragė. In this *Leutnant* Pfannenstiel failed; Soviet troops mounting a dogged defence of the border and refusing to be dislodged. With none of the confusing Red Army retreat witnessed elsewhere, there was little point in attempting to infiltrate the lines in disguise and the Brandenburgers were instead employed as shock troops. However, they were unable to reach their initial objective in time and Soviet engineers demolished the bridge. Pfannenstiel's men were then attached to a *Kampfgruppe* commanded by *Oberst* Otto Lasch of the 43rd Infantry Regiment which battered its way towards the Latvian capital Riga; Army Group North's main task being a rapid advance through the Baltic states to Leningrad, rendering Riga of secondary importance as Leeb's main force descended on Daugavpils. Nonetheless, German forces were intending to assault the city's bridges and 'Kampfgruppe Lasch' entered the Riga neighbourhood of Pārdaugava on 29 June, headed for the Daugava River. The target bridge was defended by two workers guard battalions, NKVD troops and a pair of armoured trains with supporting artillery. After severe fighting, only three *Sturmgeschütz* (self-propelled assault guns) managed to cross the bridge before Soviet engineers destroyed it. Lasch ordered Pfannenstiel to take the 7th Company on an assault against the remains of the bridge, but, using his Brandenburger prerogative, Pfannenstiel refused as he saw little chance of success. Under attack from Soviet marines who had made a night landing on the German-held bank, Lasch ordered construction of a pontoon bridge at Katlakalns and eventually crossed the river. During the night of 1 July, the Soviets finally abandoned Riga and retreated eastward. The 7th Company continued to be used as light infantry until August when the survivors were returned to Germany.

Oberleutnant Knaak's 8th Company formed two assault groups to accompany the German spearheads, coordinated with the Army Group through *Hauptmann* Walther and Knaak himself travelling in the vanguard of the 8th Panzer Division. The Daugava River provided another formidable natural obstacle to the German advance immediately before Dünaberg, though smaller waterways leading to the river also needed to be bridged and the Brandenburgers were to lead the way.

On 23 June, the assault groups prepared for action. The 1st Panzer Division fielded a motorised *Kampfgruppe* tasked with securing the railway bridge over the Dubyssa River near Lydavenai. The advance of the entire XXXXI Panzer Corps depended on their ability to cross the span with heavy vehicles and *Oberleutnant* Wichmann of the 1st Rifle Regiment formed an assault team of four armoured cars, two scout vehicles and ten Brandenburgers led by 24-year-old *Oberfeldwebel* Alfred Ernst Werner which attacked the 270m bridge at 1830hrs on 23 June. Werner and his men stormed the crossing on foot while Wichmann covered them with heavy suppressing fire. The bridge was swiftly taken and successfully held as infantrymen arrived to consolidate the gain. Although heavy KV1 tanks launched a fierce counter-attack the following day that inflicted heavy casualties, the bridgehead held and the Dubyssa was crossed. Though the Soviet armoured attack was eventually defeated, it was a foretaste of what the Wehrmacht would later face, the colossal Red Army behemoths appearing virtually impervious to anti-tank and howitzer fire.

The second assault group attacked a bridge over the narrow Šušvė River near Josvainiai, just over 50km to the south-east of the first group. The Brandenburgers were leading elements of the 8th Panzer Division that held the right flank of Army Group North. Though the bridge was taken and held, allowing the continued rapid advance of the panzers, five Brandenburgers were killed; Knaak's men being used as highly mobile shock troops rather than the covert infiltration units for which they had been trained and subsequently casualties were disproportionately high.[6]

Nonetheless, despite localised aggressive Soviet counter-attacks, the Wehrmacht rolled through Lithuania and finally stood poised to cross the major obstacle of the Daugava River, *Oberleutnant* Knaak being tasked with taking the main bridge before the outskirts of Dünaberg. On the morning of 26 June Knaak and thirty of his men boarded captured Red Army trucks, slipping through the ragged lines and merging with retreating Soviet troops. They attempted to rush the 300m bridge, hoping that the confusion of the Soviet retreat and the element of surprise afforded by their disguises would carry the battle. They wore *Halbtarnung* to maintain the façade for as long as possible, aided by the setting sun being behind Knaak and his men as they approached the bridge's defenders. The first truck managed to reach the eastern bank before they were recognised and Russian troops opened fire with weapons of all calibres. Nonetheless, Knaak's men had breached the defences and disembarked with few casualties to take up their own firing positions. The second truck was badly hit while still crossing the bridge, its occupants forced to jump out prematurely although, despite the heavy bombardment, the survivors also reached the far end on foot. Covered by their comrades, a small group of men disabled the prepared explosives and the bridge was held for the twenty minutes it took for the first armoured spearhead to begin crossing. Red Army troops attempted several times to rush the bridge in order to seize control and destroy it, but were beaten back each time with heavy losses.

Despite their success, the assault group had suffered five men killed and at least twenty others wounded. Amongst the dead was *Oberleutnant* Wolfram Knaak.[7] The fallen officer was later posthumously promoted to *Rittmeister* and finally awarded the Knight's Cross in November 1942 for gallantry in action. All five men were buried together, a cross crowned with a helmet and adorned with their names and the battalion insignia created by Grabert marking the spot.

On 28 June, *Oberfeldwebel* Werner's unit that had triumphed at Lydavenai was called into action once again, this time against another major 200m bridge over the Daugava River. The objective lay at the foot of the town of Jēkabpils and Werner's men disguised themselves in a combination of Soviet uniforms and civilian clothing, *Unteroffizier* Gert Drenger sitting in the truck's cab in uniform, with *Pionier* Strömer in dark work clothes as driver. Riding on the truck's footboard was *Unteroffizier* Purwin, who spoke fluent Russian and would act as interpreter. The truck reached the bridge in the dull grey light of early morning but was forced to pause as an improvised barricade of mined paving stones had been erected by Soviet defenders who carefully observed their approach from the north bank. In what was a careless oversight and unfortunate for Werner and his men, a motorcycle sidecar combination was following close behind the Russian truck, carrying a mortar for potential fire support. However, the motorcyclist was still in his German uniform of the 1st Panzer Division and defending Soviet troops recognised the threat and immediately opened fire with everything they had, including anti-tank guns. The Brandenburgers threw themselves out of the truck to scramble for whatever cover they could find, the driver Strömer being riddled with bullets while still inside the cab.

Several men were killed and wounded, the remainder rolling down the embankment to attempt to get below the Russians' line of fire. However, the defending barrage was relentless and within minutes all of the Brandenburgers were dead or dying except for one man, named Burrer. He had seen two Russians approaching and shot both before hiding in a shallow ditch. A Soviet officer passed nearby, apparently going to the aid of his men, and he too was shot down by machine-gun fire. Burrer's weapon jammed as he heard other Russian voices nearby, so he lay as still as possible and let them pass by as they ran parallel to the river and out of sight. Suddenly there was an almighty explosion and Burrer was showered with water and rubble as the Soviet troops successfully blew the bridge.

Burrer stayed there for over an hour until he heard approaching armour. Unsure of their nationality he remained frozen in place until the familiar sight of German panzers and accompanying infantrymen came into view. The bridge was lost, but Burrer had survived; all the remaining fourteen men of his unit were killed in the short brutal firefight, including their leader *Oberfeldwebel* Werner.

In total, seven bridges had been taken and held by the 8th Company and by 28 June elements of the company were just 80km short of Leningrad, but at a heavy cost in dead and wounded. Nevertheless, Leeb, the commander of Army Group North, penned a letter to Lahousen at the Tirpitzufer, with copies despatched to OKW and Canaris in which he praised the regiment:

> What these brave men have done on Russian soil has justified and surpassed the regiment's reputation which it acquired in the other campaigns of this war. Through their great bravery in difficult situations, they have led the panzers and troops along the path to victory and obtained results, the lack of which would have been irreplaceable for carrying out the operations . . . Their high losses are a sign of the heroic commitment and German soldiers' fame. Before the fallen we lower our flags in awe and gratitude.[8]

In the meantime, while German troops were in the outskirts of Dünaberg, *Leutnant* Hermann Lütke's *Fallschirmjäger* platoon had made their first combat jump. The small unit had been furnished with parachutes before the beginning of 'Barbarossa' though an originally planned jump to seize a strategically valuable bridge had been rendered unnecessary by the rapid ground advance capturing the target with unexpected speed. The *Fallschirmjäger* moved from Suwalki to the captured Soviet airfield at Varene, where they were briefed on Operation 'Bogdanow', the capture of two railway bridges on the line from Lida to Maladzyechna near the village manor houses of Bogdanow in Belarus. One of the bridges crossed the river Holszanka while the other was a viaduct that traversed a road 240m away along the track. Elements of the 19th Panzer Division had become bogged down and separated from the main German thrust after Soviet troops had infiltrated between the vanguard advancing towards Bogdanow and the bulk of the division. The *Fallschirmjäger* drop was of dual purpose; to secure the rail track and provide a diversionary raid in the area and relieve pressure on the separated panzer troops.

On the afternoon of 25 June, at 1630hrs, three Ju 52 aircraft carrying Lütke and thirty-five men took off and flew at low level towards the drop zone, skimming the treetops to avoid enemy anti-aircraft fire or fighter interception. The idea was to land 1,200m past the river bridge atop a small clear plateau, whereupon the men would make their way through a relatively sparsely wooded area and onwards to the bridge. As the drop zone neared, the leading Ju 52 unexpectedly attracted heavy ground fire that shattered the cockpit glass and wounded the pilot in the mouth. The aircraft radio operator (who also acted as jumpmaster) and two *Fallschirmjäger* were also injured, one shot through the upper thigh, and the embarked troops were immediately ordered to prepare to jump, despite being short of the target. At a height of only 60m they began to exit the aircraft, their parachutes barely opening before they hit the ground. As was the method with early German parachute operations, the *Fallschirmjäger* had dropped without their main weapons which were parachuted separately in containers. These were still aboard the lead aircraft and initially it appeared that the mission was doomed from the outset until the injured pilot circled slowly around to their position, attracting more heavy ground fire as the wounded radio operator threw the containers out of the door.

The *Fallschirmjäger* rapidly made contact with two armoured cars from the Panzer Division's reconnaissance unit PAA 19 (*Panzer Aufklärungs Abteilung 19*), commanded by *Leutnants* König and Watermann. The combined force immediately came under attack from two companies of Red Army troops, supported by four tanks and fire from heavy mortars. During the initial confusion, both Hermann Lütke and his deputy *Feldwebel* Eric Reichert had fallen. For three hours, the pocket of Germans that had reached the bridge fended off repeated attacks, sometimes in hand-to-hand combat, before shelling by the Russian tanks forced them to retreat into the river itself for cover. While the two armoured cars provided valuable fire support, moving position frequently to frustrate enemy gunners, the *Fallschirmjäger* fought for a further one-and-a-half hours, frequently firing while standing in breast-deep water, until darkness began to fall. Their ammunition was virtually exhausted when, abruptly, the Soviet attackers withdrew, leaving both the bridge and viaduct in German hands. The armoured car unit had lost two men killed – *Gefreiter* Hugo Ulrich and *Oberpionier* Herbert Frenzel – while the Brandenburgers had suffered four dead, four wounded and thirteen others missing in action. At midnight *Feldwebel* Rose took command of the *Fallschirmjäger* and two Russian prisoners that had been taken during the battle. With this first combat drop, the regiment had inaugurated a new form of warfare for themselves and, despite the heavy casualties, had acquitted themselves well. The surviving Brandenburger *Fallschirmjäger* were not sent back to Vilna until the beginning of July.

Battles with Army Group South

Oberleutnant Meissner's 6th Company, 2nd Battalion, was attached to Army Group South, Meissner moving from guarding the Romanian oil wells to operations alongside the 22nd *Luftlande* Division. On the morning of '*Barbarossa*' the 6th Company advanced together with Romanian forces into Bessarabia and the southern Ukraine, the Brandenburgers in the vanguard to enable capture of bridges over the Pruth and Dnestr Rivers before beginning the assault on the formidable defences of the Stalin Line.

From there they forced crossings of the Bug and Dnieper Rivers and began the attack on the Crimea with the *Luftlande* Division. Its commander, *Generalleutnant* Hans Graf von Sponeck, issued orders to his staff two days before the invasion commenced that Jewish Red Army prisoners be identified and kept separately, later commanding his division to work closely with *Einsatzgruppe* D in rounding up and shooting Jews in his operational area. Fortunately for the Brandenburgers they retained their autonomous character throughout '*Barbarossa*' and there seems to be no evidence that they were involved in those genocidal actions.

The ready companies of *Major* Heinz's 1st Battalion were also attached to Army Group South. The Battalion Headquarters, 2nd and 4th Companies as well as the Nachtigall Battalion were subordinated to *General der Infanterie* Carl-Heinrich von Stülpnagel's Seventeenth Army, operating in the region of XXI *Gebirgs* Corps, while the 3rd Company was placed elsewhere under the control of III Panzer Corps of Kleist's Panzer Group 1.

During the early morning darkness of 22 June, *Hauptmann* Dr Wolf-Justin Hartmann's 2nd Company left their forward staging area west of Przemyśl dressed in full Soviet uniforms and seized the rail bridge north of the city across the San River, a tributary of the Vistula. Hartmann, described frequently as having a 'very lively manner', had enlisted in the regiment as a 45-year-old reserve officer, having served during the previous war, fighting in Russia as an artillery commander during 1916 and later a volunteer member of the *Deutschen Asienkorps* (German Asian Corps) with the 701st Field Artillery Division where he was employed as a liaison officer with the Ottoman Army, fighting in Palestine against British Imperial forces. An adventurer by nature, he had subsequently sailed extensively during the 1920s before living for several years in South America, writing novels of his wartime adventures. A fresh European conflict brought his return to Germany and enlistment in the Brandenburgers.

The company raced east, breaking through the incomplete fortifications of the so-called 'Molotov Line'; the Przemyśl sector of the line that marked the Soviet Union's new western border comprising nine centres of resistance totalling ninety-nine bunkers stretching for 120km. They passed through the largely unmanned bunker system until caught in a savage artillery bombardment near the town of Butsiv that killed five of Hartmann's men and forced a temporary halt to their advance.

On the left flank of Army Group South, *Oberleutnant* Werner John's 3rd Company (named '*Sturmkompanie Schulze*' for the attack) stormed the defended bridge over the Bug River at Ustyluh on the morning of the invasion, supported by the 298th Infantry Division. John led twelve men that were disguised as Red Army troops, the only members of the group who spoke the native language being four Ukrainians while the remaining eight covered themselves in bloodstained bandages to discourage any attempts to communicate with them while they attempted to infiltrate the front line. During the previous night, they had stolen a calf from a local farm, though they were discovered in the act and John was forced to mollify the agitated owner with some money and a flask of schnapps. The calf was slaughtered, the meat given to the nearest German field kitchen while its blood was used to soak bandages on the Brandenburger troops. Slipping through the porous front line in two groups, they managed to mingle with retreating soldiers, many of whom shared similar bloodstained bandages after the border skirmishes that morning.

The first crossing of the Bug at Ustyluh was achieved with little problem, the Brandenburgers using the chaos caused by the start of the initial German artillery bombardment to make their appearance as retreating troops. Soviet Commissars that were shepherding the retreating rearguard towards the east attempted to order John's leading Brandenburgers onto trucks for the withdrawal, but soon left the scene before making any attempt to enforce the order. Ustyluh is situated at the confluence of the Luga and Bug Rivers and was a transit point for the grain and lumber traffic that had plied the waterway as far as Danzig. The German artillery bombardment that threw the Red Army into headlong retreat destroyed or damaged more than 80 per cent of the town's houses and killed approximately 500 people. Once the Wehrmacht established a firm hold on the ruins it was used as a railway traffic point, the local Jewish population soon being rounded up and put to work fixing minor artillery damage to the bridge over the Bug River, clearing the debris from the street and loading freshly arrived ammunition and military provisions onto trucks at the railway station.

John's company continued to head east towards two wooden bridges near P'yatydni. Their crossing of the Bug had taken place at 0315hrs and they reached their new objective by 0430hrs. Racing across the pair of bridges, they established a small defensive enclave on the eastern bank that they defended against frequent and heavy counter-attacks. At one point, Soviet engineers attempted to attack using the river itself, approaching on pontoons in an unsuccessful effort to destroy the two bridges with explosives. The lightly armed Brandenburgers were scheduled to hold the bridges for only twenty minutes, though it was one-and-a-half hours before infantry reinforcements arrived and John's exhausted men were relieved.

1. *Kampforganisation Jablunka* photographed before the attack on Poland. *Leutnant der Reserve* Dr Hans-Albrecht Herzner is the uniformed officer sitting in the front row.

2. A second, poorer-quality, photo taken at the same time, but with an additional uniformed member of the Wehrmacht.

3. Theodor von Hippel; veteran of the East African campaign of the First World War and father of the 'Brandenburgers'.

4. Officers of the *Deutsche Kompanie* in their Slovakian base at Sliač, August 1939. *Leutnant* Siegfried Grabert stands second from right.

5. *Hauptmann* Hans-Jürgen Rudloff inspecting his men of the *3rd Baulehr Kompanie z.b.V. 800* before crossing the Belgian border as the spearhead of 'Case Yellow'.

6. A bridge over the Juliana Canal, captured by *Leutnant* Hermann Kürschner's West Platoon, one of whom still wears his Dutch uniform disguise.

7. The Gennep railway bridge after its capture by *Oberleutnant* Uwe-Wilhelm Walther's *4th Baulehr Kompanie z.b.V. 800*, a feat for which Walther was awarded the Knight's Cross.

8. The Nieuport bridge after its capture by *Leutnant* Siegfried Grabert's assault group on the night of 27 May 1940.

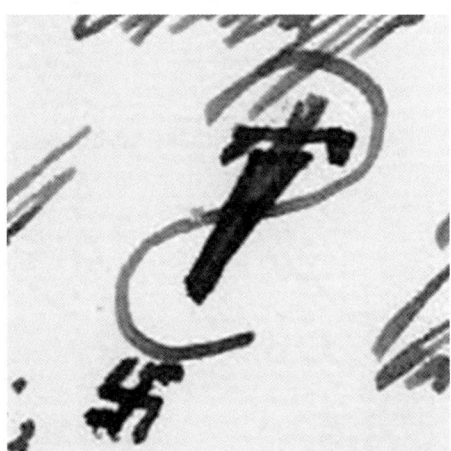

9. Grabert's original drawing of the new regiment's insignia, included in a letter to his brother written after the capture of the Nieuport bridge and sluice controls.

10. Born in Schorndorf/Württemberg in 1916, Siegfried Grabert entered the Reichswehr in 1934 before a sports injury forced an end to his military career and he embarked on medical studies. Grabert later joined *Freikorps Ebbinghaus* and gravitated to eventually lead the 8th Company, II Battalion 'Brandenburg'. Awarded the Knight's Cross on 10 June 1941, he was posthumously awarded Oak Leaves on 6 November 1943 after being killed in action in the Bataysk bridgehead on 25 July 1942.

11. Deputy Führer Rudolf Hess greeting Knight's Cross holders who had been members of the National Socialist German Student Union on its fifteenth anniversary, 27 January 1941, in Munich. Walther stands at the far end of the line.

12. Not all bridges were captured intact; this one over the Drava River was successfully destroyed by retreating Yugoslavian troops, 1941.

13. Uwe-Wilhelm Walther, pictured here in Greece during 1943. Walther was a superb soldier and gifted leader who was wounded several times and ended the war as part of Skorzeny's SS *Jagdverbände*.

(above) 14. The raising of the flag over the Acropolis in Athens by Brandenburgers led by *Rittmeister* Dr Paul Jacobi on 27 April 1941.

(left) 15. *Oberstleutnant* Paul Haehling von Lanzenauer, commander of the Brandenburg Regiment (left), and *Major* Friedrich Wilhelm Heinz (middle), commander of I Battalion.

(below) 16. Ukrainian troops of the Nachtigall Battalion in training at Neuhammer. They came under Brandenburger command for Operation '*Barbarossa*', attached to Heinz's I Battalion.

17. Operation 'Barbarossa'. A destroyed Brandenburger vehicle next to a disabled Soviet BT7 light tank. Note the new regimental insignia painted on the fender. The men on foot all appear to be wearing the *jäger* arm badge, possibly the vehicle's former occupants.

18. Brandenburger troops in Soviet uniform during the opening day of Operation 'Barbarossa'.

19. The sheer volume of Soviet prisoners taken during *'Barbarossa'* was staggering. From these masses of men, the Brandenburgers would find valuable intelligence agents, interpreters and combat recruits.

20. *Feldwebel* Willi Hein (left) and *Leutnant* Oskar Schatz of 2nd Company in full Soviet disguise during Operation *'Barbarossa'*. Schatz was later killed on 22 August 1942 near the Terek River, 100km from the Grozny oilfields.

(above) 21. Casualties within the regiment were relatively heavy, not only through their employment as assault troops but also the complicating factor of friendly fire incidents as many units went into combat in disguise, thereby running the risk of misidentification by other Wehrmacht spearheads. To compound these dangers, Brandenburger infiltration units frequently used German artillery fire to cover their penetration of enemy lines.

(left) 22. A *Fallschirmjäger* photographed wearing an early pattern army belt buckle, possibly identifying him as a member of the Brandenburger *Fallschirmjäger* platoon that made its first combat drop in an attack on two bridges near Bogdanow on 25 June 1941.

23. The grave of the *Fallschirmjäger* platoon commander *Leutnant* Hermann Lütke and his fellow *Fallschirmjäger* killed in Operation 'Bogdanow'.

24. *Oberleutnant* Hans-Wolfram Knaak photographed near Dünaberg, Lithuania, where he was killed on 26 June 1941.

25. The grave of Knaak and four of his men killed in the capture of the bridge over the Daugava River.

26. Nachtigall troops on the streets of Lviv at the end of June, enthusiastically greeted by the population. Though some members took part in the hideous pogroms that followed, the unit as a whole was not involved. The battalion was dissolved in October 1941.

27. Checking a dusty Russian road for mines. The early Brandenburger recruits were trained in the handling of explosives both offensively and defensively.

28. An officer of the '*Azad Hid Fauj*' (Free India Army) at *Regenwurmlager*.

(above) 29. The Free India Army, otherwise designated *Infanterie-Regiment 950 (Indisches)* and later transferred to the Waffen SS (*Indische Freiwilligen Legion der Waffen-SS*), was raised in Germany and trained as part of the Brandenburgers, primarily for Operation '*Bajadere*'. One hundred legionnaires were dropped by parachute in Eastern Persia and ordered to infiltrate into Baluchistan Province to undertake sabotage operations in preparation for an anticipated national revolt against British rule. Abwehr reports from Kabul received in Berlin indicated success, but to no discernible effect.

(left) 30. Friedrich 'Fritz' von Koenen, commander of the 13th (Tropical) Company; the first Brandenburger unit deployed to North Africa.

(below) 31. Brandenburgers of the 13th Company using captured Allied vehicles.

32. *Rittmeister* Conrad von Leipzig, the one-legged officer who would serve in North Africa and later form the *Küstenjäger Abteilung*.

33. Brandenburger troops in North Africa. Their speciality of lightly equipped, fast moving operations suited warfare within this theatre of action perfectly and they ranged far to the south on deep-penetration reconnaissance missions.

34. An LWSI of the Tropical Company during rehearsals with *Kampfgruppe Hecker* for the amphibious landing at Gabr Si. Hameida that was cancelled at the last moment.

(above) 35. Tobruk finally fell to Rommel's forces in June 1942, with Brandenburg troops involved in the German advance and also security duties around the captured port.

(left) 36. *Hauptmann* Count László Almásy (left) and *Major* Nikolaus Ritter discuss plans to land agents behind enemy lines in Egypt.

37. Ritter (at right with arm outstretched) and Almásy brief Luftwaffe pilots for the disastrous flight into Egypt during June 1941.

38. Brandenburger troops returning to German lines with flag stretched out to aid aerial recognition.

39. Odo Wilscher, Koenen's adjutant and later member of the Brandenburger *Fallschirmjäger* Battalion. He is pictured here after his transfer to the Waffen SS and Skorzeny's SS *Jagdverbände*, commanding the sniper school in Zeithain.

40. Light vehicle of the 13th (Tropical) Company, equipped with a single 20mm flak cannon.

41. Car emblazoned with the emblem of *Sonderkommando Blaich*, a single Heinkel He 111 that bombed the French stronghold of Fort Lamy south of Lake Chad.

42. A soldier of the 'Free Arabia Legion', part of the KODAT command that was ultimately headed by Theodor von Hippel before the collapse of Axis forces in North Africa.

43. Brandenburger recruits for the *Kustenjäger Abteilung* at the completion of training aboard the naval sail-training ship *Gorch Fock* in Swinemünde.

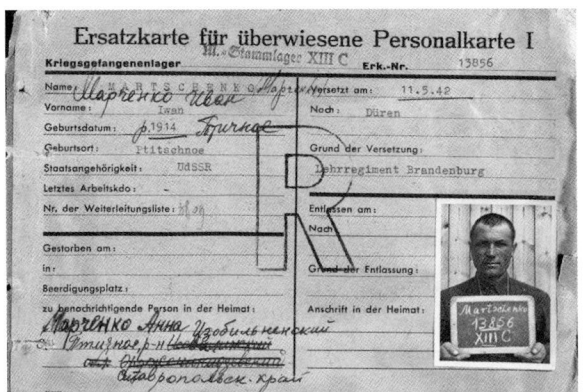

44. Identity card of a Soviet prisoner of war recruited into the Brandenburger Regiment.

45. Admiral Wilhelm Canaris on a visit to Brandenburg units at the front lines in Russian, October 1941.

46. *Leutnant* Trommsdorf and Finnish troops during the development of '*Kompanie Trommsdorf*' for the attack on the Murmansk railway line. Trommsdorf ultimately proved incapable of the physical demands and returned to Germany, his unit taken over by *Oberleutnant* Otto Hettinger.

Sturmkompanie Schulze continued fighting alongside the 25th Motorised Infantry Division, also seizing a railway bridge across the Styr near Rozyszce 80km to the east on 28 June, establishing another bridgehead that came under severe Soviet pressure but never buckled. However, Soviet snipers and infantry attacks had taken their toll; sixteen men had been killed from the 3rd Company and *Oberleutnant* John wounded by shell splinters after being caught in a bombardment by Soviet tanks. Hospitalised, he was replaced as company commander by *Leutnant* Dieter Weithoener until the remains of the company returned to Brandenburg an der Havel during August.

Meanwhile Heinz led the 4th Company and Nachtigall troops through Russian lines in the vanguard of the 1st *Gebirgs* Division. Local villagers recounted stories of Soviet border guards fleeing at the first sign of German troops, which could account for the lack of serious resistance encountered by Heinz at that point.[9] Heinz had led his troops across the San without serious casualties and by 28 June '*Kampfgruppe Heinz*' stood before a strongly fortified Russian position near the city of Lviv (known as Lemberg to the Germans). Flushed with the success experienced thus far and with the Soviet defenders reeling back in confusion, the Brandenburgers were poised at the gates of the city and mounted their attack on the strongpoint at 0300hrs on 29 June. The Nachtigall Battalion led the assault and, despite the apparent complexity of the defensive works, met only moderate resistance before the Red Army lines collapsed.

As the Nachtigall Battalion marched into Lviv they were greeted enthusiastically by the local populace who generally harboured little ill-will towards their Wehrmacht 'liberators' from the severe and unrelentingly oppressive Soviet yoke that had historically degraded the Ukraine. Heinz himself arrived in the city at the head of thirty men on motorcycles and sidecars. Heading at full speed for the city hall, he was apparently responsible for rescuing Bishop Graf Czepticki from the adjacent cathedral, the Bishop of the Ukrainian Unity Church having been chained inside the building by retreating NKVD men who then set fire to the ornate interior. By 1400hrs the first elements of the 1st *Gebirgs* Division were in the city and Lviv firmly under German occupation.

With Heinz's approval, the next move made by the Ukrainian Nachtigall troops was to proclaim the beginning of an independent Ukrainian state at 2000hrs on 30 June during a 'liberation ceremony' conducted by Bandera's representative, Yaroslav Stets'ko. He declared to an assembled audience in a small meeting room in the building belonging to the Prosvita Society – dedicated to the preservation of Ukrainian culture and shut down by Soviet rulers in 1939 – that the newly independent Ukraine would cooperate fully with 'National Socialist Greater Germany, which under the leadership of Adolf Hitler, is creating a new order in Europe and the world and is helping the

Ukrainian nation liberate itself from Muscovite occupation'. Lviv's radio station, occupied by enthusiastic Nachtigall troops, was later used to relay the message over the airwaves, giving hope to nationalists who heard the proclamation.

However, while Heinz may have encouraged the Ukrainians, two other German officers present – *Hauptmann* Hans Koch (an Abwehr II officer who acted as an OKW consultant for Ukrainian affairs) and Engineer *Hauptmann* Wilhelm Ernst zu Eikern (Army Corps Staff) – were quick to inform the enthusiastic Ukrainians that only Hitler himself could proclaim the nation's independent statehood and pointedly reminded them that the war was not yet won and such a declaration of independence was somewhat premature. Yet there were precedents for the Ukrainian announcement; the Slovakian Hlinka Party had declared a Slovak state on 14 March 1939 following the German annexation of Czechoslovakia and the Croatian Ustaša had proclaimed theirs on 10 April 1941 after the German entry into Yugoslavia. Both claimed liberation, the former from Czech occupation, the latter from Serbs as the oppressors of Croatia. Both states were recognised by the Axis powers, though not as truly independent countries, but rather satellites of the Greater German Reich. A more foreboding precedent was that both also unleashed extreme bouts of ethnic violence immediately afterward.

Indeed, into this heady mix of emotions in Lviv came news that at least 2,800 bodies had been found in the city's prisons, murdered by the retreating NKVD, many showing obvious signs of torture. Caught surprisingly off-guard by the German attack – despite frequent and explicit warnings from collected intelligence – Stalin had ordered the immediate liquidation of anybody suspected of espionage or subversive activities against the Soviet Union. Killings took place predominantly in prisons and labour camps, particularly in the Baltic states, the Ukraine, Belorussia and annexed Polish territories. On the day of the German invasion, many 'ordinary criminals' were released and the shooting of political prisoners began. Troops of the NKVD dragged prisoners from their cells and executed them, killing others in their crowded cells with grenades and pistol fire. Wehrmacht doctors, lawyers and the Ukrainian Red Cross were all swiftly coordinated in collecting information on the NKVD's crimes in Lviv, though the events that swiftly followed were no longer the responsibility of Stalin's murderers.

Shukhevych, the Ukrainian head of the Nachtigall Battalion, helped to organise local militia groups who, with the encouragement and connivance of incoming SD *Einsatzgruppen*, unleashed a horrifying wave of anti-Jewish pogroms throughout the city, the Jewish community being falsely accused of collaborating with the Bolshevik NKVD killers. The Nachtigall Battalion and other Wehrmacht units did not, as a whole, take part in the violence, though individual members almost certainly did and altogether an estimated 4,000 Jewish civilians were killed during the first of Lviv's pogroms. Within days the Nachtigall Battalion left the city, marching in the direction of Vinnytsia on 7 July alongside the Brandenburger's 1st Battalion, led by *Hauptmann* Hartmann. Both units were soon in ferocious action and suffered heavy casualties in fighting against fanatical troops of the Red Army's Komosol Regiment.

Heinz had been outraged by what he witnessed in Lviv, though found himself unable to intervene to any significant degree. On 1 July, he sent a clear report on the capture of the city to his superiors, mentioning the behaviour of local residents as well as German police units:

> The Ukrainian population, partly even the poorer Polish population, dating from the Austrian period, took the troops as liberators and the massacres committed by the Reds fuelled their rage to the utmost. Violence began on 30 June and 1 July against the Jews which adopted the worst character of a full pogrom. The police were controlling events and the most brutal and repugnant behaviour took place against the defenceless . . . The population considers the Bolsheviks criminally guilty due to their massacres, but now does not understand the torture and shooting of indiscriminately condemned Jews, including women and children. This makes a particularly discordant impression on the Ukrainian Companies. They cannot distinguish between the power of the Wehrmacht and the police and, as they see examples in the actions of German soldiers, are generally wavering in their assessment of Germany. It is the same force which yesterday ruthlessly shot down Jewish looters, but rejects cold-hearted cruelties.

The report, plus his support for the Ukrainian independence movement, soon cost Heinz his position in the regiment. On 19 July, he received the clasp for his EK II, six days later the clasp for his EK I and the Infantry Assault Badge in silver before he was ordered back to Brandenburg's *Generalfeldzeugmeister* barracks by Canaris, not least of all to keep him away from potential repercussions for his actions from more devout National Socialists. There he received a new assignment: command of the Abwehr School near Meseritz (the *Regenwurmlager*) for the training of *V-Leute* and foreign troops. After his departure, the Brandenburg Regiment's 1st Company which had functioned as a holding unit for *V-Leute* was renamed '*V-Abteilung*' and transferred during November 1941 to Meseritz. Subsequently, *Oberleutnant* Babuke's 17th Company, still in the process of forming, was redesignated and moved to Brandenburg an der Havel to become the new 1st Company. Heinz for his part remained at the *Regenwurmlager* for a year but would later return to the regiment during November 1942.

The Nachtigall and Roland Battalions were subsequently dissolved during October 1941. Bandera's premature declaration of Ukrainian independence had not been warmly received by his German overlords as Hitler's vision of the Ukraine was as a vassal state to the Greater German Reich, not an autonomous region. Bandera was arrested on 15 September 1941 and imprisoned in Sachsenhausen concentration camp until 1944.[10] Both dissolved battalions were regrouped at Neuhammer and merged to create the auxiliary police unit *Schutzmannschaft Bataillon 201*. Attached to the SD and *Einsatzgruppen*, this unit spent time then engaged in fighting partisans and murdering Jewish civilians in Belarus.

Though Nachtigall was no more, both Herzner and Oberländer remained active with Ukrainian forces, the latter reporting to OKW during 1942 that the key to mastering the Ukraine was by 'winning over the masses and pitilessly exterminating partisans as deadly to the people'.[11] He was later named head of the mixed German and Caucasian *Sonderverbänd Bergmann*, which was actively involved in brutal anti-partisan warfare. However, in May 1943 he was dismissed from the Wehrmacht on Hitler's orders after distributing a political paper that called for the mass recruitment of Eastern volunteers by the Wehrmacht, a policy to which Hitler was opposed. Oberländer returned to Prague, a year later joining the staff of Andrey Vlasov's Russian Liberation Army.[12]

Heinz's was not the only Abwehr voice to call for, at the very least, greater restraint in dealing with what had euphemistically been described in the Third Reich as the 'Jewish problem' as Nazi perceptions of racial superiority were resulting in catastrophic outrages leading to what is now known as the Holocaust. Of course, there was also a pragmatic reason for restraint. The Wehrmacht had been hailed in many Soviet regions as liberators from Stalin's brutal regime and while the opportunity existed to mobilise entire populations in concert with Germany's war aims, the behaviour of occupation troops and subsequent political policy against all non-German populations, not just Jews, would rapidly undo any accrued goodwill, Furthermore, Hitler had issued specific instructions that Red Army Commissars were to be immediately shot upon capture. Soviet prisoners were poorly treated at best and, once the facts of these executions became common knowledge, Red Army resistance perceptibly stiffened as there was clearly no benefit in surrendering to such a pitiless enemy. Lahousen later related this fact to American interrogators after the war:

> The treatment of Russian prisoners and commands regarding this, with which alone the German Wehrmacht befouled itself forever, were the object of several written and oral protests of Amt Ausland/Abwehr, all of which had Canaris' signature or were issued in his name . . . So, to give one example of many, in

the 'sorting-out' of Bolshevist infected Russian prisoners, Crimean tartars or Azerbaijan men from the Caucasus were liquidated by the '*Sonderkommandos*' of the SD solely because as Mohammedans they were circumcised and therefore were regarded as Jews by the race-fanatics of the SS and SD. Precisely from these peoples of the Soviet Union, however, had Abwehr *Abteilung I* and *II* especially gained valuable volunteer helpers (agents and combat units) . . . With the statement that this war was not a military dispute of two states or armies, but an ideological conflict of two concepts of life and that the political objectives of National Socialism were to be given preference over all military or other considerations, these and similar protests (especially from the front) were rejected by some generals who were all too subordinate to Hitler. Canaris had protested and warned here too. It was in vain.[13]

There was indeed little appetite in OKW for criticism of what had become policy on the Eastern Front. *General* Hermann Reinecke – head of OKW's General Office of the Armed Forces (*Allgemeines Wehrmachtamt*) and the office for the NSFO (*Nationalsozialistische Führungsoffiziere*) responsible for political propaganda in the Wehrmacht – issued regulations for the treatment of Soviet prisoners of war on 8 September 1941, which read in part:

> The Bolshevist soldier has therefore lost all claim to treatment as an honourable opponent, in accordance with the Geneva Convention . . . The order for ruthless and energetic action must be given at the slightest indication of insubordination, especially in the case of Bolshevist fanatics. Insubordination, active or passive resistance, must be broken immediately by force of arms (bayonets, butts and firearms) . . . Anyone carrying out the order who does not use his weapons, or does so with insufficient energy, is punishable . . . Prisoners of war attempting escape are to be fired on without previous challenge. No warning shot must ever be fired . . . The use of arms against prisoners of war is, as a rule, legal.[14]

The war in the East was being characterised as an ideological and racial struggle for survival and would be punctuated by massacres perpetrated by both sides. In the interim, the Red Army's stubbornness in defence was already perceptibly increasing.

By 17 July *Hauptmann* Dr Wolf-Justin Hartmann's 2nd Company had reached the small village of Lyudavka that lay on the main road to the city of Vinnytsia which was less than 30km to the east. They had already advanced 400km as the crow flies from their jumping-off point on the Polish–Soviet frontier, forging ahead as the spearhead for 4th *Gebirgs* Division. Resistance before the Ukrainian city had noticeably stiffened and light artillery fire and aircraft attacks disrupted the German advance as Hartmann summoned his five company officers for a situation briefing.

Under cover of darkness the company advanced in a two-pronged attack to dislodge Soviet troops, amongst whose number were fanatical Komsomol members. Hartmann was attempting to break their defensive bulwark that had been established along a tree-lined road only 1.5km away. Support for the Brandenburger assault troops came from three *Sturmgeschütz*, the German plan to envelop the enemy positions with simultaneous approaches from north and south. During the early morning of 18 July, the attack was launched into heavy small arms and mortar fire. Following heavy fighting, the Soviets were finally forced to retreat, leaving over one hundred dead and wounded men behind them. However, for the 2nd Company the result was catastrophic; over fifty men wounded, including Hartmann, who was taken to the rear midway through the assault and twenty-eight killed, including four of the five officers subordinate to Hartmann; only *Leutnant* Oskar Schatz remained alive and unscathed.[15]

The dead were buried in a ceremony during the following day attended by the commander of the 4th *Gebirgs* Division. His unit also had lost men, amongst them the commander of 13th *Gebirgsjäger* Regiment, *Oberstleutnant* Franz-August Sorko, killed by a stray bullet during fighting immediately to the north. The Brandenburgers' decimated 2nd Company continued to be used in further bitter fighting, though their strength was pitiful and morale had slumped to a new low. Canaris himself visited the survivors of the company on 30 July with regimental commander *Oberst* Haehling von Lanzenauer, restoring some self-confidence in his men, though they had also reached the point of material exhaustion. On 4 August, they were finally ordered out of the line, moving to Lviv where they were reunited with their recovering commander Dr Hartmann. From there they returned in stages to Germany, via Przemyśl, then Kraków and finally reaching the barracks in Brandenburg an der Havel on 17 August 1941, whereupon they began the task of rebuilding their shattered unit.

CHAPTER **6**

War in the Desert

'Mortal danger is an effective antidote for fixed ideas.'
Generalfeldmarschall Erwin Rommel

While the Wehrmacht were preparing for the ambitious invasion of the Soviet Union, the Brandenburgers had already become involved in several smaller deployments to both North Africa and the Middle East. German intelligence work in North Africa had been the domain of the French-based *Abwehrstellen* at St Germain and Bordeaux, augmented by Abwehr officers attached to the German Armistice Commission in the Vichy-controlled cities of Algiers, Oran, Tunis and Casablanca. Indeed, it was to the latter that Hippel had been transferred after his departure from the Brandenburg Regiment. However, as intelligence reports from these sources necessarily passed through the hands of Wehrmacht officers of the Armistice Commission before dissemination, they were frequently judged 'alarmist and exaggerated' when they predicted potential Allied activity and correspondingly dismissed out of hand, leading to major intelligence failures throughout the German North African campaign. Perhaps the most notable example of this was the disregarding of intelligence that showed preparations to be underway for the Anglo-American landings in the Casablanca area and subsequent failure to anticipate Operation 'Torch' in 1942. The Abwehr also suffered from a shortage of officers capable of understanding and dealing with Arabs. To counter this deficiency, several French North African prisoners of war were recruited by the Abwehr as agents but their selection and training was so poor that they immediately deserted upon arrival back in their homelands.

During early 1941, the Abwehr established *Aussenstelle* '*Wido*' in Tripoli. British forces had checked the Italian advances after their declaration of war in June 1940 and then pushed Italian troops as far west as El Agheila, threatening the existence of an Axis presence in North Africa. However, the diversion of British forces to Greece resulted in a German opportunity to reinforce the flagging Italians in Libya. In concert with the arrival of combat troops, the new Abwehr post was created to supply intelligence in support of General Erwin Rommel's fledgling Afrika Korps. The 41-year-old commander of the '*Wido*' station was *Rittmeister* Witilo von Griesheim, a former cavalry officer before his attachment to the Italian Army as part of an exchange programme between the Axis partners. Subsequently he was moved to the General Staff although his 'abnormal sexual disposition' forced his resignation in 1937. Griesheim volunteered once more for active military service in 1940 and was swiftly recruited by Canaris into the Abwehr. Working with the Italian intelligence service, Griesheim supplied a steady stream of valuable information simultaneously to both Berlin and Rome and his opposites in Allied intelligence characterised him as 'an able and dangerous man'.[1] He made effective use of Arab agents and Tuareg tribesmen, one of whom acted as his permanent interpreter. The '*Wido*' station relocated at least twice, moving from Tripoli to Nalut and then eventually Zuara near the Algerian border where they shared an office with the Italian intelligence service in a house only 200m from the Mediterranean Sea.

Supervising Griesheim and the entire operation was *Major* Franz Seubert (codenamed 'Angelo') of Abwehr I, while assisting him on the ground were *Wachtmeister* Hans von Steffans and *Unteroffizier* Holzbrecher, both members of the Brandenburg Regiment and both assigned to a small radio station at Nalut, 200km south-west of Tripoli. Steffans had previously served in the French Foreign Legion for seven years beginning in 1923 and it is thought that he did not particularly get along with his superior Griesheim, finally being transferred back to the regiment during 1942. The posting of both men to Libya illustrates the fact that the Brandenburg Regiment was frequently used as a convenient pool of trained men from which all three branches of the Abwehr could draw drivers, interpreters, wireless operators and, on several occasions, actual field agents. For example, *Unteroffizier* Beilharz, born in Jaffa, Palestine, was posted to Tripoli as an Arabic interpreter. He had previously been part of the Brandenburger 2nd Company before transfer to North Africa in September 1941 and assignment to the small 'Hoesch Group' camped near Tripoli, later attached to a *Panzergruppe* headquarters. This minor unit was tasked with scouting beyond the German–Italian lines for periods of up to three or four days at a time, contacting Arabs and gathering as much information about the enemy as possible before returning. Beilharz was later part of Count László Almásy's Operation '*Salam*' in 1942, which we will look at shortly. Often, civilian Abwehr personnel were also transferred to the regimental strength for training and to obtain nominal military rank before posting overseas, generally attached to the *V-Leute* Company that had been amalgamated with *Major* Heinz's 1st Battalion.

The Middle East

It was not only North Africa that attracted Abwehr and Brandenburg attention, but also turbulence in the Middle East. At the beginning of April 1941, a pro-Axis *coup d'état* had taken place in Iraq, overthrowing the government that had maintained a pro-British stance since the country had been granted partial independence nine years previously. Four nationalist generals mounted the successful coup which installed the former Prime Minister Rashid Ali al-Gaylani as leader of the country. Gaylani had resigned dismissed from the post earlier that year under pressure from Great Britain due to his overt alignment with the German and Italian governments. The coup had been assisted and encouraged by the German Consul, Fritz Grobba and three Abwehr II men; *Hauptmann* Wilhelm Kohlhaas and Palestinian-Swabians *Unteroffizier* Brass and *Unteroffizier* Krautzberger of the Brandenburg Regiment. Hitler issued a secret directive on 23 May 1941 – *Weisung Nr. 30* – regarding the future prosecution of war in the Middle East. In the text, he described the 'Arab liberation movement' against the United Kingdom and potential German involvement therein.

> In this context, an uprising in Iraq is particularly important. It strengthens forces hostile to the British beyond Iraq's borders, disrupts English communications and ties down English troops and English ships at the expense of other war reserves. I have therefore resolved to push forward developments in the Middle East by supporting Iraq . . . I order the sending of a military mission, assistance from the Luftwaffe, arms deliveries for the support of Iraq . . . The Military Mission (codename: *Sonderstab F*) is to be commanded by *General der Flieger* Felmy.
>
> Their tasks are
> a) to advise and support the Iraqi armed forces,
> b) to make military connections with England hostile forces outside Iraq as far as possible,
> c) to gain experience and documents for the German Armed Forces in this area.
>
> . . . The members of the military mission shall initially be regarded as volunteers (per the Legion Condor). They wear tropical uniform with Iraqi insignia. The latter also to be used by German aircraft.

Just under one month later, on 21 June, the eve of '*Barbarossa*', Felmy's responsibilities were defined:

Sonderverbänd F is the Central Field Office for all questions regarding the Arab world, which concern the Wehrmacht. [Felmy] is included in all plans and measures taken in the Arab world.

General Hellmuth Felmy had begun his military career in 1904, joining the Imperial German Army before moving on to the fledgling air force. He began the Second World War as commander of *Luftflotte 2* before his dismissal in January 1940 following the debacle of the Mechelen Incident. During the First World War, he had commanded *Fliegerabteilung 300* in the Palestinian theatre, working alongside the Turkish military. His expertise and familiarity with the Middle East resulted in Felmy being called back into active service following his 1940 dismissal and tasked with taking charge of the German mission to Iraq. '*Sonderverbänd F*' was created in Potsdam by an amalgamation of several units, one of which was *Oberleutnant* Fendt's 11th Company of the Brandenburger Regiment, nine 37mm PaK being taken on company strength after attachment to Felmy's command. The remainder of the *Sonderverbänd*'s combat units were sourced from various parent units, each of a specialist service branch. Alongside Fendt's Brandenburgers *Sonderverbänd F* comprised: 2nd Company (Mountain troops), 3rd Company (Infantry), 4th Machine Gun Company, 5th Artillery Company (with three StuG IIIDs), 6th Flak Company (twelve 20mm cannon), 7th Engineer Company and 8th Anti-Tank Company (nine 50mm PaK 38s). A Luftwaffe component would later be added for the impending Iraqi operation.

Felmy's Orderly Officer *Leutnant* Stocky had been instrumental in assisting with the original formation of *Sonderverbänd F*, aided by Kurt Wieland who had been born in Württemberg, but had lived most of his life in Palestine. Wieland had been a weapons instructor for the *Gebirgsjäger* elements of the Brandenburg Regiment in Baden before transfer to the headquarters of Felmy's new unit with the rank of *Gefreiter*. After creation in Potsdam, Felmy's formation was to transfer to conquered Ukraine for training, Wieland being sent ahead with a skeleton staff from the *Sonderverbänd* to prepare a holding camp near Stalino (now Donetsk). They were not to be used in combat while events of the Iraqi *coup d'état* unfolded, instead being held in readiness for despatch to the Middle East. However, events on the Eastern Front intervened and they were finally committed to the fighting against the Red Army after the advance on Odessa had bogged down against strong resistance. Wieland was wounded during the fighting and subsequently returned to Berlin where his qualities were soon recognised and he underwent officer training once fit for duty again.

While his ground troops were diverted to the Eastern Front, Felmy's immediate concern was a Luftwaffe element that was still bound for Iraq. Two squadrons of aircraft – twelve Bf 110 twin-engine heavy fighters (4/*Zerstörergeschwader*

76) and twelve He 111 medium bombers (4/*Kampfgeschwader* 4) – were flown via Athens to Damascus, Aleppo, Mosul and ultimately Baghdad for what would transpire to be a short and unsuccessful tenure. The German Luftwaffe personnel (named *Sonderkommando Junck* after their commander *Oberst* Werner Junck, designated *Fliegerführer Irak*) soon discovered that they lacked spare parts, sand filters, tyres suitable for the soft desert sand and modifications to their aircrafts' cooling systems that the harsh climate required. Ammunition and fuel were also in short supply, as were local geographical knowledge and military intelligence for the planning and execution of bombing raids. Though they did indeed fly several combat missions, the aircrafts' Luftwaffe insignia being overpainted with Iraqi colours, their impact on the fighting was negligible and before long British troops were advancing virtually unhindered on Baghdad to quell the nationalist uprising.

The first ground skirmishes in the city took place at the end of May 1941 and as the coup had obviously failed the Luftwaffe aircraft returned to Mosul before they were finally abandoned for shipping to Greece aboard Italian transports. While British forces were being hounded out of Greece and then Crete, the former pro-British Iraqi regent had returned to his homeland and on 4 June 1941 the last pockets of resistance in Mosul were crushed. With Iraq again firmly in Allied hands, British and Commonwealth troops were now ideally poised for future operations against Vichy-controlled Syria.

Following the end of the Iraqi revolt, *Sonderverbänd F* was repurposed for future deployment to North Africa after its brief tenure at Odessa. Composed entirely of ground troops, the unit was redesignated *Sonderverbänd 288* and some members transferred ahead of the main body to North Africa with the purpose of training Arabs, the addition of the Brandenburger men having brought a strong cadre familiar with the Middle East and North Africa, including several ex-members of the French Foreign Legion. During November 1941, the initial wave of troops under Felmy's overall command departed an Italian port on troopships bound for Benghazi. The motorised unit was intended to take part in the planned Axis advance through Libya and onwards to the Caucasian oilfields by way of Persia, Iraq and Palestine after a successful seizure of the Suez Canal. However, it was not to be. They and the later creation *Sonderverbänd 287* operated under direct OKW command in action, eventually being formed into standard Panzergrenadier units and therefore no longer part of the Brandenburger story.

Despite failure in Iraq, the Middle East remained a fertile area for special operations and undercover work, though there appears to have been little successfully undertaken by the Germans. Both the Abwehr and SD were active in Iran, the latter attempting to oust OKW influence from the region during 1943 by inserting a swathe of new agents by aircraft. Heydrich's SD was actively attempting to usurp Abwehr dominance of international intelligence operations, though by comparison they were still an immature service and lacked the established manpower pool provided by such highly trained and skilled organisations as the Brandenburg Regiment. However, the SD's resolute ambition extended their reach into what had been the Abwehr's Middle Eastern domain and *Hauptmann* Wilhelm Kohlhaas later remembered the German Consul Fritz Grobba's telling statement regarding what the diplomat perceived as lacklustre Abwehr support for the Iraqi insurgency.

> [The two Brandenburgers] had, during the winter, appealed to the ambassador as a well-known oriental activist, but now they did not want to give up their regiment. Dr Grobba soon became rude with the words: 'If the Abwehr does not do it, I'll hand it over to the SD.'
>
> I eventually succeeded, but it was not the last time that he had relations with our, still vague, black competition and he let us feel that he was no longer so highly attached to Canaris to whom he owed his fate in diplomacy and his Baghdad post.[2]

Current printed mythology seems to accredit the Brandenburgers with an attack on the Iranian refinery at Abadan (Operation '*Amina*') but there is no documentary evidence that I can find to support this. The refinery, owned by the Anglo-Iranian Oil Company, produced 8 million tons of oil in 1940 and was a crucial part of the Allied war effort. A tangible pro-German stance in the country, coupled with the presence of an estimated 3,000 German nationals, led to the August–September 1941 Anglo-Soviet invasion of the country that secured not only the oilfields but also the Persian Corridor of the Trans-Iranian Railway; one of the safest routes for Allied Lend-Lease supplies to the Soviet Union free from Axis interference.

The Abwehr did indeed develop a plan for sabotaging the refinery as the invasion of the Soviet Caucasus appeared to nearing success. The Abwehr believed that if the refinery were threatened with potential capture it was likely to be destroyed by the British Army who held it. Charles Bedaux, economic adviser to Vichy and the Reich, developed a plan whereby to save the refinery it would be deliberately pre-emptively sabotaged, but in such a way that it appeared destroyed to its British operators but capable of being rapidly repaired. Bedaux's idea was to fill the bores and pipelines with fluid sand available from the grinding of locally sourced sandstone, rather than using coarse desert sand that would cause serious internal damage. In this way, the pipelines could be filled within three days and then cleaned out within two. However, the operation never left the drawing board as the failing invasion of the Soviet Union and disaster at El Alamein consumed resources beyond expectations, including the men of the Brandenburgers. The Anglo-Soviet invasion did, however, produce some benefit to the Abwehr as noted by British intelligence in 1944:

> It appears that when Russian troops entered Persia, many Persian students in Germany remembered stories which they had heard of Russian behaviour in their country in the last war and were hoodwinked by German propaganda about Russian atrocities. Several of them were so indignant that they wrote letters to Hitler and other Nazi leaders, demanding to be allowed to serve in the German Army . . . Dr Wagner of the Abwehr, who was then working under the cover name of Wendel, therefore wrote himself to all Persians in Germany – to those who had not written letters as well as to those who had – inviting them to a meeting in Berlin. Thanks to the promises of Shahrukh that they would all be given important posts when the Germans entered Persia, many of the students accepted the offer and went to train at Meseritz. Here the Free Corps formed a part of the *Sonderkommando Bayader* [sic], which included other peoples like Uzbeks and Indians.[3]

Afghanistan also attracted the attention of the Brandenburger Regiment. *Leutnant* Witzel of the 4th Company, rated by the Allies in subsequent intelligence reports as 'one of the ablest men of the Abwehr', was attached to the German legation in Kabul during 1941 alongside two dedicated radio operatives. It was Witzel who coordinated the planning for a German expedition to the North-West Frontier with India to attempt to initiate tribal sabotage against British forces in the region. Contemporary documents of the NSDAP record that 'the Führer wishes the study of a deployment in Afghanistan against India following Operation "*Barbarossa*"'.[4] The leading Nazi ideologist Alfred Rosenberg also wrote in his political diary that 'it would be possible in an emergency to use this country on the German side if necessary for actions against British India or Soviet Russia.' During February 1941, the head of the German Army, Alfred Jodl, suggested that 'an uprising of the mountain peoples along the Indian frontier, probably also in Afghanistan' could be fuelled to 'create a difficult trouble spot for England'.

Economic cooperation between Afghanistan and Germany was already well underway by the time that war had broken out in Europe. The Organisation Todt was active in the country, planning and supervising the construction of improved infrastructure including roads and bridges. German engineers were also conducting the joint exploitation of mineral reserves and later still, Germany purchased large quantities of cotton and wool for the manufacture of uniforms while during 1939 there were secret German arms deliveries to

Kabul destined for the Afghan military. By that stage, Germany had become Afghanistan's largest trading partner and in 1937, *Deutsche Lufthansa* had begun scheduled flights to Kabul.

However, while Hitler may have defined clear objectives for cooperation with Middle Eastern and Arab countries in his war, he was far less enthusiastic about India, which he saw as naturally subject to British rule. On 17 October 1941, he remarked in conversation with his inner circle of confidants that 'If the English were to be driven out of India, India would perish. Our role in Russia will be analogous to that of England in India.' The logic of the encirclement of oil-producing regions through operations in the Middle East and Caucasus was apparent to the dictator; the need for military adventures to conquer the Far East was not. Nonetheless, the Brandenburgers had already attracted some Indian members by the time that the noted nationalist Subhas Chandra Bose arrived in Germany to appeal for assistance in his fight against British rule. Bose, the former Mayor of Calcutta, had escaped house arrest that had resulted from his anti-British agitation and the organisation of civil disobedience. Crossing the Afghan border assisted by Abwehr men posing as road builders, he had departed Kabul on 18 March 1941 to Samarkand and thence onward to Moscow by train and to Berlin by aircraft, arriving in the German capital on 3 April 1941. While Hitler may not have altered his position on India to be any more sympathetic to Bose's cause, there were those in OKW, the Foreign Ministry and even Heinrich Himmler, head of the SS, that desired more tangible cooperation between Germany and Indian revolutionaries.

Bose sent two of his most trusted men to the town of Annaberg to search for potential recruits to an Indian Wehrmacht unit during 1941 – N.G. Swami and Abid Hasan – who had both served at some point in the *Lehrregiment 'Brandenburg'*. Their drive was successful and Austrian Abwehr *Hauptmann* Walter Harbich was placed in command of a company of approximately 100 men of this newly created '*Azad Hid Fauj*' (Free India Army) and together with Hasan travelled to the *Regenwurmlager* near Meseritz. There they found Tajik, Uzbek and Persian recruits already training with similar ambitions for their homelands. Harbich's Indian troops were all former prisoners of war and began training in the arts of sabotage, radio construction and use, parachuting, climbing and cipher methods. Their eventual purpose was to parachute into India, particularly the area of the North-West Frontier and begin operations to destabilise British colonial rule through acts of sabotage while also recruiting and training fresh converts to their cause with the methods they had learned. What became known as Operation 'Tiger' had been born.

Ribbentrop authorised 1 million marks for the support of 'Tiger' and plans were made to construct an airstrip in tribal territory for use by Fw 200 Condor aircraft carrying supplies for the Indian commandos. However, those ambitious plans never came to fruition and parachute drops remained the method of insertion for both men and material. Meanwhile, as the Indians trained, the lawless North-West Frontier appeared to already provide a fertile area for German-backed insurrection as early as 1941.

In April, the Abwehr sent Witzel to Kabul to form a forward intelligence station for operations against British India. He arrived in Afghanistan via Moscow and passage through the Uzbek town of Termez, disguised as a courier of the Foreign Office. High on his priorities was the establishment of a dialogue with the Pashtun tribal leader Mirza Ali Khan, who had managed to loosely unite various tribal factions against British colonial rule in 1936 after a series of British legal judgements had enraged Muslim tribesmen.[5] Calling for 'jihad' against the British, Mirza Ali Khan instigated a brief conventional war, before adopting guerrilla tactics that continued until the end of British rule in 1947. Known as the 'Fakir of Ipi', the Muslim leader was considered by Witzel a potential tool to be used by German interests in the intended war against British India. British journalists had already leapt to much the same conclusion, already claiming that European fascism was the root cause behind the unrest, the *Daily Herald*'s headline of 16 April 1937 reading: 'Mussolini was behind the revolt in north Waziristan.'

During 1941 Witzig was joined in Afghanistan by two other Brandenburgers; Manfred Oberdörffer and Fred Brandt. Oberdörffer was the son of a Hamburg merchant, remembered by a fellow student as 'blond, blue-eyed, robust, uncompromising . . . a volcanic soul . . . an equally ingenious and vulnerable human being'. Oberdörffer completed his medical studies and departed Germany for journeys through Africa and Asia as a researcher into leprosy. The young man was a devout National Socialist and had been horrified to discover a Jewish grandfather in his family tree, deciding to work outside Germany rather than be subjected to the scrutiny of his heritage required for NSDAP membership.

Following the outbreak of war, he returned to Germany and was recruited into the Brandenburg Battalion during June 1940, unable to be called a Wehrmacht doctor (*Arzt*) due to his non-Aryan background, but instead known as a 'medic' (*Sanitäter*). Following the usual intensive training, he reached the rank of *Gefreiter* and was stationed in the north of France where some leprosy cases had been discovered amongst French-African prisoners of war. By November 1940 he had returned to Brandenburg an der Havel until, during May 1941, he was abruptly posted overseas to join Witzig, his regimental comrades unaware of what his destination had been until a package arrived from Kabul carrying 1,000 cigarettes as a gift from Oberdörffer to his former comrades.

Fred Brandt was a German-Latvian who had been born in St Petersburg, Russia. Brandt had been occupied as a lepidopterist in Iran before the outbreak of war and had become fluent in both Persian and Arabic as well as the languages of his birth. Recruited by the Abwehr in 1940 he had trained with the Brandenburgers in *Quenzgut*, being promoted to the rank of *Gefreiter* and sent with Oberdörffer to serve as translator and to utilise his familiarity with local customs.

Their part of Operation 'Tiger' was to supply the Fakir of Ipi with money; in this instance, a suitcase full of forged banknotes from the printing presses at Sachsenhausen concentration camp. They departed German on 21 May 1941, travelling as leprosy researchers despite the disease being almost completely unheard-of in Afghanistan. Their journey was to Moscow by railway sleeper-car, south to Baku on the Caspian Sea before the pair sailed by steamer to the Iranian port of Bandar Azali from where they hired a car and local driver to take them onward to Kabul.

Oberdörffer possessed something of a tempestuous personality, with a profound weakness for women, and relations between the two men quickly became strained due to his somewhat cavalier manner in dealing with their various contacts. He had spent days in brooding silence as their driver spoke only a local dialect that Brandt could understand but Oberdörffer could not. The German's mood finally lightened with the addition of two extraneous passengers that joined them for their journey as far as Herat where the original Persian driver departed, to be replaced by an Afghan of whom Brandt harboured severe mistrust. The two Abwehr men had not established any genuine rapport and Oberdörffer refused to listen to his concerns about their new driver, seemingly enthusiastic that he could at last converse in English with the new man.

In Kabul, Brandt was disconcerted to learn that their arrival was widely expected and after contacting Witzig, the pair also visited the representative of their Axis ally in Kabul, Italian Consul Pietro Quaroni. A skilled diplomat, Quaroni had clashed with his own government over his disagreement at their departure from the League of Nations in 1935 and thereafter had been 'relegated' to the Middle East, far away from the fascist government's obvious displeasure. Oberdörffer was apparently captivated by Quaroni's wife Natalia, the woman claiming to be a 'White Russian' though Brandt's conversations with her soon revealed her to be a Bolshevik. Brandt maintained a professional detachment and conducted his own investigations into the Fakir, encouraged by stories he had learned which all shared the same common thrust: the warlord of the Waziri tribe was deeply untrustworthy as his primary concern was purely the benefit of his own people, not international affairs or relations with other warring nations. However, Brandt was unable to influence Oberdörffer with his acquired knowledge and instead despatched messages to Berlin pleading for freedom of independent action away from his distracted companion, who Brandt believed was inept at every aspect of successful espionage. However, his pleas were firmly rebuffed by Berlin, who curtly reminded Brandt that he was on active service and under Oberdörffer's command.

Though it was strictly forbidden for foreigners to leave Kabul's city limits, the two quietly departed the city bound for a rendezvous with the Fakir during July along with six Afghan escorts armed with rifles. Travelling on foot towards the tribal lands, they were within sight of the frontier and a manned Afghan border post on 19 July. Resting during the hours of darkness before attempting to slip through the border, a sudden flurry of gunfire took them completely by surprise, with Oberdörffer hit in the stomach and chest and Brandt badly wounded in his thigh by a rifle shot. His scalp had been severely lacerated by flying rock splinters and he was bleeding profusely. The nearby Afghan border guards immediately came to their aid, though not before they had been robbed of the money and all their possessions. Apparently abandoned and left to die by their assailants, the injured men were given a jolting truck ride towards hospital in Kabul by the border guards, though it was in vain for Oberdörffer who died along the way. A Turkish surgeon eventually removed the bullet from Brandt's thigh and thirty-five rock fragments from his neck and head.

Uncertainty still remains as to who killed Oberdörffer, men in the pay of the British authorities perhaps being most likely, the pair having been under surveillance since their arrival in Kabul. However, German intelligence maintained that they had been betrayed and shot by Afghans who considered the Germans to be emissaries of the previously overthrown regent King Amanullah who had been living in exile in Rome since 1929 but who had pursued economic cooperation with Nazi Germany in order to promote his return to power. Brandt, however, believed that it was in fact the Italian Consul and his wife who paid 'bandits' to murder the pair. For his part Quaroni, later in September 1943 after the fall of Mussolini's government, scoffed at the very idea that the Fakir could have been influenced by German money and power, accusing Hitler's intelligence service of 'being extremely stupid and bungling in their methods and ready to be led up the garden path by every petty intriguer'.[6] While Brandt was returned to Germany and would later be posted by the Abwehr to Albania, Oberdörffer was buried in Kabul's international cemetery, where he continued to upset people even decades later. The very presence of his grave managed to cause a minor uproar in the Bundestag in 2010 when the left-wing politician Inge Höger discovered the resting place of a 'fascist physician' that was in the same graveyard that now contained German members of the International Security Assistance Force (ISAF) killed in action in a new Afghan war. Somewhat ironically, it was also Witzel who had written the *Handbook on Afghan History* handed out to those same modern-day German soldiers by the Military History Research Office (MGFA, Bundeswehr).

Ultimately, Axis propaganda and intelligence efforts in the region were ineffective and characterised by a fairly constant and almost startling inefficiency. The three main Axis powers frequently mounted divergent operations that compromised the potential efficacy of each other's, while 'men on the ground' displayed great ignorance of local affairs and customs. Pietro Quaroni had been the first to prompt Bose to instigate sabotage missions and was also the first to develop solid plans for the opening of tribal insurrections against British rule in 1940, but his ideas were rejected by Berlin who did not want to diminish the 'prestige of the whites in the Middle East or India'. Following the opening of '*Barbarossa*' in June 1941, the Soviet Union closed its border with Afghanistan and after Iraq was occupied by British and Commonwealth troops, the country was effectively isolated from the Axis countries. Its sole trade route now lay through British India and the despatch of food and material from there subsequently softened attitudes towards Great Britain.

North Africa

Away from the Middle East, the commitment of German combat troops to North Africa had already begun in February 1941 when Erwin Rommel arrived with the vanguard of what would become the Afrika Korps. *Major* Seubert of Abwehr I requested the addition of a Brandenburg unit to enhance the intelligence capabilities of Rommel's forces and the despatch of a specially trained and equipped formation was planned for the same year. Many men of the regiment had returned to the Reich from both Africa and the Middle East and a drive was undertaken for volunteers from the ranks, approximately sixty men being screened and accepted within weeks, predominantly from the 2nd and 3rd Companies. Twenty-five-year-old *Oberleutnant* Friedrich 'Fritz' von Koenen was placed in command. He had been born in Danzig in 1916 but his family had fled from Polish persecution and emigrated to German South-West Africa where they became major landowners. As a child, Koenen became fluent in not only German, but English, Afrikaans and native African dialects while also choosing to study Arab languages as part of his schooling.

Koenen's new unit was designated the 13th 'Tropical' Company, which continued to expand during 1941. On 28 October, the first half of the Tropical Company departed Brandenburg an der Havel, transported initially by train for Lucrino Bagnoli near Naples. From there, Koenen, eleven NCOs and approximately seventy men were carried by aircraft to Tripoli disguised as a Wehrmacht supply and procurement unit (*Versorgungs und Beschaffungseinheit deklariert*) while the administrative 'second half' of the company remained in

Germany under the command of the company adjutant, *Rittmeister* Conrad von Leipzig, sifting new recruits and continuing training for African operations.

During the period in which the Tropical Company was created, there appears to have been an Abwehr presence already gathering recruits from those Germans still present in the Italian colonies, particularly those of Palestinian origin. Codenamed Operation '*Kleeblatt*' ('Clover Leaf'), there are only sparse references in available post-war records to both it and the related *Kommando Bisping*, the latter a component of the Tropical Company after Koenen's arrival. *Oberleutnant* Ferdinand Bisping had been born in South-West Africa in 1917 where his father had owned a large cattle farm. During 1936 he had travelled to Germany and became an officer in the Wehrmacht before volunteering for the *Baulehr-Bataillon z.b.V. 800* in 1940. Placed in command of a motorcycle unit, he had transferred to North Africa to collect recruits for the Brandenburgers, accumulating an estimated sixty men. Bisping was placed in command of Operation '*Kleeblatt*' in May 1942, the gathered men renamed '*Kommando Bisping*', though known amongst its members with wry humour as the 'BBC' ('Bisping Bicycle Company') presumably due to a continued motorcycle component. According to later Allied interrogation reports of *Feldwebel* Hans-Jürgen Kirchner, it was Bisping's first assignment for the Abwehr as the 'authorities, who did not think much of him, wanted to get rid of him'. He remained in charge of his *Kommando* until the end of the war in Africa.[7] Whether directly subordinate to the Brandenburg Regiment or operating semi-autonomously, the large number of Brandenburgers known to have been part of *Kommando Bisping* during its existence attest to the connection. For example, Sudeten-German *Oberleutnant* Franz Krautzberger had enlisted in the Brandenburgers in 1940 and was posted to North Africa as part of *Kommando Bisping* in May 1942. Wounded in a 'private shooting match', he was sent to Germany to recover before returning to North Africa to take charge of a separate *Kommando* in Tunis. Wounded once more while leading a raid, he was posted to Salonika, Greek-based Abwehr commanders being 'very annoyed at him for leading such dangerous expeditions on his own initiative, thereby unnecessarily endangering the lives of valuable Abwehr members'.[8]

The administrative trail of Operation '*Kleeblatt*', as a separate entity, is difficult to trace. It appears to have been an Abwehr initiative to recruit Arab volunteers directly into Abwehr – and perhaps Brandenburger – units. Headed by a civilian, Dr Scheuermann (designated *Sonderführer* for the task), it seems to have existed in North Africa from autumn 1941 until its personnel became Bisping's motorcycle unit. Scheuermann returned to Germany in 1943 to apply for military officer training.[9]

In the meantime, once Koenen's men were in Libya they began intensive training and were placed under Rommel's direct command. As early as March

1941 OKH had passed on to Rommel a proposal by *Rittmeister* Friedrich von Homeyer for the formation of a fast-moving, dual-purpose raiding/reconnaissance troop of a dozen men using six Kübelwagen. Homeyer advocated missions deep into the desert via Kufra and Auwenat and into the Nile Valley at Dereut. Although he was granted permission to form a larger unit – *Aufklärungs Abteilung 580 (mot)* of the 90th Light Division – in August 1941, his force only reached North Africa during 1942, Homeyer subsequently being killed by British artillery fire on 3 July at El Alamein and his unit was later upgraded to an armoured reconnaissance battalion and attached to 21st Panzer Division.

Rommel harboured some mistrust towards the newly arrived Brandenburgers, professing an aversion to 'war in the shadows' and strictly forbidding the use of disguise in enemy uniform, which he believed a direct contravention of the rules of war. Nonetheless, the forward elements of the 13th Company were swiftly despatched to the front line after their arrival and soon began operating as forward reconnaissance troops for the German forces. It appears that '*Abteilung von Koenen*' was initially divided into two components, half in and around Benghazi by the end of November while the remainder stayed in Agedabia under the command of *Feldwebel* Doehring.

It appears that Rommel's harsh opinion of German special forces may have softened somewhat after British commandos attempted to kill or capture him on 17 November 1941 – the same night that a small unit of Brandenburgers launched a disastrous mission near El Dabaa after being put ashore from a U-boat. The British were determined to eliminate Rommel, his legend amongst friend and foe already burgeoning as he swiftly and dynamically reversed Axis fortunes in the Western Desert. On the night of 17 November, a small commando force, led by 24-year-old Lieutenant Colonel Geoffrey Keyes, was landed from the Royal Navy submarines HMS *Torbay* and *Talisman* and attempted to penetrate what they presumed was Rommel's headquarters at Beda Littoria and either take him prisoner or assassinate him. However, Operation 'Flipper' was a complete disaster, two men being killed (including Keyes whose body was found a mile away after attempting to crawl away, one foot shot off and the other injured), twenty-eight captured and only three escaping back to Allied lines. Three Germans were killed. To compound the Allied tragedy, Rommel was not even in North Africa at the time, still on his way from a planned visit to Rome. Even if he had been, his headquarters was not at Beda Littoria as he had moved to a location near Tobruk to be closer to the fighting. Keyes was buried by the Germans with full military honours, Rommel sending his personal chaplain to conduct the service.[10]

Nearly 700km to the east, seven Brandenburger men were landed that same night by *Kapitänleutnant* Hans-Dietrich von Tiesenhausen's *U-331* between

Cape Ras Gibeisa and Cape Ras el Schaqiq. *U-331* had sailed with the extra men aboard from Salamis, Greece, at 1900hrs on 12 November, the Brandenburgers tasked with Operation '*Hai*' that was intended to cut the coastal supply railway that had been constructed by the 16th and 17th New Zealand Railway Operating Companies. The New Zealanders had originally been earmarked for service in France before the country's fall and were subsequently diverted to the Western Desert where their expertise was required. Their task was to help run and extend more than 400 miles of railway lines, easing the logistical burden of moving quantities of men and supplies from Egypt into Libya.

The sabotage troops were landed as planned by rubber dinghy, a single U-boat crewman helping row them ashore and guarding the dinghy as they raced inland. The U-boat then stood off to sea before a scheduled return the following night inshore to pick up the raiding party. A pair of patrolling British sentries discovered the tracks of the main raiding party but were killed by the U-boat crewman and a single Brandenburger who had remained with the dinghy. The charges were laid and, with dawn breaking by the time they reached the coast once more, all eight men hid in a cave to await darkness and the planned rendezvous with *U-331* on 18 November. However, the two sentries were clearly overdue and a heavily armed search party ran headlong into the Germans that evening after an abortive attempt to row from the beach to the rendezvous point had resulted in their dinghy capsizing in the heavy surf. Struggling back ashore through the breaking waves, the Brandenburgers were captured without a fight and subsequent interrogation revealed the pressure-fused charges they had planted which were soon disarmed. It was an inauspicious start for German commando operations in North Africa.[11]

The first official deployment of Koenen's Brandenburgers by *Panzerarmee Afrika* was made on 22 January 1942, when they were tasked with a combined reconnaissance and commando mission ahead of the German advance. Rommel's rapid movement east had allowed little time for the Abwehr to establish useful intelligence networks beyond those already operated by the '*Wido*' station. In its stead, Koenen's men fulfilled this role, ranging ahead of the German lines in a combination of Axis and captured British vehicles and gathering valuable information.

In February 1942, the second half of the 13th Company arrived in Libya with *Rittmeister* von Leipzig. The 22-year-old had been severely wounded in action with his cavalry unit during the first day of the invasion of the Soviet Union, resulting in his right leg being amputated. Though a much-admired and respected commander who always shared his men's trials and privations at the front, his wound had never healed properly and caused him extreme discomfort for the remainder of his life, requiring constant painkilling injections. Following his wounding, rather than leave the Wehrmacht he had volunteered for reconnaissance duties and enlisted in the Brandenburg Regiment where his drive and determination more than compensated for his physical disability. Leipzig had been born in German South-West Africa, the son of an ex-Imperial Navy officer who had served in the area during the First World War. After 1918, his father had married and established a successful sheep farm in Africa – *Farm Blaukohl* – Conrad the first of three brothers born to the couple in the German colony. Coincidentally, his youngest brother, Hellmut von Leipzig, was also in North Africa, having been assigned as Rommel's driver after volunteering for the Afrika Korps. Later, following the demise of the German forces in North Africa, Hellmut would also transfer to the Brandenburgers as an officer candidate, his officer training arranged by a grateful Erwin Rommel before the two men parted company.

The fortunes of war in the desert had ebbed and flowed ever since the arrival of German forces, but by May 1942 Rommel was advancing against the Allied defensive line at Gazala and the German assault on an isolated Allied garrison at Tobruk began. An initial amphibious operation was planned that utilised Koenen's men as part of *Kampfgruppe Hecker* (led by *Oberst* Hermann-Hans Hecker, *Pionier Führer Afrika*). Rommel's orders for 26 May outlining the Axis attack on the Allied defensive Gazala Line closed with instructions that: 'On X+1 *Kampfgruppe Hecker* will land at Gabr Si. Hameida to block the Via Balbia around Kilometre 136.'

Hecker's battlegroup included men of the 13th Brandenburger Company, 33rd and 39th *Panzerjäger* Battalions 778th Engineer Landing Company and Italian 3rd San Marco Marine Battalion. Their brief was to sever the Allies' Via Balbia supply route by landing 30km east of Tobruk while Rommel's forces attacked the Gazala Line directly. The troops were embarked on *Marinefahrprähme* (MFPs – landing craft) and sailed on 28 May under escort by mixed S-boats and R-boats (motor minesweepers). However, after only a few hours at sea the operation was cancelled by radio after Allied resistance proved unexpectedly fierce on the Gazala Line and all boats returned to Derna to unload. The company was subsequently used for guard duties under the command of *Major.i.G.* (*im Generalstab*, signifying an officer of the General Staff) Josef Zolling, Ic of *Panzerarmee Afrika*, before rejoining *Kampfgruppe Hecker* and moving towards Bir Hakeim where they took part in the attack on the fortress that was held by Free French troops. It was during this period that the 13th Company suffered its first losses.

On 6 June *Gefreiter* Reinhold Eichhorn was killed in action in the southern foothills of the Jebel Akhdar on the old Trig al Abd camel track that led to Tobruk. *Kampfgruppe Hecker* fought its way along the track to maintain contact with rapidly retreating Allied troops, while also headed south-east to join the battle for Bir Hakeim. This Allied strongpoint was on the site of a former Ottoman Empire fort that had been built around an ancient Roman well. Comprised of little more than a small elevation in the flat desert landscape, it had been impressively fortified by the French defenders, three gates allowing traffic in and out by way of marked paths through the extensive minefields that contained 130,000 anti-tank and 2,000 anti-personnel mines. Bir Hakeim anchored the inland end of the Gazala Line and was held by an original garrison of 3,703 men of *Général de brigade* Marie Pierre Koenig's 1st Free French Brigade, formed largely of colonial and French Foreign Legion troops and later becoming one of the most decorated French units of the war. To their north, unbeknownst to the French, a battalion of 400 poorly armed minelayers held a position near Bir-el Harmat at the northern fringe of the French minefields, the smaller force comprised of Jewish Palestinians of Major Liebmann's Jewish Brigade.

While the Allies expected a frontal assault against the coastal portion of the strongly defended Gazala Line, Rommel instead chose to sweep southwards, hoping to skirt around the French position while making a feint attack along the coast road. The main Gazala Line was made up of extensive minefields and 'boxes' of troops that in total outnumbered Rommel's forces and he hoped to nullify this advantage by concentrating where the line was thinnest. His initial success almost proved his downfall as German panzers swiftly moved beyond the reach of the supply columns that had difficulty finding them in the swirling maze of dust and Allied minefields. German trucks were forced to travel long distances around Bir Hakeim, limiting the Axis forces' offensive power. Both the French and Jewish positions were directly attacked on 26 May after appeals to surrender were rejected. Expecting the outnumbered defenders of Bir Hakeim to be overrun in short order, the fierce battle instead became a protracted slugging match that dragged on for two weeks, the Luftwaffe flying 1,400 sorties against the exposed target and the equivalent of four German and Italian divisions being engaged in the assault. By 7 June Axis forces had completely encircled Bir Hakeim and the following day Rommel arrived to take personal command of operations. *Kampfgruppe Hecker* was folded into the 90th Light Division for the attacks that followed, Koenen's men acting in the role of traditional infantry.

The 90th had started life as a 'special purpose unit', the *Divisions-Kommando z.b.V. Afrika*, which had come into being on 26 June 1941 primarily for the purposes of the siege of Tobruk and the expected assault to capture the port city. Over the months that followed, during which the Germans were unable to break the Australian garrison, the unit changed first into *Division z.b.V. Afrika* and then 90th Light Infantry Division by the time that the Axis forces were beaten back from Tobruk during November 1941 before Rommel's new counteroffensive. Amongst the division's units was the 361st Infantry Regiment that had been formed primarily from German ex-French Foreign Legionnaires.

At 1000hrs on 8 June the first of the day's two direct assaults on Bir Hakeim was preceded by artillery barrages and a Luftwaffe raid. By the end of the day one French observation post had been overrun and a 75mm gun captured, but both Brandenburger *Gefreiters* Ernst Schweim and Herbert Vosswinkel had been killed in action. Two days later *Gefreiter* Manfred Lawicki was also killed during a day's fighting where the Brandenburgers and grenadiers of the 90th broke into the main defensive perimeter in three direct assaults. By the end of the day's fighting the French defenders had only a single 75mm artillery shell left. That evening, Pierre Koenig signalled the Eighth Army Commander Major General Neil Ritchie: 'Am at the end of my tether. The enemy is outside my HQ.' Ritchie promptly ordered the French garrison to break out that night, issuing the same instructions to the one hundred surviving Jewish troops to the north. The delay they had inflicted on Rommel's advance had allowed the British Eighth Army to retreat in good order to their new defensive line at El Alamein and their own evacuation began at 2330hrd that same night, involving fierce clashes in the dark with the surrounding Germans. By the end of the battle, the surviving French troops successfully reached Allied lines, they and their supporting units having suffered 141 dead, 229 wounded and 814 captured as well as the loss of 53 guns, 50 vehicles and 110 aircraft. Axis forces had suffered 3,300 dead or wounded, 227 captured, 164 vehicles destroyed – including 52 tanks – and 49 aircraft shot down.

Meanwhile the remainder of the Gazala Line had crumbled and Tobruk was attacked on 20 June, falling after less than a full day's fighting. However, the gallant defence of Bir Hakeim had imposed a severe delay on the Axis advance and influenced Hitler's decision to cancel Operation '*Herkules*', the proposed invasion of Malta. With time to organise the main defensive line at El Alamein, Rommel would be stopped at the very gates of Alexandria in the first battle, which brought about an uncomfortable stalemate until October 1942. Afrika Korps *General* Bayerlein later recalled the effect of the French stand:

> We were in a really desperate situation, our backs against a minefield, no food, no water, no petrol, very little ammunition, no way through the mines for our convoys; Bir Hakeim still holding out and preventing our supplies from the south. We were being attacked all the time from the air. In another 24 hours, we should have had to surrender.[12]

Count László Almásy and Operation '*Salam*'

Before their commitment as shock troops in the battle at Bir Hakeim, Koenen's Brandenburgers had already begun operating in their planned unconventional role. The Hungarian Count László Almásy headed an operation to insert two Abwehr agents behind British lines in April 1942 with the purpose of contacting pro-German Egyptian military officers. Almásy, a veteran of land and air combat from the First World War, was an aristocrat, motorist, desert explorer, aviator and sportsman who had spent years during the 1930s exploring parts of the Egyptian and Libyan desert. After Hungary joined the Tripartite Pact in November 1940, Almásy was recruited into the Abwehr in Budapest by Luftwaffe *Major* Nikolaus Ritter, chief of the Luftwaffe's section of Abwehr I and commissioned with the rank of a Luftwaffe *Hauptmann*. His initial work entailed cartography before his commitment to the plan to deposit two spies in Egypt, codenamed Operation '*Kondor*'.

Almásy was in North Africa in May 1941 and had already used his flying skill on behalf of the Abwehr, including the retrieval of two Hungarian agents from a landing strip 40km from the Giza pyramids. Ritter requested permission to mount a similar undertaking and land spies by aircraft in Egypt, as reliable information was urgently needed regarding British troop movements to Egypt from Palestine, Iraq and India and information about the flow of supplies through Red Sea ports. In June 1941, he was in Benghazi finalising details of his plan that involved the use of two bombers, one to be piloted by Almásy, the other by *Hauptmann* Hans Bleich. The Hungarian was to lead the way to the landing ground that he had used previously, though a quarrel between himself and Ritter over the condition of one of the aircraft (the Luftwaffe ground crew reporting a damaged tyre rendering it unfit for landing on an improvised airstrip) led to him resigning from the project, followed shortly afterward by Bleich. Ritter, undeterred, took one aircraft himself, the second flown by a replacement pilot as they carried a 40-year-old Egyptian-born spy named Muehlenbruch and a 45-year-old Jewish spy from Hamburg named Klein towards Egypt.[13] Arriving at the area indicated by Almásy, neither aircraft could see the landing zone and were forced to attempt to return without fulfilling their mission. However, through either faulty navigation or an unplanned diversion that was required due to their home airfield being under attack by British bombers, Ritter's aircraft went miles off its planned course and he ran out of fuel, making a forced landing in the sea nearly 4km from the coast. Though the Egyptian spy was killed, Ritter suffered only a broken arm and was later rescued with the remainder of his complement by German forces. Returning to Berlin, the project was taken from his control and Almásy asked by the Abwehr whether it was feasible instead to insert two spies by travelling overland. Though Ritter was keen to be involved, the Abwehr had lost confidence in him and *Rittmeister* Hoesch was brought in to take his place as coordinator.[14] As far as Almásy was concerned it was eminently possible, the same are having been the subject of an expedition that he had made in 1932, mapping the region that had been previously unrecorded by Western explorers.

The two agents concerned, Johann Eppler (alias Hussein Gaffar) and Heinrich Gerd Sandstede (alias Peter Muncaster), had been enlisted in the Wehrmacht as part of the Interpreter Company at Meissen, though Sandstede (and possibly Eppler) was also employed by the topographical department (*Kartenstelle*) of OKW in Berlin working on maps of the areas of Africa that he was familiar with. Eppler had been born in Alexandria, the illegitimate son of a German woman, Johanna Eppler, and a British officer. His mother later married an Egyptian named Gaffar though he was raised between 1915 and 1931 in Germany before returning to Egypt. He left North Africa for Germany once more in 1937 and married a Danish woman, Sonia Eppler-Wallin, the couple living in Copenhagen until September 1940. Eppler had become fluent in German, French, Egyptian and Arabic and possessed adequate English and a smattering of Scandinavian languages. Conscripted into the Wehrmacht, he was first transferred to a supply unit before his linguistic abilities brought him to the Interpreter Company. Sandstede, on the other hand, was a German national from Oldenberg who had lived between 1930 and 1939 in Uganda, Kenya and at Dar-es-Salaam, Tanganyika. He was an office manager for Texas Oil Company, and British authorities interned him at the outbreak of war as a hostile alien but he was repatriated to Germany in an exchange of civilians in January 1940. His linguistic skills included mastery of German, English and Swahili as well as some French and Italian. After attachment to the interpreter service, Sandstede and Eppler transferred to the Brandenburgers' 13th Company during summer 1941 after being recommended by their NCO, *Wachtmeister* Odo Wilscher, who would subsequently become Koenen's adjutant and later transfer to the Brandenburger *Fallschirmjäger* Battalion.[15] Their tenure with the company, which consisted primarily of African-Germans training for deployment to North Africa, was brief before both men transferred back to Berlin and the topographical department; an example of the method by which the regiment was used more as a depot for *V-Leute* than a military formation.

The pair were recruited for their mission to Cairo by *Rittmeister* Ulrich Otto Hoesch in August 1941. Hoesch had also lived in Africa before the war and it was with him that the two prospective agents met Almásy in Vienna's Grand Hotel. Hoesch departed for a separate mission to North Africa and was later killed in action at Gazalla on 7 October 1941, his role as coordinator of the planned mission being taken over by Abwehr *Hauptmann* Pretzl, a frequent pre-war visitor to Egypt where he worked as a professor at the Azhar University. Pretzl oversaw W/T (radio communications) training for the two agents at his home in Munich before they attended a four-week Abwehr W/T course in Berlin-Stahnsdorf. Pretzl in turn was killed in a plane crash on the way from Munich to Vienna in November 1941 and Almásy took direct charge of the operation. At the end of December 1941 Almásy and *Feldwebel* Enthold travelled to Africa to begin preliminary arrangements for their mission, coordinating with the '*Wido*' station for logistical support. The remaining six men associated with the operation would not arrive until February: Eppler and Sandstede, *Unteroffizier* Wöhrmann, *Vizeadmiral* Rolf von der Marwitz (German Naval Attaché in Ankara), *Feldwebel* Hans von Steffans and *Gefreiter* Waldemar Weber who would be their radio contact with Rommel's headquarters. Once in Libya they were joined by *Gefreiter* Munz and *Feldwebel* Beilharz and later *Unteroffizier* Körper and medical NCO *Unterarzst* Stringmann. The presence of the high-ranking 53-year-old Marwitz is unusual, though the veteran naval officer, who had served in the First World War before diplomatic postings from 1937, appears to have been involved in German espionage in the Middle East as a conduit by which Abwehr agents were paid. Though not a member of the intelligence services, his position in Ankara made him responsible for the embassies in Athens, Bucharest and Sofia and therefore a useful ally for Canaris' Abwehr. His role in '*Salam*' was advisory and, perhaps, financial.

The men were prepared and acclimatised within seven weeks and during April 1942 vehicles were obtained from the *Fallschirmjäger* '*Kampfgruppe Burckhardt*' based in Marawah, Libya. *Major* Burckhardt was returning with his men to Germany after having stood guard duty at an aerodrome located at the Jalu oasis that they had seized from the Allies in a ground assault during February. The transport consisted of two captured British Ford V8 trucks and three Bedford 1½-ton trucks with German markings. This was not to be a covert mission; all men wore German uniforms and the vehicles remained plainly marked, though dust and the relative similarity of desert clothing added layers of obscurity to identifying marks and insignia. At Jalu Almásy's group proceeded to load water containers for the upcoming operation, only to be told by local Arabs – as British Long Range Desert Group (LRDG) members had been before them – that the water of the Jalu wells was too brackish and would last only three days before becoming undrinkable. A sample sent to the Afrika Korps' 659th Water Supply Company (*Wasserversorgung Kompanie*) confirmed this information and Almásy was compelled to travel to Bir Bettafel 20km away to refill their supply.

The men and vehicles of what was now known as Operation '*Salam*' were assembled at Jalu and made their first attempt to depart for Egypt on 12 May.

While Steffans and Marwitz remained behind, Almásy, the two agents, Wöhrmann, Körper, Munz, Beilharz and Stringmann followed the Kufra track for 60km where Italian military maps suggested the hardened surface was that of a load-bearing gravel desert – a '*serir*' – before heading into softer sand. After 30km more, a sandstorm created difficulties for the trucks in shifting dunes and one was abandoned with a broken axle. Four of the remaining trucks returned to the Kufra track while Beilharz – who apparently developed the 'galloping shits' – and Stringmann retraced their steps to Jalu. After 30km of the Kufra track Almásy swung east along the most northerly of three camel tracks and began to periodically establish supply dumps of fuel and water for use on their return journey. Their expedition continued, crossing the tracks of heavy British traffic bound for the garrisoned Kufra oasis (captured by French troops from the Italians in March 1941) of which Wöhrmann transmitted details to their base. The small column encountered difficulties in finding the correct passes through the Gilf Kebir (Great Barrier), a rugged and remote plateau that marked the boundary between Libya and Egypt. A single vehicle was left abandoned in a wadi in order to extend the fuel of the remaining three. Six derelict British vehicles were found which yielded eight extra cans of fuel, though the '*Salam*' men did not linger to investigate their find further. Shortly thereafter they encountered a supply dump that Almásy had left during the course of a 1932 expedition over the same ground, containing four canisters of still drinkable water and ten petrol canisters from which the fuel had leaked and evaporated away.

Their position as far as water and fuel were concerned was becoming desperate as Almásy searched for the correct pass. They possessed insufficient fuel to skirt south of the mountainous range blocking their way and when all hope appeared lost Almásy finally found traces of his 1932 trail, following it between two peaks that had only been committed to cartography during that original exploration that Almásy had made nearly ten years previously. Only approximately 100km short of their destination of Asyut on the banks of the Nile, they left yet another truck behind that had broken down and continued along their way loaded on to the remaining two. At Rommel's headquarters, Weber acknowledged a wireless message from Eppler, the last transmission he was to receive from either of the two agents. After bluffing their way past British sentry posts and other small units encountered along their path, Almásy and his group reached the area of Asyut and the two agents – codenamed 'Max' (Sandstede) and 'Moritz' (Eppler) – disembarked to continue their journey alone. They buried their uniforms and one of the W/T sets, marked the spot and headed into Asyut on foot, arriving on the morning of 24 May and taking a train bound for Cairo at 1pm. Their part of '*Salam*' was now over and their mission reverted to Operation '*Kondor*'.

Meanwhile, Almásy and his '*Salam*' men retraced their path to successfully reach German lines once more, whereupon the Hungarian aristocrat reported in person to Rommel. For his successful part of the operation he was promoted to *Major* and decorated with the EK I before being discharged from the Wehrmacht as per his request and returning to his native Hungary. It had been originally proposed by the Abwehr that if Almásy completed his expedition safely, he take control of Koenen's half of the 13th Company and train them in the methods of the LRDG, equipping them with captured Bren carriers, Ford V8 trucks, machine guns and mortars and operate in the Kufra region as both reconnaissance and a harassing force against British supply lines. However, as far as Almásy was concerned, he had done enough. His war was over.

In the end, the remarkable journey that they had made to deliver the two agents was futile. Both men were arrested on 24 July after achieving nothing except the squandering of their supplied fortune (£3,000 in forged pound notes). Early attempts at making wireless contact with Rommel's headquarters failed and after money became scarce, they met with Viktor Hauer, a German national, though Austrian by birth, working at the Swedish Embassy to administer the interests of interned German civilians with the approval of British authorities. Through Hauer they accessed a transmitter that Hauer had hidden in the embassy basement, disguised as packing crates belonging to a pre-war German archaeological team. The agents transmitted a single message towards Rommel's headquarters:

> To Section 1 H west of the Abwehr, Angelo.
> Please guarantee our existence. We are in mortal danger (or it is exceedingly urgent, according to Sandstede). Please use the wave-length No. 1 at 0900 hours Tripoli time.
> Max and Moritz[16]

There was no reply and unfortunately for the two agents, Hauer was playing a double game and working not just with British approval but in the interests of the Allied intelligence services. While he distracted the pair by introducing them to sympathetic Egyptians, who included Anwar el-Sadat from the Egyptian Signals Corps (later President of Egypt in 1970), Hauer warned the British authorities that he had been contacted by German spies. A staged kidnapping of Hauer was mounted so that he could be fully interrogated and after British intelligence had learned all he knew he was interned in Palestine 'for his own protection'.[17] Eppler and Sandstede were finally arrested on 24 July 1942, along with the rest of their small network including el-Sadat. The British authorities were less than impressed.

Both Sandstede and Eppler had a diary; they both claim that these diaries were written to cover themselves if ever they should have to explain their achievements in Egypt to the Germans. A large number of the entries in the diary were true, but many were false . . . The diaries were written up when it seemed likely that Rommel would arrive in Cairo . . . In fact, Sandstede and Eppler had, so far as can be ascertained, achieved nothing. This may be accounted for by the fact primarily that their transmitter got no response from Weber, that they were unable or unwilling to make certain contacts which they had been told to make and because they were too intoxicated with the possession of so much money and too intent upon enjoying the fleshpots of Egypt in the form of women and wine.[18]

Ironically, Eppler and Sandstede would have been unable to communicate with their Abwehr contact who had been attached to *Panzerarmee Afrika* even if they had managed to establish a reliable wireless station. *Major.i.G.* Josef Zolling was Rommel's Intelligence Officer (Ic) and the small staff of his '*Abteilung I*' numbered just six junior officers and only one qualified Abwehr radio operator, *Gefreiter* Waldemar Weber of the 5th Company, *Lehrregiment 'Brandenburg'*. He, together with driver and fellow Brandenburger Walter Aberle, were jointly known as '*Funktruppe Schildkröte*'. Weber had arrived as part of Almásy's group and transferred to the *Panzerarmee* Ic, referring all subsequent information received directly to Zolling who in turn was supposed to pass the raw material through to *Unteroffizier* Holzbrecher at the Zuara '*Wido*' station, maintaining the link with the Abwehr and, by extension, the Brandenburger Regiment. The cipher data that Weber required to effectively communicate with Almásy would be provided by Zolling, consolidating his position as a vital intermediary between Almásy and Weber. Similarly, there was to be no wireless traffic between Eppler, once in position in Egypt and the '*Wido*' station; all messages were to be relayed by Weber to Zolling for subsequent dissemination.

Rommel was an avid consumer of radio intelligence and demanded 'hands-on' control of his front-line units via a busy radio net. He had personally ordered the two '*Salam*' operators to join his headquarters during the difficult Gazala battle as he suffered from a shortage of wireless operators and needed every asset he could accumulate. *Funktruppe Schildkröte* was accommodated aboard a 3-ton Citroën truck which was patently unsuited to traversing the rough desert landscape. While attempting to keep pace with the advancing troops of the 90th Light Division the vehicle's sump plate was damaged by sharp rocks, bringing them to a standstill as engine oil drained out over the sand. While awaiting recovery, Marmon-Herrington armoured cars of the 4th South African Armoured Car Regiment arrived on the scene first and the two men were captured. Both Brandenburgers were of Palestinian birth and could speak fluent Arabic and English. Weber had transferred to the regiment in the spring of 1940 and taken part in the covert operations in Bulgaria, before further cipher training and posting to Istanbul and ultimately Tripoli. Aberle had also transferred to the regiment during the spring of 1940, spending time on the Belgian coast during preparations for '*Seelöwe*' before posting to Tripoli in October 1941.

Alongside the capture of '*Funktruppe Schildkröte*' there was another problem that dogged the Abwehr, though one of which they remained blissfully unaware: from the winter of 1941 Bletchley Park had managed to break the Abwehr Enigma code. A conversation between a captured U-boat radio man and Brandenburger prisoner of war recorded by British interrogators in September 1942 provides a telling example of German unwillingness to believe the impossible had been achieved:

Radio operator: We have cracked the British code, during the Norwegian campaign for example, but they will never crack the code we had in the navy. It's absolutely impossible to crack.

Abwehr commando: Everyone says that of their own code.

Radio operator: What!? They can't crack it.

Abwehr commando: There's only one method that can't be deciphered and even that can be deciphered by expert mathematicians: I think they can break a code in the course of two years . . .

Radio operator: No, they can't crack it . . .

Abwehr commando: Oh, that's just one of those silly ideas people have.

Radio operator: No.[19]

By December 1940 the Abwehr's hand cipher had been broken, but it was another year before Alfred Dillwyn 'Dilly' Knox cracked the Abwehr's Enigma settings, providing up-to-date priceless information. For example, the British were aware of '*Salam*', through the successful decrypting of the complex 'Chaffinch' code belonging to the Afrika Korps (also compromised by Bletchley Park operatives) coupled with intermittent radio contact from Almásy's column. It was only the infrequent nature of messages from '*Salam*' that kept the British several steps behind the German vehicles. Nonetheless, Enigma information greatly assisted in the capture of the two agents in Cairo and subsequent foiling of numerous Abwehr operations in the Levant.

Under interrogation, Eppler and Sandstede provided as much information as they could, helping destroy the so-called Egyptian 'fifth column' and bargaining to save their own lives from the gallows that traditionally awaited captured spies. On 4 August 1942 British authorities recorded a conversation between Eppler and Sandstede that seems a fitting footnote to their fumbled espionage attempt.

> Eppler: Those bastards Almásy and the others. All of them have received the Iron Cross First Class. To hell with them. That is why I decided to tell everything to save our lives. [Talking of Weber and Aberle] Aberle is 100 per cent Nazi.
>
> Sandstede: They have treated me awfully well and I have told them everything. What else do they want of us?[20]

Amongst the information obtained from Eppler were indications of a new German expedition into southern Libya. He informed his interrogators of the possibility of another mission planned for the southern fringe of the North African desert.

> While preparations were made in Berlin for the Almásy expedition . . . the equipment accumulated was stored in a private building on the Mattheikirchplatz [i.e. near HQ *Lehrregiment 'Brandenburg'*]. In the same building was also stored the equipment being accumulated for an expedition under Schulz-Kampfhaenkel. [Eppler] saw there, he estimates, eight to ten medium machine guns, several light machine guns, .08 pistols, beds, chairs, tents, tables, etc. There was also a generator for electric light and power which was to go on this expedition . . . Working together with Schulz-Kampfhaenkel was *Oberstleutnant* Haeckel (Heckel) (*Major* until December 1941). He is to oversee land reconnaissance in south Libya and French Equatorial Africa . . . [Eppler] does not know how many men Haeckel has under his command, but assumes the number to be at least fifty, possibly drawn from the *Lehrregiment 'Brandenburg'*.[21]

Otto Schulz-Kampfhaenkel was a noted geographer, filmmaker and airman who had previously led the Amazon-Jari Expedition of 1935–7 that explored the Amazon basin, sponsored by both the Brazilian government and the Nazi Party's Foreign Service. Commissioned into the Luftwaffe as a *Leutnant*, his new proposal was to reconnoitre the area south of Kufra as far as the Belgian Congo, providing cartographic details while also monitoring the region for signs of enemy activity. The Allies had an established air supply route through French Equatorial Africa against which Germany had already violently protested in Vichy, urging Marshal Pétain to take Chad back from the Free French. The route was immensely valuable to the Allies, material being shipped from North

American industries, through Brazil and across the Atlantic under American and Brazilian air and sea cover. Once in Dakar or Takoradi, the cargo would pass through forts occupied by Free French troops until they reached Khartoum, Wadi Halfa and finally Cairo. In Berlin, OKW were concerned also about the possible threat of a rumoured French Army under formation by De Gaulle in French Equatorial Africa. There was insufficient cartographic information to determine the ability to move large bodies of men and mechanised units from the south to threaten Rommel's right flank.

To that end, a special detachment codenamed '*Theodora*' of the *Abwehrstelle VI*, Münster, had already begun a somewhat academic examination of poorly mapped African territory, largely performed by university professors temporarily assigned as *Sonderführer* to the Abwehr in order to put their scientific knowledge at the disposal of military intelligence. This work was directed by Dr Konrad Voppel who had been the peacetime head of a state cartographical institute in Leipzig.[22] The work was carried out in close cooperation with the Military Geographical Department of OKW, though '*Theodora*' enjoyed far greater powers than the OKW department, able to issue completely new maps based on a combination of fresh scientific surveys and aerial photographs while OKW's department could only revise existing maps. The interrogation of prisoners from French colonial troops also yielded some information, but a reliable physical exploration of the territory between Equatorial Africa and the North African zone of operations was demanded, dovetailing with Schulz-Kampfhaenkel's proposition. He would lead a group of approximately thirteen scientists – astronomers, geographers, geologists, cartographers, surveyors, palaeontologists, zoologists, botanists and other scientists plus an engineer from Zeiss – supported by approximately sixty soldiers with pre-war African experience, equipped in Tripoli and supported by both the '*Wido*' station and the Italian War Ministry. Luftwaffe *Oberstleutnant* Haeckel was placed in military command while Schultz-Kampfhaenkel oversaw the scientific work.

Correspondingly, he also established an office in Berlin codenamed '*Theo*' equipped with modern scientific instruments for the preparation of maps, which would compile the information transmitted from the expedition itself named '*Sonderkommando Dora*'. The *Sonderkommando* took fifteen Steyr 1500 A trucks, six V Kübelwagen, two Horch 901 (Sdkfz 15) trucks, two Horch 901 *Funkwagen* (Sdkfz 17), nine Opel Blitz trucks – including one equipped as a photo laboratory – six Mercedes trucks, one captured Ford V8 Truck, two Horch Sdkfz 222 *Panzerspähwagen* (armoured cars) and a heavy BMW R75 sidecar combination. A powerful aerial component was also included that numbered two Heinkel He 111s, two Focke-Wulf Fw 58s, one Henschel Hs 126, a Fiesler Storch, a motorised Go 244 and two gliders, a Gotha Go 242 and a DFS 230. All powered aircraft were equipped with towing gear, cameras and powerful radio transmitters for the collection of data.

Though defensively equipped, '*Sonderkommando Dora*' was not intended as a fighting unit. They established a base at the oasis of Hon, launching expeditions as far west as Ghat and as far south as the Tibesti Mountains (the Dohone Region at Bir Sarfaya), the Tummo Mountains south of Bir Mushuru and along the Gebel ben Ghnema. The results of their labours were twenty-three highly accurate sketch-maps, Nikolaus Benjamin Richter's astronavigation being found in modern times to have been accurate to within 300m. They also confirmed the unlikelihood of French attack from the south, although by the time their findings were collated the situation for Rommel's African campaign had already changed irrevocably.[23] The scientists were eventually evacuated to Germany during January 1943 while the attached combat troops were transferred to Koenen's 'Tropical Company'.

Operation '*Dora*'

Somewhat confusingly, the second half of Koenen's 'Tropical Company' launched a parallel mission with a similar cover name. Under the command of the one-legged *Oberleutnant* Conrad von Leipzig the force of approximately a hundred men mounted Operation '*Dora*', charged with travelling south through the Sahara to Chad in order to harass and potentially sever Allied supply lines while also reconnoitring established camel tracks, searching for water sources and marking out potential airstrips. Leipzig's men were equipped with twenty-four captured British trucks – including twelve 2-pdr Portee vehicles – four captured jeeps with Flak guns, a command vehicle, one radio car and various German trucks and were accompanied by an experienced vehicle maintenance crew. The operation was also bestowed the use of a captured British fighter aircraft, a Spitfire reported as having been 'borrowed' by Canaris from a Luftwaffe testing facility and listed as flown by a Brandenburger *Hauptmann* Gerlach, though particulars of his identity remain scarce.[24]

Most of Leipzig's men could speak English, French and various Arabic dialects to varying degrees, the use of subterfuge essential for the completion of their mission. The entire '*Dora*' group departed Tripoli in a single column amidst heavy Arab road traffic of overburdened camels and shepherded livestock, heading south for nearly 1,000km towards Murzuq deep in the Libyan desert and home to a small Italian border garrison. Gradually traffic thinned and the '*Dora*' column began to make good time.

> We travelled through the Gefara, the broad built-up plain south of Tripoli. Before me in the car sat *Oberleutnant* Conrad von Leipzig, the leader of our operation . . . a task which required at the same time the maximum amount of physical effort and planning skill; exactly the mission for a Brandenburg officer.
>
> A splendid Italian road went through developed land, which the industriousness of Italian colonists had wrested from the plain. Before us lay Garian with its white houses and barracks. It was the gateway to the Jebel, the mountains. Gradually the road became worse and narrower. It snaked through mountains free of vegetation to Mizdah, a small village of dilapidated Berber huts and an Italian garrison post.
>
> For nearly 1,000 kilometres we passed over the plain through Hun and Socna until we reached Misurata. During late afternoon, we reached our first objective in Murzuq, a wretched nest of Arabs with dilapidated huts and an Italian barracks. But whoever, like us, arrived there after a long trek through the desert waste found the place rather comfortable.[25]

There they established themselves in the Italian garrison, guests of the desert veteran Major Matteo Rinaldi who had arrived in the region with Marshal Graziani during his brutal campaign against the Senussi tribes in 1931. His garrison amounted to four Italian infantrymen and 150 Meharis, tribal militiamen named after the Mehari camels they rode. Leipzig was also planning to establish an airstrip in order to make his rendezvous soon with the captured Spitfire. Scheduled to arrive from Italy before the '*Dora*' men continued their mission, it disappointingly failed to materialise. From Murzuq, Leipzig divided his force. A single column, '*Trupp III*', under the command of *Leutnant* Becker, would take three of the heavier vehicles and head west across the Wadi al Hayaa to the Algerian border at Ghat. From there, Becker would swing to the south and head towards French West Africa, skirting the western fringe of the Sahara Desert. The remainder of the force would proceed south-east to Gatrun (Qatrun) before crossing the border into Chad. There, it would divide once more; '*Trupp II*', under *Feldwebel* Stegmann moving along the Tibesti Mountains of northern Chad in the direction of the Sudan, to interdict Allied supply lines, while '*Trupp I*' under Leipzig headed south to Lake Chad.

Following advice from Rinaldi, a small party left Murzuq during the following morning to head to firm ground near Qatrun and begin preparation of an advanced airstrip. After several days' effort, the strip was built though the aircraft had still not arrived and Leipzig opted to move onwards. The remaining two *Truppen* established a forward operating base at Qatrun, where the two columns split, leaving a signal station, the maintenance troop and two armoured cars behind as protection against marauding Arab tribesmen.

Trupp III pushed west to Ghat through often pathless country in which the three vehicles frequently bogged down. They finally reached their immediate objective.

> Only natives live here, who surveyed us with ample mistrust. Our translator had to summon up all his language skill to get anything out of them. Suddenly, a tall scraggly man in an unspeakably dirty Burnous came up to us and said '*Hummel, Hummel!*' We were shocked. Who was this son of the desert and how did he come by the typical greeting of the Hanseatic cities? Soon we learned the answer: the man was Ernst Niebuhr, a genuine Hamburger from the suburb of Barmbeck, for whom a lust for adventure had taken him into the French Foreign Legion in 1920. One day he up and left [i.e, deserted]. He found shelter amongst the Berbers, went with the caravans into the deep desert, wed a desert beauty with smouldering eyes, had a dozen kids and worked here for God only knows how many years with a lively trade, using camels to go from oasis to oasis. He had not the slightest desire to return to the Alster lakes of Hamburg.[26]

For Becker's *Trupp*, the discovery of a German so deep in the desert was heaven-sent as he furnished them with information and the kind of local detail that they had been sent to find, amassed over the decades since his desertion from the Foreign Legion. Though they were bemused by his apparent indifference to Germany's war, they spent the evening around a fire recording as much material as they could obtain. Before long, Becker and his men returned to Qatrun to report their findings to the '*Dora*' base and await news from the remaining two columns.

Oberleutnant von Leipzig's *Trupp I* had probed south to the Tummo Mountains that marked the borders of Libya, Niger and Chad. The Germans had opted for *Volltarnung* and were equipped with British uniforms to match their vehicles. While crossing the first foothills they encountered a French reconnaissance vehicle, each party waving to their 'allies'. However, approximately 15km into French West Africa (now northern Niger) the Brandenburgers entered a small village which transpired to be a French military outpost. Challenged, they were soon identified despite their disguise and a sharp firefight followed during which the Brandenburgers lost two vehicles. In the confusion that followed, Leipzig and his men retreated into Libya, the weak French force that chased after them soon abandoning pursuit. However, with a German presence now identified, the Tummo mountain passes were reinforced with additional French troops, ruling it out as a potential covert route for the Brandenburgers to repeat their penetration of French West Africa.

Feldwebel Stegmann's *Trupp II* had meanwhile advanced to the south-east along the Wadi Arahi to the foot of the Tibesti Mountains that lay on the border with Chad. There they met with local Tibbu tribesmen who related stories of a German aircraft bombing Fort Lamy south of Lake Chad, the regional headquarters of the Free French forces. The raid, of which the Brandenburgers had been unaware, had been mounted by *Hauptmann* Theodor Blaich, an adventurer and plantation owner in West Africa who had flown back to Germany in his own aircraft to enlist in the Wehrmacht at the outbreak of war. He had recognised the strategic location and importance of Fort Lamy after its occupation by Free French forces in 1940 and recommended its capture. Unable to obtain official support he changed tack and proposed a bombing raid which found approval from Erwin Rommel, the idea forwarded to *Fliegerführer Afrika* who allocated a single Heinkel He 111 – designated *Sonderkommando Blaich* – that flew from a remote natural airstrip in southern Libya for the mission on 21 January. Sixteen bombs were dropped, destroying 80,000 gallons of stored fuel, stocks of oil and ten French aircraft without any return fire. However, in bad weather and low on fuel the Heinkel made an emergency landing on its return journey, eventually being found by Italian search aircraft six days later. Resupplied with food, water and fuel, the Heinkel managed to take to the air again and returned to base successfully. The raid had slashed available supplies for Free French and RAF units in the area by half, though it also provoked an increased tempo in French hit-and-run raids on Italian outposts as well as strengthened French regional defences, bolstering their forces and establishing a string of observation posts on the heights of the Tibesti range along the border.

Meanwhile, *Hauptmann* Gerlach had finally arrived in Qatrun with his Spitfire, having nearly been shot down by German Flak gunners near Tripoli after the transit flight from Sicily. Arriving at the forward Brandenburg airstrip three weeks after the patrols had already left, Gerlach commenced reconnaissance flights of the region and remained unmolested by French anti-aircraft gunners as the Spitfire had been repainted with RAF markings. He determined that the mountains to the south were heavily occupied by Free French troops, who appeared to have their headquarters in Bardai and Wour, near the border. During flights as far as Lake Chad, Gerlach observed a steady stream of military traffic on the roads headed north.

By the time that the last ground column had returned to Qatrun, Leipzig could compile a clear estimation of enemy dispositions and strengths to the south. He was also able to confirm to Rommel that any attempted German advance against the Free French positions would require a large conventional force of at least three divisions with substantial air support. Anything smaller would be unable to seize the mountain passes and would face danger from flanking attacks. However, his radioed report coincided with the battle at Alam el Halfa as Rommel attempted – and failed – to outflank the Allies' El Alamein positions. With his reports despatched and no clear indication of what to do next, Leipzig flew to meet with Rommel in person and request reinforcements to conduct operations aimed at seizing the Tibesti heights. However, there were no forces to be spared as the Afrika Korps had already exhausted almost every last reserve. It was during this meeting with Rommel that Conrad was able to greet his brother Hellmut, Rommel later wryly observing to his driver that 'That brother of yours must get out of North Africa quickly! Otherwise the English will think that we have to send cripples to the front.'[27]

Despite their success, the situation to the south as reported by Leipzig was of little concern to Rommel. He had battered his exhausted Afrika Korps against the withdrawing Allies relentlessly, capturing Mersa Matruh by the end of June and driving his men forward to try to overrun the disorganised remains of the Eighth Army before they could regroup at El Alamein. The German supply lines were stretched to breaking point, his men asleep on their feet and his few remaining functioning tanks and vehicles in desperate need to refit. Though plans were in the early stages of preparation for Koenen's 'Tropical Company' to revert to their traditional role and begin infiltrating British lines in order to capture bridges for the final advance on the Suez Canal, it appears that they returned as infantry to the operational area of the 90th Light Division. The division took severe casualties as it stumbled forward in a front assault against entrenched South African troops as part of Rommel's diversionary attack against the El Alamein defensive perimeter. He was employing his now-familiar technique of feint combined with a flanking manoeuvre, but this time to no avail. The 90th was beaten to a standstill as the Allies took the initiative during what is now known as the 'first battle of El Alamein'. During the afternoon on 10 July, the 90th, reinforced with whatever strength was available, possibly including Koenen's company, fought along the coast road and railway track, *Oberleutnant* Otto Müller of the 13th Company killed in the fighting. Helmut Spaeter lists four other Brandenburgers killed between 15 July and 6 August in the region of El Alamein: *Gefreiter* Hans Lohse (15 July; though the only Hans Lohse shown in official German records to have died on that day was killed aboard *U-576* off the North American coast); *Oberschütze* Jaspar-Hans Lütje (15 July); *Gefreiter* Hans Kleckers (15 July); and *Pionier* Heinrich Meili (5 August). He also records the death of *Stabsarzt* Dr Wolfgang König at the Sismanoglion military hospital in Attika, Greece, on 1 August.

By then, both sides had fought to a halt in the oppressive heat of the Egyptian summer. Though constant patrolling and artillery harassment kept men alert and never fully released the pressure of enemy contact, exhausted stalemate had been reached as a new commander arrived to take charge of the British Eighth Army. The Brandenburgers that had been involved in the fighting dug in, *Oberleutnant* Bisping's *Kommando* positioned in slit trenches on the coastline and augmenting their food supplies with fish retrieved by hand after being stunned and brought to the surface with hand grenades. The Axis supply network had still not managed to catch up to the front line and was under increasing pressure from Allied air attacks.

Coupled with those difficulties was the fact that Malta had not yet been attacked and conquered, despite assurances by OKW that it would be dealt with once Tobruk had fallen. Rommel was requested to go on the defensive during the planned attack (Operation '*Herkules*') to allow Luftwaffe assets to be redirected to the Malta operation, but his relentless pursuit of what he perceived to be a broken Allied army as it retreated pell-mell towards Alexandria meant that he refused to relax his offensive pressure. Nevertheless, in preparation for '*Herkules*', the Brandenburgers of 1st Platoon of the *Leichte Pionierkompanie* (Light Engineer Company) under the command of *Oberleutnant* Armin Kuhlmann had been assigned to the attack on Malta originally scheduled for 30 June 1942, Kuhlmann and his men held on standby while transferred to the Adriatic for amphibious training.

The Light Engineer Company had begun their metamorphosis into seaborne raiders during February 1942, led at that time by *Hauptmann* Max Horlbeck who, in turn, handed command to *Oberleutnant* Herbert Kriegsheim. The complement of one officer, twenty-six NCOs and 163 men had transferred to the naval training vessel *Gorch Fock* in Swinemünde during that month. Though undergoing naval training, they remained firmly under the command of Lahousen's Abwehr II as an independent component of the Brandenburger Regiment – the Kriegsmarine operated their own amphibious units that would later evolve into naval infantry and the *Kleinkampfverbände* (Small Battle Units). Within the Light Engineer Company were five frogmen (*Kampfschwimmer*), led by the celebrated pioneering German diver Friedrich Hummel. These specialists constituted a smaller sub-group within the company that concentrated on the demolition skills required for their trade while the remainder learned the specific techniques required for effective amphibious operations. It was this company's 1st Platoon that transferred under the command of *Oberleutnant* Armin Kuhlmann to Brindisi in preparation for '*Herkules*', the planned invasion of Malta, while the remainder of Kriegsheim's unit eventually moved to Odessa once their time aboard *Gorch Fock* was over, rebased later at Nikolayev to complete their training on the Black Sea coast from where they would eventually mount their first combat operations. By late 1942 the company had relocated back to Langenargen on Lake Constance where they were officially designated the *Küstenjäger Abteilung z.b.V. 800 'Brandenburg'*, remaining at roughly battalion strength and an equivalent of the British Special Boat Service. The *Abteilung* comprised a headquarters, two companies equipped with Type 41 *Pionierlandungsboote* (Engineer Landing Craft) and Type 42 *Sturmbooten* (Assault Boats), a third with former French private motor yachts and the 4th (Heavy) Company equipped with twelve '*Linsen*' explosive motor boats and two control boats, as well as a small group of trainee frogmen (though these men would later be grouped together as the *Meeresjäger Abteilung 'Brandenburg'* in 1943). They also operated a number of small torpedo boats (*Schneiderboote*).

Kuhlmann's platoon, meanwhile, had been tasked with a seaborne assault on the defences of Valletta, but they were left in an extended training limbo as the operation was continually postponed. Malta and its British naval forces that used the island as a base remained a thorn in the side of Axis supply lines across the Mediterranean, somewhat ironically due to Rommel's unwillingness to halt his advance in order to allow the switching of air support to '*Herkules*'. That same advance had now run out of supplies, due in no small part to the effect of a functioning naval and air base at Malta, and was brought to a halt virtually within sight of Alexandria.

In the meantime, the men of Operation '*Dora*' were recalled from Qatrun to the north where they were reunited with the remainder of the 'Tropical Company' and began to receive reinforcements as Koenen's formation was expanded during the lull in combat operations. The ambitious and successful '*Dora*' was finally over and *Oberleutnant* Conrad von Leipzig was indeed transferred from North Africa, posted back to Germany to take command of the now fully formed *Küstenjäger Abteilung*. It was during their journey north from Qatrun on 15 January 1943 that Leipzig's men encountered a Rhodesian patrol of the LRDG. Captain Ken Lazarus was leading sixteen men in five Chevrolet trucks, designated 'S1', when Gerlach's Spitfire sighted them.[28] The Brandenburgers laid an ambush in the inhospitable terrain of the steep-sided Wadi Zemzem and successfully attacked the Rhodesian LRDG group, the only time that the two specialist formations fought in direct combat in North Africa. At least half of the Rhodesian trucks were destroyed and a Rhodesian navigator named Hendersen killed, while the '*Dora*' men lost an armoured car.

CHAPTER 7

Rebuilding

'Guerrilla war is a kind of war waged by the few but dependent on the support of many.'

Basil H. Liddell Hart

Far to the north of the North African battleground, the invasion of the Soviet Union had, inevitably, cost the Brandenburg Regiment their highest casualties of the war thus far. However, it was not just the Red Army that had inflicted such losses but a great many 'friendly fire' incidents, with Brandenburgers in Soviet uniforms killed by their own side in a mixture of poor communication with local Wehrmacht units and the unavoidable 'fog of war'. There was also a worrying trend of deploying the Brandenburgers as traditional light infantry or shock troops rather than capitalising on their specialised strengths as infiltration and commando units. Wherever possible, once the initial missions of *'Barbarossa'* were complete, Canaris had the companies withdrawn to Germany for refitting and restructuring.

By September 1941 most the regiment had returned to their respective bases. In North Africa, Koenen's men were active alongside the Afrika Korps. The 6th Company was still engaged in the drive on the Crimea alongside the 22nd *Luftlande* Division and *Oberleutnant* Dr Kniesche's 9th Company had gone into action during the middle of September. In the Baltic Sea, the regimental 16th Company took part in Operation *'Beowulf II'*; a combined air-landing and amphibious assault on a Soviet heavy coastal artillery emplacement on the Estonian island of Saaremaa (known to the Germans as Ösel).

Near the shores of the Black Sea, the 6th Company operated in the vanguard of the 22nd *Luftlande* Division. *Oberleutnant* Meissner left the company during July, to be replaced temporarily by Siegfried Grabert, before the more permanent commander *Oberleutnant* Hans-Gerhard Bansen was promoted from command of the 1st Half-Company to take charge in August. Bansen's company was then detached from the 22nd Division and transferred east as Odessa was bypassed and placed under siege. On 28 October, Bansen was tasked with taking part in the breakthrough on the Perekop isthmus that linked the Crimean Peninsula with the Soviet mainland. The company continued to fight in the grinding Crimean battles that followed, including the initial failed attacks on the fearsome Soviet Maxim Gorki artillery emplacement in December 1941. As Sevastopol came under siege, Bansen's men were moved to the coast where they were repeatedly engaged in eliminating small Soviet landing parties attempting to infiltrate behind German lines and prevent the advance to the Kerch Peninsula.

The 6th Company was also augmented with volunteers from the *Tamara II* unit that had been formed by the Abwehr from Georgian volunteers, most of them captured during '*Barbarossa*'. Lahousen originally envisioned the unit as a sabotage troop for actions behind enemy lines in Georgia, *Tamara I* numbering sixteen men trained by an NCO from the 5th Company, *Lehrregiment 'Brandenburg'* and *Tamara II* of eighty men commanded by *Leutnant* Dr Kramer of Abwehr II. After formation in Austria and initial training in Romania, '*Tamara*' was transported to the Crimean to the area of the mountain Demerdzhi, between Simferopol and Alushta. Once there they underwent further training in conditions as close as possible to those found in the Caucasus, improving their reconnaissance and sabotage skills. Special attention was also placed on weapons training, mountain guerrilla warfare tactics and night navigation.

Kramer's men took part in fighting in the Crimea, the unit increasing in numbers and adding an additional thirty men mainly drawn from the Brandenburger Regiment. In December 1941, approximately twenty members of *Tamara II* were transferred to 6th Company for insertion behind enemy lines in Sevastopol. However, Soviet amphibious landings on the Crimean coast during January 1942 acted as a spoiling attack and the company was involved in defensive fighting against the new threat, bloody combat taking place at Yevpatoria. After the attackers were repulsed, *Tamara II* was stationed around Yevpatoria as security troops, before moving towards Kerch with the 6th Company during April.

During early August, *Tamara* recruited further members from prisoner of war camps in Feodosiya, 120 men now amalgamated into the ranks of 6th Company, which was withdrawn for a period of training before moving to Simferpol while the remaining *Tamara* men were later made part of the 'Bergmann Battalion'. Manstein was determined to break Sevastopol's defences and wanted to use Russian-speaking members of 6th Company with sabotage and intelligence-gathering experience. Bansen led a group of his men in an attack on the northern side of Sevastopol, held by the Soviet 8th Marine Brigade. To achieve surprise, the Brandenburgers dispensed with the customary preliminary artillery bombardment and infiltrated the Soviet positions before a follow-up main assault began. The Brandenburgers posed as Soviet reconnaissance troops returning from German lines and successfully opened gaps in the defences and, by the morning of 17 December 1941, attacking troops were able to drive strong wedges between the Soviet marines and adjacent infantry units on the northern side of the Sevastopol pocket.

The siege of Sevastopol had months left to run and the 6th Brandenburg Company were involved alongside the reconnaissance battalion of the 22nd *Luftlande* Division, Bansen being awarded the German Cross in Gold on 9 July 1942. The shattered city of Sevastopol finally fell that month, after which Bansen's company returned to its base at Baden bei Wien. Manstein later remarked: 'The Brandenburgers I've met on the battlefields of Russia, were not just soldiers, but patriots who, hearing the call, came together under our flag, wherever they may be.'

Meanwhile, *Oberleutnant* Dr Kniesche's 9th Company had arrived at the Eastern Front from Düren during the middle of September. Attached to the 2nd SS Division (motorised) 'Reich', they would take part in Operation '*Taifun*' ('Typhoon'), the assault on Moscow. The 'Reich' Division had already fought huge encirclement battles that had destroyed swathes of Red Army units and had earned the distinction of being the German unit to have penetrated furthest to the east, while also absorbing terrific punishment from increasingly stubborn defenders. By the time of '*Taifun*' they were already exhausted and understrength, but the offensive began on 2 October, 'Reich' and the 9th Company beginning to move two days later. Their advance led them through Gshatsk (now known as Gagarin), bludgeoning through dogged defence from the Red Army. On 8 October, snow began to fall. Snow turned to sleet which turned to autumn rain and soon the Brandenburgers and SS troops were battling through thick glutinous mud towards their goal. The destructive fighting decimated battalions of the SS division until it was virtually unable to function as an effective fighting force. Finally, on 4 December, with the harsh Russian winter setting in, the SS Motorcycle Battalion's 1st Company reached the terminus of the Moscow tram system, the Soviet capital appearing to be on the brink of falling. Exhausted, Dr Kniesche's accompanying Brandenburgers were redeployed away from the front line, *Leutnant* Ramstetter taking the 1st Half-Company and *Leutnant* Kirnich the 2nd Half-Company to safeguard the rear areas of LI Army Corps near Volokolamsk, north-west of Moscow. It was a fortuitous posting as the Soviet forces counter-attacked and hurled the SS division back from Moscow, beginning a winter defensive ordeal for which the German forces were woefully ill-prepared.

During September 1941, before the arrival of winter in the sector of Army Group North, mainland Estonia was largely under German control. However, there remained strong Soviet garrisons on the islands of Saaremaa, Külasema and Hiiumaa (Dagö), the location of which allowed control of naval transit to and from the Gulf of Riga with heavy artillery. The low-lying islands had been heavily fortified by their Soviet garrison that comprised over 20,000 men, including naval troops, engineers and regular infantry.

For the capture of these islands, Army Group North formulated two distinct plans; *'Beowulf I'*, to be launched from Latvia, or *'Beowulf II'* from the western coast of Estonia. While the battle for Tallinn was still raging, the decision was made to launch *'Beowulf II'* using elements of three infantry divisions and men of *Hauptmann* Benesch's 16th Company *Lehrregiment 'Brandenburg'*. Three diversionary attacks would also be mounted – *'Südwind'*, against Koiguste Bay, Sutu Bay and Kuressaare on Saaremaa; *'Westwind'* against Vormsi and Saaremaa's offshore islands; and *'Nordwind'* directed against Hiiumaa Island. *'Beowulf II'* was finally launched on 8 September with an attack on Külasema Island, the Brandenburgers being held in reserve until the assault on Saaremaa that began on 14 September, their mission being the neutralisation of Soviet coastal artillery on the eastern Kübassaare peninsula.

Benesch divided his company into two sub-units, the first fifty men to be landed aboard five DF S230 gliders towed by Ju 52s from the airstrip at Pärnu, their short flight covered by Messerschmitt Bf 110s of ZG26 'Horst Wessel', which were also tasked with neutralising Soviet anti-aircraft batteries. The second part of his company was to land by sea from various small craft, the main German amphibious landings taking place to the north. Benesch himself was aboard the first glider to put down, the landing smooth though they came down 800m short of their expected landing zone and under immediate sustained fire from well-entrenched Soviet troops. There was no sign of the seaborne force which had, in fact, been forced back to port by strong currents and rough seas. Elsewhere, the weather conditions badly affected the main German infantry landings, although, in larger landings vessels, they continued nonetheless.

The Brandenburgers that had landed were immediately thrown on to the defensive as extra Soviet troops arrived by truck to join the fight. The heavily defended bunkers facing the Germans proved impossible to approach and before long Benesch had his men form a defensive hedgehog position under heavy counter-attack as they began withdrawing slowly towards the eastern coast. The supporting Bf 110s were relatively ineffectual and at 1600hrs a message was flashed from the cockpit of one aircraft by semaphore that boats would shortly attempt a landing to retrieve the Brandenburgers, though the men ashore saw none. Meanwhile, two of the Luftwaffe glider pilots were dead and casualties were mounting amongst the assault troops. Kriegsmarine gunfire and attacks by Junkers Ju 88 aircraft helped keep the Soviet troops at bay until, approximately two hours later, three Ju 52 aircraft passed overhead and dropped nine rubber dinghies, four of them straight into Soviet hands. Benesch was instructed to use the vulnerable boats to head eastwards at sea where they would be met by *Vorpostenboote*.

With too few boats for the number of men, Benesch and his troops waited until darkness and used the inflatables as stretchers for the wounded, sporadic enemy fire causing few problems as the Soviets appeared unwilling to give chase. The five rubber boats – designed to carry four occupants each – were launched from the long sandy beach, nine wounded men placed aboard with as many other men as they could carry while the remainder took turns swimming alongside. Battling strong currents, they made their way out to sea, one dinghy becoming separated and drifting back towards land where the occupants were reportedly captured and all but two of them executed. The remainder finally contacted German ships at 0700hrs the following morning. As well as the two glider pilots, eleven of Benesch's men had been killed in the attempted attack. Despite their failure, the Baltic islands were finally secured by German troops on 21 October and by the end of the battle the Soviets had lost approximately 19,000 men captured and 4,700 killed while German casualties amounted to 2,850 men. Benesch's company was pulled out of the action and returned to their base and later reconstituted as the 11th Company, though their commander was detached to spend time in Finland as liaison officer for '*Kompanie Trommsdorf*' (see below).

Brandenburgers in Finland

Finland had declared war on the Soviet Union three days after the launch of Operation '*Barbarossa*' and in the Arctic Circle they played a major role in Operation '*Silberfuchs*' ('Silver Fox') that comprised a two-stage pincer attack to take and hold the vital Soviet port of Murmansk. The first phase began on the opening day of '*Barbarossa*' when, in the Arctic Circle, Germany committed two *Gebirgs* Divisions (2nd and 3rd, who together constituted the Wehrmacht's *Norwegen Armee Korps*) to move east from Kirkenes and occupy the Finnish nickel mines at Petsamo. From there, they began the second phase on 29 June together with Finnish forces, making initial headway before becoming bogged down in an entrenched stalemate that would remain virtually stagnant for the next three years.

To the south, the Wehrmacht's XXXVI Army Corps (169th Division and 6th SS *Gebirgs* Division 'Nord') attacked towards Kantalahti on 1 July, launching a frontal attack on Salla that was taken within a week while the Finnish II Corps advanced from Kuusamo in support, their goal being to cut the Murmansk railway at Kandalaksha. However, once again despite initial success, the offensive eventually stalled by September in the face of strong Soviet defences as well as unexpected diplomatic pressure from the United States. While the Finnish military was keen to retake territory lost to the Soviet Union during the 1940 'Winter War', it appears that they had far less appetite for any kind of war of conquest beyond their original borders. Whatever motivation may have existed for such an undertaking was surely subdued following receipt of a diplomatic note from the United States to Finland's President Risto Heikki Ryti in which Finland was urged to 'stop all offensive operations and withdraw to the 1939 border'. Furthermore, the note declared, 'should material of war sent by the United States to Soviet territory in the north by way of the Arctic Ocean be attacked en-route either presumably or allegedly from territory under Finnish control, in the present state of opinion in the United States, such an incident must be expected to bring about an instant crisis between Finland and the United States'.[1] Though they loudly protested such an ultimatum, Ryti's government knew that they could not risk antagonising the United States and Finnish troops were quietly reined in, demands also being made to the Wehrmacht that any Finnish units 'on loan' should be immediately placed back under direct Finnish military command. Both Murmansk and the Murmansk railway continued their operations unimpeded.

The double-track railway line that linked Leningrad to Murmansk was a major conduit of Allied Lend-Lease supplies during the first year of the Soviet war, predominantly, though not wholly, American. Indeed, by December 1941 British tanks landed in Soviet Arctic ports comprised over 25 per cent of the Red Army's medium and heavy tank strength. Luftwaffe attacks on the line periodically managed to cut the track, but these breaks were soon repaired and were a nuisance rather than a serious threat. In Berlin, the Abwehr's *Leutnant* Trommsdorf had already formulated plans for the establishment of a specialised mountain troop unit to undertake missions on the Finnish front; particularly the cutting of the Murmansk railway.

Training of the specialised unit was carried out in Wünsdorf (Zossen) south of Berlin. The *Heeressportschule* at which the German Olympic team of 1936 had trained was located there and Trommsdorf attempted to recruit several of the finest skiers in the German armed forces. Some accounts have cited that this included a skiing gold medal winner of the 1936 Winter Olympic Games, but Franz Pfnür (Gold Medal for Alpine Skiing) subsequently joined the SS and there remains no record of his being seconded to the Brandenburgers. Between eighty and ninety men were gathered for '*Kompanie Trommsdorf*' including demolitions specialists, water purification engineers, a meteorological technician and dog handlers who looked after forty sled dogs provided by the *Heereshundeschule* (Army Dog School) at Sperenberg.

During early 1942, they were transported to Finland and placed under the command of General Dietl who attended the company's initial exercises in their new environment. He was apparently not very impressed with what he saw and ordered Trommsdorf to move his troops north of Rovaniemi, the administrative capital of Lapland. There they were to properly acquaint themselves with the conditions of the northern front, six Finnish NCOs from the *SS Freiwilligen-Bataillon Nordost* being taken on board to provide further and more effective instruction for the Brandenburgers.² Their first combat assignment was finally given at the end of March when they were detailed to be part of Operation 'Lutto', an attack to disrupt the lines of communication used by General Vladimir I. Shcherbakov's Fourteenth Army on the Karelian front. Trommsdorf's unit was combined with *Gebirgsjäger* of the 3rd Battalion/136 *Gebirgsjäger* Regiment (2nd *Gebirgs* Division) and Finnish troops under the command of *Hauptmann* Otto Stampfer. The Brandenburgers were to forge ahead of the main body of '*Kampfgruppe Stampfer*' and infiltrate behind Soviet lines, cutting communications and generally interfering with logistics between the Russians' supply depot at Ristikengt and their front-line troops. However, poor coordination in heavy snow meant that by the time the Brandenburgers arrived at the planned rendezvous point with the *Kampfgruppe*, Stampfer's men had already gone into action and mounted a frontal assault on Soviet positions rather than wait for the Brandenburgers. Casualties were heavy with little gain and Stampfer retreated, leaving Trommsdorf's men to also fight their way back to German lines, becoming disorientated and lost before being rescued by a *Gebirgsjäger* patrol. Trommsdorf, a former university lecturer in civilian life, had shown commendable theoretical knowledge of operations in such a harsh environment. However, he was soon shown to be clearly unsuited to the physical task itself, described by Spaeter as 'an intellectual type with thick metal-rim glasses' and already past the age of 30 and so he subsequently returned to Germany, his initial replacement as company commander the South Tyrolean *Leutnant* Alfred Sölder who in turn was superseded by *Oberleutnant* Otto Hettinger.

Almost as soon as the Brandenburgers had returned to the German lines they were involved in fighting against a new Soviet advance near the town of Kiestinkiand and distinguished themselves in the defensive combat by shoring up a flagging battle line. In June, they were withdrawn to rest and refit at Rovaniemi, taking the opportunity to analyse the failings of their previous mission. The Finnish SS men were on hand to offer winter survival advice as well as improving the Brandenburgers' cross-country speed and limiting use of weapons to a level comparable to Finnish methods of silence before action. Men were taught how to pack all personal utensils and equipment in such a way as to create no noise while moving. Finnish troops could move in relatively large formations with minimal sound. A favoured Finnish technique for attacks was to do so in small bounds; moving several yards, lying down, moving on again and repeating until they had reached close range, and the Brandenburgers perfected the skill.

Their planned raid against the Murmansk railway line began on 18 August 1942. By that stage, the company had been redesignated 15th (Light) Company, *Lehrregiment 'Brandenburg' z.b.V. 800* (made official on 2 August) and though Hettinger remained company commander, the most experienced man of the group, SS *Scharführer* Kaarlo Paananen, led the incursion. Alongside a small number of Soviet deserters, there were several more Finns attached to the raiding party, thirteen from the Finnish Army's long-range patrol unit *Osasto Paatsalo* (Detachment Paatsalo) that had been formed for such guerrilla operations behind enemy lines. In total, three loosely grouped teams departed from the area of Juumo in collapsible kayaks supplied with small outboard motors, the first party comprising most of the company headed by *Oberleutnant* Hettinger, then *Feldwebel* Schneider and finally a group led by the overall leader, *Scharführer* Paananen. They travelled along the interconnected rivers and lakes of central Karelia, the two-man kayaks connected in pairs by rope as they headed east. The company was armed with a mixture of German, Finnish and Soviet automatic weapons, fighting knives and close-combat weapons and heavier machine guns, wearing Soviet uniforms, rubber boots and camouflage jackets without insignia.

Progress was slow, with the kayaks carried overland between the rivers and tributaries. They eventually reached the Knyazhegubskoye Reservoir whose expanse they crossed in low-lying mist that concealed them from Soviet patrols. After travelling nearly 160km over extremely inhospitable terrain, the Brandenburgers had reached striking distance of the Murmansk railway line and established a camp on a small island near the lake's western bank on 24 August. Patrols were despatched by Hettinger to scout the railway line itself and three bridges were chosen for destruction. The attacks took place under cover of darkness. However, sentries at the northernmost bridge sighted the approaching Brandenburgers, who only managed to set fire to the wooden structure with reserve petrol from the kayaks before being forced to retreat by Soviet reinforcements, their explosive charges remaining unused.

Security troops at other bridges and tunnels were immediately placed on alert, Hettinger intercepting the Soviet radio messages and thus able to warn his remaining two teams. The second bridge measured nearly 400m in length, Finnish commandos killing the sentries silently at the southern end before explosives were planted in three places along the span. Despite nearby Red Army troops becoming alerted to their presence at the last moment, a stretch of nearly 75m of bridge was demolished as the Brandenburgers successfully withdrew with two men slightly wounded. The third bridge was also successfully destroyed, the central span blown to pieces along with several Russian troops at 0230hrs.

Returning to their island camp, their retreat was hindered first by a strafing Soviet aircraft that injured two men and then by large motor boats carrying Red Army troops that swept by the concealed kayaks later that night. Despite later brushes with ambushing Soviet troops and weather that alternated between sleet, fog and rain, on 29 August 1942, the Brandenburgers once again reached Finnish lines east of Lake Seyeminki, but not without further casualties. During the voyage on Paanajärvi, Sölder's group began by carrying their kayaks which had taken damage from Soviet gunfire. Attempting to cross the lake in two groups using two motorised pontoons as propulsion, strong winds blew up that capsized the pontoons, throwing the men into the frigid water where some were drowned, dragged under by their heavy equipment. Robert Kauder and one other were hauled ashore unconscious, Sölder using artificial respiration to revive Kauder. At severe risk of exposure, the men struggled to light a fire with wet matches, though eventually a flame took hold and they began to dry out. Most of their equipment had been lost and they were stranded for six hours in the lakeside forest before help arrived.

All surviving Brandenburger and SS members of the raiding party were awarded the EK II. However, as with the air raids on the railway, the damage was soon repaired though the maintenance stretched from initial estimates of hours to two weeks, after which over-hasty and inexact restoration unintentionally derailed at least two locomotives. Nonetheless, the effect on the Soviet military machine was negligible. The 15th (Light) Company remained in Finland until December 1942 as a reserve unit for the Twentieth Army before returning to Neuhaus in Austria

Reorganising the Regiment, June 1942

By the end of the 1941 it was obvious that Operation *'Barbarossa'* had fallen short of its goals. The Soviet Union had not collapsed. On the contrary, the Wehrmacht had been forced onto the defensive after suffering tremendous losses in their advance to the suburbs of Moscow. To *Oberstleutnant* von Haehling, it had become equally apparent that the covert nature of Brandenburger deployment was becoming a secondary consideration and they were being more frequently used as light infantry and therefore entirely dependent on the 'parent' unit to which they were attached for conventional heavy-weapon support. The Abwehr appeared to be taking less interest in the direction of the regiment and how it was employed and so began a period of restructuring and internal redirection to enable the regiment to continue to function while also creating elements equipped with standard heavier weapons more familiar to Wehrmacht infantry units. On 26 June 1942, he submitted a report to Lahousen at Abwehr II detailing the steps that he had taken during the first months of the year in reorganising those units that had returned from the front and listing the 'ten commandments' of Brandenburger employment that he hoped the Wehrmacht would follow.

General Duties.

The mission of the *Lehrregiment 'Brandenburg' z.b.V. 800* is that of covert military operations against targets of tactical, strategic, or military-economic importance. These take place where other units of the fighting forces cannot yet operate . . . The taking of transportation facilities, especially bridges, is of primary importance.

The special operations of the *Lehrregiment 'Brandenburg' z.b.V. 800* require military stratagems of all kinds to deceive the enemy and seize from him objectives of military importance. Exploiting the success of these special operations tactically and strategically is the role of the commanders of troops following.

Guidelines for operations:
1. The units of *Lehrregiment 'Brandenburg' z.b.V. 800* are exclusively combat instruments of a war of movement. Their employment in the vanguards of motorised and armoured units is therefore the rule. Their employment in rearguards can be appropriate and necessary in some cases.
2. The units of *Lehrregiment 'Brandenburg' z.b.V. 800* are to be withdrawn from the front upon instigation of positional warfare. Lengthier periods of defensive fighting are to be used by elements of *Lehrregiment 'Brandenburg' z.b.V. 800* for accelerated testing of and conversion to, new methods of fighting. Only in this way will the element of surprise be assured in the future against an 'alerted' enemy.
3. Since its troops have been selected for special operations, are specially trained and are difficult to replace, the employment of the entire regiment or its units in the role of standard infantry is warranted only in extreme emergencies and, then, only temporarily.
4. The combat unit for special operations by the *Lehrregiment 'Brandenburg'* is the company. It is divided into two 'half-companies' each capable of independent action and one heavy platoon. The total strength of the company is 300 men.
5. The companies of *Lehrregiment 'Brandenburg'* are placed at the disposal of Army Groups or Armies. The focal point of combat determines their use and this can change accordingly.

6. Whenever possible a company of the *Lehrregiment* is to be assigned to only one division. Dividing the company between more than two divisions endangers its fighting strength and is to be categorically rejected.
7. The strength and composition of forces assigned to each combat mission depends on the situation and the objective.
8. From the moment companies of the *Lehrregiment 'Brandenburg'* enter an Army's zone, they are tactically and, as far as the operation is concerned, disciplinary subordinate to it. Otherwise responsibility for the welfare and care of personnel stays with the regiment even during the operation.
9. Commitment of Brandenburger units occurs exclusively and responsibly per the directives of the fighting forces.
10. As a rule, as part of each mission, the *Lehrregiment 'Brandenburg'* will assign a liaison officer [*Verbindungs-Offizier*] to the command responsible for that action. The liaison officer will inform the operationally responsible unit command of the strength, organisation and fighting method of the regiment's units.[3]

The gulf that had been developing between the Abwehr and the *Lehrregiment* was becoming increasingly apparent. Canaris' initial desire to have the Brandenburgers as a potential backbone to any kind of anti-Nazi insurrection was clearly misguided as the regiment employed highly motivated and frequently idealistic young soldiers. The original 'old guard' of ex-*Freikorps* men and First World War veterans had started to give way through transfer or casualties to younger officers as the regiment became entangled in the large-scale battles in the Soviet Union and North Africa. Haehling successfully formalised the alteration of the regiment's composition and Spaeter's unit history provides an illustrative breakdown of the 5th Company following his reorganisation:

Commander: *Oberleutnant* Zülch
Medical Officer: *Oberarzt* Dr Schmid
Company Headquarters: *Feldwebel* Ladendorff

1 Half-Company
(*Leutnant* Lau)
I *Einsatz* (approx. platoon size):
Leutnant Seuberlich
1st Rifle Squad
2nd Rifle Squad

2 Half-Company
(*Leutnant* Steidl)
I *Einsatz*:
Leutnant Pils
1st Rifle Squad
2nd Rifle Squad

Pionier Group	*Pionier* Group
Anti-Tank Rifle Troop	Anti-Tank Rifle Troop
Flamethrower Troop	Flamethrower Troop
Light Mortar Troop	Light Mortar Troop
II *Einsatz*: *Oberfeldwebel* Schmalbruch	II *Einsatz*: *Leutnant* Lorencuk
(Organised as I Einsatz)	(Organised as I Einsatz)
Half-Company Logistic Train	Half-Company Logistic Train
(*Feldwebel* Wolfsberger)	(*Oberfeldwebel* Goller)

Heavy Platoon
(*Oberfeldwebel* Martl)
Heavy Machine Gun Platoon: *Feldwebel* Ortner
Heavy Mortar Platoon: *Feldwebel* Majoni
Anti-Tank Rifle Platoon: *Feldwebel* Stemmberger

Company Logistics Train: *Hauptfeldwebel* Röttges
Paymaster: *Oberzahlmeister* Stein

Replacements were brought into the regiment and by June 1942, those units still in Germany began to deploy to the East to take part in the planned summer offensive.

In the interim, the 197 men of the *Leichte Pionierkompanie Brandenburg* had begun their naval training aboard the *Gorch Fock* in Swinemünde under the eye of Kriegsmarine instructors. It was a diverse group of men that included volunteers from each of Germany's three Wehrmacht service arms and the SS. Alongside the small craft specialists were a core of men trained in amphibious assault, primarily of Caucasian and Baltic ethnicity. Their landing exercises that took place on the Baltic coast at Bansin earned them the nickname '*Küstenjäger*'.

By June 1942 the 1st Platoon was in Brindisi preparing for the invasion of Malta while the remainder of the special company were transferred first to Odessa and then on to Nikolayev to prepare for impending amphibious operations. They arrived in transport belonging to 2nd Battalion and were soon involved in exercises for a planned offensive across the Kerch Strait. The *Leichte Pionierkompanie* was intended for coastal raids and river crossings, initially equipped with *Sturmboote* and small landing craft. By the time of 'Case Blue' (the summer 1942 offensive), it was commanded by *Hauptmann* Horlbeck and, with 1st Platoon in Brindisi, 2nd Platoon (*Oberleutnant* Kriegsheim) and 3rd Platoon (*Oberleutnant* Dr Wagner) made their way with all their equipment to the Crimea by rail. Amongst the men was a Kriegsmarine liaison officer and the colourful Friedrich Hummel. A former long-distance yachtsman, merchant navy sailor, Hamburg police officer and member of the SD, Hummel had been recruited by the Abwehr in November 1939, transferred to the *Lehrregiment* shortly thereafter and working as an instructor on all matters nautical. He would later form the first German frogman units – *Kampfschwimmer* – and eventually end the war with Skorzeny's SS *Jagdkommando* alongside other former Brandenburgers. His role with the *Leichte Pionierkompanie* remained instructional as they underwent final training in conquered Soviet territory.

The *Leichte Pionierkompanie* – or *Küstenjäger Abteilung* as it would be known from the end of 1942 – was related to, but different from, another nautical branch of the Brandenburg Regiment established later. In December 1943 Hummel was involved in the formation and training of the *Meeresjäger Abteilung 'Brandenburg'* that comprised solely frogmen for sabotage and demolition missions. Initial volunteers numbered approximately sixty and included twenty-one men from the Kriegsmarine and twenty-four from the Abwehr, as well as *Fallschirmjäger, Gebirgsjäger* and Waffen SS troops who had been members of *Sondereinsatzverbande z.b.V. 'Oranienburg'*. Amongst the naval recruits, the majority were world-class champion sportsmen, several who had taken part in the 1936 Olympics. The initial intake began training at Valdagno, Italy, using a swimming pool within a restricted military area. The intense training and sporting activities were concealed by the Abwehr using the pretence of a rehabilitation unit for wounded troops.

Hauptmann Fritz Neitzert – a Brandenburger *Gebirgsjäger* – was the *Abteilung*'s commander, ground-breaking frogman Alfred von Wurzian the chief instructor and his 'right-hand' *Obergefreiter* Richard ('Ritchie') Reimann. During March 1944, Friedrich Hummel took command of the *Meeresjäger* and by order of OKW on 15 April, the *Meeresjäger Abteilung* were amalgamated with the newly established *Kleinkampfverbände der Kriegsmarine* commanded by *Konteradmiral* Hellmuth Heye, the Brandenburger unit becoming *Lehrkommando 700* and all men transferred officially into the Navy which would specialise in such units.

CHAPTER 8

'Case Blue'/Operation '*Braunschweig*': The 1942 Summer Offensive in the Soviet Union

'Never forget that no military leader has ever become great without audacity.'
Carl von Clausewitz

The bane of Hitler's ability to wage war was a lack of resources, particularly oil, either refined or unrefined. Pre-war German oil supplies originated from three sources: imported crude or petroleum products from overseas, domestic production in Germany and Austria, and synthetic oil produced domestically, primarily from coal. During the last full year of peace, 1938, German consumption of oil totalled 44 million barrels. Although well below the level of other industrialised nations such as Great Britain or the United States, at least 60 per cent of that total was derived from foreign imports. The outbreak of war resulted in increased demand while also cutting off supply from most foreign sources following the institution of the British naval blockade. In September 1939, German stockpiles totalled 15 million barrels. Despite some measure of seized stock from the campaigns of 1940 and the first half of 1941, OKW estimated in a study made during May 1941 that Germany's oil supply would be exhausted by August. Romania's Ploieşti oilfields became Germany's chief external supplier, their 2.8 million barrels provided in 1938 increasing to 13 million barrels in 1941, almost half of the nation's entire output. Nonetheless, it was below German expectations and there was no sign of available increase as the oilfields themselves were gradually becoming depleted. Hitler was forced to put the seizure of oil at the top of his list of military objectives or face inevitable defeat. On 1 June 1942, he told the assembled officers of Army Group South that 'if I do not get the oil of Maykop and Grozny then I must end the war'.[1] Before the invasion of the Soviet Union, Stalin had also supplied limited quantities of oil from the rich fields of the Caucasus and by summer 1942 it was these fields that became the object of a renewed German military drive.

On 15 April Hitler issued Directive Number 41 in which he outlined the general plan for the summer offensive designated *Fall Blau* ('Case Blue'). The central

Wehrmacht forces were to stand on the defensive before Moscow while in the north Leningrad was captured, linking German and Finnish forces. Meanwhile a two-pronged attack was to be mounted by Army Group South which was divided in half; Army Group A making the crucial drive into the Caucasus towards the Baku oilfields via those in Maykop and Grozny (Operation *Edelweiss*) while Army Group B advanced towards Stalingrad to cover the former's northern flank (Operation *Fischreiher*). The Caucasus possessed plentiful supplies of other resources such as coal, peat, nonferrous and rare metals, wheat and corn, but the ultimate prize was oil. To the north, Stalingrad remained a secondary concern, its value that of a Soviet logistical hub. In the Führer directive were clear objectives suited to the *Lehrregiment 'Brandenburg'*:

> Should opportunities arise during these operations to establish bridgeheads to the east or south of the Don River, particularly by the capture of undemolished bridges, advantage will be taken of them. In any event, every effort will be made to reach Stalingrad itself, or at least to bring the city under fire from heavy artillery so that it may no longer be of any use as an industrial or communications centre.
>
> It would be particularly desirable if we could secure either undamaged bridges in Rostov itself or other bridgeheads south of the Don River for later operations.

In spring 1942 the regiment was almost entirely devoted to 'Case Blue', the order of battle in June 1942 being as follows:

Commander: *Generalmajor* Alexander von Pfuhlstein.
Adjutant: *Leutnant* Adrian von Fölkersam.
Operations Officer: *Oberleutnant* Wülbers.
Intelligence Officer: *Oberleutnant* H. Pinkert.

1st Battalion (*Major* Wilhelm Walther), based in Brandenburg an der Havel.
  1st Company (*Hauptmann* Babuke), to be attached to 14th Panzer Division/ III Motorised Corps.
  2nd Company (*Oberleutnant* G. Pinkert), to be attached to 23rd Panzer Division/XL Motorised Corps.
  3rd Company (*Hauptmann* John), to be attached to 3rd Panzer Division/ XL Motorised Corps.
  4th (Light) *Fallschirmjäger* **Company** (*Oberleutnant* Kürschner), placed on alert in Roven'ky.

2nd Battalion (*Major* Paul Jacobi), based in Baden bei Wien.
5th Company (*Oberleutnant* Zülch), to be attached to III Motorised Corps.
6th Company (*Oberleutnant* Bansen), engaged in fighting in the Crimea (later transferred to France).
7th Company (*Oberleutnant* Oesterwitz), to be attached to SS Division 'Wiking'/XIV Motorised Corps.
8th Company (*Oberleutnant* Grabert), to be attached to 13th Panzer Division/XIV Motorised Corps.

3rd Battalion (*Rittmeister* Franz Jacobi).
9th Company (*Oberleutnant* Dr Kniesche), still deployed with LI Army Corps near Smolensk.
10th Company (*Oberleutnant* Ronte), to be attached to V Army Corps/Seventeenth Army.
11th Company (*Oberleutnant* Hütten), reconstituting from 16th Company, deployed in August.
12th Company (*Oberleutnant* Schäder), to begin anti-partisan operations for Army Group Centre.

Regimental Units:
Leichte Pionierkompanie Brandenburg (*Hauptmann* Horlbeck), soon to be designated *Küstenjäger Abteilung*, training on Lake Constance (transferred to Crimea in July).
Tropical Company (*Oberleutnant* von Koenen), in action in North Africa.
15th Company, 'Light Company', engaged in Finland (the redesignated 'Trommsdorf/Finnland Company').

The regiment had also lost men to the establishment of several 'foreign legions' for use by the Wehrmacht during the pending offensive. The Abwehr's *'Tiger B'* was one such, formed on 18 October 1941, at a training camp in Rembertów. The organisation comprised six companies of troops – one Caucasian and five others of Central Asians – that had been built around a cadre of trained troops of the Brandenburg Regiment. *Tiger B* was created as a unit to undertake sabotage missions behind enemy lines, gather intelligence and attempt to induce regional uprisings against Soviet rule in their various homelands. Though bolstered with Brandenburg troops they were – and remained – separate from the regiment itself; redesignated the *Turkestanisch-Kaukasisch-Mohammedanische Legion* (Turkistani-Caucasian-Mohammedan Legion) on 13 January 1942. Towards the end of March, they were subdivided into three constituent parts all initially active in the General Government of Poland: *Turkestanisches Infanterie-Bataillon 450* (later transferred to the Waffen SS), *Kaukasisch-Mohammedanische Legion* (subsequently renamed once more as *Aserbeidschanische Legion* on 22 July 1942), and the *Turkestanische Legion*.

The Brandenburgers would not be the only German commando forces in operation for 'Case Blue'. During mid-April, Lahousen had attended a meeting with Adolf Hitler and Alfred Jodl in which the Abwehr were directed to make full use of their own 'partisans', former prisoners of war who had been recruited into the German forces. Soviet prisoners who volunteered were either used in their original uniforms or outfitted as civilians and began filtering behind enemy lines as early as May to wreak havoc in Red Army rear areas. On 22 May, Abwehr agents were also parachuted into Voronezh, Stalingrad, Krasnodar and other key areas where they sabotaged railway lines, power stations and pipelines while Operation '*Hannover*' was launched by 350 White Russians of *Sonderverbänd Graukopf* on 22 May around Army Group Centre. Though they inflicted heavy casualties on the Red Army, the savage fighting left only a hundred survivors to return to the German lines. In the Caucasus, the *Sonderverbänd Bergmann* was formed from 200 Germans and 550 former Soviet prisoners of war or deserters who were ethnically Georgian, Armenian, north Caucasian and Azerbaijani. Commanded by Theodor Oberländer, the Bergmann troops remained part of the standard Army hierarchy, their apparent designation as an Abwehr force purely made as a form of cover.

The Brandenburger troops who were to take part in 'Case Blue' moved east to their respective operational areas during June and July. Walther's 1st Battalion was subordinated to Army Group B for the drive towards Stalingrad while the remaining battalions would accompany Army Group A into the Caucasus. The 2nd Battalion entrained in Vienna and headed east via Odessa, gathering in the region of Nikolayev in the southern Ukraine by 10 July, while the 3rd Battalion's 10th and 12th Companies and their Battalion Headquarters reached Stalino (now Donetsk), north-west of Rostov-on-Don. The regimental staff assembled first at Roven'ky before also moving forward to Stalino.

'Case Blue' began on 28 June 1942 with Army Group B's Fourth Panzer Army beginning its advance from the vicinity of Kharkov towards the Soviet transport and communications centre of Voronezh on the Don. *General der Panzertruppe* Friedrich Paulus' Sixth Army also began to move, *Oberleutnant* Gerhard Pinkert's 2nd Company leaving Kursk on the first day of July and racing ahead of the armoured columns to seize bridges over the Don River, frequently merging with the familiar sight of retreating Soviet troops. On 30 June, 'Case Blue' was renamed Operation '*Braunschweig*' as initial advances encouraged German hopes for the offensive, the Red Army once again seeming to be falling back in chaos. However, as the Brandenburgers penetrated up to

100km behind enemy lines using the confusion as cover, it was not just the Soviets who frequently mistook them for Red Army troops and Pinkert's men were repeatedly shelled by their own approaching forces, causing needless casualties and affecting morale.

Hauptmann Werner John's 3rd Company was at the spearhead of the 3rd Panzer Division in *Volltarnung* of Soviet infantry uniforms aboard two American Dodge trucks that had been captured from the Red Army. Ranging up to 80km behind enemy lines, the company was stopped at the entrance to a small village near Millerovo by a vigilant Soviet guard post and subsequently questioned by a Red Army Political Commissar. John was amongst those men of the party who did not speak Russian and posed as a battle-weary truck driver while those men fluent in the language disembarked to chat with local villagers and enemy soldiers milling around. The party's combat interpreter explained their presence as a special unit returning from a covert mission against the advancing Germans. For three quarters of an hour the suspicious Commissar interrogated the interpreter until the latter exclaimed in frustration: 'If you don't believe me, ask the Army!' 'If I had a telephone connection, I would have already done so!' came the reply.

Nonetheless, he was finally satisfied and the Brandenburgers re-boarded their truck for departure, fully briefed on local Soviet strongpoints in order that their journey might be conducted securely. Ironically, it appears to have been the American trucks that had attracted the Commissar's attention as they were still relatively scarce in the Soviet front lines. John and his men in due course successfully returned to German lines with valuable information obtained without once firing their weapons and further operations were planned based on this intelligence.

The 3rd Panzer Division established a bridgehead over the lower Don River near Konstantinovsk on 23 July and the 2nd and 3rd Companies continued to take and hold small bridges as they swung south towards the Caucasus. John's 3rd Company took the bridge at Konstantinovsk before racing on and capturing a crossing of the smaller Sal River to the south, where *Hauptmann* Babuke's 1st Company was advancing steadily east in front of the 14th Panzer Division which had pushed its way into the northern outskirts of Rostov-on-Don. The 13th Panzer Division and SS 'Wiking' Division of XIV Motorised Corps were bludgeoning their way into the city itself through gaps torn in the Soviet defensive lines by supporting infantry formations. Both the 2nd and 3rd Companies (attached to 23rd and 3rd Panzer Divisions respectively) would be redirected south towards Grozny alongside their 'parent' units as Hitler began an unnecessary chain of logistical changes and shifts of objective that would only serve to dilute his offensive. Such micromanagement at the very highest level would become the bane of Wehrmacht operations.

The Don River posed a major barrier before the solid terrain of the Caucasus that was well-suited to armoured operations. At its narrowest point, the river was still 250m wide, though five substantial bridges capable of bearing heavy German vehicular traffic spanned its width in Rostov and for their capture, *Oberleutnant* Grabert's 8th Company was brought into operation, having been attached to the 13th Panzer Division. In the division's vanguard was *Oberstleutnant* Harald Stolz's 43rd *Kradschützen* Battalion, a reconnaissance unit of combined motorcycles and armoured cars. Fighting their way through the confusing urban battle in Rostov, Stolz attempted to reach the main railway bridge but reached the river to the east of the span which Soviet engineers had partially demolished though the adjacent road bridge remained intact. Unable to force a crossing, Stolz established a strongpoint and awaited reinforcements.

As resistance faded in the city of Rostov itself, Grabert's company made its way to the river by truck, carrying inflatable boats as part of their equipment and established itself with Stolz, crossing the northern branch of the Don River along with twenty-eight volunteers from the *Kradschützen* Battalion's engineer platoon. Ferried across the river, they immediately established a command post on the far bank. In sweltering summer heat, heavy machine-gun and mortar fire caused a small number of German casualties, the first half-company of Brandenburgers already making their way across using their inflatables under the command of *Oberleutnant* Dr Oskar Hüller. Securing a larger bridgehead on the river's south bank, the remainder of the 8th Company soon followed and Grabert planned his assault on the bridge itself.

The southern bank was more sparsely built upon than the northern, a small harbour east of the bridge fringed with warehouses, while the terrain near the bridge lay exposed; a single slightly raised causeway leading to Bataysk, but swept by Soviet gunfire. After establishing his position, Grabert awaited darkness before beginning his assault. Covered by supressing fire from the northern bank, the Brandenburgers pushed through intense defensive fire, illuminated by drifting parachute flares and a burning truck on the bridge itself. They stormed the southern end of the bridge and captured it intact. Grabert was grazed in the head by a ricochet and his men were low on ammunition as he planned to continue the attack and take the next bridge downriver. Flares signalled his men to move their heavy weapons forward as his assault group prepared to rush forward, capitalising on their speed to keep pressure on the retreating defenders and keep them off balance. The bridge they held was still swept with heavy machine-gun fire and unusable and the seizure of further crossings would serve to push the defenders away from the river bank that they still held in isolated pockets.

Leading from the front, Grabert took his company in a direct assault at 0230hrs as dawn approached, though Soviet machine guns that had previously been concealed opened fire and took them by surprise. Several men were hit, but the momentum of the attack carried the Brandenburgers through and the next bridge was soon secured, though only with a tenuous grip. However, amongst those men that had been seriously wounded was Grabert himself, shot in the stomach and bleeding profusely. In severe pain, he was dragged under the bridge superstructure onto the sloping river bank and into cover. *Stabsarzt* Dr Helmut Weber of the company headquarters injected him with morphine to ease his pain, though he already knew the severity of his wound, reportedly saying: 'Don't do anything to me, Doctor, I am a medical doctor myself and know that I will die.'[2]

Casualties were steadily mounting as ammunition, morphine and medical supplies began to run out for the remaining Germans. With the heat of the midday sun tormenting the Germans, *Unteroffizier* Fohrer was despatched to swim back across the river and request aerial and artillery support as soon as possible and it was only the timely intervention of Stukas that allowed the remaining Brandenburgers to hold their position until elements of the 13th Panzer Division crossed the captured bridge. The way to the Caucasus was now cleared of its last natural barrier. However, Siegfried Grabert was not alive to savour the triumph, dying under the bridge as reinforcements arrived on 25 July 1943. The attack had virtually destroyed the 8th Company. *Leutnant* Hüller was also killed, his body being found in a mud-filled ditch 100m from the bridge along with the *Sanitätsunteroffizier* Weber who had been shot in the head. In total seventeen men were killed (two officers, two NCOs and thirteen men), sixteen men were missing (two NCOs and fourteen men) and fifty-four men were wounded (eleven NCOs and forty-three men) of whom thirty-four were hospitalised. Grabert was posthumously awarded the Oak Leaves to his Knight's Cross and promoted to *Major*. On 9 August 1942, Haehling issued a communique to his regiment:

> The commander of 8./*Lehrregiment 'Brandenburg' z.b.V. 800*, our Knight's Cross holder *Hauptmann* Siegfried Grabert, was killed at the head of his company in heroic combat in the Bataysk bridgehead on 25 July 1942.
>
> *Hauptmann* Grabert had given his soldiers, who were wholeheartedly attached to him, an example of an enthusiastic, intrepid and brave German soldier in both everyday life and against the enemy. His soldierly duties and combat successes are a glorious chapter for the *Lehrregiment 'Brandenburg' z.b.V. 800*.
>
> He endured his mortal wounds with complete equanimity and gave the orders for his company's continuing battle to the last moment.

The *Lehrregiment 'Brandenburg' z.b.V. 800* thanks its faithful and dear comrade for his successful deeds and exemplary courage. He will always remain a shining and inspiring model for the Regiment.

The shattered company was withdrawn for a brief period of rest and refit, newly promoted *Leutnant d.R.* Ernst Prochaska, who had served outstandingly as a platoon commander since the company's inception, given command. He would lead his men back into action during August as a new phase in the advance into the Caucasus began, codenamed Operation '*Edelweiss*'.

On 11 July, Directive 43 had been issued from Hitler's headquarters that described the 'continuation of operations from the Crimea'. Amongst the plans, Manstein's Eleventh Army was ordered to cross the Kerch Strait and occupy the Taman Peninsula by early August at the latest in Operation '*Blücher*'. This thrust was designed to capture the Black Sea ports of Anapa and Novorossiysk before heading into the Caucasus Mountains and along the coast to Tuapse and ultimately Poti. With Poti in German hands, the Black Sea would be secured and the last Soviet naval bases destroyed. There were specific tasks for the *Lehrregiment* outlined in Hitler's directive:

> The following special operations (Abwehr II) have been prepared. These special operations are to be examined by the General Staff of the Army with the Office of Foreign Intelligence, Security Section II [Abwehr II] and, if approved, to be included in Operation '*Blücher*'.
> (a) Parachute drop of a commando detachment in the Maykop area to protect oil installations ('Operation '*Schamil*').
> (b) Sabotage operations against the triangle of railways Krasnodar–Kropotkin–Tikhoretsk and against the bridges over the Kuban in that area.
> (c) Participation of a light engineer company of the Brandenburg Training Regiment, raised for operations of this kind, in attacks on enemy ports and coastal installations.

With the Don delta cleared of Soviet resistance, the next stage of Operation '*Edelweiss*' began with the push south towards Krasnodar, Maykop and into the Taman Peninsula. Leading the Wehrmacht advance were the 5th, 7th and 8th Brandenburg Companies. On 1 August, a *Kampfgruppe* of the 13th Panzer Division had reached Novoalexandrovsk, capturing the town on the bank of the Rasshevatka River which lay within the fertile grain-producing lands of the north Caucasus. Maykop and its scattered oilfields lay less than 150km away and German patrols reported strong Soviet troop concentrations between the panzer spearheads and those vital oilfields. The risk of sabotage and destruction before the Germans could capture them was too great and *Leutnant* Adrian von Fölkersam of the 3rd Company was tasked with infiltrating behind Soviet lines and capturing the oilfields or at least preventing their demolition.

Adrian Baron von Fölkersam – known as 'Arik' to his friends – had been born into an aristocratic Baltic German family who had long served the Imperial Russian military: his grandfather Admiral Dmitry Baron von Fölkersam of the Tsar's Imperial Navy and his great-grandfather General Gustav Baron von Fölkersam of the Imperial Army. Fölkersam's family fled Russia following the Russian Revolution in 1917 and settled in Latvia when he was a young child. Growing up in Riga, from 1934 he attended university in Munich, Königsberg and Vienna studying economics, after which he became a journalist on the *Rigaschen Rundschau* and joined the SA. Known as a charismatic team leader, Fölkersam then joined the Brandenburgers in which his brother Patrick had already enlisted. Both men were part of the 2nd Company, comprised of *Volksdeutsche* of Baltic, Russian and African origin.

He had risen through the ranks to become *Leutnant* adjutant of 1st Battalion before being posted to take part in '*Edelweiss*'. Fölkersam appears to have been eminently suited to his role, Wolfgang Herfurth of *SS-Jägerbataillon 502* later described him:

> He was a man of few words and able to play many parts well. He could distinguish exactly what was important from the unimportant. He always had reservations about orders coming from above and each order was examined and checked for its feasibility. So, he sometimes changed orders without further approval. He was completely convinced of his family's tradition and lineage and a supporter of the elite ideals as well as a follower of Stefan George's poetry, which brought us closer to humanity. He carefully prepared his subordinate commanders with exercises and difficult question and answer contests. He put great emphasis on individual training and strengthening. And though he clearly had a great deal of confidence, he was no arrogant superior.

For his mission, Fölkersam selected sixty-two men, mainly Baltic *Volksdeutsche* whose Russian was perfect, plus a scattering of hand-picked Sudeten Germans. For their mission, they would be in *Volltarnung*, without the usual precaution of a German uniform underneath. Given the nature of the deep penetration of enemy lines that was planned it was felt an unnecessary danger to carry any form of identifiable Wehrmacht equipment. They were equipped instead as NKVD troops of the 124th NKVD Rifle Brigade, Fölkersam taking the guise of Major Truchin.

Because of the rapid German advance and corresponding retreat of the Soviet Ninth Army, the Russian front line was extremely porous and Fölkersam's group marched under bright moonlight south through acres of sunflower fields, headed for Krasnodarskiy, 10km from Novoalexandrovsk. The small village of Feldmarshalskiy that lay astride the narrow road was packed with a mixed bag of retreating Soviet troops that had become separated from their parent units, including Kuban Cossacks – who had been responsible for holding the front line – Ukrainians, Kyrgyz groups, Caucasians and Turkmen, Georgians and finally Russians and Siberian units. From careful observation, Fölkersam's patrols reported a sense that only the Russian and Siberian men were keen to return to the fighting, the remainder either favouring defection to the Wehrmacht or melting away to their homes, the few Soviet officers present struggling to retain control. Fölkersam's men surrounded the village in the darkness, noting that alongside the enemy's horses and camels were trucks and fuel supplies that the young *Leutnant* wanted to acquire before continuing to Maykop.

Once the enemy troops were surrounded, Fölkersam and his men fired their weapons into the air and quickly moved in to disarm the startled troops. The power exerted by their NKVD uniforms cowed the dispirited men who were herded together in the centre of the village. There, Fölkersam jumped on to the bonnet of a truck and began haranguing the group, accusing them of desertion in the face of the enemy. Two dissenting Cossacks who responded with loud sarcasm were quickly manhandled away from the village square for 'execution'. Fölkersam ordered all Cossacks separated from the remainder and, along with a small part of his force, marched them out of the village for proclaimed summary execution as traitors and cowards. Away from the prying eyes of the remaining Red Army men, Fölkersam rounded on the Cossack leader and asked whether they genuinely intended to defect to the Wehrmacht, causing confusion and suspicion amongst their prisoners. Fölkersam offered them the opportunity to head towards Anapa, mingling with refugees and making their way to the German lines, while he and his men fired volleys into the air that would satisfy the listening men in Krasnodarskiy. The deal was struck and after the Cossacks' departure and ensuing gunfire, Fölkersam and his men returned to the village. They ordered the Russian and Siberian officers present to head south towards Maykop while they remained to deal with the remaining prisoners. Once the others had hastily departed, no doubt grateful to be alive and away from the NKVD bloodbath, Fölkersam extended the same offer to those left behind, before commandeering trucks for the journey to Maykop.

The journey was long, hot and dusty as the main road south soon became clogged with refugees and retreating troops. Reaching Armavir on the Kuban River on 3 August, genuine NKVD troops stopped them, attempting to restore order amongst the teeming throng of people. Fölkersam swung down from the truck cab and presented his forged credentials to the NKVD colonel in charge, claiming to be on special assignment on behalf of Aleksei Zhadov, commander of Sixty-Sixth Army at Stalingrad. Unwilling to admit ignorance of the order, the colonel chastised Fölkersam for being a day later than expected and directed him to continue towards Maykop, while warning him to remain vigilant against 'fascist spies' disguised as Soviet infantrymen.

The Brandenburgers continued south and finally reached Maykop, driving immediately to Red Army headquarters where Fölkersam was introduced to the NKVD lieutenant general charged with local defence, referred to in subsequent accounts as General Perscholl.[3] Fölkersam was warmly greeted, news of his execution of traitorous Cossacks having preceded his arrival, and the Brandenburgers were provided with a confiscated villa and adjacent garage for the duration of their stay. Perscholl invited Fölkersam to dinner and, over a full meal accompanied by large quantities of vodka, the German *Leutnant* established himself as a welcome guest in the city. During the days that followed he and his men were able to reconnoitre Maykop's defences, Fölkersam going as far as using his NKVD position to order well-positioned anti-tank positions moved away from the main road lest panzers take a 'less obvious' axis of attack.

By the evening of 8 August, German armoured forces were only 20km away and chaos had overtaken Soviet troops in Maykop. Perscholl had departed with his staff and there was widespread looting by roving bands of leaderless men. The time had come to execute the final stage of his mission and Fölkersam divided his men into three parties. The first and most numerous, under the command of *Feldwebel* Landowski, was charged with heading south-west towards Neftegorsk to prevent the destruction of oil installations being prepared for demolition. The Brandenburgers were to kill the genuine demolition parties and take their place, masquerading as a Soviet sabotage troops. A second smaller group headed by Franz Koudele was to sever telephone and telegraph communications between Maykop's defenders and the outside world. Fölkersam himself led the third group that was intended to meet two Soviet brigades of Guards that had arrived from Tiblisi and Baku as reinforcements and attempt to persuade them to fall back from the town.

German artillery fire was landing in the city as the third team planted explosives at a small artillery communications centre, the subsequent explosion taken to have been a lucky shell hit. Fölkersam then forcefully persuaded defending artillery troops that the German threat lay to the south and had them abandon their defensive positions while he and his 'heroic' NKVD men covered their move. He next presented himself to the Soviet general commanding one of the reinforcing brigades and attempted to also persuade him that the front line now lay to the south. His opponent was initially sceptical and suspicion began to transform into hostility before word of the retreating artillerymen swung the issue in Fölkersam's favour and the first brigade was ordered to withdraw; its movement convincing adjacent troops to also leave their positions and head south.

Meanwhile, Koudele had managed to bluff his way into the central communications centre and browbeat the officer in charge to evacuate the building and retreat to the new defensive line at Apschetousk. Once the Soviet operators had departed, Koudele's men manned the telephones and radios, redirecting Soviet troops towards Tuapse as they relayed the disinformation that Maykop was cut off and surrounded. By noon, panzers had reached the northern outskirts of the city and the Brandenburgers evacuated the building and destroyed the Soviet equipment with grenades.

To the south-east Landowski attempted to contact Soviet authorities by field telephone to order a withdrawal from the oil installations but without success. Divided into 'NKVD squads', his troops raced into individual facilities and ordered Soviet troops stationed there to retreat while they handled the demolitions themselves as a 'rearguard'. However, though largely successful, in at least one place a Soviet security officer had attempted to contact Army Headquarters and, after being unable to get through due to Koudele's demolitions, sabotaged the machinery and wells at Makdse. In fact, despite some measure of success for the Brandenburgers, Hitler's ambition of quickly plundering Maykop's oil reserves was to be frustrated by widespread Soviet sabotage. However, against the city defences Fölkersam's men had succeeded spectacularly and on the evening of 9 August, the 13th Panzer Division stormed into Maykop and took over 1,000 prisoners against relatively weak opposition. The men of Fölkersam's command gingerly made their way towards approaching German troops and 'surrendered' themselves lest unnecessary casualties were caused. Fortunately, the leading elements had been fully briefed and there were no accidents, *Oberst* Haehling soon arriving by Kübelwagen to oversee the return of his men, and Fölkersam's mission was over. He and his men had achieved a remarkable feat and Fölkersam was awarded the Knight's Cross on 14 September 1942.

The day after Fölkersam's mission ended, *Leutnant* Prochaska was tasked with capturing the road bridge over the River Belaya at Belorechensk to the north-east. The reconstructed 8th Company used *Volltarnung* as they travelled ahead of armoured elements of 13th Panzer Division. They departed the German lines in four captured Russian trucks, mingling with the last wave of retreating Red Army troops as fighting continued at the city fringe. Challenged when approaching the bridge by a Soviet officer, Prochaska claimed that they had been assigned the task of protecting the crossing and they were waved onwards. Upon reaching their objective they were halted again, this time by a Soviet military policeman attempting to thin the flow of traffic. As the policeman waved them onwards, the leading truck's starter failed and several Brandenburgers dismounted to attempt to push start the truck once more, assisted by the Russian policeman. After the engine sparked into life, they continued over the river, reaching the far bank where the entire company rapidly disembarked to overwhelm the crew of a stationary tank as well as engineers that had rigged the span for demolition while a small number of Brandenburgers raced across the bridge itself, removing demolition charges and throwing them into the water below.

Prochaska fired two white flares to signal success to the waiting panzer spearhead, which appeared shortly on the northern bank. As Soviet fire broke out from the opposite river bank, Prochaska sprinted across the bridge to guide oncoming armoured vehicles past an abandoned panje wagon and a long black limousine that had recently been vacated by its officer occupant. Running towards the German tanks, he was hit in the head by enemy fire and killed instantly. Six other men from the 8th Company were also killed: Fritz Erstürung, Sepp Schöfer, Hans Gruber, Max Galauf, Willy and Fritz Renz. The German tanks continued across, relieving the hastily entrenched Brandenburgers and racing onwards towards the oil installations that had been captured by Fölkersam's men to the south-east. *Leutnant* Renner took temporary charge of the 8th Company – replaced by *Hauptmann* Helmut Pinkert on 1 October – and Ernst Prochaska, who had led the company for only a matter of weeks, was posthumously awarded the Knight's Cross on 16 September 1942.

To the west, *Oberleutnant* Karl-Heinz Oesterwitz's 7th Company moved ahead of the SS Division 'Wiking' disguised in Red Army greatcoats over their uniforms and side caps adorned with the infantryman's red star. Aboard three trucks they overtook the advancing SS column, narrowly missing being fired on by jumpy crewmen of the leading 'Wiking' armoured vehicles. Passing over the newly named 'Prochaska Bridge', they infiltrated the Soviet front line where they caused a localised rout ahead of the advancing 'Wiking' troops by feigning panic which spread infectiously through hastily prepared defensive works. Reaching Pshekhskaya, the Brandenburgers removed their disguises and attacked an artillery battery, killing most of the crews before the rest fled and abandoned the guns to the Germans. In short order, Oesterwitz and his men stormed both the road and rail bridges over the Pshekha River with three men wounded during the fighting but none killed. For this he would later be decorated with the German Cross in Gold and the road appeared open for the 'Wiking' SS troops to advance on Tuapse.

Near Dondukovskaya, on the banks of the Fars River, *Oberleutnant* Zülch prepared to lead the 5th Company south-east towards Cherkessk, a town that had grown up during the previous century around a Russian fort on the Kuban River. Beyond lay the foothills of the Caucasian Mountains, the summit of Mount Elbrus only 100km away, and the town marked a midway point between Maykop and the Grozny oilfields. The company advanced in the heat of the Caucasian summer in German vehicles as light reconnaissance infantry. *Leutnant* Konrad Steidl, commander of one of the half-companies, recorded the advance in a personal diary, this extract from 10 August later reproduced in Spaeter's book:

Burnt-out vehicles, German and Russian and the fresh corpses of horses and Red Army soldiers lined the sides of the road. From time to time we could hear gunfire. There was trouble brewing so we travel cautiously, though over great distances. We were aiming for the town of Dondukovskaya. Suddenly, from there are loud bangs from all the shrubs and bushes. Grenades land on the roadway. Wounded scream, the first of our vehicles burn. Zülch is at the head of the column with his Kübel. I leave my seat, get my half-company in cover and race with my motorcycle to Zülch.

From the houses, enemy mortar fire whistles. My commander gives me my orders: Move immediately to attack the west edge of Donukovskaya and storm the adjacent village.

There is already an '*Ölkompanie*' [technicians tasked with taking charge of the captured oil installations] in the village, its survivors involved in a difficult struggle as the village has been attacked. I stormed with my soldiers to the left and right of the street and, using smoke, fought hand-to-hand from house to house and bunker to bunker. In a couple of hours, I had taken back control of the road with my men and we prepared for a second attack against the village itself. Martl already has a heavy machine-gun platoon ready in the corn field. He digs in and is quite nervous, because Russian machine-gun fire and grenades land all around us. He sits about 200m from the edge of the field. My attack goes over an open space. It will be hard. I lie with my platoon at the edge of a ditch and discuss the attack with them. Heavy shells are exploding close to us. A sudden scream; a direct hit on the street amidst one of my groups, *Leutnant* [Dr Hans Adolf Rudolf] Pils, Walter Perntner, *Feldwebel* Schink and five of our best men are killed instantly. There is also a large number wounded.

I give the signal to attack and jump up, firing my submachine gun, and with a 'Hurra' I'm first from the ditch to charge the supressed enemies. Behind me on a broad front, wide apart, are my soldiers. At the same time, our heavy weapons keep the Russians' heads down. It crackles like hell. Already I only have 20m to go. The bullets whistle in front of my nose into the dry ground. When we reach them we rushed forward against the Russians with hand grenades. The sweat runs in streams. My people are breathless, yet I urge them on against the enemy's positions in the village. My bunch is quite scattered – Schmied Sepp looks after the wounded. With a few men, amongst them one of my biggest daredevils Vladimir Mark, I stormed the Russian huts with hand grenades and took eighty prisoners.

Walter Ladendorff reached me with an order from Zülch to withdraw and take secure positions on both sides of the road. Strong Russian forces are reported on all sides, we must form a 'hedgehog'. It is said that we are surrounded. *Oberjäger* Felix Graf Schaffgotsch, one of our best, is also dead. The losses are great after half a day's fighting.

I let them build deep emplacements, as we expect a Russian attack with artillery support in the early morning. In the evening, I was ordered with Sepp to report to Zülch. In the candlelight, we sit together briefly and lie down in the holes. At midnight, I squat in the foremost hole with my pack and await the attack predicted by Zülch. In one hand I have a flare gun, in the other a pistol as I squat freezing next to *Feldwebel* Ortner's heavy machine gun.

The expected attack doesn't come. In the morning, an armoured section from the 13th Panzer Division arrives. This is a 'food' for me. I immediately contact a 'box' [tank] with a 7.5cm cannon, take a few men and act as their reconnaissance. Shortly, a sniper shoots at us. As we open fire in our attack, the village, in which a Russian company has again taken up position, is set on fire. I return with sixty prisoners.

In the afternoon Zülch and I mount a daring escapade: we roar into a Russian infantry battalion with two tanks and beat it into flight. Thereupon, three of us are going to storm a collective farm – we are racing without breath over an open field. There are still 200m to the finish line. Zülch's elegant boots are smeared to the top with dirt, heavy clumps of clay cling to my mountain boots. We can hardly do more, the 'chorus' is getting increasingly angry, it whistles and crackles around us, it would be madness to go on without cover. So, we lie a few hours before the collective farm until darkness falls. With our hands, we dig holes in the clay ground – I really got to know *Oberleutnant* Zülch's iron calmness and cold-bloodedness. On the following day, the company reunited with us in Dondukovskaya. Zülch speaks. It feels strange; the fresh graves are in front of us, simple wooden crosses with the tattered steel helmets. Our daring *Leutnant* Hans Pils will no longer move with us over the endless steppe into the distant Caucasus. But we roll on and, with heavy hearts, leave our dead behind.[4]

The Brandenburgers continued to lead the advance into the Caucasus, both in plain German uniform as light infantry and in disguise, as infiltrators. Casualties continued to mount against increasingly desperate Soviet resistance. Maykop and its surrounding oilfields had been taken, the smallest of the three oil-producing areas and the drive towards the remainder needed to be made with consolidated force. Unfortunately for the Germans, Hitler's micromanagement of his forces caused unnecessary logistical shuffling and a swirling change of offensive focus. With Luftwaffe air cover removed to support Sixth Army at Stalingrad, progress in the Caucasus slowed still further and on 9 September, Army Group A commander *Feldmarschall* Wilhelm List was relieved of his command, Hitler assuming direct control. Meanwhile, news had been received that all was not well in the Maykop oilfields.

The *Technische Brigade Mineralöl* (Mineral Oil Technical Brigade) had been formed as a specialised Wehrmacht unit during the winter of 1941/2. Their express purpose was to take charge of the oilfields of Maykop, Baku and Grozny and begin immediate production for German usage. After ordinary infantry training, the brigade had been posted to Ploieşti for advanced technical instruction before heading towards Rostov-on-Don alongside the German advance. The unit comprised 6,500 men divided into three specialised battalions – Drilling, Processing and Transport – and was commanded by Luftwaffe *Generalleutnant* Erich Homburg, assisted by chief technician Dr Günther Schlicht. Amongst their heavy equipment were one hundred deep bore drills and ten mobile distillation plants.

A full month after the capture of Maykop, German forces took control of the wells at Neftegorsk and Khadyzhensk where large-scale sabotage had already taken place. Concrete or scrap metal had been used to block wells, pipelines blown up and compressor installations destroyed by the retreating Red Army. Although the brigade moved in to begin immediate repairs Dr Schlicht reported that, despite progress, the extensive damage would take years to fully repair. To make matters worse, bands of Soviet partisans, whose ranks had been swollen by isolated groups of Red Army troops, had begun harassing attacks that killed members of the brigade and destroyed valuable technical equipment. The Soviet road and railway system made replacing heavy machinery virtually impossible, choked as it was already with military supplies. With the Black Sea ports not yet in German hands, this latter fact also begged the question of how, if significant quantities of oil or petroleum were successfully produced, it was to be transported to fuel-hungry troops elsewhere. What limited oil production was considered possible would not begin again until 21 November 1942, while to the north the Red Army completed its encirclement of Stalingrad and the complexion of Germany's Eastern Front changed irrevocably.

To complete the imbalance between German and Soviet oil production, Hitler had also refused to allow Luftwaffe bombers to raid the oil installations at Baku that supplied most of the Soviet military. With the Red Air Force struggling against Luftwaffe strength and freshly captured German airstrips within bombing range, Hitler demanded instead that Göring divert his forces to concentrate on the capture of Stalingrad, a subsidiary target at best in the original offensive plans. Not until 7 October 1942, when it became obvious that the thrust towards Baku and Grozny had failed, did he authorise the bombing of the oilfields 'as strongly as possible', calling for 'massive attacks' on Grozny on 22 September. By this time the Luftwaffe was exhausted and Soviet aerial strength in the Caucasus had been given time to recuperate. The German raids that followed certainly inflicted damage and left plumes of smoke towering above the refineries, but with bomber strength split between the oilfields and Stalingrad, the impact on overall Soviet oil production was negligible. The ultimate prize of Baku was beyond reach of bombers operating from the nearest secure airfields and though Grozny suffered severe damage, it was all too little and too late.

During August *Oberleutnant* Hütten's 11th Company had been deployed in Aramawir, securing the town which lay at the junction of the III and LVII Panzer Corps. Moving east, Hütten advanced through Voroshilovsk (now known as Stavropol) before swinging south-east towards Prochladnyj and beyond over the Terek River that flows through Georgia from the Caspian Sea. The 4th (Light) *Fallschirmjäger* Company was also prepared for a possible airborne operation in the Terek region as *Oberleutnant* Oskar Schatz and eighty men of the 2nd Company reached the town of Maysky. After crossing the Nalchik River, they were preparing to bridge the Terek, the final water barrier before the Grozny oilfields a little over 100km away. There, on 22 August, as panzers rolled into the village in support, a direct hit from enemy shellfire killed Schatz and his radio operator as they joined a forward artillery observer studying Soviet positions. The observer was badly wounded and died later that night. The two Brandenburgers were buried in the soft ground of a local school. His parachute drop cancelled, *Hauptmann* Kürschner's *Fallschirmjäger* would be thrown into the maelstrom at the Terek River during October, acting as light infantry before being hastily withdrawn to the north.

Operation '*Blücher*': the German Attack across the Kuban Strait

During July, all except the 1st Platoon of *Leichte Pionierkompanie Brandenburg* had transferred to the Crimea in preparation for the Eleventh Army's attack across the Kerch Strait on to the Taman Peninsula. The Crimean Peninsula had finally fallen completely to German forces with the surrender of the last defenders of Sevastopol on 4 July, only partisan activity and small Soviet coastal raids remaining. Across the strait, Soviet troops had been virtually trapped within the Taman pocket since the forces of Operation *'Edelweiss'* had passed Rostov-on-Don headed south towards the coastal port of Novorossiysk. The Soviet Black Sea Fleet began evacuating troops from the Sea of Asov while OKW planned the assault, designated *'Blücher'*, by five entire infantry divisions with Kriegsmarine support. *Hauptmann* Horlbeck took 2nd Platoon under the command of *Oberleutnant* Kriegsheim and 3rd Platoon commanded by *Oberleutnant* Dr Wagner to Mama Tartarskaja on the Sea of Asov coast north-west of Kerch. There they prepared for their mission at the spearhead of the attack across the Kerch Strait.

At 0200hrs on 2 September, the long-awaited – and frequently postponed – Operation *'Blücher'* began. Horlbeck's men were tasked with three separate and simultaneous missions. The first was the neutralisation of Soviet positions at Cape Pekly on the Sea of Asov, next was the occupation of the straggling exposed island of Tusla that lay between the Kuban and Taman peninsulas and last the storming of a stranded freighter SS *Gornjak* that lay in shallow water off the Bay of Taman and aboard which a Red Army observation post had been established.

A six-man raiding party approached Cape Pekly unobserved and disembarked successfully before being spotted by an enemy sentry. The attackers opened fire and stormed the small string of bunkers and trenches with grenades and satchel charges, quickly overwhelming the defenders. The attack on the *Gornjak* was also successful, a single guard quietly killed while the rest of the raiding party slipped aboard and captured the remaining Russians. On Tusla, three *Sturmboote* landed after a final approach to shore without engines. Nearing the low coastline at separate points, they were spotted before making landfall. However, the Soviet defenders that had been protected by their squat bunker made the mistake of emerging to engage the first boat sighted and were shot by the second landing party. As the Brandenburgers rushed their enemy, two of them were killed by gunfire and two wounded before the small island was taken.

Brandenburgers then marched inland to attack Soviet artillery batteries at Zaporozhskaya, as the main German infantry landings began. Three assault detachments of the 46th Infantry Division were put ashore from MFPs, Siebel ferries and *Sturmboote* covered by the 3rd R-Flotilla with S-boats and Italian MAS flanking to the south. With strong Luftwaffe support, German troops quickly took several villages south and south-west of the bridgehead while MFPs provided covering artillery fire. By 1500hrs the northern part of the Taman Peninsula was in German hands, followed by landings on the promontory south-west of Tamanskiy that encountering little resistance. Romanian cavalry advanced from Temryuk and it appeared that the battle for the Taman bridgehead would be over within days; possibly leading to the wholesale collapse of Soviet forces in Krasnodar as, to the south, German forces battled into the outskirts of Novorossiysk, Brandenburgers of *Oberleutnant* Ronte's 10th Company involved in the advance.

However, Kriegsmarine Black Sea strength was almost exhausted, the flotillas of various craft in a sorry state compounded by damage from Soviet fire and the elements. Their effective artillery support and transport capabilities were essential for the success of '*Blücher*' and, as the inevitable Kriegsmarine offensive pressure slackened, Soviet submarines and aircraft gradually gained the upper hand. Nevertheless, during the night of 9 September, all of Novorossiysk harbour was finally under German control, tiny but fiercely resisting Soviet enclaves at Mount Myskhako the sole remaining enemy presence. While Novorossiysk harbour storage facilities had been destroyed, the main pier, coal yards and railway siding were intact and promptly requisitioned for naval use.

Horlbeck's men returned to Kerch after their missions and were not deployed again until 10 September in an attack on the coastal road that ran between Novorossiysk and Gelendzhik and which remained in Soviet hands. The *Leichte Pionierkompanie Brandenburg* had moved to the recently captured port at Anapa as a forward base and it was from there that they sailed for the raid intended to block the line of retreat for Red Army units falling back from Novorossiysk. However, the assault group encountered heavily armed small craft of the Soviet Baltic Fleet and were forced to return to Anapa without attempting their landing.

In November Horlbeck was assigned a long-range reconnaissance mission, being ordered to make a landing behind enemy lines at the small promontory of Cap Penaj. From there the Brandenburgers were to conduct sabotage missions to the south at Gelendzhik, but as the date for the operation neared it became apparent that the regional military situation had altered and his orders were cancelled as unnecessary before the raid could be mounted. On 12 December, the *Leichte Pionierkompanie Brandenburg* was finally withdrawn from Anapa, which was under increasing pressure from enemy air attacks. Sailing to Kerch they suffered their most serious casualties after one of the Engineer Landing Craft carrying them struck a mine laid by Soviet motor torpedo boats (MTBs) and exploded, killing thirteen men. The survivors entrained in Kerch for the return by rail to Langenargen on the Bodensee.

On the situation maps success in the Caucasus appeared to be tantalisingly close for Germany during early September. Elements of the 101st *Jäger* Division and SS 'Wiking' were less than 50km from Tuapse, and the eastern seaboard of the Black Sea as far as Sokhumi appeared to be on the brink of falling to the Wehrmacht. In North Africa Rommel's forces stood facing the last Allied defences before Alexandria and a final advance on the Nile. The spectre of a direct German threat to the Middle East, possible Turkish entry into a war of Axis triumph and the subsequent linking-up with Wehrmacht troops in the Caucasus suddenly loomed large in the imagination. But, situation maps do not tell the full story of weariness, actual effective fighting strength or supply. The Axis military machine was, in fact, at the end of its tether, even if not yet fully aware of that fact.

Far to the north – too far as events would soon demonstrate – on Monday 7 September, the German Sixth Army attacked and captured the Mamayev Kurgan, the dominant height overlooking Stalingrad. Within a week, Army Group B had begun the grinding house-to-house fighting to capture the city.

Walther's 1st Battalion had been leading the advance towards Stalingrad with small mobile groups that forged ahead to capture river crossings and transportation hubs while gathering information on retreating Soviet units. With regular restructuring of Wehrmacht units, the 2nd and 3rd Companies had been stripped from Sixth Army leaving just *Hauptmann* Babuke's 1st Company attached to Army Group B and reaching the small town of Tsatsa and its namesake lake by 24 August, operating in the vanguard of the 29th Motorised Infantry Division south of Stalingrad. Sharp Red Army counter-attacks continued to cause casualties, *Leutnant* Peter Bachmann being killed that day and *Unteroffizier* Baron posted as missing: only fragments of his uniform were found and the NCO assumed to have been captured. Sleep was becoming a rare commodity at night as Soviet aircraft mounted harassing bombing raids under cover of darkness. On 28 August Babuke handed over command of the company to *Leutnant* Schulte as he was transferred back to Germany. The company's situation report of the time makes grim reading:

> Sunday 30 August. Grab 'Tarne' clothes. At 0200hrs accompany *Leutnant* Hebler to a small village. Russians had come with Panjewagen in the night and had been captured. Large rocket launcher attack [*Nebelwerferangriff*]! 0700hrs with attacking spearhead . . . to attack in disguise and in enemy vehicles. Anti-tank fire. Hits on vehicle belonging to '*Gruppe Fuchs*'. Own tank flies into the air! *Feldwebel* Garling gets large splinters through his big toes! Down from the vehicle and into hedgehog position! Forstenhäusler killed. Reinecke and Kurz wounded. Start of the big battle! Ten aircraft attack despite fighters and Flak! Two of our own fighters. What the hell is going on!
>
>   Monday 31.8 Drive all night across Russian line. '*Stoi!*' Russian post! Is disarmed and taken. Prisoners, prisoners, even women. – At dawn, a strong breakfast in the farm with eggs, milk, cream and fresh bread. Get out quick!

To the right of us Russian infantry attack with 'Urrah!' Buried by aerial and artillery bombardment. Rain in the night. Tents.[5]

The 1st Company battled north alongside the 29th Motorised Infantry Division until by the middle of October they had reached the approaches to Stalingrad itself and halted at the Don Canal that linked that great river with the Volga. There they were taken out of the line as Fourth Panzer Army fought to contain and destroy Soviet units pinned with their backs to the Volga in Stalingrad's southern suburbs. The company was then withdrawn completely, travelling by road to a military railhead and entraining for return to new quarters at the *Erbgrossherzog-Friedrich-Kaserne*, Freiburg im Breisgau.

The Advance on Grozny

With the Grozny oilfield firmly in Wehrmacht sights, the 3rd Company spearheaded attacks by the 3rd Panzer Division against the town of Mozdok sandwiched between the Lenin Canal and Terek River. After heavy fighting against three Soviet brigades a small bridgehead was thrown across the Terek, the 3rd Company being involved in the battle and joined by the 5th and 8th Companies of the 2nd Battalion, hurriedly thrown into the fray after travelling at full speed from the western battles.

Leutnant Werner Lau led his 5th Company together with a *Kampfgruppe* from 13th Panzer Division in an attack on the 120m-long combined road and railway bridge west of Arik, invaluable for Soviet oil transport from Baku and Grozny to Rostov-on-Don. The bridge was wired with 4.5 tons of explosives and ready to be demolished. Lau led his men in *Volltarnung*, infiltrating alone ahead of his company and spending the night amidst Soviet reconnaissance troops. At dawn the following day the remaining Brandenburgers stormed the bridge using their disguise to get close enough to remove the demolition charges and kill all the defenders. Lau personally captured several bunkers single-handedly before the bridge was secured. He was justifiably recommended for the Knight's Cross, which he finally received on 9 December 1942.

Wehrmacht troops poured across the captured bridge to reach the planes beyond, though resistance was fierce and nearly suicidal from some Red Army units. Heavy minefields destroyed several vehicles of the 13th Panzer Division near Nizhniy Akbash and the division's commander *Generalmajor* Traugott Herr was seriously wounded after being struck in the head by shrapnel from a mine explosion on 31 October and evacuated to Germany to recuperate. At the eastern end of the German line, units had reached as far as Chervlennaya before unrelenting Soviet air and land attacks forced them gradually back. Less than 25km from Grozny and 130km from the shores of the Caspian Sea, the Wehrmacht had reached the furthest east that they ever would in the Caucasus.

In the records of the FSB (Federal Security Service of the Russian Federation) in Moscow are impressions that were taken by NKVD troops during the entire German campaign in the Caucasus. By November they recorded a new pessimism amongst Wehrmacht troops.

> According to the testimony of prisoners, the 23rd Panzer Division numbers no more than thirty-five tanks. Remnants of 13th Panzer Division has been moved to the rear, obviously to re-form . . . At present [17 November] the enemy is on the road Ardon, Dzuarikau but has moved onto the defensive, awaiting reinforcements for action.
>
> The morale and political status of the enemy is negative. Heavy losses in the Caucasus, the tightening of war conditions and poor nutrition have led to a significant decrease in the mood of the soldiers. Amongst the soldiers of the enemy, there is talk about the difficult situation in Germany and a deterioration of living standards for their families. Soldiers say that winning the Caucasus is impossible, because Germany does not have enough strength left. Many German soldiers are sure that the war will end in the defeat of Germany.[6]

Nonetheless German pressure continued. On 25 October, the 13th and 23rd Panzer Divisions of III Panzer Corps mounted a renewed attack to capture Nalchik from the direction of Maysky with scattered Brandenburger companies attached. From the 1st Battalion came the 2nd Company, from 2nd Battalion the Battalion Headquarters plus 5th and 8th Companies and from the 3rd Battalion came the 11th Company. From the area of Baksan, Romanian and German mountain troops made a southward thrust in support. Preceded by strong Luftwaffe bombardment, principally Stuka attacks, the advance began against seven defending Red Army divisions. Fighting was fierce and brutal as the Axis forces battered their way to Nalchik. The fighting in the urban area was protracted and difficult as both panzer divisions swung south to make for Lesken and Chikola. The Romanian 2nd Mountain Division took control of Nalchik by 28 October after suffering 820 casualties in desperate house-to-house fighting. Over a thousand Soviet prisoners were taken and marched back to makeshift holding pens behind the lines and many of the passes leading into the Caucasus mountain range were now under Axis control. *Leutnant* Helmut Neugebauer and a party of men from the Brandenburg 10th Company were tasked with combing through the prisoner of war camps in search of volunteers for the regiment, having found ninety potential volunteers by 20 October. He, his men and new recruits were then transported to Düren to begin the formation and training of a new company, eventually to become the 8th Company, 3rd Regiment, Brandenburg Division in 1943.

On 2 November, the German-Romanian attack was resumed after a brief pause. The Brandenburgers were concentrated for Operation '*Darg Kokh*', named for the small municipality through which the axis of advance would pass. German forces had swept south following the bend of the Terek River as far as the outskirts of Vladikavkaz, capital city of the Republic of North Ossetia, while the 370th Infantry Division had stalled at Ekhotovo. The Brandenburgers' 5th Company was tasked with blasting over the river and lancing east against Darg Kokh, combined with a battle group from the 13th Panzer Division and under the direct command of 2nd Battalion commander, *Major* Dr Jacobi.

The company was ordered to seize and hold four road and rail bridges over the Terek until relieved. However, it was to be a costly failure. Of four separate assault groups, only *Leutnant* Steidl appears to have captured the bridge assigned to him, which carried the road that stretched from Ardon to Darg Kokh. After taking hold of one end against light resistance, he and his thirty men ran headlong into heavy fire from Red Army troops protected by bunkers on the far shore. Battling forward they cleared each position in hand-to-hand fighting and the defenders retreated in disorder, the bridge finally taken as the last Soviet troops ran. However, the lull that followed was brief as heavy artillery fire began falling around the small German bridgehead, Steidl clearly able to see troops reforming in the distance with newly arrived enemy tanks. The counter-attack, when it came, was relentless until only three of the Brandenburgers remained uninjured, grimly holding on and repulsing every enemy attack while awaiting promised reinforcements.

Just as they were on the verge of exhausting their ammunition, a brief pause in the fighting allowed a runner to reach Steidl and he was ordered to retreat. The other attacks had failed with heavy losses and Steidl and the lightly wounded survivors who were mobile fell back by rushes. The bridge itself remained under artillery bombardment and appeared on the verge of physical collapse as the Brandenburgers retreated to prepare fresh defences in Ardon.

They remained there for several days, fighting off occasional night attacks, though their enemy appeared unwilling to press their hard-won advantage. Losses to the company had been severe, not least the commander *Major* Dr Jacobi who had been wounded in the attack against the railway bridge across the Terek and subsequently died in hospital after his weakened body contracted jaundice. *Hauptmann* Gerhard Pinkert took command of what remained of the battalion, which suffered another grievous loss on 7 November, when veteran *Oberleutnant* Johann Karl Fürchtegott Zülch was also killed after being shot in the head by a sniper while observing enemy forces.

On the Soviet side, the day that Zülch fell marked the beginning of their resurgence. Alexey Mikhailovich Buchukury had been drafted into the Red Army during August 1942 to protect his Ossetia homeland. A member of the 319th Rifle Division and then the 276th Georgian Infantry Division, he recalled:

> The Nazis were near Vladikavkaz. On 2 November 1942, Gizel' was occupied. The fascists behaved as though they had already won. The town was constantly bombed, fired at from guns. Hitler's aircraft flew over our position, dropping leaflets, the content just insulting words: 'Surrender! Your days are numbered, resistance is futile, on 7 November, the town will be at our feet' etc. etc. At lunch bombers appeared; day and night bombing our positions, attacking our trenches with their horrible howl, but we were well hidden, we had good bunkers, so there was almost no loss. Bombing and shelling continued every day from 30 October to 7 November 1942.[7]

On that November day, the Wehrmacht finally conceded the battle in the south. Defeated in Vladikavkaz, the Wehrmacht began its retreat, though it fought for every metre of territory that the Red Army regained. Gizel' was reoccupied by Soviet troops on 11 November, *Oberleutnant* Renner's 8th Company being involved in the stubborn defence of the town. Soviet forces launched a counteroffensive and managed to interdict Axis communications on the Nalchik–Beslan–Ordzhonikidzevskaya and Nalchik–Alagir–Ordzhonikidzevskaya roads. This isolated a part of the III Panzer Corps still fighting in Ordzhonikidzevskaya only 50km west of Grozny, part of 13th Panzer Division trapped and encircled until relieved by Romanians of the 2nd Mountain Division on 12 November and continuing the retreat during the following night.

The Brandenburger's 1st Battalion had been reduced to a composite battlegroup of the 2nd and 4th (Light) *Fallschirmjäger* Company – designated '*Kampfgruppe Walther*' – after *Leutnant* Schulte's 1st Company had returned to Germany. On 16 December, the *Fallschirmjäger* commander *Hauptmann* Kürschner was severely wounded and replaced by the 1st Battalion adjutant *Oberleutnant* Hans Gerlach. Of 3rd Battalion, *Major* Franz Jacobi still maintained the 10th and 11th Companies in the Caucasus, the 9th returning to Mödling south of Vienna for transformation into a 'Tropical Company' and attachment to Koenen's forces in North Africa. *Hauptmann* Horlbeck gathered the remains of the 5th and 11th Companies into his own namesake *Kampfgruppe* that defended Ardon allowing other Wehrmacht units to withdraw through the town. Meanwhile the 12th Company continued its anti-partisan operations near Smolensk and the *Leichte Pionierkompanie Brandenburg* was in action along the Black Sea coast.

On 19 November 1943, the Red Army exploited the gap left between Army Groups A and B as they chased diverging objectives and launched Operation 'Uranus'. While the German Sixth Army lay partially paralysed by the onset of winter and battle exhaustion in Stalingrad, the offensive broke through Romanian forces north of the city and the following day a second major offensive smashed Romanian lines to the south. By 23 November the two prongs of the Russian advance met at Kalach and the Sixth Army was surrounded in the rubble of Stalingrad.

Fearing that the Soviet advance could isolate the entire Army Group A in the Caucasus and with the southern advance stalled before Grozny and beginning to ebb slowly back, Axis forces throughout the entire region were thrown onto the defensive with a strong Soviet attack expected against the Taman Peninsula. On 16 December, the Red Army launched Operation 'Little Saturn' that hammered Axis forces in the Ukraine, pushing them further away from Stalingrad and sealing the fate of the Sixth Army, while the German First Panzer Army was pushed steadily back towards Rostov-on-Don. In the Caucasus, the Seventeenth Army retreated towards the Taman Peninsula, Brandenburg units frequently employed as rearguards. Quite uncharacteristically, Hitler authorised his men to fall back into the Taman Peninsula not only to protect the eastern approaches to the Crimea but also to provide a potential launching point for renewed offensive operations against the Caucasus during 1943. Luftwaffe reconnaissance noted a steady build-up of Soviet forces in ports along the Black Sea and a fresh storm finally broke on 4 February 1943, when elements of three Soviet infantry brigades landed at the tiny Red Army enclave at Cape Myskhako that had defied attempts to remove it and were soon firmly lodged ashore inside an expanding beachhead.

The high tide of Wehrmacht conquest had been unequivocally passed. In many ways 'Case Blue' had been doomed virtually from its conception. Adolf Hitler ignored advice from his senior commanders to maintain a single strong thrust against consecutive objectives and divided his Army Group South to chase diverging objectives simultaneously. The Wehrmacht had been unable to conquer the Soviet Union during 1941 on one continuous front; it was highly unlikely that, after suffering the grievous losses of the winter's defensive fighting, they would achieve two separate parallel military ambitions. The depleted Wehrmacht was forced to rely more heavily than ever before on Hungarian, Romanian and Italian troops alongside their own on the Eastern Front. While elements of these armies were highly motivated and effective soldiers, they were generally less committed and qualitatively inferior to their German counterparts, many of whom were fresh recruits by 1942 and lacking the ability of their predecessors. By sending spearheads in different directions, Hitler opened the middle ground to Soviet counter-attack, which was what encircled the Sixth Army and forced a retreat from the Caucasus lest those southerly forces became cut off from the west, whereupon they could be destroyed piecemeal.

Hitler and many Wehrmacht chiefs also underestimated the value of accurate intelligence which reported substantial numbers of uncommitted Red Army troops at the time that 'Case Blue' got underway. Stalin's generals had adopted a strategy of retreating before the German advance, trading physical territory for time and not allowing the Germans to succeed in their attempts to replicate the hugely destructive encirclement battles of *Barbarossa*. Where Soviet prisoners of war had numbered millions in 1941 and whole armies were destroyed, the prisoners taken in 1942 numbered instead in the hundreds of thousands. By the standards of the North African desert or Western Europe those numbers would be catastrophic; on the Eastern Front, they were not. The Wehrmacht had expected to encircle and destroy what they believed remained of the Red Army in the Don bend during the first months of 'Case Blue', but the Soviets retreated before they could be trapped. Though the retreat was frequently chaotic and lost huge quantities of equipment to the invader, it nonetheless preserved troop numbers that could be added to the vast reserves about to come into action. Hitler's fixation on Stalingrad can perhaps be explained by his mistaken and ill-informed belief that the Red Army was at its last gasp despite the warnings of some intelligence officers. Events soon proved otherwise.

CHAPTER 9

Regeneration, 1943

'He often said to me, "Schellenberg, always remember the goodness of animals. You see, my dachshund is discreet and will never betray me. I cannot say that of any human being..."'

Walter Schellenberg on Wilhelm Canaris

The New Year brought yet another organisational change to the *Lehrregiment 'Brandenburg' z.b.V. 800*, this time a lasting transition that enabled a complete 'repurposing' of the entire organisation. Since their inception, the Brandenburgers had been intended for commando operations in advance of Wehrmacht offensives. They had proved their guile and worth on all major fronts to which German land forces had been despatched. Through their combination of bravery and deception they had acted as effective 'pathfinder' troops that frequently allowed the Blitzkrieg to function at its optimum capability. Speed of movement was a hallmark of Germany's wars of conquest until the end of 1941. The Brandenburgers had also provided a skilled pool of men from which the Abwehr could draw potential agents and saboteurs who would act independently behind enemy lines. In this, they were less successful, although there are strong cases for a popular opinion that the highest echelons of the Abwehr were potentially acting against Germany's best interests; the determination of men like Canaris, Oster and Lahousen to see Hitler deposed and the Nazi regime destroyed before German was dragged into an abyss would, after all, require military failure. This, in turn, was best enabled by a comprehensive failure of military intelligence. Though this theory is disputed, there is certainly a degree of logic to it.

Regardless of the motivation, while the political machinations of those in command were unfolding in Berlin, the Brandenburg Regiment suffered accordingly. With increasingly infrequent use of the Brandenburgers as infiltration troops – both in disguise and not – on the Eastern and North African fronts during 1942, the regiment was more frequently utilised as a traditional light infantry unit. Bereft of heavy weapons, the Brandenburg companies were organised differently from traditional *Jäger* units, generally smaller and therefore more vulnerable when committed to standard infantry battles. They relied entirely on 'parent units' for the necessary supporting elements such as artillery and vehicles in order to function effectively, though such support was frequently either not available or not provided. By the end of 1942 casualties had risen accordingly as the Brandenburgers were thrown into the attritional battles of the front line. The staff at Abwehr II appeared to take little further interest in the Brandenburgers' deployment, either through distraction by more pressing intelligence concerns or a belated acknowledgement that the original covert dual-purpose edge Canaris envisioned the Brandenburgers providing for anti-Nazi rebellion was completely out of the question. If anything, the regiment had managed to attract an idealistic membership to replace those original members that had been either killed or rotated elsewhere. Canaris' original brief to Lahousen regarding its potential as a revolutionary weapon was moot after three years of war.

An interesting insight into the fragmenting of the Brandenburg Regiment's purpose can be read in a passage from the historical section of Herbert Kriegsheim's post-war book. It demonstrates a basic misunderstanding of the method of operation employed by the Brandenburgers – by their leader, of all people.

> It became increasingly apparent how the absence of a clear, uniform leadership led to a dispersal of our forces and endless creation of plans. On the one hand, Abwehr II, as well as the staff of the 'Brandenburg' Division, developed a truly worldwide plan on the globe, while, on the other hand, the parts of the 'Brandenburg' Division used at the front were thrown in 'everywhere' that gaps arose.
>
> The connection between the regiments, battalions and companies employed in action was completely inadequate. The Commander-in-Chief himself, for example, visited the regiment 'Brandenburg', which had been deployed in heavy partisan warfare in 1943, only three times in six months and then only for hours. Thus, at the Division Staff on the Lochowdamm in Berlin, a false picture about the type of deployment and the fighting power of the 'Brandenburgers' was increasingly developed. These visits also had a depressing effect on the troops deployed. One episode can illustrate this:
>
> The divisional commander landed at a battalion of the 4th Regiment, which had just finished a heavy battle in Tunis. The battalion commander presented the battalion and spontaneously, but in this front-line situation understandably, stretched his hand out to the divisional commander. The Commander-in-Chief shook his hand before the assembled battalion, but said to the battalion commander:

'It is I who will determine who offers a handshake.'

He then visited the company. When he saw a series of 'Brandenburgers', who were obviously unshaven and had already begun growing beards, he went to the company commander:

'Why are those people unshaven? These men are to leave immediately and get rid of their beards.'

The company commander tried to explain but received the 08/15 response:

'Keep quiet, I did not ask you!'

The battalion commander and the commander of the regiment are told the same harsh way. At the next meal, when the freshly shaved 'Brandenburgers' report to the divisional commander, he is also told that the next 'Brandenburg style' operation must fail because it was planned to put these men behind English lines disguised as bearded Arabs.[1]

The Brandenburgers had been created as an unorthodox unit of the Wehrmacht and clearly this irregular nature had become increasingly at odds with traditional military discipline and structure. Undoubtedly the gradual decline of the Abwehr did nothing to eliminate this apparent confusion and the Abwehr's failings – whether by design or not – had also served to irretrievably isolate the Wehrmacht's intelligence service. The competitive nature of inter-department relationships within the Third Reich had provided an opening for the power-hungry men of the SD to exploit. Reinhard Heydrich had long eyed Canaris' crown as Germany's intelligence chief and developed offices in the SS accordingly, the rise of his service motivated by naked ambition as much as a distrust of the Abwehr's loyalty to Germany and its Führer. Even Heydrich's death at the hands of Czech SOE agents on 4 June 1942 and subsequent replacement by Austrian *Obergruppenführer und General der Polizei* Ernst Kaltenbrunner did not end the SD–Abwehr contest.

One of Heydrich's most industrious protégés was Walter Schellenberg who in March 1942 with the rank of SS *Obersturmbannführer* was given command of *SD-Ausland* (officially known as 'Amt VI'); the civilian foreign intelligence agency of the Third Reich that had been established at the outbreak of war in 1939. The *SD-Ausland* was divided into sections similar to those of the Abwehr:

- Department A (Organisation and Administration);
- Department B (Espionage in the West);
- Department C (Espionage in the Soviet Union and Japan);
- Department D (Espionage in the North and South American Sphere);
- Department E (Espionage in Eastern Europe);
- Department F (Technical Matters).

Determined to engage in foreign missions, Schellenberg established Operation 'Zeppelin' as part of Amt VI C; an intelligence unit formed in 1942 to train and employ Caucasian and Asiatics from the Soviet republics of Central Asia, who had been recruited as prisoners of war, as agents against the Soviet regime. While sabotage was the key mission, the accumulating of essential information regarding the Soviet Union's military-industrial capability and spreading of anti-Bolshevik propaganda were all allocated to 'Zeppelin'. However, despite a considerable number of men being enlisted and trained at 'Sonderlager T' in Breslau-Oswitz, only a minority dropped into action and with little overall success. Through German operational inefficiency, security was poor and most men deployed were killed or captured soon after reaching their assigned areas.

A second major military intelligence-style operation was launched by Schellenberg during 1942 because of the arrival of the US Army's 34th Infantry Division in Northern Ireland, the first such unit to be shipped overseas after the declaration of war on the United States by Germany in December 1941. German plans for Eire had previously been limited to a brief idea of occupation that was soon abandoned in favour of keeping a wary eye on British attitudes towards the neutral Irish state while also providing limited support to the IRA. The neutrality of both Iceland and Greenland had already been compromised by US forces and an occupation of Eire was thought possible, which would open new ports and coastline to Allied forces to aid their Battle of the Atlantic. Schellenberg was involved in the planning of Operation 'Osprey' that entailed the use of volunteer commandos trained in sabotage and the use of British weaponry to land in Eire in the event of American occupation to train Irish volunteers of the IRA and any Irish Army units that had determined to resist the Americans.

Approximately one hundred SS volunteers were gathered together at the Totenkopf barracks at Oranienburg, appropriately named *Sonderlehrgang z.b.V. 'Oranienburg'* (Special Unit for Special Assignments 'Oranienburg'). Dutch SS-*Hauptsturmführer* Pieter van Vessem was placed in command and the men awaited training instructions for nearly a month before officially activated. Though ostensibly gathered for 'Osprey', the head of the SS-*Führungshauptamt* (SS Leadership Main Office) SS-*Obergruppenführer* Hans Jüttner, responsible for all organisational aspects of the Waffen SS, saw an opportunity to establish a counterpoint to the Brandenburg Regiment. With assistance from two Irish prisoners of war that had been recruited from Friesack Camp (Stalag XX-A (301)) – Fusilier James Brady and Private Frank Stringer – the SS volunteers were given English-language training, as well as instruction in the use of British weaponry, sabotage and explosives.

Nonetheless it was still to the Abwehr that the SS turned for advice regarding their newly established commando unit and its preparedness. Two

Brandenburgers were brought to Oranienburg, ostensibly to give English lessons, but in fact to evaluate the SS unit for its suitability for employment in Ireland. The pair, Bruno Reiger and Helmut Clissmann, had already participated in Hollmann's abortive Operation 'Seagull' during 1940. Clissmann was well suited to the task. He had first travelled to Ireland as a young student during the 1930s where he studied at Trinity College Dublin on a doctoral thesis. Before the outbreak of war, he returned to Dublin as representative of the German Academic Exchange, contacting the IRA and marrying Budge Mulcahy, from a strongly Republican family in County Sligo. After war was declared he returned to Germany and worked for the Abwehr on all matters pertaining to Ireland, enlisted into the Brandenburgers as a non-commissioned officer. He was involved in many Irish plans, though without any notable success.

His expert opinion was sought regarding the SS men and, though he did not doubt their fighting ability as they were all decorated and seasoned veterans, he found their general demeanour to be one of arrogance and contempt for all things foreign. Their English was generally poor and Clissmann doubted they would make any favourable impression on potential Irish recruits. He and Reiger returned an unfavourable report as well as encouraging the cancellation of 'Osprey' as the strategic situation appeared to already be changing in Ireland. There now appeared little chance of an Allied invasion and so the SS leadership acquiesced to their recommendation.

However, the SD decided to retain *Sonderlehrgang z.b.V. 'Oranienburg'* for other purposes. Though they would remain on the SD roster, they were seconded to the Waffen SS for training. Now that they had established their own version of the Brandenburg Regiment, the SS were able to step into the arena of secret operations that had previously been the domain of the Abwehr. Six of the Oranienburg volunteers were dropped into Persia (Operation '*Franz*') where they contacted hill tribes and attempted unsuccessfully to foment trouble against the British. Meanwhile the remainder continued sabotage training with an eye to potential deployment in the Balkans while Schellenberg awaited military developments in the region.

There were some in the SD who opposed this move into irregular operations and to circumvent potential problems Schellenberg removed the *Sonderlehrgang* from the office of Department F where they had been administratively placed and instead created a new 'Department S' for sabotage. To take charge of his new section, Schellenberg also placed in command a man who would have a profound impact on the future of many from the Brandenburg Regiment: *Obersturmführer* Otto Skorzeny. During the early summer of 1943, SS *Sonderlehrgang 'Oranienburg'* moved to a purpose-built facility in nearby Friedenthal and was redesignated SS *Sonderlehrgang z.b.V. 'Friedenthal'*. By this stage *Hauptsturmführer* van Vessem commanded one full company of volunteers and other smaller elements that included an independent transport element. Comprising a total of 300 Waffen SS men, the complement included fifty Dutchmen and Flemings and a few Hungarian *Volksdeutsche*. Skorzeny immediately set about expanding his unit which in October 1943 was renamed 502nd SS *Jagderverbänd*.

The development of an independent specialist commando unit by the SD echoed profoundly in the corridors of OKW. The need for the Brandenburgers to retain their original purpose was deemed to have now been considerably diminished, not least of all by the general war situation. The Abwehr had lost motivation to deploy the regiment as before, though their use as infantry had merely caused unnecessary casualties. The decision was therefore taken during November 1942 to raise the Brandenburg Regiment to the size of a division while also beginning the process of transferring direct command from Abwehr II to OKH in Berlin. The Brandenburgers were to become the 'house unit' of the German Army Staff.

The growth was to be managed in stages beginning on 1 January 1943 when the regiment would be renamed. From that date, it would be known as *Sonderverbänd 'Brandenburg'*, each existing company providing a nucleus for a battalion (*Abteilung*), each battalion that of a regiment until the new unit had reached full strength. The nomenclature and structure for this new unit was as follows:

Sonderverbänd 800 (former Regimental Staff).
Verband 801 (former 1st Battalion, Freiburg), *Major* Wilhelm Walther.
I, II and III *Abteilung*.
Verband 802 (former 2nd Battalion, Baden Unterwaltersdorf), *Oberstleutnant* von Kobylinski.
I, II and III *Abteilung*.
Verband 803 (former 3rd Battalion, Düren), *Oberstleutnant* Franz Jacobi.
I, II and III *Abteilung*.
Verband 804 (formed from newly enlisted elements in Brandenburg and fragments), *Hauptmann* Hollmann.
I, II and III *Abteilung*.
Verband 805 (formed from V-Leute), *Major* Ernst von Eickeren.

Regimental units remained outside of the formalised *Sonderverbänd* structure as this was intended purely as a temporary 'hold-all' title until divisional strength was attained over the first four months of 1943. Major Friedrich Heinz was also soon returned from his exile at the *Regenwurmlager* to take charge of *Verband 804*, created from the remnants of *Abteilung von Koenen* after its return from North Africa as well as members of the *V-Leute Abteilung* and other fragments of existing units, including *Leutnant* König's which had been active on the Danube.

With elements of the new *Sonderverbänd* still in combat both in the Soviet Union and North Africa, the build-up was conducted in a manner that was, at best, disjointed. As new units were formed they were also thrown piecemeal into action, predominantly against partisans. The first of these was the newly established *I Abteilung/Verband 801*, despatched towards the communications lines of Army Group North on 30 January 1943, when *Rittmeister* Plitt received orders to get his men on trains travelling from Frankfurt to Tilsit, East Prussia. After two weeks in Tilsit infantry barracks, they were instructed to join anti-partisan operations near Kretschy, Novgorod. There they went into action in heavily wooded marshland against fortified partisan groups, suffering a steady stream of casualties from direct enemy action and landmines.

Retreat in North Africa

While the full reorganisation to *Sonderverbänd* began in Germany, the decision was taken to raise Koenen's North African force to roughly battalion strength. Kuhlmann's coastal raider platoon, which was clearly no longer required for an attack on Malta, was to be sent to North Africa, coupled with the 9th Company of the 3rd Battalion, currently engaged in anti-partisan operations near Dorogobuzh in the Smolensk area. The men were to be immediately transferred to Germany for medical examination and inoculation to determine their fitness for tropical warfare before flying to Trapani in Sicily and then onwards to Tunisia. The existing Brandenburger presence in North Africa had already begun to withdraw westwards, when Montgomery's heavily reinforced army launched Operation 'Lightfoot' on 23 October with a five-and-a-half-hour artillery barrage. Though this second battle at El Alamein would rage for nearly two weeks, it resulted in a final collapse of the Axis lines, beginning the start of a general Axis retreat from which they would ultimately not recover.

Allied forces then landed in Morocco and Algeria in Operation 'Torch' on 8 November 1942 and the Axis found itself fighting on two North African fronts. From Chad, General Philippe Leclerc de Hauteclocque began his advance into Libya following the victory of El Alamein and on 16 December 1942 with 500 European and 2,700 African troops in 350 vehicles he began his move north. On 12 January 1943, he took the oasis town of Sabhā and Mizdah ten days later before finally reaching Tripoli on 26 January, where he linked up with the advancing Eighth Army.

Meanwhile on 12 November, Koenen's forces received the nomenclature *'Tropical Abteilung von Koenen'*. Kuhlmann and his men had arrived by Ju 52 transport in Tunis by 8 November and by Christmas 1942, Koenen's forces were on coastal guard duties in Tunisia while undergoing advanced training to increase both the cohesiveness of his unit as a whole and to allow specialised training for those men who had been earmarked for further operations against Allied communications and supply lines. By 21 December, *Tropical Abteilung von Koenen* was declared operational.

At Koenen's villa headquarters in the town of Hammamet south-east of Tunis, plans were made for the best method by which to accomplish fresh missions assigned to the Brandenburgers by *Oberst* Fritz Bayerlein, Rommel's Chief of Staff. Their objectives were three Tunisian bridges that spanned rivers and wadis at Sidi Boubaker (Gafsa), Kasserine and Tozeur, carrying railway lines vital to Allied supply routes and which had proven impervious to Stuka attacks. Combined with the railway track itself, telephone and telegraph wires also followed this route and cutting them had the potential to cause major disruption to the Allied offensive. Tunisian topography varied between verdant date plantations, marshland, mountains and wadis, and a complicated network of roads and bridges were essential for military forces to traverse the country in strength. A US Army report of the North African campaign describes the difficulties of Allied logistical concerns in Northwest Africa.

> Morocco is dominated by the Atlas Mountains . . . the coast line is rugged; it offers no natural harbors and strong winds cause heavy swells and surf, making landings precarious. The artificial ports of Safi, Port-Lyautey and Casablanca were essential, with Casablanca the key port. The limited railroad system consisted of a standard gauge main line . . . Algeria is dominated by high plateaus with steep-sided valleys and large rocky areas. Movement is principally confined to roads or railroads, except along the coastal rim. Vehicular movement from west to east is limited to the coastal road and one parallel interior route. These roads were capable of handling approximately 25-ton loads; most other roads would not handle heavy traffic even in dry weather . . . Tunisia, like Algeria and Morocco, presents war fighters with a challenging terrain. Cross-country movement along the coast was favorable, but in the interior, movement was confined to primitive roads through the passes. The interior was dominated by rocky alluvial plains connected by gorges and high mountains. The principal interior ranges were the western and eastern Dorsals. These dominating ranges would force operations along roads or railroads linking the towns, from north to south, of Beja, Le Kef, Thala, Kasserine and Gafsa in western Tunisia; with Mateur, Port du Fahs, Faid and

Gabes in eastern Tunisia; to the critical coastal towns of Bizerte and Tunis. The main railroad and highway followed the coastline from Tunis to Algeria.[2]

Koenen and his officers finalised their plans. The first of three attacks was made on 27 December 1942 on the bridge at Wadi el Kbir and was led by Koenen in three DFS 230 gliders, towed by Ju 52 transport aircraft. Due to the lack of large landing sites, barbed wire was wrapped around the gliders' skids to reduce the space required for a successful touch down. *Unteroffizier* Heinzel piloted the lead glider which carried Koenen, interpreter Reginald Bade and seven other men. The floor between their cramped bucket seats was filled with weapons and explosives. The remainder of the small attack force was carried in the two remaining gliders which were all airborne by midnight of Boxing Day.

Their course crossed Cape Bon and headed south towards Sfax and then Gabes, before heading west to the landing zone, the path masked by a squadron of Ju 88 bombers that accompanied their flight for a large part of the journey. However, one glider mistakenly followed the bombers beyond the planned separation point and was compelled to make a forced landing north of Sfax once their error was realised. Koenen's assault group was now reduced to two gliders.

The remaining DFS 230s released their tows at the agreed distance from their target at approximately 0200hrs, using thermal currents from the cooling earth to drift silently towards the objective and landing on target near the clearly visible 300m bridge span. Rapidly unloading, the men took nearby cover while Koenen and *Stabsfeldwebel* Neumann went ahead to reconnoitre the target. It was only then that they realised that they were a glider short due to absolute radio silence having been observed while airborne. The bridge appeared deserted and virtually unguarded, the French sentries sheltering from the cold night air in and around the small station building of Sidi Boubaker.

The subsequent planting of explosives was directed by Neumann; two 8lb charges on the bridge upper works; a further 6lbs on the track at each end of the bridge; the final 160lbs in two separate charges attached to the bridge's centre pile. A Bavarian member of the team climbed a telegraph pole and hacked down the lines with a hatchet, swearing loudly as he nearly fell to the ground with them, provoking frantic arm-waving from his commander urging him to be quiet lest he attract guards to the scene. However, all remained silent.

It was only once they had attached all the charges that the Germans realised that their fuses were still packed in the third glider. The exasperated Koenen was placated by Neumann who habitually carried several spare fuses, though only of sixty seconds duration each. While the remainder of the party retreated, three men at each explosive point simultaneously lit the fuses under Neumann's direction and jumped into the wadi below. As Neumann himself attempted to run, his feet became entangled in the scattered telegraph wires and he fell, *Feldwebel* Norbert Slouka jumping from the bridge into the wadi to assist him but spraining his ankle as he did so. Neumann recovered and untangled himself to drag Slouka clear just before shattering explosions blew their bridge apart.

Koenen immediately ordered all men to rendezvous at the gliders which were then set on fire. Two men were missing but with French troops arriving on the scene there was no time to wait for them and the Brandenburgers withdrew, guided by two Arabs. The injured Slouka apparently volunteered to await the arrival of the two men and became separated from the group, never to be seen alive again.[3] The escaping Germans had nearly 130km to cross and opted at first to travel by night and rest during the hours of daylight. Near dawn the following morning they had halted in a small wadi near Djebel bou Ramli when a small group of Arabs were spotted approaching their position. Koenen's Tunisian guide made cautious contact and discovered one of the Arabs actually to be one of the missing Brandenburgers, a German Palestinian named Berger whose mastery of the language had enabled him to contact anti-French Arabs who subsequently reunited him with Koenen. The second missing man, Hannes Feldmann, would later arrive in Gafsa six days after the attack, riding an Arab donkey and looking particularly well fed. Koenen's men force marched for six days until finally reaching the Italian garrison at Maknassey from where they returned by truck to Hammamet. Following the success of his mission, on 1 January 1943, Friedrich von Koenen was promoted to *Hauptmann*.

A second Brandenburger glider attack also took off from the Bizerta airfield at the same time as Koenen's men. Their target was a road and rail bridge northeast of Kasserine, though the raid would ultimately be a significant failure. Helmut Spaeter's book on the Brandenburgers includes a letter written to him by one of the mission's survivors, Willi Clormann:

> For my operation: we also flew with ten men in a glider. The glider pilot was a Luftwaffe *Oberleutnant* from the *Fliegerführers* Staff in Tunis (name unknown). Operation commander was a *Leutnant* who came to us before the mission, *Leutnant* Hagenauer, *Führer der Pioniergruppe* nicknamed 'Poldi'. We were supposed to have three gliders, but only ended up with two because one had to back out. In the two remaining gliders, engineers were needed primarily and so I, who was a leader of a security group, had to leave my people behind and could only take with me one man as cover for the engineers armed with an MG42 machine gun.
>
> We landed in a different valley as planned on 26 December 1942, after being towed by Ju 52 aircraft at a height of about 2000m following violent

anti-aircraft fire that made our *Oberleutnant* pilot throw some wild manoeuvres. The pilot broke both wrists and had to be left behind at the crate. [Arabs discovered him the next day and he was then captured by Allied troops.] We nine had a lot of trouble, our leader was heavily wounded as well as the Engineer NCO and we took them on our march with us. I had taken over leading the company, because I knew the map and the course of our planned action. We were able to orientate ourselves the same night that we landed and we were about 20km south-west of the target. During the day, we rested, tended our wounded and divided all the crates, explosive cords, ignition cables so that we could carry them in the early afternoon. At dusk, I was able to find a dromedary rider with his animal, who naturally had to take over our load. This knowledgeable guide took us in the right direction, but unfortunately he did not miss a trick and after he had already received a lot of Francs from us, betrayed us to the Frenchmen in Kasserine and was probably paid money for our heads there.[4]

After reaching striking distance of their target, the struggling group remained hidden by day following the Arab's departure. Hagenauer ordered Clormann and his subordinate *Obergefreiter* Franz Wodjerek to move ahead independently and reconnoitre the bridge and the two men dutifully crept forward with only the essentials to study the objective through field glasses. After about two hours they heard gunfire from behind them and observed French troops moving towards their comrades' position. The firing did not last long and it was obvious that the remainder had either been killed or captured. With little choice, the pair opted to strike out for German lines. With 180km to cover they carried only sixty-seven cigarettes, two boxes of matches, one can of the sugary drink Cola Dalma, one tin of heavily caffeinated Chocacola chocolate, and two pistols with seven bullets between them. After six days, their hunger was acute, though a sympathetic Bedouin they encountered shared couscous and chicken with them before leading them to a German outpost at Pichon. After the two gaunt and bearded men managed to convince the sceptical garrison that they were members of the Wehrmacht, they were transported back to Tunis.

Attempts to attack a pair of railway bridges between Morsott and Tebessa on 30 December by men of *Fallschirm-Pionier Bataillon 11* (airborne engineers) also failed after inexperienced pilots put the Germans aground miles from their targets, resulting in their swift capture. Only the commanding officer, *Oberleutnant* Friedrich, and one Tunisian guide escaped captivity by jumping over the tailboard of an Allied truck as they were hauled away. However, one further Brandenburger raid was successfully mounted, on 10 January 1943 against the railway bridge over Wadi el Melah north-east of Gafsa.

Leutnant Luchs planned to take eight men for the mission, using two captured British 1.5-ton Bedford trucks, known to the Germans as '*Flitzers*', rather than using glider assault. Travelling via the Italian outpost on the elevation Djebel el Morra, Luchs was informed by the garrison's commander of French horsemen – *Spahis*, drawn from the indigenous population – and armoured vehicles near the bridge. Following a difficult journey over frequent patches of loose sand in which the trucks became periodically bogged down, they arrived to within 2km of the bridge. Leaving the remainder of his men in concealment, Luchs and *Feldwebel* Klima approached on foot clothed in Arab garb. They surveyed the bridge, but also spotted *Spahis* behind them that had discovered their tyre tracks and were approaching the concealed trucks. Quickly rejoining their men, a brief firefight followed before the Brandenburgers successfully escaped with their vehicles intact.

Rather than abandon the mission, Luchs opted to regroup at el Morra before repeating the attempt, reasoning that the French would be celebrating their victory over the foiled German raid and unlikely to expect a second attempt. In this he was correct. Retracing their path, the two trucks halted 1km from the bridge and the men disembarked to approach on foot and scout the situation, finding their target completely undefended. Returning later with one of the trucks loaded with explosives, Luchs, Klima and two others attached explosives to the central span, upper bridge works and tracks while the remaining five men fanned out to act as lookouts and provide covering fire if required. Unhindered by the enemy, they eventually drove away leaving ten-minute fuses burning behind them. Even though the captured British chemical fuses burnt slower than expected in the cold night air, turning them unexpectedly into twenty-five-minute fuses, the resultant blasts destroyed the bridge completely, a locomotive and two wagons later seen by aerial reconnaissance photos to have subsequently crashed into the wadi below.

Though the effect of these sabotage missions was negligible to the outcome of the North African campaign, they played on the nerves of Allied railwaymen. The existing French railway system in their North African territories was small and inadequate throughout. Within Tunisia, the topography arguably placed even greater demands on transport infrastructure than neighbouring regions. Though new American rolling stock was arriving in North Africa, the railway's capacity remained limited and trains were overburdened to make the best use of what was available. Unable to effectively counter German sabotage operations, railwaymen were never sure if bridges were standing or track undamaged as they hauled their cargos without lights through the Tunisian nights.

The British too attempted a commando mission to destroy a valuable bridge still in German hands: this time a high, vulnerable, sixteen-span Roman viaduct near Bouficha over which Axis supplies were taken by rail from Bizerta and Tunis to the southern front. The bridge had withstood air attack, being heavily defended by Flak and so Operation 'Felice I' (sometimes called 'Felicity') was launched. Eight commandos led by Captain J. Eyre of the Royal Engineers were to land from submarine HMS *Unbroken* in four folboats, make their way inland and sabotage the span. Eyre's second in command was Lieutenant P.M. Thomas of the Royal East Kent Regiment (The Buffs) while the remainder of the raiding group were Free French commandos.

> Through the periscope, the town of Hammamet looked tired, sun-baked, empty and lazy; a cluster of white, low-roofed buildings dried up by the desert sun. As I swept the shore towards Bou Ficha where the commandos were to be disembarked, however, the scene changed. The road was alive with heavy traffic moving south. The beach was filled with patrols, marching singly with bayonets fixed, or driving backward and forward in lorries and open trucks.[5]

The eight commandos successfully landed on the night of 28 January. Unfortunately, men of the *Küstenjäger Abteilung* were watching the coast and *Gefreiter* Heinrich Müller detected the approach of the enemy kayaks and subsequent disembarkation of the men and their explosives. Brief flurries of gunfire followed that raised a general alert, flares fired which illuminated the beach and kayaks and, offshore, the outline of HMS *Unbroken* that was still surfaced. With no option but to retreat from the area, the submarine fired a single star shell to signal their intention to the men ashore before diving away from approaching German patrol craft and returning to Malta. All eight commandos were captured.

A second landing that night in the Hammamet area was made by *MTB307* that dropped Squadron-Leader Hugh Mallory-Falconer, an ex-French Foreign Legionnaire and Royal Corps of Signals officer before he had enlisted in the Royal Air Force in April 1940. Mallory-Falconer was an SOE signals officer who had been based in Gibraltar and had previously established the North African signals system for the regional SOE and OSS agents and handlers. Codenamed 'Blue', Mallory-Falconer and two other men were put ashore but captured almost immediately by Brandenburger men who were by that time on high alert.[6]

It soon became apparent to the Germans that the British officer was intended to organise resistance around Tunis and subsequent radio messages were sent masquerading as Mallory-Falconer – his headquarters radio contact comprehensively fooled by the ruse as adequate security checks had not been put in place before the disastrous landing. Reinforcements were requested by the

Germans and ten Corsican agents and saboteurs were later landed by sea near Kelibia, all of them dressed in civilian clothes.

A local Abwehr officer was given the task of intercepting the scheduled landing: *Major* Hans-Joachim Rudloff, who had left the Brandenburg Regiment back in November 1940. Following service in Spain and the Soviet Union, Rudloff had been transferred to Tripoli in October 1942 for counter-intelligence duties. It was then that he first encountered the SD in his official capacity. The competition between the Abwehr and SD had intensified by the beginning of 1943 and the regional SD commander *Obersturmbannführer* Walter Rauff was a particularly unpleasant man to work with. Rauff was the head of an SS *Einsatzkommando* that had been transferred from Athens to Tunis to implement the Third Reich's policy against Tunisia's Jewish population. Fortunately, conditions in the bridgehead were never conducive for Rauff to properly begin his work, not least due to outright hostility towards him and his mission from the Italian authorities. Rudloff clashed with Rauff on several occasions regarding the treatment of captured agents and commandos and fortunately it was Rudloff who was responsible for the interception of the Corsican landing party.

Two MTBs transported the Corsican agents from Malta and they made landfall on 6 April after the correct recognition signals were received from the darkened shoreline. After landing, as the party attempted to leave the beach, they were lured into an ambush by one of Rudloff's men and swiftly captured. Despite specific orders that none of the saboteurs were to be harmed, their commander Captain Brun was shot in the heat of the moment by an excited soldier, dying in hospital of his wound several days later. Obeying specific instructions, Rudloff handed the captives over to the SD, though on the strict agreement that they would only be interrogated in the presence of Abwehr officers. Intervening directly with Rauff against the Corsicans' execution – and in direct contravention of Hitler's 'Commando Order' – Rudloff was able to virtually smuggle the men to Europe and subsequent internment as prisoners of war. Rudloff took possession of their wireless equipment and continued to transmit false information to the Allies that included fictitious attacks on ammunition dumps, grounded aircraft, transport units and Axis communication links.

The troops that Rudloff had used to intercept the Corsicans were Arab volunteers of the *Kommando Deutsch-Arabischer Truppen*. In 1942, *General* Felmy and his Chief of Staff, together with *Admiral* Canaris, had held a conference in Berlin with the former Iraqi Prime Minister Rashid Ali and then another in Rome with the Grand Mufti of Jerusalem, a Palestinian Arab nationalist and Muslim leader in Mandatory Palestine. During these talks the future of Felmy's existing German-Arab *Sonderverbänd* troops was discussed, both Ali and the Grand Mufti believing them misplaced in their current position in the Soviet Union as they had been trained and ideologically equipped for war in the African desert. However, despite these opinions relayed to Hitler by Felmy in conference at the Führer's Ukrainian headquarters, the situation remained unchanged for some time. The increasingly disgruntled Arab troops had been in action in the Soviet Union until the Allied 'Torch' landings fortuitously prompted the transfer of at least the Arab training battalion (3rd Battalion, *Sonderverbänd 287*) to Palermo, Sicily. Meanwhile, the remainder of *Sonderverbänd 287* and *288* were scheduled for transfer back to North Africa, its members given permission to wear an insignia bearing the emblem of a sun rising behind palm trees. Felmy's *Sonderverbänd F* was also renamed *Generalkommando z.b.V.* (Corps Headquarters for Special Employment) on 25 September at Stalino in line with its impending change of theatre.

Meanwhile, in Africa, the arrival of large numbers of German troops in the Tunisian bridgehead resulted in an unexpected increase in the number of Arab volunteers for Wehrmacht service; a combination of idealists and unemployed opportunists. During December 1942, *Oberbefehlshaber Süd*, *Generalfeldmarschall* Albert Kesselring, created an administrative command called the *Kommando Deutsch-Arabischer Truppen* (KODAT). The Arab training battalion was then moved from Sicily to Tunisia to supervise the induction and instruction of recruits, the men equipped with Wehrmacht uniforms wherever possible, though most were outfitted in captured stocks of French 1935-model khaki uniforms without badges and with a white armband on the right arm bearing the words '*Im Dienst der Deutschen Wehrmacht*' ('In the Service of the German Armed Forces'). Sleeve shields emblazoned with the words 'Free Arabia' were also issued as quickly as they could be manufactured.

Recruits were organised into separate companies for Tunisians, Algerians and Moroccans, each commanded by German senior NCOs or officers with a small number of Wehrmacht ex-Foreign Legionnaires rated as NCOs in the company to provide a professional backbone to each cadre. Though equipment and training facilities were limited, each company numbered approximately 150 men by the end of 1942. With no heavy weapons and most small arms taken from captured French material, the KODAT troops were predominantly tasked with guarding the coast. By February 1943, sufficient quantities of German weapons had reached Tunisia for the companies to be expanded each to battalion strength; two Tunisian battalions, one Algerian battalion and one Moroccan battalion, each of three infantry companies and one heavy weapons company equipped with mortars and heavy machine guns. Attached to the 5th Panzer Army, KODAT's training was severely disrupted when the unit's commander *Major* Hans Schober and *Oberstleutnant* Hermann Meyer-Ricks of *Generalkommando z.b.V.*, who had been given the original task of raising the formation, were killed by low-flying enemy aircraft on 24 February. With Felmy's other Arab units still involved in unexpectedly heavy fighting along the Mius River in southern Russia, there were no current staff available to replace the two dead officers and so, with men experienced in Arab–German relations difficult to find, *Oberst* Theodor von Hippel was transferred from his Abwehr post to take command.

During mid-February, Hippel's men took part in Fifth Panzer Army's attack towards Tebessa which bogged down in short order, before the KODAT troops were forced on to the defensive. Tunisian soldiers were placed in the centre of the Mareth Line but with disastrous results due to their inexperience and lack of training. Taken to their positions during the hours of darkness, the troops lit fires to keep warm and were immediately shelled by German artillery. Alarmed by the gunfire, Allied units facing them were placed on immediate alert and soon attacked, overrunning the Tunisians who were withdrawn from the front line and thereafter used for constructing defensive positions towards the rear.

During mid-April, some of the KODAT German personnel and all trained Muslims were reinforced by ex-Foreign Legion troops and consolidated as a *Kampfgruppe* near Ferryville, comprising two infantry companies and one heavy company with howitzers, Flak weapons, heavy machine guns and an anti-tank platoon.

The troops appear to have fought effectively in the northern sector of the Tunisian front until disbanded in the last chaotic days of the German presence in North Africa. On 8 May 1943, the unit's supply train was disbanded and records destroyed and the survivors, numbering less than a hundred men, awaited evacuation to Italy or were later taken into captivity. Amongst those captured by American troops was Theodor von Hippel, father of the Brandenburgers.

The End in North Africa

Before the destruction of the Germans' remaining Tunisian bridgehead, Koenen's 'Tropical Battalion' saw action against both British and American troops. During February, his Brandenburgers took part in Operation '*Frülingswind*' as part of *Generaloberst* Hans-Jürgen von Arnim's Fifth Panzer Army, the operation launched on 14 February in northern Tunisia. Attacking along the Faid pass, German and Italian troops initially mauled the Americans at the battle of Sidi Bou Zid and subsequent recapture of the strategically located town of Sbeitla. The Brandenburgers lost four men killed in the fighting but accumulated twenty-seven captured medium tanks, sizeable quantities of ammunition, twenty-three guns and 700 prisoners at the peak of the battle. To the south, Rommel had launched his own offensive on the following day, Operation '*Morgenluft*', that shattered

American forces at Kasserine, his master plan being to push on and capture Tebessa. However, despite their respective successes both offensives gradually petered out, largely as a result of personal hubris. The relationship between Arnim and Rommel was particularly frigid; Rommel regarding his counterpart who had recently transferred to North Africa from Russia as 'a traditional Reichswehr soldier, addicted to a monocle and high boots' while the latter viewed Rommel as a 'jumped-up, publicity-seeking second-rater'. Their individual egos and ambitions caused both offensives to be completely uncoordinated operations, when a single decisive stroke might well have inflicted lasting damage to the Allies. Rommel had indeed devised an offensive scheme that could have hit the British First Army with enough force to send them reeling back into Algeria, while the overstretched and exhausted Eighth Army advancing from Libya would have been relatively powerless to intervene. However, Arnim refused to endorse the idea and relinquish control of what was his first independent command. Correspondingly, one combined armoured strike became two mismatched attacks, both beaten back to their starting lines. Despite Rommel thereafter being promoted to overall command of the newly ordained '*Heeresgruppe Afrika*' to defend Tunisia with Fifth Panzer Army and Italian First Army, the last meagre opportunity to hold the position had been squandered.

Nonetheless, Axis forces continued to fight. Bad weather that hampered Allied operations assisted the fighting defence, the area held by Koenen's Brandenburgers facing the advancing British First Army. During early April, the 2nd Lancashire Fusiliers attacked and captured the heights of Djebel Ang, struggling over the difficult terrain. General Sir Kenneth Anderson, GOC First Army, wrote in his despatches:

> This mountain land is a vast tract of country, every hill in which is large enough to swallow up a brigade of infantry, where consolidation on the rocky slopes is very difficult, in which tanks can only operate in small numbers, where movement of guns and vehicles is very restricted and where the division had to rely on pack mules for its supplies and to carry wireless telegraphy sets, tools and mortars.

As a combined group of Fusiliers and 5th Northamptons then attempted to push on to take the dominating mountainous area known as Tanngoucha and its key village of Heidous, they were hit by a severe counter-attack in thick mist at about 0430hrs on 15 April by the 1st Battalion of the 962nd *Afrika* Regiment and Koenen's Tropical *Abteilung* (operationally attached to 334th Division, Fifth Panzer Army). In the fierce fighting that followed, two British companies suffered severe casualties and virtually a third of them were captured in the thick fog, the

47. Brandenburgers kayaking towards the Murmansk railway line, August 1942.

48. Adjusting the small outboard motor aboard one of the Brandenburgers' kayaks while headed towards the Murmansk line.

49. Brandenburgers in Finland used a mixture of German, Soviet and Finnish uniform and equipment, such as the Finnish Suomi KP/-31 submachine gun as pictured here.

50. Fritz Babuke, pictured here as *Oberleutnant* following his receipt of the EK I.

51. Chief instructor *Leutnant zur See* Alfred von Wurzian (left) at the first parade of the newly formed *Meeresjäger Abteilung*. Brandenburger *Gebirgsjäger Hauptmann* Fritz Neitzert (middle) was the Abteilung's first commander.

52. The Brandenburger *Meeresjäger Abteilung* on parade in Piazza Dante, Valdagno, 1944. The recruits included men from all military branches, including the Waffen SS.

53. 'Case Blue', the advance into the Caucasus in pursuit of oil, marked the greatest penetration to the south-east by the Wehrmacht, spearheaded by Brandenburger units. This NCO carries a Russian map case.

54. Alexander von Pfuhlstein (left), pictured here as commander of 154th Infantry Regiment, attending a ceremony honouring fallen troops of the 58th Infantry Division at Novogrod, 1942. At right is the divisional commander, *Generalmajor* Karl von Graffen.

55. *Admiral* Canaris inspecting Brandenburger troops with Friedrich Wilhelm Heinz (middle) and regimental commander Alexander von Pfuhlstein (right). Pfuhlstein's antipathy towards Heinz is well documented, though Heinz was a confidant of Canaris and the anti-Hitler circle within the Abwehr.

56. An NCO briefing during the advance of 'Case Blue'. The *Oberfeldwebel* (third from left) carries the helmsman (*Steuermann*) qualification badge for engineer assault boats.

(right) 57. Cooperation between Brandenburg and Romanian forced had begun before the invasion of the Soviet Union, with Brandenburg units posted as security for Romanian oilfields. A large Romanian commitment fought alongside the German advance into the Caucasus.

(below, left) 58. Siegfried Grabert's death in action announced in the newspaper *Die Bewegung*, the central publication of the National Socialist German Student Union.

(below) 59. Adrian Baron von Fölkersam following the award of his Knight's Cross. His unit's infiltration behind Soviet lines to Maykop remains one of the Brandenburgers' most remarkable exploits.

60. Fighting for the oil transport depots in the Caucasus, 1942.

61. The bridge over the Bjelaja named after *Leutnant d.R.* Ernst Prochaska, the young commander of 8th Company killed immediately after its capture from Soviet troops. Prochaska was awarded the Knight's Cross posthumously.

62. *Oberleutnant* Karl-Heinz Oesterwitz (left), pictured during the advance into the Caucasus.

63. Kurt Konrad Steidl, commander of the 1st Battalion, 2nd *Jäger*-Regiment. He was awarded the Knight's Cross on 26 January 1944 for action against Greek partisans around Klisoura during the previous December in which his unit broke through the partisan lines, stormed and captured the bridge in Prijepolje and established a bridgehead in the town, destroying two partisan brigades. In 1944 he transferred to Skorzeny's SS command.

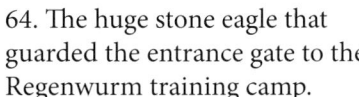

64. The huge stone eagle that guarded the entrance gate to the Regenwurm training camp.

65. A snapshot of personnel in training at *Regenwurmlager* shows the diverse ethnicity from which both the Brandenburgers and the Abwehr as a whole drew members whom they considered best suited to operations within different geographical areas.

66. The brutality of anti-partisan warfare became an increasingly common theatre of action for the Brandenburgers. Ambushes on vulnerable road and rail communications networks were frequent and reprisals swift.

67. Brandenburgers were used in the inhospitable forests and marshes that surrounded the Prip'yat' River to fight Soviet partisans in 1944 as the Wehrmacht retreated. Here a casualty is fortunate to be evacuated by air.

68. *Jäger* of the Brandenburger Division receiving fresh winter clothing.

69. Men of the *Kustenjäger Abteilung* at sea on the Adriatic aboard a heavy *Sturmboot*.

70. *Leutnant* Helmut Demetrio (in glasses) and his French men of the 8th Company, II Battalion, in the south of France.

71. An Italian soldier of the Blackshirt III 'M' Assault Battalion '9 September (Pontida)', commanded by Major Carlo Zanotti, which placed itself under Brandenburger command following the armistice between the Allies and Italy.

72. Brandenburger troops were committed to searching for and fighting Greek guerrillas, which were themselves verging on civil war between opposing political ideologies. The Balkans became a morass of difficult and brutal operations for the German commandos.

73. Brandenburgers and Chetniks, uneasy allies of convenience – most of the time.

(above) 74. Brandenburgers question captured Yugoslavian Partisans. Tito's troops were accorded the status of combatants, rather than guerrillas, by the Germans.

(left) 75. Well armed, disciplined and well organised, the communist Partisans that followed Marshal Josip Broz Tito were formidable adversaries for Brandenburger units.

76. Brandenburgers in action in Yugoslavia, 1943.

(left) 77. Brandenburger *Fallschirmjäger* rowing ashore on Levitha from a Junkers Ju 52 floatplane, 18 October 1943.

(below) 78. Brandenburger troops during the fighting for Leros, November 1943.

(below) 79. Troops of the 1st Company, *Kustenjäger Abteilung* at the 150mm battery on Monte Racchi, Leros.

80. Relaxing once the fighting had ended on Leros; the last great success for German forces in the Aegean.

81. Brandenburgers displaying an interesting mix of uniforms, Leros, 1943.

82. Wilhelm Walther (left) is seen here with *Oberleutnant* Max Wandrey and *General der Flieger* Helmuth Felmy at Wandrey's Knight's Cross ceremony, 9 January 1944.

83. Brandenburger troops boarding a *Marinefahrprähme* in the Dodecanese, 1943.

84. *Oberleutnant* Werner Lau, II Battalion, 4th Regiment 'Brandenburg'.

(left) 85. Austrian-born *Major* Karl-Heinz Oesterwitz, pictured here after the establishment of Panzer Grenadier Division 'Brandenburg'. During October 1940 he commanded the 7th Company of the Brandenburg Regiment, later taking part in the Balkans campaign and Operation '*Barbarossa*'. He was awarded the German Cross in Gold for capturing an important bridge at Belorechensk as part of the advance into the Caucasus in August 1942. During fighting in the West Caucasus he was awarded the Knight's Cross, the Oak Leaves following on 10 February 1945.

(right) 86. Friedrich 'Fritz' Kühlwein, last commander of the Brandenburg Division, before its conversion to Panzer Grenadier status.

(below) 87. Brandenburger PaK40 of the 2nd Regiment in action against Yugoslavian Partisans.

(above) 88. Otto Skorzeny in Budapest, 1944. His commando mission to the Hungarian capital was carried out by his SS *Jägdverbände*, which included a large cadre of transferred Brandenburgers. In the middle is Adrian Baron von Fölkersam, one of the first Brandenburgers to join his command.

(below) 89. Dawn on the Eastern Front.

(right) 90. The Brandenburg cuff title; somewhat ironically not awarded until 17 August 1944 after the division was passing out of the realm of special forces.

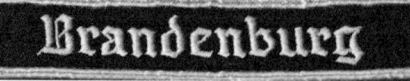

remaining British troops being forced to retreat. At 2000hrs the next evening as a fresh British battalion prepared to mount a renewed attack, Brandenburg men reached an escarpment immediately above the British headquarters and began to throw grenades into the midst of the men below. In the confused melee that drew in British engineers, anti-aircraft gunners, clerks and drivers, the Germans were finally dislodged and forced to retreat. The slugging match that was the battle for Tanngoucha continued until 3 May when it was finally taken by 38th (Irish) Brigade.

During February, the dramatic reorganisation of the Brandenburg Regiment as it evolved to divisional level was well underway when yet another change was forced upon them. On 8 February *Oberst* Haehling von Lanzenauer died in hospital in Schömberg in the Black Forest, from a lung infection and jaundice that he had contracted on the Eastern Front.[7] As a replacement, the former commander of 154th Infantry Regiment and Knight's Cross holder *Generalmajor* Alexander von Pfuhlstein was confirmed.

> He had been proposed to Canaris by General Oster. A very obstinate Prussian, typical Reichswehr officer, though he was an unconcealed foe of the Nazi regime. I know that Oster, with and via Pfuhlstein, followed a special purpose with the Brandenburg Division.[8]

Pfuhlstein was a man of strong convictions and character, though those principles did not include belief in National Socialism or its ambitions for Germany. The eldest of three children, Pfuhlstein had served in the First World War as a *Fähnrich* in the Prussian 4th Foot Guards Regiment before being commissioned and going on to win both classes of Iron Cross and the wound badge in black. After joining the Luftwaffe in 1933 he returned to the Army in August 1935. However, his reputation was for pessimism that manifested itself in often bitter sarcasm, *General der Infanterie* Kurt Brennecke labelling him a 'difficult character'.

During the 1930s he had served as part of Oster's *Abwehrstelle Hannover* and had engaged in conspiratorial discussions with his chief, examining the options that existed for the removal of Hitler and destruction of his regime. However, wartime posting to combat and the award of the Knight's Cross as commander of the 154th Infantry Regiment following heavy fighting in the Demyansk pocket had transformed Pfuhlstein into a purely military-minded officer, unbeknownst to Oster and Canaris. He later went as far as disavowing any attempts to 'politicise' his Brandenburg unit, which led to much animosity towards such officers as Friedrich Heinz whom he viewed as a Machiavellian intriguer, rather than an effective combat officer.

After his confirmation as commander of the *Sonderverbänd*, Pfuhlstein visited Koenen's command in Tunisia, assisting in the restructuring of the 'Tropical Company'. During February, fresh men and equipment for the *Küstenjäger Abteilung* had arrived, transported by rail from Germany to southern Italy, then onwards by freighter to Palermo and ultimately Tunisia. Included in the new intake was *Oberleutnant* Dr Kurt Wagner who took command of the company which was now provided with two heavy *Sturmboote* – originally intended for use by the fledgling *Küstenjäger* for Caspian Sea operations and crossing the Volga River – and a pair of small torpedo carriers, the 'Schneider boats'.

When Pfuhlstein left North Africa, he took Koenen with him for return to Germany and use of his front-line expertise in the expanding *Sonderverbänd Brandenburg*, overall command of the 'Tropical Company' passing to *Oberleutnant* Hoffmann who was assisted by his adjutant *Oberleutnant* Blödern. Dr Wagner continued to direct the *Küstenjäger* based at Ferryville under the tactical control of *Korvettenkapitän* Friedrich Kemnade's 3rd S-boat Flotilla. The Brandenburger boats patrolled the Tunisian coast near Bizerte on security duties and mounted minelaying off Tabarka near the Algerian border, at least three men killed and five seriously wounded during the latter operation. When Tunis fell to the Allies on 7 May, the *Küstenjäger* assisted in the operation of Luftwaffe Siebel Ferries to evacuate sick and wounded men across La Goulette under enemy artillery fire to German lines in the north and evacuation aboard the last available Ju 52 aircraft leaving the Tunisian bridgehead.

Rommel's final offensive was launched on 6 March 1943, when he attacked the Eighth Army at the Battle of Medenine using three panzer divisions. However, forewarned by Ultra intelligence from Bletchley Park, Montgomery deployed a daunting screen of anti-tank guns that destroyed fifty-two irreplaceable panzers. The offensive was called off after three days and Rommel transferred back to Germany, his command handed over to his rival Arnim and the 'Desert Fox' never returning to Africa.

With the final Axis collapse only days away, both Schneider boats were blown up by their crews while the *Sturmboote* began ferrying escaping troops to Sicily, using the cover of darkness to avoid the overwhelming Allied air superiority. They sailed, led by Dr Wagner, from Ferryville through Lac de Bizerte on the morning of 8 May as French troops entered the outskirts of Bizerte itself. Wagner headed east towards Cap Zabib, bringing his boats alongside the small fishing harbour's pier, where they came under repeated air attack by B 26 and P 40 aircraft though suffering only minor damage. The collapse of *Heeresgruppe Afrika* was evidenced by the hundreds of disorganised men that arrived at the coast, abandoning vehicles and heavy weapons as panic set in upon the realisation that there was no great 'sea lift' to take them to Sicily. The two Brandenburger boats were apparently threatened by armoured troops demanding passage at gunpoint before some form of military discipline was restored.

Wagner was ordered to collect the staff of Fifth Panzer Army, now under the command of General Gustav von Vaerst, in headquarters bunkers near Bizerte. While he remained with the boats, *Oberleutnant* Kuhlmann made the collection overland, returning after two hours to find both Kurt Wagner and his boat's *Oberbootsmannsmaat* Rudolf Ludewig dead, killed in continuing air attacks. Assuming command, Kuhlmann finally left the bitter scene of German defeat in Tunisia. As the two Brandenburg boats sailed for Sicily they transported fifty-three staff officers of the Panzer Army – primarily specialists and General Staff officers bound for the Eastern Front – though their commander Vaerst was not amongst them. After sharing a last fine cigar with Kuhlmann he had politely asked him to communicate a message to Berlin: 'A *General* will not leave his command post when tens of thousands of Germany's best soldiers are uselessly consigned to captivity and facing an uncertain fate. My presence with them is now more important than the return to a home in which this German *General* no longer believes.' Kuhlmann also took an unassuming Arab with him; Achmed el Bedoiu who had been Dr Kurt Wagner's batman and who, with no desire to remain in North Africa, subsequently became Kuhlmann's.

After a successful crossing, the *Sturmboote* made landfall in Trapani, the Brandenburger men and their boats later transported by rail to Langenargen on Lake Constance, where the *Küstenjäger Abteilung* was undergoing training with Conrad von Leipzig and beginning further expansion. On 26 May *Vizeadmiral* Eberhard Weichold (*Marinegruppenkommando* Italy) subverted any potential intended role for the Brandenburger's *Küstenjäger* in operations against what was now Allied-controlled North Africa:

[VA] Weichold has investigated how attacks on the enemy communication lines in North Africa could be carried out by harassing squads. The operations can be carried out on an extensive coast and would tie down considerable enemy forces. Vice Admiral Weichold considers the men of the special division 'Brandenburg' unsuitable for this task, since it is a question of purely military offensive actions for which dashing volunteers are needed. The Chief of Staff, Naval Staff considers it necessary that the command of operations of this type be in the hands of a naval officer with a staff of officers from all the armed services. The operations must be conducted over sea and will consequently be dependent on this element so that successful execution of such operations could only be expected if under the responsible command of a naval officer. The Chief of Staff, Naval Staff is going to submit suggestions to the Chief, Naval Staff accordingly.[9]

Meanwhile, amongst those men left behind in Tunisia were the last remnants of the Brandenburger 'Tropical Company'. They had been repeatedly thrown into the line as light infantry during the Tunisian retreat, occasionally infiltrating the enemy lines on short sharp patrols and were gradually whittled down in numbers as they did whatever they could to hold open the last pockets of German troops and enable evacuation of as many as possible. The final survivors awaited captivity with some measure of peace, gathered in an olive grove with their commander *Oberleutnant* Hoffmann, singing regimental songs before the arrival of the enemy. Their unit's epitaph can best be summed up by a quote frequently attributed to the former leader of the Afrika Korps, Erwin Rommel, when he reputedly said: 'Koenen and his men are as much to me as a whole regiment.' On 12 May, at 0040hrs, German high command received the final radio transmissions from *Heeresgruppe Afrika*. The Axis war in North Africa was finally over.

OKW Diverts Brandenburger Strength

Following Allied landings in North Africa and the German occupation of Vichy France in November 1942, fears arose once more of a potential Allied invasion of Spain. While requests to withdraw those parts of *Verband 803* that were committed to the Eastern Front were denied, elements of *Verband 802* were requested and approved to take part in Operation '*Gisela*', the planned pre-emptive occupation of northern Spain and its ports from the French border to Vigo. *Generaloberst* Alfred Jodl, OKW Chief of Staff, was convinced there would be an Allied attack on 22 February, though the deadline passed without incident and '*Gisela*' was finally abandoned as the threat posed to Spain from potential Allied invasion receded.

On 30 January, Austrian Luftwaffe *Generaloberst* Alexander Löhr, who occupied the newly established post of *Oberbefehlshaber Südost* responsible for all forces in south-east Europe, requested the transfer of Brandenburg units to his command but was refused by both the Abwehr and OKH. Those units in Germany were considered at that stage to be understrength either through incomplete formation or having recently returned from being mauled on the Eastern Front. Although Löhr's initial request was turned down, the battlefield of the south-east was to become the focal point of Brandenburg deployment in the immediate future. In Yugoslavia, Marshal Tito's communist partisans were barely contained and growing in strength daily. The entire region was riven by nationalist, ideological and religious divisions that resulted in fierce and unrestrained warfare hallmarked by extreme brutality. The Brandenburgers were proving their adeptness at anti-partisan operations on the Eastern Front and would soon be redirected by the Wehrmacht to Löhr's uncompromising battleground.

After the final Axis collapse in North Africa, the Italian peninsula and islands appeared extremely vulnerable as the next stage of the Allied re-entry to Europe. After the predicted invasion of Spain failed to appear, Canaris twice warned that the Allies would attempt to occupy Sicily, Sardinia and Corsica during March; either convinced by Allied false intelligence or using his own 'fog of war' approach to undermine Hitler's military position. OKW subsequently informed *Oberbefehlshaber Süd*, *Generalfeldmarschall* Albert Kesselring in command of all Mediterranean and North African forces, that on 18 March 1943 '*Sturmbrigade XI*' would be formed on Sardinia with the addition of the 14th 'Unit' (*Einheit*) of *Sonderverbänd 'Brandenburg'* which was to be brought to Livorno as soon as possible. This new formation, part of *Verband 804* was *Oberleutnant* Hettinger's 15th (Light) Company that had returned from Finland in December 1942. Barracked in Neuhaus im Triestingtal, Austria, they had officially been redesignated 14th *Einheit* on 3 December 1942 and were loaded on to transport at Weissenbach on 29 March, issued with tropical uniforms though they did not know their destination. After three days, they crossed the Italian border, reaching Livorno on 2 April where they were housed in the barracks of an Italian parachute unit. After a week in Livorno, Hettinger's men were taken in the early morning to the harbour alongside other elements of the *Sturmbrigade* to board the passenger liner *Corsair* that had been impressed into service as a troopship.

> 9.4 . . . The 'Einstmann Brigade' is still loading, funny bunch . . . Each group gets a bottle of schnapps, which soothes some of the nervous stomachs!
> 10.4. Sardinia! Arrive in Porto Aranci, with a jetty built in the bay and a small train station, 'Terra Nova'. Our platoon commander is *Leutnant* Gutweniger (the Finns named him 'Wehän Hüver' – 'Less Good'!)
> 12.4. Food is scarce, so 'special operations (*z.b.V. Einsatz*)!' The Einstmann Brigade has too much of it. Our 'Gasparone Group' – that is Manfred Stoll and other robbers – organised for the company fourteen tins of Bierwurst. We stowed it in rifle ammunition boxes![10]

The company remained on Sardinia until the island was evacuated in September, although on 20 April Hettinger was injured in an accident and was evacuated to hospital, being replaced by *Hauptmann* Benesch.

On the Eastern Front the end of the year had brought retreat for the Wehrmacht. Brandenburg units were caught in the Elchotowo bottleneck of escaping Axis forces from the southern Caucasus. The Red Army's 'North Caucasus Operation' had launched on 1 December, two armies of over 1 million men smashing into a weak Axis flank. The decision to retreat from the southern regions had already been taken to avoid encirclement as the offensive crashed into hard-pressed and overextended Axis lines. Heavy fighting followed and by the beginning of February Soviet troops had reached the southern and eastern approaches to Rostov-on-Don and the Sea of Azov. Troops of the Soviet Black Sea group reached Maykop on 29 January and by 4 February were on the banks of the Kuban River. Instructions were issued for a withdrawal of the Brandenburg troops:

3 January 1943
Situation Report:
   On Hitler's orders, Corps for Special Assignments (General Felmy) and elements of the 'Brandenburg' Special Unit will be withdrawn from the Eastern Front and transferred to Tunisia.[11]

However, in practice it was difficult to disengage those units fighting as *Kampfgruppen* against the tremendous strength of the Red Army offensive. Not until the end of March was the German front line stabilised north of Taganrog and the active Brandenburgers began to be withdrawn. By then Stalingrad had fallen and the Sixth Army had been destroyed.

During March 1943, the Kriegsmarine safely transported 22,026 men, 1,655 prisoners, 1,551 civilians, 19,835 horses, 5,534 horse-drawn vehicles, 930 transport vehicles and 1,650 tons of military supplies across the Kuban Strait away from the advancing Soviets and back into the Crimea. Additionally, a ropeway had been built by the Organisation Todt allowing a total load capacity of 1,000 tons to cross per day. Orders from Berlin to construct a road-rail bridge never advanced beyond the early stages, though ironically the project was later finished off by the Red Army using materials abandoned by the Wehrmacht after their withdrawal from Kerch, but destroyed by drifting ice. In March 1943, the harbours of Anapa and Novorossiysk were still in German hands though rigged for demolition, and to stabilise German lines on the Taman Peninsula, the Soviet beachhead at Myskhako was attacked by the Seventeenth Army with Kriegsmarine support as Operation '*Neptun*'. After frequent postponements due to bad weather, the attack began on 17 April but was called off after a week in the face of mounting casualties and little headway.

By then '*Kampfgruppe Walther*' – formed from elements of 2nd, 3rd and 4th (Light) Companies – had returned to Germany. They had retreated to Rostov-on-Don, frequently fighting off Soviet infantry and armoured attacks with little more than desperate defiance. *Hauptmann* Werner John, leading the 3rd Company, was wounded while attacking a Soviet tank with a satchel charge, hit in the foot by machine-gun fire from another tank following behind. Nonetheless, the armoured vehicles were driven away or destroyed by the remainder of the company, which continued the retreat in good order although nearly completely out of ammunition. Their commander evacuated to hospital, the remaining forty-three men were led by *Leutnant* Geisenberger back to Germany during March after crossing the frozen Don delta. With the rest of *Kampfgruppe Walther* that had covered the withdrawal of the last panzers across the Don, they were grouped at Freiburg where *Verband 801* was forming, minus its 1st Battalion that remained in action in Latvia.

Kampfgruppe Horlbeck fought in plummeting temperatures north-west of Ardon defending retreating forces as they withdrew past the Terek River. *Leutnant* Steidl later recounted a damning judgement on Horlbeck's last days with the *Kampfgruppe*, saying that as they were involved in severe fighting at the line of the Malka River, Horlbeck 'like a commanding General, did not meet with his troops', leadership of the battlegroup being handled by *Hauptmann* Dieter Weithoener of the 2nd Battalion, Brandenburg Regiment. Steidl's last mention of their previous commander is that the 'fat, carefree Horlbeck wanders away.'[12] Whatever the circumstances of Horlbeck's departure, the *Kampfgruppe* was certainly renamed '*Weithoener*' in January and fought its way back through Armavir and Kalnibolotskaya. The battered remains of 5th and 8th Companies were combined with '*Kompanie Mertens*' and a Flak company commanded by *Oberleutnant* Wichmann and, covering the retreat of the 3rd Panzer Division, they fought off repeated Soviet attacks on the German bridgehead south of the frozen Don River delta at Asov.

Frequently using the cover of blinding snowstorms, Soviet tanks and infantry continued to assault the Brandenburger lines, their flank held by men of *Sonderverbänd Felmy*. Repeatedly the Red Army were repulsed, extraordinary feats of heroism committed by Brandenburger units in hand-to-hand combat as they compensated for their lack of heavy weapons by hunting and destroying armoured vehicles using grenades and explosives. By the time that they withdrew across the Don River they had accumulated 650 Soviet prisoners which were herded to the north-west to an uncertain fate. By 18 February the last Brandenburg men were across and the bridge behind them destroyed. *Kampfgruppe Weithoener*, alongside the remaining scattered Brandenburg units from the Caucasus retreat, returned to bases in Germany and Austria. Only the 12th Company remained committed from those forces that had begun 'Case Blue', combing the German rear areas for partisans.

Pfuhlstein had thrown himself energetically into the task of rebuilding and restructuring his new command. On 27 March, he submitted formal proposals to

OKW on the future use of the Brandenburgers after they had fully transformed into a division; his designs endorsed by the Army General Staff who claimed at least partial control over the new Brandenburg Division for OKW. Jodl is recorded as writing at the beginning of April:

> The Wehrmacht's Operational Staff lacks its own unit for OKW theatres of war. For every division, we must go begging, cap in hand, to OKH, often with considerable difficulty. This is both an unworthy and unbearable situation! The newly formed Brandenburg Division will therefore be directly subordinate to the Wehrmacht's Operational Staff as its 'house unit' and therefore I will decide on its deployment.[13]

Though Canaris and the Abwehr had not been completely removed from the Brandenburg hierarchy, they no longer had autonomy – another indication of the Abwehr's general loss of prestige and reputation. Canaris now had only a partial say in Brandenburger activities, only the '*Kurfürst*' Regiment – originally intended as 5th Regiment of the division, but removed from its structure – remained under Canaris' sole control. On the date of Jodl's words, the official order of battle of Pfuhlstein's new unit was formalised. The 'z.b.V.' suffix that denoted the Brandenburgers' special operations usage – and a final link to its original purpose – was no longer deemed applicable and thereafter they were simply entitled '*Division Brandenburg*' (referred to hereafter in its anglicised 'Brandenburg Division' form). A new '*Wappen*' was also to be used on divisional transport: a large white helmet with the red eagle of the Brandenburg region emblazoned upon it.

Pfuhlstein, however, remained frustrated by a seeming ambivalence from the Abwehr's top echelons towards his command. Later, Pfuhlstein related his conviction that Canaris remained motivated primarily by his desire to control a military formation that could either act as a personal bodyguard or protection for the Abwehr should the shifting sands of German political power struggles cause a 'critical situation'.

> I received absolutely no help towards refurbishing the unit, neither from the department nor from Admiral Canaris. I gradually concluded that Admiral Canaris was quite uninterested in speedily returning my unit to the front.[14]

Though the division still had no organic heavy weapons unit and therefore remained reliant on 'parent' formations, the order of battle had come to resemble more the lines of an 'ordinary' *Jäger* division; more heavily armed than a *Gebirgsjäger* division, but less than a standard infantry unit and therefore still capable of operating in adverse terrain.

Regeneration, 1943

Brandenburg Division.
Division Staff (Berlin).
Commander: *Generalmajor* Alexander von Pfuhlstein.
1st General Staff Officer: *Major* Frankfurth.
Ia: *Hauptmann* Wülbers (from 31 May 1943).
IIa and Division Adjutant: *Hauptmann* Helmut Pinkert.

1st Jäger Regiment 'Brandenburg' (*Major* Walther).
Regimental base: Freiburg im Breisgau.
Regimental units: One company from **Signals Battalion 'Brandenburg'**.
1st Battalion (*Rittmeister* Plitt, later replaced by *Hauptmann* John after the latter's wounds healed).
1st, 2nd and 3rd Companies plus 4th (Light) Company (later transferred).
2nd Battalion (*Hauptmann* G. Pinkert, later replaced by *Oberleutnant* Rosenow).
5th, 6th, 7th Companies (8th Company never established).
3rd Battalion (*Hauptmann* Gustav Froboese, later replaced by *Oberleutnant* Wandrey).
9th, 10th, 11th, 12th Companies.

2nd Regiment 'Brandenburg' (*Oberstleutnant* Wolfgang von Kobylinski, developed severe illness and died on 19 June; replaced by *Oberstleutnant* Franz Pfeiffer).
Regimental base: Baden bei Wein (later moved to Admont).
Regimental units: One company from **Signals Battalion 'Brandenburg'**.
1st Battalion (*Hauptmann* Weithoener).
1st, 2nd, 3rd Companies plus 4th (Light) Company (later transferred).
2nd Battalion (*Hauptmann* Oesterwitz).
5th, 6th, 7th Companies plus 8th (Light) Company (later dissolved).
3rd Battalion (*Hauptmann* Renner).
9th, 10th, 11th Companies (12th Company never formed).

3rd Regiment 'Brandenburg' (*Oberstleutnant* F. Jacobi).
Regimental base: Düren/Rhld
Regimental units: One company from **Signals Battalion 'Brandenburg'**.
1st Battalion (*Oberleutnant* Kriegsheim).
1st, 2nd, 3rd Companies plus 4th (Light) Company (later dissolved).
2nd Battalion (*Hauptmann* Bansen).
5th, 6th, 7th, 8th Companies plus Italian III 'M' Assault Battalion '9 September'.
3rd Battalion (*Hauptmann* Grawert),

9th, 10th, 11th, 12th Companies.

4th Regiment 'Brandenburg' (*Oberstleutnant* Heinz).
Regimental base: Brandenburg an der Havel.
1st Battalion (*Hauptmann* Hollmann – recalled from early retirement – later replaced by *Hauptmann* Gerlach).
1st, 2nd, 3rd, 4th Companies (5th Company never formed).
2nd Battalion (*Hauptmann* Dr Hartmann, later replaced by *Oberleutnant* Lau).
6th, 7th, 8th Companies plus 9th (Light) Company (10th Company never formed).
3rd Battalion (*Hauptmann* von Koenen).
11th, 12th, 13th Companies.
Independent Companies
14th Company (*Oberleutnant* Hettinger), redesignated 16th (Light) Company in July 1943.
15th (Light) Company (*Oberleutnant* Oschatz); *Fallschirmjäger* Company. This parachute unit was later expanded into the '*Fallschirmjäger* Battalion' of four companies in March 1944, based in Stendal and commanded by *Hauptmann* Weithoener.
Translator Company.

Divisional Units
Nachrichtenabteilung (Signals Battalion) (*Hauptmann* Eltester), headquarters in Berlin, divided between the regiments.
Lehrregiment (Training Regiment) '***Brandenburg***' (*Major* Martin).
   1st Battalion based in Brandenburg an der Havel.
   2nd *Gebirgsjäger* Battalion based in Baden bei Wein and later Veldes/Oberkrain.
Küstenjäger **Battalion** based at Langenargen/Bodensee (*Rittmeister* Conrad von Leipzig).
   1st, 2nd, 3rd, 4th (Heavy) Companies.
***Legionärbataillon* 'Alexander'** (*Hauptmann* Alexander Auch).
   1st 'White Company' and 2nd 'Black Company'.
***Lehrregiment* 'Kurfürst'** (briefly held on divisional strength, this regiment comprised training personnel from the *Quenzee* establishment and was in effect a last attempt by the Abwehr to maintain some control over the division. It was, however, withdrawn from the Brandenburg Division on 1 April 1943 and replaced by *Major* Martin's *Lehrregiment* above).

There was also an important distinction to make between the strength of a Brandenburg and Wehrmacht infantry unit, as evidenced by this example from August 1943 written by Pfuhlstein:

Battalion Strength:	Infantry	Brandenburger
Officers	22	15
NCOs	135	81
Men	698	322

Recruiting was still strong for the division; Koenen's 3rd Battalion/4th Regiment recorded 28 NCOs, 81 NCO candidates and 541 other ranks taken on from four military districts in Germany at the beginning of June 1943.

The *Küstenjäger Abteilung* had also had its order of battle confirmed on 10 January 1943. Formed from the Light Engineer Company with additional volunteers from all Wehrmacht services and the SS, the *Abteilung* mustered the following strength:

Abteilung Headquarters (*Oberleutnant* Kriegsheim, superseded by *Rittmeister* Conrad von Leipzig);
   Naval adviser: *Kapitänleutnant* Martiny.
1st Company to 3rd Company, each having approximately 230 men:
   1st Platoon – one heavy *Sturmboot* 42, one *Pionier* Landing Boat 41, two light machine guns;
   2nd Platoon – two heavy *Sturmboote* 42 (six planned), two *Pionier* Landing Boat 41, nine light machine guns;
   Two light Flak weapons, two medium mortars.
4th (Heavy) Company:
   Two craft of the Italian X Flotilla MAS Borghese;
   Six heavy *Sturmboote* 42;
   Twelve *Linsen* explosive motorboats with one light machine gun and various Flak weapons.

The mission brief for the *Küstenjäger Abteilung* was for anti-partisan operations at sea and missions behind enemy lines against harbours and shipping. The Heavy Company contained the first German attempt at using explosive motorboats such as those established by the Italian Navy and would later be handed over to the Kriegsmarine's *Kleinkampfverbände*.

The *Legionärbataillon 'Alexander'* had been formed from the pool of Russian volunteers that had been gathered in Freiburg, though they later trained at Kranepuhl south of Brandenburg where they inhabited barracks of a Luftwaffe

Flak unit. The 1st 'White' Company was composed of Russians and Ukrainians while the 2nd 'Black' Company was chiefly made up of men from Turkestan, Armenia and other regions of the Caucasus. *Hauptmann* Alexander Auch had been born in St Petersburg and spoke flawless Russian and while the initial cadre around which his battalion formed were German veterans from the Brandenburgers' old 2nd Company, the remainder were eastern volunteers.

Many German recruits who had been taken into the Brandenburgers during early 1942 were only now being attached to combat units as the formation reached divisional strength. Take for example the experience of Hinrich-Boy Christiansen. Born in Kiel in 1924, he finished his schooling at a Hamburg *Gymnasium* and enlisted in the 90th Motorised Reserve Battalion on 28 January 1942, beginning his training in Hamburg.

> A few days before the end of basic training [during March], I was suddenly ordered into the orderly room, where, in an adjoining room, I reported to a *Leutnant*. I was briefly asked for my CV, family, why I volunteered for the Wehrmacht, a few language skills were tested and then I was asked, to my joyful surprise, if I did not want to report to a special unit. Naturally, without the slightest idea of what this meant, I wanted to see what kind of special tasks it might be. What 17-year-old volunteer could resist such an offer? . . .
>
> But while most of my fellow recruits were being sent to the Eastern Front, we were sent back to Berlin by a *Feldwebel*, who did not give us any information about our trip's destination. From there we continued by train the next day, until we arrived somewhere late in the evening and were loaded into a truck. In the dark, we could still see that it was a large-scale complex of barracks that lay in a forest setting. To our question of what was happening, we got the completely unmilitary answer: 'Sleep for now. Roll call tomorrow morning is at about ten o'clock, then you will see.'
>
> Our suspense grew and we were not to be disappointed. We had just got up the next morning, when we heard a marching song on the road outside our barracks, but in a language we didn't know. We staggered to the windows and saw to our weary astonishment a unit doing a stiff Prussian march, but in Russian uniforms. As soon as that had disappeared, something even stranger came along. The first thing we saw was a lean, proud rider in a *Hauptmann* uniform, whose narrow brown face was decorated with a mighty moustache. Behind this German officer, who had the appearance of a most unusual officer, were about forty or fifty men, who were eagerly trying, but without great success, to achieve something like a proper march without dropping their rifles. The most amazing thing was the fact that this troop was wearing German uniforms, but on their heads . . . a green turban.

> We were beginning to realise what a strange mob we had landed in. The place was the so-called '*Regenwurmlager*' near Meseritz. This 'near', however, was slightly exaggerated. If we wanted to go to the cinema on Sunday afternoon, we had to walk about two hours there and back. Otherwise, there were only heath, forest and sand in the area.[15]

Christiansen transferred to Brandenburg an der Havel for the completion of his training, a member of the 1st Battalion, and had volunteered to join the *Fallschirmjäger* Company during February 1943. However, as the wearer of spectacles, he was rejected much to his disappointment. Instead he was transferred to Düren and after two weeks' guard duty in Berlin, he joined the 2nd Company, 1st Battalion, 3rd Regiment, Brandenburg Division. His first combat posting would soon be to Witebsk, Belarus.

Before the division had completely formed, *Rittmeister* Plitt's 1st *Abteilung/Verband 801* had already gone into action against partisans on the Eastern Front though following the final establishment, Plitt became commander of the redesignated 1st Battalion, 1st Regiment 'Brandenburg', still fighting partisans in the rear areas of Army Group North. His battalion was spread across a wide area and took part in extremely heavy fighting against strong enemy groups which were becoming bolder in their tactics. Partisan activity in Soviet territories under German control reached new heights during the second half of 1942 and into 1943. German-led pacification operations had begun from the moment of occupation but reached an intensity during autumn 1941 and managed to quell much partisan activity. With the front line moving east, the guerrillas found their situation intolerable with growing shortages of weapons and ammunition as well as medical supplies and food. The Red Army or Air Force could offer no support and there was virtually no radio communication possible to coordinate operations due to a lack of radios and operatives trained in their use. Scattered piecemeal attacks were little more than nuisances to the Wehrmacht by late 1941, generally brought under control by harsh reprisals from security and SS units.

However, between February and September 1943 the so-called 'Vitebsk Gate' was opened by the Soviet 4th Shock Army after it ripped a hole 40km wide in the densely forested and marshy territory marking the junction between Army Groups North and Centre. The Soviet Toropets–Kholm Offensive encircled German forces at Kholm and Demyansk, while the breach created in the German lines allowed widespread reinforcement of partisan groups in Belarus, as well as considerable supplies of weapons, ammunition and 150 radio sets. It also allowed a flood of harvested food to flow eastwards to feed the Red Army. In anticipation of its eventual closure by German counter-attack, Soviet engineers were also able to transport enough materiel through the 'gate' to construct nearly fifty secret airstrips for future partisan supply missions. However, German forces were unable – and initially unwilling – to counterattack in an attempt to close the gaping hole in their front line as they were both understrength following an exhausting winter and more concerned at relieving forces trapped in the Kholm and Demyansk pockets. Though the gap was finally closed in September 1942, guerrilla forces in Belarus had replenished fighting strength and improved organisational skills that would remain undiminished for the remainder of the war.

From Plitt's battalion, *Leutnant* Heinemann took forty volunteers from his 4th (Light) Company behind enemy lines in *Volltarnung* to attempt to infiltrate Soviet partisan positions. The company was comprised of ex-Soviet prisoners, now considered Wehrmacht 'legionnaires' and beginning on 13 May, they made their way deep into enemy territory before an unexpected mutiny in the ranks derailed the mission. Heinemann's position was perilous and, possibly aware of the rising number of defections amongst foreign Wehrmacht and SS personnel to the enemy, he had the nine ringleaders shot and returned with the remainder to German-held territory where twenty-four others deemed untrustworthy were reinterned as prisoners of war.

Meanwhile, the battalion's 3rd Company was involved in a surprise raid on a partisan bunker complex on 15 May in which *Hauptmann* Fritz Babuke was wounded during close-quarters fighting. His place was taken by *Oberleutnant* Schulte who, after being killed in an ambush that left his company with four dead and several injured, was in turn replaced by *Leutnant* Hebler.

By July 1943 two more Brandenburger battalions had been sent to the Soviet Union: *Oberleutnant* Kriegsheim's 1st Battalion and *Hauptmann* Grawert's 3rd Battalion of the 3rd Regiment. Their primary purpose was initially the security of supply lines that straggled through forested marshland in which partisans had become increasingly active. The Brandenburgers were given the temporary designation of '200th *Jäger* Regiment' as a cover with a more orthodox Wehrmacht service history should they be taken prisoner and, along with Jacobi's regimental staff, both battalions were engaged in heavy fighting against guerrilla bands. The fighting was brutal and any captured Germans could expect little mercy from their enemy. Conversely, there was little compassion towards the partisans either. Vitebsk itself had been largely destroyed by the fighting, Kriegsheim's 1st Battalion operating mainly to the south-west of the city. Hinrich-Boy Christiansen was involved in these battles:

> [Diary extract] 17.09.43: Afternoon mission. I see two dead women burning, which I had seen alive just a few minutes ago, it was not a pretty sight. One must get used to hitting civilians hard, especially women. Additionally, from

my memory: It was two women who were captured with weapons in their hands, had tried to flee again and were wounded. There was also a young girl with them, whom I had to return to the company command post. It was one of the worst moments I had experienced as a soldier; this young, handsome girl, with whom I would have preferred to go out, now driving her through the forest with a gun, but at the same time knowing that she had probably tried, shortly before, to shoot me or a comrade.[16]

Kriegsheim's battalion had also suffered the unexpected blow in July of a mutiny by Soviet legionnaires of *Oberleutnant* Kohlmeyer's 4th Company that had been billeted in a large collective farm at Sarethsje. Kohlmeyer had already had one narrow brush with disaster when he had been stopped by two *Feldgendarmerie* on the road between his own headquarters and that of the battalion command. Engaging the leading military police *Feldwebel* in conversation, it was perhaps an inbuilt sense of danger that first raised his suspicions before a small incorrect uniform detail confirmed it. Within seconds of being attacked themselves, Kohlmeyer and his driver opened fire and killed both men, later identified as German communists who had enlisted with the Soviet partisans.

The Soviet mutineers of Kohlmeyer's company were led by Alexander Lewa, a Russian who had emigrated to Serbia following the Bolshevik revolution and married a German woman. Believed above suspicion as a loyal Wehrmacht soldier, he had formed small intelligence sections in the company for transmitting information to partisans before launching his own surprise attack. A stunned survivor escaped the bloodbath that followed and raced to Kriegsheim's headquarters by motorcycle, the battalion commander immediately taking his 2nd Company in full combat order towards Sarethsje. Approaching the stockaded farm stronghold, the first body to be found was that of Karl Kohlmeyer; the 28-year-old officer's body had been riddled with bullets, a pistol near his open hand.

All fourteen German members of the company had been shot, several after being captured while wounded and the signs of battle gave no doubt to experienced eyes that the attack had come from within the camp. Two trucks and forty-six legionnaires were missing, leaving eighty-two men, half of whom were dead or wounded and the remainder cowering in fear as the Germans approached. A reinforced platoon followed the tyre tracks and found both trucks abandoned in the forest, tracking the escapees until around midday on 19 July when they came under heavy fire from German MG42s. The mutineers had clearly been reinforced by partisans and the Brandenburgers were forced to withdraw.

Morale in the battalion sank with the revelations, some officers asking for the remaining Russians to be shot as an example until Kriegsheim angrily reminded them that those who remained had not defected despite the risk of execution by their erstwhile comrades who had deserted to the partisans. An uneasy peace descended, though the 4th Company was ultimately disbanded, its survivors grouped into a new platoon. Kriegsheim was removed as battalion commander and transferred, his place taken by *Hauptmann* Wasserfall who in turn was later succeeded by *Hauptmann* Pinkert.

Hundreds of kilometres to the south-east the battle of Kursk was fought and lost by German forces in late July, the Wehrmacht's last attempt at regaining the initiative on the Eastern Front a failure. From that point onward they would be forced to constantly be reacting to Soviet advances rather than making their own. *Hauptmann* Grawert's 3rd Battalion had been earmarked for operations against Soviet bridges as part of the Operation '*Zitadelle*' Kursk offensive but these were cancelled as the attempt failed. The battalion was instead sent to the defensive fighting west of the Desna River at Zhokovka, 55km north-west of Bryansk, during September 1943.

The Brandenburgers were visited personally by *Generaloberst* Walter Model, commander of the Ninth Army, on 12 September who reinforced them with *Sturmgeschütz* support as they protected the supply lines to the 296th Infantry Division at Foshnya, the main road under fierce Soviet attacks under cover of darkness. Over the next three days Grawert's company took numerous prisoners, killed at least eighty enemy troops and destroyed an enemy tank. They also managed to recapture two German 88mm Flak guns that had fallen into enemy hands during the Wehrmacht's retreat as well as other weapons and ninety horses.

By 2 October Grawert's men had been in action continuously and suffered casualties of two officers, three NCOs and twelve men killed, six officers, eleven NCOs and fifty-seven men wounded; only a single officer remaining unscathed. Reaching exhaustion, Grawert's men were finally withdrawn to the area south-west of Minsk, to rest and undertake anti-partisan operations along the area's railway lines and supply routes.

Wasserfall's 1st Battalion was involved in heavy fighting against enemy armoured units near Nevel as part of Third Panzer Army. They would not be withdrawn from the front-line trenches until the end of October and even then, it was only for a brief respite during which they engaged partisans behind the lines. Returning to the chaotic front they were shunted around as a 'fire-brigade' unit to plug holes torn in the German defences by relentless Soviet attacks. Luftwaffe field divisions that occupied adjacent sectors required occasional stop-gap groups of Brandenburgers to shore up their own lines. *Hauptmann* Gerhard Pinkert led '*Kampfgruppe Wagner*' comprised of Brandenburg troops and elements of the 211th Infantry Division against Soviet spearheads in the severe defensive fighting as German troops struggled back towards the Polish frontier.

The Russians of the 'Alexander Battalion' were committed to violent battles against partisans near Teterevino as part of Operation 'Zitadelle' before being forced to retreat following the Soviet counteroffensive. By November Auch's men had been pushed as far back as Zhitomir, which fell to Soviet troops on 13 November. In a ferocious counter-attack, Auch's troops stormed into house-to-house combat in support of the 7th Panzer Division that retook the burning city. Within his 'Christmas Order' (*Weihnachtsbefehl*) for 1943, *Generalmajor* von Pfuhlstein singled out the battalion for praise, noting that:

> Our veteran Russian legionnaires under *Hauptmann* Auch made possible the ordered withdrawal of German troops from the Zhitomir area by providing cover. Our legionnaires were the last to leave Zhitomir and they were the first to re-enter the city during the counter-attack.

In January 1944, the two Brandenburg Battalions of the 3rd Regiment were sent to the vast swampland known as the Pripet marshes. During the invasion of the Soviet Union, the German armed forces had a marked tendency to avoid large areas of forest or wetlands as they were unsuitable for mobile warfare. Correspondingly there was little formal training in the close combat typical of such environments. Artillery support was nullified by swampy soil and required specialist training that was frequently lacking amongst artillery observers. Likewise, aerial bombardment required the attaching of extension-rod fuses (*Vorsatzzuender*) to produce any useful results. Armoured vehicles were clearly of no use in such terrain and therefore it was left to infantrymen to shoulder the burden. During the heat of summer, men were in constant humidity that rotted boots, uniforms and equipment while the fetid atmosphere produced swarms of mosquitoes. Amidst the pools of stagnant water, diseases such as diarrhoea, dysentery and typhoid became commonplace and spread almost unchecked. Digging-in became next to impossible in waterlogged soil and life was miserable for all but the hardiest troops. During winter the alternative hardships caused by sub-zero temperatures brought new misery.

The forests and marshes that surrounded the Prip'yat' River that flowed from west to east and drained into the Dneiper protected the central part of European Russia from any military invader. From the outset of '*Barbarossa*' the marshes separated Army Group Centre from Army Group North with a gap that was never fully closed. Early SS operations in the area murdered thousands of Jews and executed scattered partisans but failed to hold the area for any length of time.

It was from this direction that Soviet forces had attacked Rzhev and Vitebsk on the left flank of Army Group Centre.

While the German advance had bypassed the marshes, the retreat was unable to do so. Brandenburgers were sent into the area centred on Haradnaja skirting the border between Belarus and the northern Ukraine. There they fought scattered partisan bands as several German divisions retreated into Poland. It was a miserable battlefield of small victories and constant casualties. Christiansen's diary provides an example of one minor operation from March 1944:

> 9.3.1944. Twenty-four hours of fighting lies behind me. On the evening of the 7th it started. We wanted to surround the village Jeziersk, which we are to attack. 4 km through the swamp . . . At a wide ditch which we must cross, [water comes up] to the belly. Later again we go through swamp and forest. When we leave the marsh on the road we are shot at. None of us return fire. But, we therefore do not have to wait for the agreed signal, since our intended surprise had probably failed. Nevertheless, at daybreak, we launch a storming attack. Everyone shouts a loud 'Hurrah!' In a cemetery, we hit the first strong resistance and suffer losses. Shooting at Ivan's heavy machine gun with a telescopic sight. Heavy machine gun position is taken. Continue into the trenches. The first prisoners. Carry on with two men. Trench battle. Two more comrades are coming. Three prisoners. Then settling down. You can hardly walk on the return march.[17]

While the *Legionärbataillon 'Alexander'* remained in action on the Eastern Front, 1st Battalion/3rd Regiment, was in Derevna until spring 1944 after which, on 30 May, it entrained for transfer south to Italy. The 3rd Battalion was likewise ordered to Italy after having been in action attached to the Panzergrenadier Division 'Feldherrnhalle' at Haradnaja. The remaining battalion of the 3rd Regiment – *Hauptmann* Bansen's 2nd Battalion – had already been sent to France and was subsequently the first to transfer to Italy during October 1943, but not before bringing destruction to some small villages near the Franco-Spanish border.

France, 1943

Following the landing of Allied troops in North Africa in Operation 'Torch', Hitler ordered a previously prepared occupation of Vichy France ('Case Anton') put into effect. Between 8 and 12 November, Germans moved into Corsica and all of southern France apart from a narrow demilitarised zone bordering Switzerland and a small area of the south-east that was seized by Italian troops. The Vichy military was disbanded and though French officials still retained some semblance of power over metropolitan France, it was now without any pretence of autonomy and closely monitored by German officials.

During spring 1943, *Hauptmann* Hans-Gerhard Bansen and his 2nd Battalion/3rd Regiment was transferred to Aquitaine in southern France. There, the 5th and 6th Companies were established in the region of Navarrenz, while the 7th and 8th were quartered around Mauléon-Licharre. With the 8th Company composed of ex-Soviet troops, their unsuitability to the new environment was obvious and the decision soon made to enlist French volunteers instead. In Paris, a recruitment centre was established in the Grand Hotel on rue Scribe facing the Opera House that would funnel men to the south-west.

Early recruiting was difficult; the first six volunteers having already resigned by June 1943 shortly after enlisting. However, German persistence triumphed and numbers gradually increased to a steady stream of volunteers, recruits beginning to trickle in to the Brandenburg Regiment's headquarters. They were a mixture of fresh idealists who perhaps had graduated through the ranks of the various anti-communist youth groups, men wishing to avoid the forced labour of the *Service du travail obligatoire* (STO – forced recruitment and deportation of French workers to Germany), veterans of the *Légion des volontaires français contre le bolchevisme* (LVF) who had fought on the Eastern Front and been repatriated through injury, and former Vichy *Milice* members looking to join the Wehrmacht. Before long the Brandenburgers began operations along the French border with Spain, their primary targets communist and Gaullist resistance groups as well as associated escape networks for Allied personnel on the run in occupied France.

The first recorded raid mounted by the 8th Company took place near Barcu, led by *Oberfähnrich* Hans Schwinn with almost the entire French strength at that point in time of around thirty men, and resulted in one young French civilian being shot for 'assisting the enemy'. Schwinn, an instructor with the Brandenburg Regiment, appears to have had an authority that was belied by his rank. In post-war OSS documentation provided by the interrogation of Ludwig Nebel, one of Otto Skorzeny's principal agents in France who was later captured by the Allies and betrayed his former colleagues to avoid the firing squad and was later used as a double-agent codenamed 'Ostrich'.

> Ostrich and [*Obersturmführer* Charles] Hagedorn had a conversation in October 1944 with Oberst Berle, Chief of Staff of the 85th Army Corps at Belfort, who told them that he was working with some groups of the

Brandenburg Division. A few days later Ostrich met the officers in charge of these groups: they were *Hauptmann* Träger, *Leutnant* Striefler and *Oberfähnrich* Schwinn. Although he is only an *Oberfähnrich*, Schwinn was certainly head of the group. Description: Height about 1m 74; average build but very athletic; dark brown wavy hair; wore glasses. He has a Swiss mother and was a student in Switzerland and he has a Swiss dialect. He speaks excellent French, knows France and understands the French people. He was active in the south of France in the area of Marseilles and Nice, using P.P.F. men in German uniform. He is critical of the SD and is alleged to have sent a report to Himmler on its work in France. Ostrich says that Schwinn is the only really intelligent Brandenburg man he has met and believes that he will be used again in espionage or sabotage in France.[18]

The 8th Company relocated to Eaux-Bonnes in the Pyrenees where further training included use of captured British weapons as well as infantry or engineer instruction by experienced Brandenburg personnel. Punitive missions against suspected resistance or evasion locations were mounted, aided by intelligence gathered by French Brandenburgers in the cafes and bistros of the region.

Leutnant Neugebauer had been superseded as head of the 8th Company by *Oberleutnant* Träger, the former moving to specifically handle recruitment and training from a requisitioned office in the Hôtel Continental in Eaux-Bonnes.[19] The 2nd Battalion was officially placed at the disposal of the Nineteenth Army on 26 August 1943, moved to Provence as OKW became increasingly concerned about the fidelity of their Italian brothers-in-arms on occupation duty in the region. *Leutnant* Fischer was given control of a unit of Italian-speaking Brandenburgers, disguised in Italian uniforms and taking up position near the Mont Cenis tunnel as a precautionary measure against possible Italian defection from the Axis. This tunnel beneath the European Alps – also known as the Fréjus Rail Tunnel – was nearly 14km long and carried the Turin to Modane railway line that linked Bardonecchia in Italy to Modane in France. In the event of an Italian surrender, Fischer and his men were to seize control and prevent any attempts at destruction by Italian troops. Allied forces had landed in Sicily and Wehrmacht plans had been discreetly drawn up in the event of Italian surrender, originally codenamed Operation '*Alaric*' but later renamed '*Achse*'. On 25 July Mussolini was deposed, voted out of power by his own Grand Council of Fascism and arrested, and several German divisions were brought into Italy under the reasonable façade of preventing Allied landings on the mainland itself. Unbeknownst to the Germans – but completely predictably – the new Italian government headed by Pietro Badoglio signed an armistice on 3 September (the Armistice of Cassibile), which became public knowledge five days later after British troops had crossed the Straits of Messina and landed on Calabria. German retaliation was swift and Italy and Sardinia were occupied, as were former Italian possessions in the Balkans and southern France.

Bansen's entire 2nd Battalion had been stationed at Aix-en-Provence at the border of the Italian zone and as Operation '*Achse*' was triggered they moved to Toulon and began disarming Italian troops. A fully motorised unit of Italian-speaking Brandenburgers in Italian uniforms and vehicles, commanded by *Leutnant* Rahn, secured the road to Nice and the Mont Cenis pass for German mobile units (Operation '*Kopenhagen*'). However, Fischer's disguised platoon from the 7th (Heavy) Company that attempted to seize the Mont Cenis tunnel failed. The northern exit was blown up by Italian troops and Fischer's men were caught inside the tunnel alongside a trapped locomotive. High levels of carbon monoxide poisoned the Brandenburgers, four of them fatally, while the remainder were captured and interned by the Italians. Elsewhere, the occupation of Italian-held French territory was generally more successful; Italian forces were disarmed and in one instance, the Blackshirt III 'M' Assault Battalion '9 September (Pontida)' commanded by Major Carlo Zanotti placed itself under German command. They were initially attached to Bansen's regiment before being later reallocated to an Italian fascist division.

Träger's Frenchmen were soon split into four separate sections and spread across southern France: company headquarters were in Marseilles on the Boulevard de la Roseraie; one section in Saint-Estèphe in the Dordogne (*Leutnant* Demetrio); another near Lyon (*Leutnant* Striefler); a third at Toulon and later transferring to Bandol (*Oberfähnrich* Schwinn); while the last, composed primarily of Spanish volunteers, was based in the lower Pyrenees under the command of *Feldwebel* Baudach, where they operated alongside German police units.

From October onwards, Träger's men remained the sole Brandenburg presence in France. Bansen had received orders to take the remainder of his battalion to Abruzzo in central Italy where they were subordinated to *Oberbefehlshaber Südwest*, actively combatting newly established Italian guerrilla bands on the Adriatic coast. While the remainder of the battalion prepared to move on 2 October, Träger's French company was detached and placed under the tactical control of Nineteenth Army, logistically subordinated to the signals battalion *Nachrichten Abteilung 445*.

In Saint-Estèphe, *Leutnant* Helmut Demetrio's section comprised two German NCOs, a German medical NCO and around twenty Frenchmen, housed alongside a GFP unit in l'Hôtel des Voyageurs. Demetrio had been born in Zeitz, Saxony, a professor of languages before the war who could speak Spanish and French fluently. He had spent five years teaching in Chile and time in Madrid, joining the Nazi Party in 1933. His grasp of languages drew him to the *Sonderverbänd 'Brandenburg'* which he joined in March 1943, assigned as Bansen's adjutant before assuming command of 1st Platoon while also acting as company adjutant.

Demetrio's men relocated several times as they hunted for resistance members, their raids on farms frequent and brutal, more often than not resulting in suspects being taken away for interrogation. The bitterness between Frenchmen on either side of the ideological divide sometimes rivalled that seen in Russia. Roger Verdier, a wealthy 38-year-old man of definite social ambitions, apparently assisted the Brandenburgers in their quest for guerrillas in order to ingratiate himself with the occupying power. An ex-member of the *Parti Populaire Français* (PPF – French fascist party) and staunch Vichyite, Verdier was responsible for several denunciations that had led to arrests, interrogation and imprisonment. He had already been the subject of at least two FFI assassination attempts, the latest at the beginning of December when nineteen bullets hit his car, though he received only a minor wound in the arm. Nonetheless he was hospitalised in Sainte-Foy and it was here on the night of 3 December 1943 that a small group of resistance fighters disguised as Gendarmes broke into his room through an unguarded garden door and killed Verdier, as well as his wife and sister-in-law as they slept in the hospital room.

Reprisals were swift as four of Demetrio's men drove to the Sainte-Foy-la-Grande Gendarmerie during the early hours of 7 December. At approximately 0245hrs they hammered on the door, ordering it opened in the name of the Wehrmacht. Constable Maurice Métais, one of the five Gendarmes present, unbolted the door whereupon all five were herded into the small office to face aggressive questioning by at least three Brandenburgers regarding the murders. Apparently dissatisfied with their answers, the attackers opened fire without warning, killing Métais and Constable René Barraud, wounding Adjutant Pradier and Gendarme Peleuse and leaving only MDL Chief Castets unharmed. In their haste to get away, they mistakenly believed all their victims dead and the four assailants drove off.

This was the first time that members of the French police force had come under attack by representatives of the Wehrmacht and marked a serious transgression by the Brandenburgers. By first light that morning Wehrmacht *Feldgendarmerie* had arrived at the scene accompanied by German civil police officers. Demetrio was not present at the time, on temporary leave in Germany while his section was handled by *Feldwebel* Barke, but he soon received instructions to report immediately to the headquarters of *Generaloberst* Johannes Blaskowitz's First Army that was responsible for the French Atlantic coast. Local SD officers demanded that the perpetrators be severely punished, not only for abusing the power attendant with their uniform but also for encouraging the anticipated FFI response and endangering an already fragile security situation in the occupied territory. The four were soon identified: Jacques Ronzier-Joly, Fernand Cogrel, Yves Bossy and Jean Mouton, all recruited in Paris.

The Wehrmacht authorities, including company commander Träger, demanded harsh punishment after their cases had been heard in rapidly arranged courts martial and the four found guilty. Ronzier-Joly, a former French sailor and veteran of the LVF, and Cogrel were shot at the beginning of 1944 after imprisonment in Pont-Saint-Espirit citadel. The two were executed by the 8th Company's armourer, *Feldwebel* Hollmann, the circumstances of their death officially listed as shot while 'attempting to escape'. Mouton was sentenced to imprisonment but after the liberation of France was retried by a Paris court and also faced a firing squad. Only Yves Bossy survived; he was sentenced to an indefinite term of hard labour after convincing the court that he had not actually taken part in the shooting but had remained outside as the driver of the car.

During the night of 4 December, Träger's company carried out an anti-Maquis sweep near Banon in the Alpes-de-Haute-Provence region, capturing a dozen resistance members and torching several farms during the operation. Over subsequent weeks, Träger frequently relocated elements of his company on the basis of effective intelligence information received from informers, the GFP and SD. To enhance perception of the lawless nature of such fighting, the Wehrmacht strictly forbade use of the word 'partisan' by its troops. All such resistance fighters were to be known as 'bandits', the Wehrmacht being engaged in *Bandenbekämpfung* (the fight against bandits). Suspects taken prisoner were generally handed over to the GFP or SD for subsequent interrogation, trial and punishment. The Brandenburgers too suffered losses: one man killed and two wounded, including Träger, when their column of seven trucks was ambushed on 27 February 1944 by Maquisards of the 'Bir Hakeim' group, known as '*Biraquins*'. Despite French claims to have killed 'a commander and three officers', Träger was the only officer injured in the attack before the guerrillas retreated. However, their timing was not fortuitous. The day following Träger's wounding, a strong detachment of the 9th SS Panzer Division 'Hohenstaufen' arrived in Pont-Saint-Espirit, technically for recuperation after heavy fighting on the Eastern Front, but in reality to assist attempts to crush local resistance once and for all. The 20th SS Panzergrenadier Regiment, reinforced with reconnaissance vehicles and attached *Feldgendarmerie*, had been subordinated to the Ninteenth Army for operations against the '*Biraquins*'.

The men of the 8th Company were attached to this powerful *Kampfgruppe* which began a series of hard-hitting thrusts into the Maquis heartland in Provence; summary executions, hostage-taking and the burning of villages becoming increasingly frequent as the Germans attempted to break the *Biraquins*. If able to encircle their slippery enemy, the SS men and Brandenburgers generally prevailed in combat. However, the difficult nature of this type of warfare caused increasing German frustration as the resistance fighters frequently melted away into the population, resulting in random excesses against local inhabitants. Träger's men were involved in these punitive expeditions, which reached an unwelcome climax in the days following the Allied landings in Normandy.

At the opening of Operation 'Overlord' on 6 June 1944, French resistance groups were encouraged to increase sabotage efforts in order to disrupt German reinforcement of the Normandy front. Skirmishes took place throughout occupied France and at approximately 0600hrs on 8 June, Maquis fighters entered the town of Valréas just east of the Rhone River, immediately cutting telephone and telegraph lines and barricading the road in an effort to impede German transport north. The resistance fighters occupied the Hotel de Ville, Hotel des Postes and Gendarmerie, local Gendarmes helping to deliver arms and ammunition before taking up weapons themselves after changing into civilian clothes. Firmly in position, they then awaited the Germans.

Though the Hohenstaufen Division had left the south of France, the Maquis faced yet another powerful armoured unit. *Major* Heinz Unger commanded a *Kampfgruppe* centred on the 2nd Battalion, 10th Panzergrenadier Regiment, 9th Panzer Division, once again stationed in the south of France for rest after combat on the Eastern Front. Counted on the strength of his *Kampfgruppe* were thirty-two armoured cars of the division's reconnaissance battalion, GFP officers from Montélimar accompanied by 250 *Reichsarbeitsdienst* (RAD – Reich Labour Service) troops and about a hundred men of the Luftwaffe 200th *Sicherungs Regiment* as well as Träger's 8th Company. The Brandenburgers were already familiar with Valréas thanks to previous operations and, on 12 June, at least nine of Demetrio's men were present as elements of Unger's *Kampfgruppe* surrounded the town.

With news of the approaching Germans, the Maquis that had confidently taken control of Valréas informed the town mayor Jules Niel that they would withdraw towards Nyons to spare the town any potential reprisals. German forces had already begun searching outlying farms and several civilians had been arrested, with some being executed. As the Maquis withdrew, a number of them were captured by the encircling German forces and brought back into Valréas for questioning as the *Kampfgruppe* moved in to the town, their prisoners taken to the Hôtel Thomassin in which Unger quickly established a headquarters.

Mayor Niel immediately requested an audience with the German commander, Unger brusquely warning him that if weapons were found during the house-to-house search that had begun, then executions could likely follow while any sign of resistance would result in the town being razed to the ground. The population was ordered to assemble in the Place de la Mairie and once they had gathered an unidentified German officer harangued them, while a member of Demetrio's squad translated his words to the frightened populace. Dejected Maquis prisoners were led into the square and made to face a wall of the 'Maison Clarice' opposite the Hôtel Thomassin, soon joined by twenty-six civilian hostages that had been taken during the search of outlying dwellings. With a dread sense of foreboding, Niel desperately tried to avert what he knew would follow before events overtook him.

Though there remains, to this day, some measure of confusion over what exactly happened next and on whose orders it was done, the results are clear as shooting began. In small groups, the people lined against the wall were shot and by the day's end fifty-three people were dead. Of those killed, twenty-six were local hostages and twenty-seven captured Maquisards. Following the cessation of the executions, the departing Germans ordered the remaining villagers to leave the bodies where they had fallen, though under cover of darkness four were found to be alive and were spirited away and subsequently recovered while a fifth died from his wounds.

Demetrio was later captured during the German retreat from France in September 1944 and stood trial after the end of the war for the massacre at Valréas, representing himself as defence counsel against the French prosecution. Found guilty, he was sentenced to death, though this was commuted and he was eventually released at the end of 1953 whereupon he returned to West Germany to be reunited with his wife and daughter.

In 1951, a French military tribunal attempted to assign guilt for the massacre to at least one of the various officers present that day. Through Niel's testimony it was established that Demetrio was not in the square when the shooting started. He was involved in interrogating prisoners in the hotel and by the time he emerged there were already ten people lying bleeding in the dust. Likewise, Unger was elsewhere when the executions began. His subsequent request for transfer from the division was seen by some to indicate that he perhaps felt a subordinate had undermined his authority by issuing such grave orders. Suspicion fell on *Hauptmann* Wilhelm Hentsch, the leader of Avignon's GFP, though he maintained that he was not present that day in Valréas. *Oberleutnant* Gerhard Blank of the 9th *Panzeraufklärungsabteilung* later testified that he saw a civilian Peugeot car with two officers – a *Hauptmann* and *Leutnant* – arrive at Valréas with a bullet hole in the windscreen. Later the two were seen to be discussing with Unger the fact that an attack had wounded their driver outside the town and reminding him that: 'the Führer had ordered all bandits shot'. His testimony, quoted here, would seem to be damning for Demetrio:

> During a battle with Maquisards in Valréas, *Leutnant* S., a group leader in my unit, captured about twenty resistance fighters. These were handed over to us by *Leutnant* S. I directed them to the command of *Major* Unger, the head of the operation in Valréas.
>
> A few days later, *Major* Unger reported that the executions were done without his knowledge. We then asked through the ranks and to all the officers who had carried out the execution or given orders to begin them.
>
> Finally, a *Hauptmann*, whose name I do not know and who probably belonged to the SD and a *Leutnant* Dimitreff or Dimitroff. Both can be considered as authors or at least as instigators. These presumptions were based on the fact that I heard them later discussing prisoners that had not been shot, saying that they had shot them and then squandered a small amount of gasoline from their transport to Avignon.[20]

Blank's statement appears to clearly assign guilt to Demetrio and perhaps even Träger, though suspicion continued to focus on *Hauptmann* Hentsch of the GFP. Demetrio's defending accounts muddied the water somewhat, though he perhaps confirmed that the vehicles both he and Träger used could match Blank's description.

> I do not know the ex-lieutenant Gerhard Blank, whose statements about Valréas you have informed me.
>
> I can only repeat that *Hauptmann* Hentsch was not present.
>
> I do not see at all at what time a discussion might have arisen between me and *Hauptmann* Träger on the one hand and *Major* Unger on the other. In fact, by the time I reported to *Hauptmann* Träger, there had already been seven or eight shots. This proves that the decision to shoot the prisoners had already been taken. *Hauptmann* Träger used a sedan Peugeot 402. I drove a khaki-coloured Peugeot 403 with red lining.[21]

The events at Valréas may have been the largest regional example of Brandenburg involvement in punitive measures against French civilians, but it was not isolated. As the fighting in Normandy intensified so too did German attempts to quell uprisings in the south. *Oberfähnrich* Schwinn's 1st Section of four Germans and a dozen Frenchmen appears to have been relentless in pursuit of this objective. The small group were stationed in the Spendid-hôtel in Cavaillon, between Marseilles and Avignon. From there they mounted several covert operations, using disguises that ranged from that of a British paratrooper – as they attempted to infiltrate Maquis escape routes – and French civilians in a bid to find local resistance groups and their headquarters. In effect their missions now appeared to have more in common with SD operations than those traditionally associated with the Brandenburgers and, of course, Schwinn would go on to later join the SS. Is it possible that he was serving two masters during his tenure with the Brandenburgers? Regardless, the division had come to be considered guerrilla warfare specialists and were therefore now being assigned to a hotbed of Partisan activity. They quickly discovered that there was no more challenging – and brutal – theatre in which to wage such a war than the Balkans.

CHAPTER 10

Partisan Warfare in the Balkans

'Those Chetniks up there who are now firing on us will have joined us within a year.'

Josip Broz Tito

Yugoslavia was a heterogeneous state of Serbs, Croats and Slovenes of whom German occupation troops harboured an inherent distrust. The most numerous demographic was Serbian, occupying what had been the former Kingdom of Serbia and the provinces of Bosnia, Herzegovina and Dalmatia and split between the Muslim and the Orthodox faith. It had been Serbian protest that had unseated the country's royal household following Yugoslavia's accord with Hitler in 1941 and precipitated the German invasion. From amongst the Orthodox Serbian population rose the Chetniks who, under the leadership of royalist former-Colonel Draza Mihailović, resisted both German and Italian occupation forces though initially only moderately. The next-largest ethnic group were the Croats who inhabited the north-west of Yugoslavia (now Croatia). Generally, more 'westernised' than Serbs, they tended towards Catholicism as a religion. The final ethnic group were the Slovenes who inhabited northern Yugoslavia (now Slovenia) that bordered Italy and were of similar characteristics to Croatians.

Following the occupation of Greece and Yugoslavia in 1941, most garrison duty had been the responsibility of the Italians. This arrangement not only honoured Italian commitments to the Tripartite Pact, but also released German forces for '*Barbarossa*'. In addition to Albania, which they had held since 1939, Italian forces assumed control of most of Greece, excepting Athens, Thessaloniki, Crete and a scattering of Aegean islands while western Thrace had been occupied and annexed by Bulgarian forces. The Italians soon began to dismember Yugoslavia, incorporating western Slovenia into Italy while annexing Dalmatia and Montenegro. Part of south-western Serbia was separated and added to 'Greater Albania', over which Italian troops exercised little real control, penned up in scattered urban strongholds and avoiding confrontation with aggressive Gheg and Tosk tribesmen. The newly proclaimed Kingdom of Croatia was divided into German and Italian zones of interest along the axis Višegrad–Sarajevo–Banja

Luka; Germans permitted troops east of this line and Italians to the west. Parts of Slovenia were incorporated into 'Greater Germany' while Bulgarians annexed Yugoslav Macedonia and occupied south-eastern Serbia, with Hungarians annexing the Batchka and Baranya and a small portion of eastern Slovenia

In August 1943, most Brandenburg units that had been deployed on the Eastern Front had been withdrawn to Germany and Austria, refitted, reinforced and issued with tropical equipment. They were shortly to be transferred to Yugoslavia and northern Greece where partisan activity had steadily increased concurrent with German fears of a planned British amphibious landing to recapture what had been lost to the Allies in 1941. Following the fall of Tunisia in May, Abwehr reports appeared to indicate the strong possibility of an Allied attack in the Balkans rather than the more obvious route through Italy. It was known that Churchill harboured a long-lasting fixation on the region, scene of his dramatic First World War failure in the Dardanelles that wasted thousands of Allied lives. He continued to harbour desires to invade southern Europe not through the French Mediterranean coast but via the Adriatic Sea, landing near Trieste and directly threatening Austria, while also advancing from the Aegean islands. The imminent Italian collapse appeared to intensify his desire, but at no point would his American or Soviet 'Allies' countenance the idea.

Nonetheless, Hitler had become convinced of a plan to invade through Sardinia and Greece. This was in no small part due to the brilliant Operation 'Mincemeat' that supplied fake intelligence papers planted on the supposed body of an Allied intelligence officer washed ashore in Spain. Passed to Canaris, who in turn handed them to OKW, the deception succeeded in diverting significant German forces to the Balkans before the actual invasion of Sicily began.

Major Friedrich Wilhelm Heinz had been recalled from the *Regenwurmlager* on 20 November 1942 and appointed as commander of *Verband 804*, which subsequently became 4th Regiment 'Brandenburg' from the beginning of 1943. On 1 March, he was promoted to *Oberstleutnant* and the following month led his regiment to the Balkans. Despite his previous association with the anti-Hitler conspirators, Pfuhlstein, as the division's new commander, harboured grave misgivings about Heinz, whom he viewed as a 'political figure' in a unit that required sharp military minds. Indeed, Heinz reported to Oster at Tirpitzufer that his regiment was 'ready and on call' for the conspirators by March 1943.[1] Initially inclined to relieve Heinz of his command as soon as he assumed control of the division, in deference to Canaris' wishes, Pfuhlstein left him at his post . . . for the time being.

> He was virtually incapable of commanding a company, let alone a regiment. Heinz knew next to nothing . . . about modern warfare in general. Similarly, he

had no experience or knowledge of how to train and instruct a reconstituted unit.[2]

For his part, Heinz also distrusted Pfuhlstein, regarding him as highly ambitious to the point of later betraying the division to Jodl and Warlimont at OKH and actively intriguing against Canaris and the circle of conspirators centred on Oster. Heinz levelled the accusation that Pfuhlstein appeared to give preference to devout Nazis as his aides and by appointing Wilhelm Walther as the commander of the division's 1st Regiment he had given control of the leading element to a 'full-time Nazi functionary'. Canaris, however, described Pfuhlstein on 1 November 1943 as 'tireless in increasing the efficiency of his division', his motivation for such appointments purely military. In Walther, whatever his political or ideological motivations may have been, he had an outstanding Brandenburg officer.[3]

Despite Pfuhlstein's distrust of his regimental commander, Heinz and his headquarters staff travelled to Belgrade during mid-April, preceding the combat units of his command. Koenen's 3rd Battalion would later arrive in Sarajevo, directly subordinated to Heinz. On 28 April, *Hauptmann* Dr Hartmann arrived with 2nd Battalion by rail at Raška in Serbia, before travelling 50km west to Sjenica where they were placed under the operational control of the 1st *Gebirgs* Division.

During June, *Hauptmann* Wilhelm Hollmann, who had been recalled from his military semi-retirement and promoted to take command of Heinz's 1st Battalion, moved with his men to the Peloponnese in Greece. They travelled alongside the 104th *Jäger* Division to Athens before moving west over the Corinth Canal. The battalion had been reinforced to the level of a motorised unit with modern weapons and a heavy company that boasted heavy machine guns and mortars, 20mm Flak guns, 75mm anti-tank guns and a 105mm artillery battery.

Hollmann's was not the sole Brandenburg unit in Greece. *Oberstleutnant* Franz Pfeiffer had taken command of 2nd Regiment in southern Russia in June 1943 following the death of its previous commander Wolfgang von Kobelynski through illness. Bavarian Pfeiffer was an experienced *Gebirgsjäger* who had won the Knight's Cross on 13 June 1941 while commander of 15th Company, 100th *Gebirgsjägerregiment* and was later seriously wounded in the Soviet Union and placed into Wehrmacht reserve pool. Fit for action once again, he brought his new regiment to Ptolemaida in western Macedonia, Greece. There he was concerned with the security of the industrialised region's coalmines and power stations. Huge quantities of lignite (known as 'brown coal' as it was composed of compacted peat) had been extracted since Greece had been occupied, the area at the centre of Greek industrial resurrection and the primary source of the nation's energy.

The Greek resistance movement was, like that in Yugoslavia, divided along political lines. While some groups professed loyalty to the royal government-in-exile, others were more staunchly communist. The two main factions in Greece were the royalist EDES (Greek Democratic National League), led by Colonel Zervas, a retired Greek Army officer and the numerically superior communist ELAS (Greek People's Liberation Army, the armed wing of the EAM, or National Liberation Front) commanded by Colonel Sarafis who had been dismissed from military service in 1935 for his political activities.

This, and similar conditions throughout the Balkans, created an extra dimension to the difficulties faced by the German occupiers from 1943 onwards, one of virtual civil war between local parties. In Greece during 1943 the ELAS attacked and eliminated most non-communist guerrilla groups, also putting great pressure on civilians who were not committed to the communist cause to adhere to their ideology, their threats frequently matched with violence. Walter Lucas, a war correspondent for the *Daily Express*, arrived in Greece in September 1944 following the German withdrawal and made some surprising discoveries that he revealed in an article published on 11 October:

> Three generalisations can be made with some accuracy about the clear majority of Greeks:
>
> 1. They are deeply and irrationally pro-British; 2. They hate the Germans; 3. They do not want any political interference in their country, either from friend or foe. That is the common denominator, but outside those simple facts the rest is a sizzling cauldron: Greek slaughtering Greek; so-called quislings as patriotic as partisans; and between the two the mass of the poverty-stricken population silently and fearfully praying for a murrain on both . . . So-called 'quisling troops' – such as the Security Battalion which surrendered to us so readily at Patras last Sunday – were formed partly from a desire to maintain order and give protection in the countryside . . . [They] are composed of many decent people who hate Germans but are frightened by the communist bogey. Many of the members are conscripted and have no other choice; others are there because it is their only means of eating. There are, too, just ordinary thugs. Of the two warring parties, the so-called quislings are probably more pro-British than many partisans. In fact, on both sides there are patriots, unscrupulous leaders and just ordinary people who have no other choice.[4]

It was a complex maelstrom in which the Brandenburgers found themselves embroiled. German forces began raising collaborationist Security Battalions from April 1943, though, as Lucas noted above, these were hardly pro-Axis. The minority EDES were predominantly in the Epirus mountains of north-western Greece, while the ELAS dominated the remainder of the country through conquest. Prior to 1943 both groups had achieved some successes against Italian occupation troops, but the arrival of seasoned German soldiers caused a sudden reversal of fortune.

Pfeiffer's troops had arrived by rail, delays having been caused by multiple sabotage attacks disrupting the line that straggled through steep-sided mountain passes in Yugoslavia. After finally reaching Skopje the Brandenburgers detrained and were transported in half-tracks over the mountains to Axios. Before long the regiment was in action against Greek partisans as *Oberleutnant* Konrad Steidl, commander of 1st Battalion, recalled in his diary:

> After a day-long reconnaissance, I found that strong groups of bandits were sheltering around Kleisoura. I reported to *Oberstleutnant* Heinz and was ordered to take a motorised detachment into the southern Kleisoura gorges. From the regiment, I had been sent the large half-track with '*Vierlings*' Flak weapon. With a motorcycle sidecar combination, I led the spearhead of a machine-gun group. We drove carefully as the bandits had mined the road. Approaching the village entrance, about a metre from some bushes I was fired at. The bullets whistled past my forehead. I jumped from the motorcycle, opened fire with my machine-pistol on two fleeing bandits and laid them both out. The village is full of bandits and at the same time they opened fire on my column from the heights above. We left our vehicles and charged the village. In a short time, the 'Bandit's nest' [*Bandennest*] is burning and we can see our last remaining opponents. The four-barrelled gun [*Vierling*] shoots with unbelievable force at only short distance from the enemy. Only a few manage to save themselves inside mountain caves, from where we still received heavy fire. Advancing is only possible with heavy losses and so I decide that any success achieved would not be worthwhile. Gröber was hit in the head by a low shot from the Flak weapon. We return to headquarters, our throats are completely dry, the heat is unbearable.[5]

The pattern of removing villagers from their homes and replacing them with guerrillas was a tried and tested ambush technique against the Italian occupiers. However, despite Steidl's initial reluctance to suffer the losses required to take this village, the tactics were frequently unsuccessful against highly motivated and experienced German troops. The Brandenburgers were used on 'pacification' missions to quell growing agitation from Greek guerrillas, known locally as *Andartes*. Kleisoura was later taken by *Hauptmann*

Renner's 3rd Battalion and Steidl moved with his men south, in the vanguard of 1st Battalion.

> I have several places nearby to pacify and launch daily operations with my detachment. A few days later, a company of Greek volunteers, who understand only sadism and plundering, but have no idea how to work as soldiers, arrive as support.
>
> I am launching a night attack against a few villages south of Aliakamonas. It was painstaking work wading with the company through the loamy river [Aliakamonas Potamos]. Rain showers set in. In the morning, we laboured on the other side of the river and in the morning, we were soaking wet in the open air, crossing exposed fields to get through several villages. Oesterwitz comes in from the west with his [2nd] Battalion. We meet. There are a lot of hellos as old acquaintances meet again. We had not seen each other since Baden. *Leutnant* Fred Wurst, a Palestinian man, Lenz Angeringer and old mates celebrate their reunion with us. The 2nd Battalion has suffered heavy losses from mines. A great thunderstorm sets in and hailstones come rattling down. Heinz transports my company back with his vehicles. A new mission is about to be launched: the attack on Neapoli and an advance to the south of Neapoli![6]

In blistering 40°C heat, Weithoener's battalion and Oesterwitz both attacked Neapoli on 24 July from the east, Steidl's company advancing along the left embankment of the entrance road and Oesterwitz on the right. Parched and breathless from the heat, they prepared to assault well-entrenched ELAS guerrillas. Supported by close-range fire from Flak guns and 75mm anti-tank guns, the Brandenburgers remorselessly took one hill after another, both battalions making steady progress. Under heavy fire from barricaded houses and positions lining the outskirts of the town, Steidl led the charge into Neapoli itself. Fierce hand-to-hand combat followed as each dwelling was cleared, flames licking through the streets as hand grenades ignited tinder-dry thatch. An ammunition dump in the centre of the village was found and blown up by a hand grenade thrown by Steidl. Eventually, the fighting subsided, regimental commander *Oberstleutnant* Pfeiffer arriving with personal congratulations for his men on their success.

Throughout August his men continued to battle *Andartes* though with little loss to themselves. On 18 August in an operation alongside Italian troops southwest of Florina, 3rd Battalion encountered a weak band of guerrillas and killed two, capturing five. Amongst those taken prisoner were three British officers who had parachuted into Greece to attempt coordination with the ELAS. Codebooks, maps and a working transmitter were also taken before they could be destroyed by the prisoners.[7]

Also in Greece was the newly deployed *Küstenjäger Abteilung*. Kriegsheim and his headquarters had accompanied its 1st Company to Brindisi by train whereupon they transferred to Piraeus in Greece, sailing regular patrols as far afield as Corfu, Thaka and Patras and acting as transport for any missions undertaken by Hollmann's 1st Battalion/1st Regiment against bandits near the Gulf of Corinth.

Brandenburgers also became established in Yugoslavia by the middle of 1943. *Hauptmann* Gerhard Pinkert's 2nd Battalion/1st Regiment had travelled by train during May to the area in which Heinz had established his 4th Regiment headquarters. Pinkert's attachment to Heinz's command – now known as *Kampfgruppe Heinz* – was indirectly a replacement for Hollmann's battalion that had been diverted to southern Greece. Pinkert's regimental superior, *Major* Walther, had remained on the Eastern Front with *Rittmeister* Plitt during the partisan battles in the rear areas of Army Group North and would not arrive with his staff until July.

Mihailović's Chetnik policy was the formation of strong guerrilla forces that could rise against occupation in support of an Allied landing in Yugoslavia. To achieve this goal the Chetniks opportunistically accepted weapons from both British and Italian sources.[8] However, his was not the sole underground movement gaining traction in the region. Josip Broz Tito had been born to a Croat father and Slovene mother in Kumrovec, Croatia, in 1892. After being drafted into military service he became the youngest Sergeant Major in the Austro-Hungarian Army but was wounded and captured by Russian troops in 1915. While a POW he had converted to communism during the Russian Revolution and, years after his return to Yugoslavia, had been Secretary General of Yugoslavia's Communist Party since 1937. He began gathering forces immediately after the Axis occupation of Yugoslavia, his guerrillas named 'Partisans'. They became so effective over the years that followed that their name became synonymous with underground guerrilla forces everywhere. As the Partisans were staunch anti-royalists, they were soon at war with the Chetniks following a brief period of cooperation against the Axis occupying powers.

After strong Partisan attacks against Italian troops in Montenegro during 1941, the Axis authorities reached a vague accord with Chetnik forces to keep Tito's Partisans in check, virtually relinquishing control of rural areas to Mihailović's troops while the Italians maintained urban garrisons. As further communist agitation transformed into a full-scale revolt in Serbia, German forces became involved in heavy fighting to quell dissident factions, assisted by the Croat nationalist fascist forces of Ante Pavelić's infamous Ustaše. By the time

Partisan Warfare in the Balkans

of the Brandenburgers' arrival in Yugoslavia, several major German operations had already been undertaken against guerrilla forces with high casualty figures and all hallmarked by extraordinary cruelty given the fratricidal nature of the conflict. During June 1943, German forces in the area were reshuffled. The 718th Infantry Division was stationed in Bosnia to the east; 714th Infantry Division assigned to west Bosnia; 704th Infantry Division in eastern Serbia; and 717th Infantry Division shifted from south-western to north-western Serbia. The vacuum left by this latter division's movement was filled by the newly formed 7th SS *Gebirgsjäger* Division 'Prinz Eugen', created from Yugoslavian and Romanian *Volksdeutsche* volunteers.

In Yugoslavia, Heinz was ordered to dismantle the triangular relationship that Mikhailović had established between his Chetniks and British and Italian forces. Tasked with arresting the Chetnik leader, Heinz opted to independently pursue the possibility of a rapprochement with the guerrilla force, with tacit Abwehr support. Heinz's approach was made between January and March 1943, in the aftermath of 'Case White', the fourth major drive against Partisan forces in Yugoslavia and a high point in German–Chetnik cooperation. With two Brandenburg interpreters, Heinz passed through Chetnik lines in Montenegro and met with the local commander Pavle Đurišić on 10 May. There he proposed the establishment of an alliance against Tito and possible formation of a Montenegrin Legion to fight under Wehrmacht control. Negotiations were brief but promising and Heinz returned to his regimental headquarters to report to *Befehlshaber der Deutschen Truppen in Kroatien* (Commander-in-Chief of German Forces in Croatia) *General der Infanterie* Rudolf Lüters. However, Lüters rejected the idea out of hand and instead began a series of new offensives as commander of XV *Gebirgs* Corps. On 14 May, he ordered Đurišić arrested and his Chetniks disarmed or brought under German control, beginning a major month-long drive against Partisan groups in the narrow highland area of Montenegro, Sandzak and Herzegovina. If successful, Lüters believed, he could trap and destroy Tito and the supreme military and political leadership of the 'Yugoslavian National Liberation Movement'. In a major operation against Tito's forces, Lüters aimed to eliminate the Partisan menace to German supply lines that trailed through Yugoslavia to Greece, which was still believed to be threatened by imminent British invasion. Codenamed 'Case Black', the Axis forces totalled 127,000 troops: 67,000 Germans, 43,000 Italians, 2,000 Bulgarians, 11,000 Croatians and 4,000 Chetniks with major air support from the Luftwaffe, Italian and Croatian Air Forces.[9] Facing them were 19,700 Partisans of 1st, 2nd, 3rd and 7th Divisions National Liberation Army and Partisan Detachments of Yugoslavia (NOVJ), 3rd Dalmatian Brigade, III Battalion/4th Proletarian Brigade, II and IV Battalion/5th Montenegrin Brigade and the Drina Operations Group.

Heinz's regiment was subordinated to the 1st *Gebirgs* Division for 'Case Black' and fought in the area between Mojkovac and Berane where they suffered their first casualties in the Yugoslavian war. Attacking in a southwesterly direction from the Ćehotina River, the Brandenburgers were later attached to the substantial '*Kampfgruppe Anaker*' comprised of the bulk of 738th Regiment and 118th *Jäger* Division with supporting units. Attacking through Tjentište they attempted to clear the left bank of the Sutjeska River but dogged Partisan defence held the German advance long enough for an orderly withdrawal by Tito's troops, who left 235 dead and missing behind them, including a company commander and political commissar. On 17 June, a strong Partisan attack around Vitez-Podvitez (on the Sarajevo–Višegrad railway line) made headway before being stopped by the arrival of an armoured train and the hastily formed '*Kampfgruppe Vertmiler*' of 1st Battalion/4th Regiment 'Brandenburg', 369th Anti-Tank Battalion, 12th Panzer Battalion and elements of two Ustaše brigades.

The tenor of 'Case Black', like most operations in the region, was that of ruthless destruction. The pitiless operation echoed sentiments contained in OKW orders that had originated from Hitler at the end of 1942. Lüters issued a directive on 12 January 1943, stating that: 'Every measure that ensures the security of the troops and appears to serve the purpose of pacification is justifiable . . . No one should be held to account for conducting themselves with excessive harshness.'[10] This, then, set the tone by which the Yugoslavian battle was fought.

As a response to what he saw during the operation, Heinz wrote a letter to Lüters in which he attempted to illustrate the vicious circle that harsh repression created: driving civilians into the ranks of the enemy through either resentment or a desire for retribution.

> The previous method of shooting all Partisans indiscriminately could never lead to success. Many Partisans have only become so by a combination of different circumstances: Ustaše, Muslim or Chetnik outrages, need and hunger, terror and being forced by other Partisans. They remain Partisans, because their way back is blocked by German orders. They have lost home and family, so they fight until death.[11]

It was a recurring theme of Yugoslavia's intense internecine warfare and Heinz was not the sole German voice to encourage restraint as a way of winning 'hearts and minds' or, at the very least, lose no more of them. Apparently, such pragmatic heads prevailed in Berlin and within a matter of weeks OKW issued official instructions that captured Partisans were no longer to be treated as irregulars, but afforded the protection of prisoner of war status.

Though 'Case Black' had officially ended, '*Kampfgruppe Heinz*' fought through most of July alongside the 7th SS *Gebirgs* Division and Ustaše and Chetnik units against Partisans in eastern Bosnia, possession of towns and villages see-sawing between the antagonists into well into August. A reinforced battalion of the German 373rd Division was nearly overwhelmed by Partisan forces on 24 August until Heinz's men intervened and beat back Tito's troops, killing a Partisan commander of the 12th Krajina Brigade, Milan Egić, near Kotor Varoš.

Despite his regiment's success in action, Heinz remained deeply unpopular with Pfuhlstein and he finally was relieved of his command in time to undergo a gall-bladder operation after what had been a recurring illness. While *Oberstleutnant* Christoph von Hugo took command of 4th Regiment, Heinz was placed in the officer reserve of *Wehrkreis III* Berlin-Brandenburg on 1 September 1943. From there he continued his political subversion in the pursuit of regime change, but with ultimately disastrous results for Canaris and other more active conspirators.

Meanwhile, Wehrmacht forces were faced with a fresh, though not unexpected, problem in the Balkans. Throughout the region the codeword '*Achse*' was received by all units at 0045hrs on 8 September and alongside other units of the German military, Brandenburger troops began moving to disarm Italian forces that had surrendered to the Allies.

Disarming the Italians

Allied troops had landed on Sicily in early July 1943 and the island was finally conquered by 17 August though without a conclusive German defeat as the Wehrmacht had mounted a highly successful fighting withdrawal to the Italian mainland. The expected Allied attack across the Straits of Messina began on the morning of 3 September when British troops landed on the toe of Italy in Operation 'Baytown'. Kesselring had decided to establish his defensive lines further north and the British faced no major defences in Calabria. Nonetheless, they advanced with painfully cautious sluggishness over manmade obstacles and inhospitable terrain. Five days after the 'Baytown' landing, Eisenhower announced the negotiated surrender of Italy. Mussolini had been arrested and imprisoned but was later liberated by German paratroopers on 12 September in an operation that included the SS *Hauptsturmführer* Otto Skorzeny (Operation '*Eiche*'). The dejected Italian dictator was but a shadow of his former self, though still immediately flown to Germany and browbeaten into forming a new fascist regime, the 'Italian Social Republic' proclaimed on 18 September 1943.

Meanwhile, German units activated Operation '*Achse*' just as further Allied forces landed at Taranto on 9 September; the Allied attack executed at short notice following an Italian offer to surrender the port and its military units intact. Kesselring correctly surmised that neither 'Baytown' nor the new attack, 'Slapstick', were the primary Allied invasion which landed that same day at Salerno under the codename Operation 'Avalanche'. American Lieutenant General Mark Clark's Fifth Army experienced some localised successes in the Salerno beachhead but were soon fighting a desperate battle against aggressive attacks by Kesselring's land forces and unexpectedly numerous Luftwaffe aircraft. Clark was initially thrown off balance and briefly panicked, proposing the evacuation of his troops from Salerno before Allied Supreme Command overruled him.

On Sardinia, the surrendering Italian garrison outnumbered *Hauptmann* Benesch's 16th (Light) Company and the men of 90th Panzergrenadier Division that formed the 'Einstmann Brigade' and refused to disarm as requested by their erstwhile allies. Initially, due to the cordial relations between Italian and German commanders and a confusing array of orders received from Rome regarding their proposed disposition towards the German forces, Wehrmacht troops were guaranteed safe passage off the island by the Italians. In Berlin, the decision had already been taken days before, after intelligence reports indicated an imminent Italian armistice, that reinforcement of Sicily would immediately cease and preparations made to evacuate German troops from Sicily, Sardinia and Corsica. The Sicilian evacuation had already succeeded, while units on Sardinia began embarking on transports for Corsica as a staging-post for onward transfer to the Italian mainland. The *Küstenjäger Abteilung*'s Heavy 4th Company had recently arrived in the port of Santa Lucia in south-eastern Sardinia, from where they mounted frequent anti-invasion patrols to cover the withdrawal.

However, unsure of Italian adherence to their declared non-interference in the German evacuation, Benesch's Brandenburgers initiated pre-emptive assaults on Italian strongholds and artillery positions on Sardinia, large coastal guns that would pose a significant potential threat to the German maritime withdrawal. Key positions were taken without any bloodshed and the German withdrawal from Sardinia was successful, the Brandenburgers departing the island for Corsica as the final rearguard without any interference. However, the peace did not extend to Corsica. There, French resistance fighters rose up against the occupying troops and were soon engaged in heavy fighting with troops of *Sturmbrigade 'Reichsführer SS'* and 90th Panzergrenadier Division who were supported by Italian paratroopers loyal to the fascist cause while the remaining Italian garrison had defected to the Allied side. On 15 September, an SOE-trained French battalion also landed on the island to bolster the uprising.

Despite this reinforcement, the Maquis rebellion on Corsica was largely held in check and the German decision to evacuate the island was confirmed on 17 September once the harbours of Bastia, Porto Vecchia and Bonifacio and their connecting roads were confirmed as firmly in German hands. By 5 October the German evacuation was complete and Benesch's Brandenburgers were transported to the front line in Yugoslavia.

Elsewhere, the '*Achse*' alert resulted in many Brandenburger units facing much greater Italian resistance. As well as Bansen's troops in southern France and the Sardinian company, the following units were immediately tasked with disarming Italian troops and occupying their positions:

> 1st Regiment: 1st Battalion on rail security duty near Levadia; 2nd Battalion near Sarajevo (Yugoslavia); 3rd Battalion near Thiva (Greece).
> 2nd Regiment: 1st, 2nd and 3rd Battalions spread between Florina (northern Greece) and Korçë (Albania).
> 4th Regiment: 1st Battalion in Peloponnese (Greece); 2nd Battalion near Sarajevo (Yugoslavia).
> *Küstenjäger Abteilung*: 1st Company in Athens (Greece); 3rd Company in Dalmatian Islands near Šibenik (Yugoslavia); 4th (Heavy) Company near Sardinia.
> 15th (Light) *Fallschirmjäger* Company standing by in Kraljevo (Yugoslavia). These men were used to surprise Italian forces in Albania, a *Kampfgruppe* entering Durazzo harbour at dawn on 10 September and seizing machine-gun posts, the Italian headquarters and all shipboard armaments. By 0640hrs the harbour was in German hands and 3,000 Italian soldiers and sailors taken prisoner along with two torpedo boats and seven merchant ships.

On the Greek mainland, there appeared little opposition to German demands for Italian garrisons to disarm. General Carlo Geloso commanded the Italian occupation forces and had frequently complained to his friend General Vittorio Amrosio (Italian Army Chief of Staff in Rome), that his troops 'have *armament antiquato*, lack almost any anti-tank or anti-aircraft guns, or armoured transport'. The influx of German forces that had taken place during the first half of 1943 to face the expected invasion of Greece had already tipped the balance of power in what was officially the Italian zone of control firmly towards the Wehrmacht. Furthermore, of Geloso's 93,000 troops, at least 12,000 were ill with malaria.

As '*Achse*' was triggered, defeatism was already rampant amongst the mainland Italian garrisons that submitted relatively meekly to the Wehrmacht. An officer of 3rd Battalion/1st Regiment 'Brandenburg' reported that though Italian troops were 'only partially' obeying their own officers, they were 'behaving in a disciplined and orderly way towards German officers'.[12] Within the Athens area, *Hauptmann* Kuhlmann's 1st Company of the *Küstenjäger Abteilung* had been placed under the command of *Korvettenkapitän* Dr Brand's 21st UJ-Flotilla. Upon receipt of the '*Achse*' codeword they promptly seized an Italian torpedo boat and destroyer – *San Martino* and *Calatafimi* – in Piraeus harbour which were later recommissioned into the Kriegsmarine as *TA17* and *TA19*. There had been no shots fired and no blood spilt.

Following the alert, the 2nd Regiment moved from the area of Grevena at 2210hrs on 8 September in an extended motorised column, travelling north to Kastoria where they were ordered to disarm the Italian 13th Infantry Regiment. Their primary mission went smoothly though a single vehicle of the 3rd Company's signals unit was ambushed by *Andartes* and one *Oberfunkmeister* was killed, two men captured and their Kübelwagen destroyed.

While mainland operations against Italian units generally proceeded without major problems, several of the Italian island garrisons refused to submit so easily. The feared British incursion into the Aegean had also begun with nearly 4,000 British troops spread across the Dodecanese Islands by early October. On the day that Italy had surrendered, the 30,000 Italian troops on Rhodes had been exhorted by British leaflets – and later two British majors parachuted onto the island – to subdue the island's 7,000-strong German garrison. However, after just two days of fierce fighting the Italians surrendered. New *Andarte* groups had risen on the island of Euboea and taken control of the ports, while Zante, Cephalonia, Corfu and Volos also seemed under imminent threat of takeover by Greek guerrillas as Italian troops began handing them their heavy weapons while refusing to surrender to German forces.

Immediate German moves to occupy Corfu were postponed on 16 September after an attempted landing by the 1st *Gebirgs* Division had been repulsed. Instead, the decision was taken to first tackle Italian resistance on Cephalonia and eliminate Italian heavy artillery support for both islands. The island garrison of Skarpantos surrendered unconditionally while Syra required extended negotiation. In Cephalonia, 525 officers and 11,500 men of the Acqui Division had been garrisoned since May 1943, the division's 18th Regiment being detached to occupation duties in Corfu. Acqui's commander, General Antonio Gandin, was a veteran of the Italian action on the Eastern Front and a holder of the Iron Cross. He had considerable strength at his disposal, including naval coastal batteries, torpedo boats and two aircraft. Following the Italian armistice, Gandin negotiated the fate of his command with *Oberst* Johannes Barge, commander of the Wehrmacht's 966th Fortress Grenadier Regiment also present on the island and with whom Gandin had a good rapport. While Corfu's Italian commander flatly refused to surrender, Gandin eventually agreed to give up his division's weapons to Barge by 16 September, simultaneously withdrawing from strategic positions along the island's coastline. However, at 0700hrs on 13 September, Italian artillery opened fire on their own initiative against a convoy of five MFPs carrying German artillery to the port of Argostoli, one of the landing craft capsizing and another being damaged, suffering four dead and three men severely wounded.

Negotiations immediately broke down completely and Gandin, with the backing of most of his officers and men, finally decided that his unit would fight. Troops of the 1st *Gebirgs* Division and 104th *Jäger* Division, assembled as '*Kampfgruppe Hirschfeld*' under the command of *Major* Harald von Hirschfeld, landed on the island after heavy Stuka bombardment and fighting raged ashore until the last Italians surrendered at 1100hrs on 22 September. The conscripts of the Acqui Division were no match for the veteran *Gebirgsjäger* and while 300 German troops were killed, the Italians lost 1,315 men during the battle. Beginning on 21 September, even before the end of hostilities, Hitler had ordered that due to the 'perfidious and treacherous' behaviour of the Italians on Cephalonia, no prisoners were to be taken. Correspondingly, over the week that followed, over 5,000 men of the Acqui Division were shot, including Gandin. It was a pattern repeated to a lesser degree on other islands.

The Brandenburg Division was criticised by both the commander of 1st *Gebirgs* Division and OKH's operations staff for not taking part in the assault on Cephalonia. Serious questions were asked of the division as Berlin considered them 'obligated' to offer their services to the attack. The adjutant of the 1st Regiment, *Oberleutnant* von Fölkersam, had in fact travelled to confer with both the Ia and Ic of the Army Group responsible before returning to Walther's regimental command post and briefing his commander. The Brandenburgers refused to take part in the invasion and were later fully backed by Pfuhlstein who declined to 'reproach' Walther as he was exercising the prerogative of the Brandenburgers to opt out of operations that they considered inappropriate for their men.

The Italian garrison of Corfu, which numbered approximately 8,000 men, had also rejected an agreement with the Germans after rumours circulated that surrendering Italian soldiers were being deported rather than repatriated. The Wehrmacht launched Operation '*Verrat*' ('Treason') in response, originally planned to be spearheaded by Brandenburger troops of Pfeiffer's 2nd Regiment. A company of Italian-speaking South Tyroleans, led by *Leutnant* Kessler, were being equipped with captured Italian uniforms and weapons before heading to Igoumenitsa. They also carried radio equipment and loudspeakers with which to increase confusion behind enemy lines once established ashore. However, their mission was cancelled before it began; German bombing and direct attack by 1st *Gebirgs* Division led in short order to an Italian surrender. Only some of *Hauptmann* Kuhlmann's *Küstenjäger Abteilung* operated in the sea area around Corfu before the Germans prevailed. While there was no mass shooting of Italian prisoners like that on Cephalonia, many officers – at least twenty-seven – were executed.

After the Italian garrison on Kos turned the island over to British troops, Allied forces occupied Leros and Samos on 17 September. By the following day, Symi, Astypalaia and Ikaria were also in British hands. Royal Air Force aircraft were now operating from Kos airfield and German inter-island convoys that ferried vital supplies and troops movements immediately came under attack. The Italian garrison on Syra was taken prisoner by German forces while fighting briefly continued on Andros and Euboea, fifty Italian officers and artillery men deserting to join the Greek partisans after removing the breech blocks of their guns on northern Euboa. A company of men from the 4th SS Polizei Division was transferred to the island though they were soon surrounded and required further SS reinforcements landed by sea. In Berlin, OKW feared that the British-controlled Dodecanese islands could be used as a springboard for further invasions of the Aegean islands, though they had moved fast enough to prevent Allied occupation of the biggest prize: Rhodes.

The German commander on Crete, *Generalleutnant* Friedrich-Wilhelm Müller of the 22nd *Luftlande* Division, was ordered to retake the Dodecanese, beginning with Kos, and plans were swiftly formulated for a daring amphibious and aerial assault. Kos now hosted two Spitfire squadrons and significant British ground forces as well as 3,500 men of the original Italian garrison. However, heavy bombardment by Luftwaffe aircraft of *Fliegerkorps X* soon rendered the airfield unusable and both Spitfire squadrons were withdrawn to Cyprus while such heavy casualties were caused amongst troops on the ground that an occupying British paratrooper battalion was also withdrawn. The air raids were subsequently widened to include Leros as the Luftwaffe had achieved local air supremacy.

The attack on Kos – Operation 'Eisbär' ('Polar Bear') – began on 3 October. A total of 2,000 German troops that included Panzergrenadiers and even some tanks set sail from Piraeus, Suda and Candia in three groups, rendezvousing west of Naxos to become convoy 'Olympus'. Spearheading the amphibious attack was 1st Company of the *Küstenjäger Abteilung*, which stormed ashore at 0610hrs and established a beachhead on the south coast at Camare Bay and Capo Foco. The stronger forces of *Kampfgruppe Kuhlmann* then began landing in the Brandenburger enclave and funnelled inland. At the same time *Oberleutnant* Oschatz led his Brandenburger *Fallschirmjäger* company in a landing amidst the scrubby undulating land north of Cape Tigani, near the cratered Antimachia aerodrome. Two aircraft, with their combined twenty-four *Fallschirmjäger* aboard, had failed to join the attack – one dropping out with engine damage, the other failing to meet the rendezvous point with the remaining aircraft and forced to return. Both would finally arrive during the following day. Nonetheless, the landing went as planned and Oschatz's men quickly moved into the attack, overwhelming British artillery and mortar emplacements guarding the approach to the airfield. Positioning his machine guns to cover the advance of the *Küstenjäger*, Oschatz had control of the access road to the small town of Antimachia and had taken his first British prisoners. With *Fallschirmjäger* attacking along the north of the road and *Küstenjäger* to the south, the airfield was soon under German control; a small swastika recognition flag flying over it by 1710hrs. Despite the flag, the *Fallschirmjäger* were twice bombed by Luftwaffe aircraft, the first raid ignoring the agreed upon signal of a white flare, the second arriving when there remained no more flares available to fire. Fortunately for the Brandenburgers, despite the impressive explosions of the Luftwaffe attack, only one of Oschatz's men was wounded.

Following a relatively quiet night, strong reconnaissance forces left for the town of Antimachia at 0410hrs the following morning. Moving east, by dawn organised resistance to their advance had ceased and Kos was in German hands. Oschatz's company had taken 400 Italians and forty British troops prisoner, captured seventeen damaged aircraft, fifteen heavy machine guns and quantities of small arms, eight artillery pieces and five anti-aircraft batteries of various calibres. In return they had suffered one man killed and five wounded. The Germans took 1,388 British and 3,145 Italian prisoners in total, the Italian island commander Colonel Felice Leggio and ninety-one of his officers being shot as per Hitler's instructions. The pair of late Junkers transport aircraft landed their *Fallschirmjäger* as reinforcements, but a German battalion being rushed by sea to the island in a small troop convoy codenamed 'Olympus' was intercepted and almost destroyed by the Royal Navy. The battalion had been earmarked to garrison Kos while the assault troops and Brandenburgers currently in possession were planned to immediately mount an attack on Leros, the garrison on Kalymnos already surrendering without a fight and allowing the island to be occupied by 1st Company of the *Küstenjäger Abteilung*. Though the Brandenburgers landed without firing a shot, their commander *Hauptmann* Armin Kuhlmann was severely wounded in an Allied air attack on the island, *Leutnant* Hans Schädlich subsequently taking command.

The prearranged timetable for the capture of Leros was now in serious jeopardy. While OKW raged with bitter recriminations following the 'Olympus' convoy's destruction, the attack on Leros was still ordered by 9 October at the latest. The existing plan, codenamed 'Leopard', was frustrated further by the combination of Royal Navy interceptions of men and material, bad Aegean weather fronts and the arrival of USAAF P 38 Lightning aircraft that had begun to cause the Luftwaffe problems in the area. 'Leopard' was gradually postponed in increments that ultimately delayed it until November, by which time the British garrison on Leros had swelled to about 2,500 troops. These included men of the 2nd Battalion, The Royal Irish Fusiliers, 4th Battalion The Buffs (The Royal East Kent Regiment), 1st Battalion The King's Own Royal Regiment (Lancaster), a company of the 2nd Battalion Queen's Own Royal West Kent Regiment and a small number of men from the Special Boat Service; the entire force under Brigadier Robert Tilney, who assumed command on 5 November. Additionally, the Italians had 8,320 soldiers and sailors still on the island, the majority from Captain Luigi Mascherpa's garrison, but also men from thirteen coastal batteries and twelve anti-aircraft and dual-purpose batteries.

In the meantime, despite the delay, Oschatz and his *Fallschirmjäger* were not idle. On 18 October, they attacked the small island of Levitha 60km north-west of Kos. An Italian radio station had been detected on the barren island and aerial reconnaissance reported small British ships present, carrying approximately fifty German prisoners from the shattered 'Olympus' convoy. The shipwrecked survivors were predominantly Luftwaffe ground troops and many of them were suffering from severe wounds sustained during the naval action.

The Brandenburger raid on Levitha was coordinated with the commander of the Luftwaffe maritime reconnaissance group, *Oberst* Hermann Busch, and Oschatz proposed a small shock troop of four rifle groups, one radio NCO and two radio men, the *Truppenarzt*, *Oberarzt* Dr Koepchen and three combat medics. Two Junkers Ju 52 floatplanes and a Dornier flying boat were provided as troop transport as well as an escort of six Arado Ar 196 floatplanes. The *Fallschirmjäger* were not parachuting into action this time; the aircraft would land as close to shore as possible and the assault groups disembark on rubber rafts that would be later used to ferry the liberated wounded men back to the waiting aircraft for transfer to hospital in Athens.

At 0530hrs on 18 October, the troop-carrying aircraft departed, landing the *Fallschirmjäger* on the south coast of Levitha as planned, the Dornier flanked on either side by Ju 52s while the smaller Arados provided cover. Oschatz was in the right-hand Junkers, storming ashore and inland, immediately heading towards the small Italian radio station that was on the island's high ground. One of the rafts that alighted from the large Dornier capsized and 23-year-old *Obergefreiter* Fritz Bruhn, weighed down with machine-gun ammunition, was dragged to the bottom and drowned. He was to be the only German lost that day, though two others were wounded by splinters from one of their own hand grenades.

A pair of Italians who opened fire on the approaching Germans were shot and killed before the fighting ended as swiftly as it had begun. Nine British soldiers, including one officer, were captured as well as the eleven men of the Italian radio station. Charts and radio cipher material was also seized and sent back to Athens with the wounded.

Only a matter of days later the *Fallschirmjäger* were in action again, this time landing on Astipalia in a combined operation with *Major* Walther's 1st Battalion/1st Regiment. The Luftwaffe mounted Stuka raids on the island as a prelude to the attack, targeting and destroying an Italian wireless station at Porto Scala. At approximately 0915hrs Oschatz's *Fallschirmjäger* Company was dropped by parachute at Maltezana at the island's narrow centre. Walther's troops were soon landed on the south-west coast, some also air landed at the small airstrip that had been quickly occupied by the *Fallschirmjäger*. As the Brandenburgers advanced from the coast they freed forty-eight German prisoners who had also survived the disastrous 'Olympus' convoy. The operation, though perhaps minor in the annals of Second World War history, was mounted with dash and determination and was rewarded with success achieved by minimal fighting, the small Allied presence on the island soon surrendered or in hiding.

Pfuhlstein issued his after-action summary on 23 October detailing the Brandenburger actions thus far in the Dodecanese. In it, he noted the high morale displayed by the 1st Regiment troops en-route to Astipalia, the leading pilot of one of their transport aircraft apparently remarking that he had never carried such a motivated troop of men before. Pfuhlstein's praise for the conduct of his men was justified.

The characteristics of a good surprise attack [*Handstreich*] – fast, lightning-quick appearance and hitting the enemy before he can organise his defence – have excelled here in all three cases. In addition to good preparation by officers, the troops have performed perfectly. It is only because each individual *Jäger* throws his heart and soul into it that these operations are so well handled.[13]

The Battle for Leros

'Leopard' was now scheduled for 9 November. *Generalleutnant* Müller had assembled an assault force that included Schädlich's 1st Company/*Küstenjäger Abteilung* (with elements of *Hauptmann* Gustav Froboese's 3rd Battalion/1st Regiment 'Brandenburg' as reinforcement) and three Panzergrenadier battalions with an aerial attack to be made by the Brandenburger *Fallschirmjäger* Company and Luftwaffe *Fallschirmjäger* 1st Battalion/2nd *Fallschirmjäger* Regiment. The naval plan involved twenty-five infantry landing craft, two MFPs, thirteen escort vessels as well as two ex-Italian destroyers and two torpedo boats to be used as a distant covering group. Heavy Luftwaffe Stuka and bomber support was to be provided to compensate for Royal Navy predominance in the region and preparatory raids numbered in the hundreds before the attack was launched. On 7 November, amidst security concerns, the operation was renamed '*Taifun*' and as the shipping required for the assault assembled, they suffered further Allied air harassment that damaged four escorting R-boats. Finally, after several false starts, '*Taifun*' began on 12 November.

Nearly forty Ju 52s swept towards the island from Athens. Skimming low to the waters of the Aegean, they were only an hour into their journey when they were unexpectedly recalled. Their landing zone was on the narrow waist of the island that would link amphibious landings from both east and west. However, one of those amphibious assaults had already gone awry.

As planned, the advance by sea to Leros had begun in two groups east and west of Kalymnos during the previous night. Under heavy defensive fire the first troops – including the *Küstenjäger Abteilung* – began landing on the eastern edge of Leros in and around Alinda Bay at 0521hrs, but those destined for Gourrna Bay on the west coast had been forced away at 0543hrs five miles south-west of the island under heavy artillery fire from ashore; Stukas were called in to neutralise British artillery and the western landing rescheduled for 1245hrs. However, even after several hours' delay, accurate shellfire continued to disrupt their attempted landing, one landing craft being hit by mortars, stored ammunition and fuel detonating and sinking the vessel. The attack was broken off and postponed until the cover of darkness before being entirely diverted to the eastern coast.

Meanwhile, a beachhead had been successfully established at Alinda and the parachute drop was restarted. The aircraft slowly flew in line astern to the drop zone that formed a triangle between the villages of San Nicola, San Quirco and Alinda. The *Fallschirmjäger* carried their personal weapons rather than dropping without them and having to recover them from containers, enabling them to go immediately into action once on the ground. Slow moving, the Ju 52s were flying below the level of anti-aircraft guns on flanking hilltops, though they still absorbed terrific punishment from ground fire as the drop zone was held by at least two platoons of the 2nd Royal Irish Fusiliers and the Buffs as well as some men of the Special Boat Service. Dropping from only 180m, the drop time was barely twenty seconds before the *Fallschirmjäger* hit the ground, the first landing at about 1430hrs. Casualties were high: as much as 40 per cent of the total parachute troops used. The Brandenburg *Fallschirmjäger* Company, together with two companies of Luftwaffe troops, began immediately attacking Rachi ridge which was soon taken and held against weak counter-attacks.

Below them, the *Küstenjäger* had come ashore on the north side of Mount Apetiki, though heavy enemy fire left not a single officer unwounded. Quickly ashore, they scaled the heights and attacked an Italian 150mm artillery battery, occupying the mount's summit. However, exhausted by the climb and decimated by enemy fire, they went rapidly on to the defensive as the Royal Irish Fusiliers counter-attacked. Having permanently silenced the battery's guns, the Brandenburgers retreated down the slopes to find cover and contented themselves with pinning down the Irish troops by accurate sniping.

The confusion of the landings began to subside with dusk and the last Luftwaffe raids of the day. An uneasy calm descended upon the battlefield in which both sides appeared to take stock of their situation. The thunderbolt attack envisioned by Müller had failed to achieve every objective thus far, but German forces were firmly lodged ashore. The frustrated western assault force was still at sea and had now been so for an entire day in deteriorating conditions as a bad weather front swept towards the island. They had escaped detection by the Royal Navy, but the longer they remained at sea the greater the peril became. Müller requested more Brandenburgers brought to the island and on the night of 15 November Froboese's 3rd Battalion was landed under enemy fire from two Italian torpedo boats. On the British side gloom permeated through the ranks, most men unaware that they had repulsed an attempted landing and plagued with the knowledge that German troops were now dug in on the island and would be difficult to dislodge.

The rescheduled landing of troops of the western group on the east side of Leros was finally carried out at about 0600hrs on the second day of the battle under heavy fire but covered by an all-out operation by Kriegsmarine *U-Jäger* and R-boats. In bad weather casualties were moderate but the large body of men were finally put ashore, reinforcing the beachhead and glad to be on terra-firma once more. Approximately 150 Brandenburger *Fallschirmjäger* were then dropped into the same zone as that of the previous day, while the *Küstenjäger* made a second drive on Mount Apetiki, dislodging British troops and taking hold of Kastro, a Byzantine castle on a promontory from where their own fire could dominate the surrounding area.

While the balance of the battle tilted irretrievably towards the German invaders there was still fierce fighting until, on 16 November, the Allies finally surrendered and Leros was conquered. A section leader of the reinforcing 3rd Battalion, *Oberjäger* Haake, recorded the end of the struggle in his diary:

> At about 2 o'clock we walked over a saddle and came unmolested into the village of Leros. We push through and reach the heights south of the city at day break. Strong infantry fire. I'm going for a Flak position when Klette and Berger

are wounded. I occupied the position with Lascyk and Tadewald. Huesmann is wounded. At three o'clock in the morning, the commander stormed Peak 204. The commander, *Oberleutnant* [Hans-Günter] Lenssen, *Oberfeldwebel* [Edmund] Thiele and *Gefreiter* [Robert] Hangen fell in this attack. An English General was captured, as well as about two companies of British and Italian troops. Our Stukas continually attack the English positions and the hinterland. In the evening the defenders of the island capitulate. General Müller negotiates with three English Generals. I move into a gun position which we captured with three of my group. At night, the dead are buried.

Gustav Froboese had been wounded during the attack, his place as battalion commander taken by *Oberleutnant* Max Wandrey who continued to lead the men as they stormed the hill and captured Brigadier Tilney. Froboese was awarded the German Cross in Gold on 30 December 1943 while Wandrey would receive the Knight's Cross on 9 January 1944 for his bravery leading the relentless German assault against heavy enemy fire. Four hundred and eight Germans had been killed in the attack on Leros while the defending British troops lost 357 men. Unlike some other islands, there were no summary executions of surrendered Italian troops.

The 1st Company/*Küstenjäger Abteilung* was based in the Dodecanese until the end of the war, redesignated '*Küstenjäger Kompanie Rhodos*' under the command of *Oberleutnant* Bertermann. Meanwhile the remainder of the company transferred to the Dalmatian islands to do battle against small units of the Royal Navy and Tito's Partisans.

The northern Aegean island of Samos was soon bombed into submission and occupied on 22 November 1943, by *Major* Walther leading a small group of men from the 1st Regiment. With the capture of this island and the Dodecanese now firmly in German hands, the Aegean was once again under Axis control; by early December all British and Greek forces had been withdrawn from the region apart from a tiny force left on Kastellorizo which, despite some isolated commando raids, the Germans were content to ignore. Hitler expressed his appreciation for the execution of '*Taifun*' via a message to *Wehrmachtsbefehlshaber Südost* (Commanding General, Armed Forces South-east) *Generaloberst* Alexander Löhr:

The capture of Leros, embarked on with limited means but with great courage, carried through tenaciously despite various set-backs and bravely brought to a victorious conclusion, is a military accomplishment which will find an honourable place in the history of this war.

On Samos, many of the island's small towns were now ruins after the aerial bombardment and Walther's Brandenburgers spent weeks on uneventful patrol, visited by *General* Müller on 4 December who distributed sixty EK IIs and eight EK Is amongst them. They returned to Piraeus four days later aboard the destroyer *TA15* that travelled in convoy with torpedo boat *TA16*, an R-boat and the freighter *Leda*, the procession narrowly being missed by four torpedoes from the submarine HMS *Unruly* which was on patrol in the Aegean. The remainder of the 1st Regiment also returned to mainland Greece – temporarily under the command of *Hauptmann* Hans Gerlach while Walther was on leave in Germany – and began operations against *Andartes* in central Greece along the shores of the Gulf of Euboea. They were also responsible for guarding the narrow coastal passage at Thermopylae, the area made famous by King Leonidas' Spartans centuries before. By the year's end, they had taken heavy losses in battle with the Greek guerrillas in snow-covered forests and over unfamiliar and inhospitable terrain. With a severe manpower shortage biting deep into all branches of the Wehrmacht and Waffen SS, officer replacements were now arriving directly from battle schools in Germany and by the end of 1943 the strength of the Brandenburg Division had been whittled away on all fronts.

A general reorganisation of the division's Balkan deployment took place in the final weeks of the year after a Führer Order issued on 4 October included explicit directives for *Generaloberst* Löhr as Commander-in-Chief South-east. In the order, Walther's 1st Regiment was to remain on station as coastal defence troops under the command of Army Group E in the Peloponnese (LXVIII Corps), while most of the division 'was to be employed guarding lines of communication in the rear and participate in the war against the Partisans'. *Oberstleutnant* Pfeiffer's 2nd Regiment was gradually moved in stages to Raška, Montenegro, while a complicated exchange of the *Kampfgruppe* 1st Battalion/4th Regiment, under the command of *Hauptmann* Hollmann, with Pinkert's 2nd Battalion/1st Regiment was made to take advantage of the large number of Bosnian *Volksdeutsche* among Hollmann's troops. Under the leadership of Austrian officer *Oberleutnant* Blöckl they were clearly, as Pfuhlstein put it in his movement order, 'not in the right place' in Greece and more use back with their parent battalion in Yugoslavia. By the time of their return to *Oberstleutnant* von Hugo's control near Sarajevo, the 4th Regiment, attached to XV *Gebirgs* Corps, maintained the following units: 1st Battalion/4th (*Major* Hollmann); 2nd Battalion/4th (*Hauptmann* Lau); 3rd Battalion/4th (*Hauptmann* von Koenen); 1st Battalion/1st – on attachment – (*Hauptmann* Rosenow).

On the Eastern Front, 1st Battalion/3rd Regiment was still heavily engaged in fighting Soviet troops after the Red Army had fully exploited the weakness of the boundary between Army Groups North and Centre at the transport and supply hub of Nevel on 6 October. Catching the Germans by surprise, the Soviets severely battered the 2nd Luftwaffe Field Division and captured the town. Hitler ordered Nevel recaptured immediately, the Brandenburgers holding a line that stretched between Ordovo and Jeziaryšča lakes in the Soviet guerrilla heartland.

> 7.10.1943: Lying in the front line south of Nevel. Russian armoured attack. Four were shot up. One, which I had initially taken for a German panzer, was settled by a hollow charge. Stuka, ground attack aircraft from both sides. Strong operation. 81 Stuka attacks. One dead man with us. At night, the Russians try to attack and are beaten. Two dead.[14]

The *Hauptkampflinie* (main battle line) of the battalion came under incredible pressure from armour, infantry and artillery with support from Sturmovik aircraft. Isolated pockets of German resistance faltered and the Soviet troops began to breach the line.

> 12.10.1943: The Russians have got past us and sit right behind us. Machine-gun fire spits at us from this direction, whistling around our heads. An unpleasant feeling. In the evening, Russian armour attacks to the right of us. The Luftwaffe Field Division is on the verge of running again and can only be brought to a halt and held by us by force, i.e. machine-gun fire. Our *Sanitäts Unteroffizier* is shot at close range by one of these brothers. He probably thought he was an Ivan.[15]

Throughout November and December, the Germans were forced gradually back, the Brandenburg Battalion fighting for every metre of ground using slit trenches and hastily built bunkers to try and withstand the Red Army onslaught. It was, ultimately, to no avail. While 3rd Battalion/3rd Regiment had finally been withdrawn to the area south-east of Minsk with a strength of only 360 able-bodied men, 1st Battalion continued to fight and at the end of 1943 was situated in Lepiel, Belarus. The 2nd Battalion had already been shipped south for rest in Abruzzo, Italy, where it was transformed into a mobile unit and began operations against the new threat of Italian guerrillas.

Pfuhlstein found little assistance from the Abwehr who had virtually ceased all attempts at influencing either the division's use in combat or its future development. Indeed, both Pfuhlstein and the 'political soldier' Friedrich Wilhelm Heinz would later complain of the 'unmilitary' atmosphere in Abwehr headquarters. Heinz later related that Canaris was frequently attempting to prevent the division being assigned to combat duties. Furthermore, after he had brought a newly designed silencer for automatic weapons for evaluation

Partisan Warfare in the Balkans

by Oster and Canaris, he was dumfounded to be asked what the point was of 'continuing to produce new instruments of murder – enough terrible things were happening in the world as it was'. Heinz subsequently took the silencer and its Brandenburger *Feldwebel* designer to *Reichsminister* Albert Speer for evaluation and testing.[16] Following requests for information regarding the quantity of men and equipment needed to expand the division, Pfuhlstein delivered an impassioned plea to the Wehrmacht General Staff at Führer Headquarters for sustained recruiting while his men were taken out of the line to refit. Within the statistics that he presented was a plan that would raise his troop level by 2,000 men within six months and double that within a year. But, first he painted a grim picture of the Brandenburg Division's condition:

> All parts of the Brandenburg Division have been used in combat since spring this year. Essential parts of the division have been at the focal points of the fighting for many weeks.
> a) Eastern Front.
>   1. 3rd Regiment. With 1st Battalion, again in heavy defensive fighting at the region of Nevel, the other battalions involved in severe fighting against bandits around Mogilev.
>   2. The Legionnaire Battalion of the Division is from 9 November at the focal point of fighting around Zhitomir.
> b) South-Eastern Front
>   1. 1st Regiment. 3rd Battalion, 1st *Küstenjäger* Company, *Fallschirmjäger* Company and 1st Company of 4th Regiment have been previously used to captured the Dodecanese Islands.
>   2. 2nd Regiment. In north Montenegro, in the region of Sjenica, fighting against an enemy stronger both in weapons and numerically.
>   3. 4th Regiment has had considerable losses from 'Operation Black' and the ensuing battles around Banja Luka.
>
> Unfortunately, the losses incurred so far are quite substantial. With only weak battalions (only two light companies of two platoons each and one small heavy company), these losses are of great importance. Individual companies only have a fire strength of 30–35 men. Losses in the fight for the island of Leros were particularly severe. Of the 450 officers, NCOs and men of the division, 171 men were killed or wounded, ten of them officers. Fresh casualties occur every day.[17]

The ranks of the Brandenburg Division had been severely depleted during almost constant combat throughout 1943 on several different fronts. Their war had predominantly become one of anti-guerrilla operations with little scope for the 'behind the lines' techniques at which the Brandenburgers had excelled. During October OKW had already begun considering the reclassification of the division and on 29 November *Generalmajor* Walter Warlimont, Deputy of the *Wehrmachtführungsstab* (Armed Forces Operations Staff) wrote to Pfuhlstein regarding the elimination of difficulties hindering the expansion of the division and encouragement to build 'on a "country-like" basis, following the model used by the SS'.[18] Pfuhlstein asked for permission to form four training battalions; he was granted permission for two.

There was also at least one ambitious undertaking that harked back to the original Brandenburgers during June 1943. African-born *Leutnant der Reserve* Hans Brügmann and five men of South-West and East African origin – *Unteroffizier* Bill Fesq, *Feldwebel* Wilfried Moll, *Obergefreiter* Rudolf Otto and *Obergefreiter* Otto Hand – boarded the long-range Type IXD2 U-boat *U-200* in Kiel. Their mission appears to have been sabotage in South Africa, principally the Australian-built dry-docks in Durban. Once their main mission was complete they were to coordinate with the Afrikaner pro-German *Ossewarbrandwag* to harass Allied outposts in South Africa and sow widespread discord. The U-boat commander, *Korvettenkapitän* Heinrich Schonder, was to land the sabotage troop on a deserted stretch of coastline before heading onwards into the Indian Ocean and ultimately Penang, Malaya. A brief layover on the outward voyage at Bergen allowed disembarkation practice for the Brandenburgers before they began the long voyage south.

Making good speed into the Atlantic after circling north of Britain, Schonder's desire to reach the open ocean was his undoing. Spotted while running surfaced south-west of Iceland by a Coastal Command Liberator bomber that was on distant convoy escort, the boat was straddled with two depth charges despite accurate Flak from the frantically manoeuvring *U-200*. The U-boat momentarily disappeared in spume cause by the blast as the Liberator circled for a second attack. It proved unnecessary; *U-200* was clearly seen to be sinking and at least fifteen swimming survivors were observed after the U-boat made its final dive. However, running low on fuel, the Liberator was forced to return to its base and the survivors from *U-200* were never seen again.

Yugoslavia: Operation '*Kugelblitz*'

In Yugoslavia, the Wehrmacht were about to launch Operation '*Kugelblitz*' ('Ball Lighting', known to the Partisans as the 'German Sixth Offensive'). The strategy, devised by the commander of the 2nd Panzer Army, *Generaloberst* Rendulic, was to attack Tito's main forces estimated to number 30,000 fighters of the 2nd,

5th, 17th and 27th Divisions that had assembled east of Sarajevo in preparation for a possible advance into Serbia. Rendulic's attacking forces numbered approximately 70,000 troops under the overall control of V SS *Gebirgs* Corps. The operational plan was to make a wide sweep around the Partisan enclave in order to encircle them, before constricting the pocket and annihilating the four divisions through conventional battle. Rendulic considered this a tried and trusted strategy that had accorded success previously, though this time the Partisans were not so easily trapped.

The Axis forces included Croatian and Bulgarian troops, the two primary German units the 7th SS *Gebirgs* Division and 1st *Gebirgs* Division to which Pfeiffer's 2nd Regiment was attached. Pfeiffer's initial orders were for *Oberleutnant* Steidl's 1st Battalion to take and hold the bridge at Prijepole, a town held by strong Partisan and ex-Italian Army forces that included light armour and some artillery. Prijepole marked the front line as the most forward German units held the wooded heights immediately to the south, troops quartered in the scattered houses of the village of Koševine barely 2km away. The capture of the bridge over the Lim River was of paramount importance to the entire operation and Steidl prepared his men accordingly.

At 0200hrs on 4 December, a spearhead platoon led by south Tyrolean *Feldwebel* Wladimir Mark began the descent towards the enemy, all conversation held in Italian lest they be overheard by enemy pickets. Before long they were in contact with Italian sentry lines, Mark attempting to engage them in conversation, though apparently unconvincingly as the Italian troops opposite opened fire. All attempts at subterfuge now over, the Brandenburgers attacked. The initial Italian bunker line was swiftly overcome and Steidl's battalion marched on to the town itself, taking advantage of swirling fog to obscure their identity to defending troops as they approached. Once in the town's outskirts they became embroiled in savage hand-to-hand combat as they cleared their way towards the bridge one house at a time. The night was alive with gunfire and the explosion of grenades until, at 0630hrs, Steidl radioed Pfeiffer that the bridge was undamaged and in German hands. However, the toll had been severe; only thirty Brandenburger men were still in action, the remainder either dead or wounded, Mark himself having taken a bullet in the shoulder. They had accumulated about eighty prisoners and would struggle to guard them while holding the bridge. During a brief pause in the fighting Steidl could hear the sound of the other battalions in action and as he took a moment to survey the situation with the wounded Mark, a sudden burst of fire hit the wounded Brandenburger in the head, killing him instantly and only missing Steidl by inches. The fighting resumed and before long Steidl had only eighteen men left to hold the bridge. Expecting to be overwhelmed by the desperate enemy attacks, the young officer was relieved to finally see the arrival of German armour and, alongside the first tank, his regimental commander Pfeiffer. The entire 3rd Battalion was soon holding the town as German forces funnelled over the Lim River into action. A strong Partisan force held a barracks on Prijepole's outskirts and Steidl led an attack that evening that took possession, killing 180 Partisans in the process.

Over the days that followed, German forces thrust west and north-west from Prijepole. Pfeiffer's regiment was used to block Partisan troops attempting to attack from the rear of the advance, the 1st Battalion being transported to Brodarevo to repulse this new threat. In heavily wooded undulating terrain and winter weather of snow and fog, the Brandenburgers fought their way against Partisan units attempting to break the German cordon. With periodic support from Croatian and German units, the battalion stubbornly battled until available ammunition ran low and they were forced to withdraw. Finally replaced in the line, they were put into reserve at Prijepole where they received fresh equipment and a number of replacement men. Amongst them was *Hauptmann* Weithoener, returned to take command of the battalion while Steidl was promoted to *Hauptmann* for his achievements; he was subsequently awarded the Knight's Cross on 26 January 1944 for courage in the face of the enemy.

Ultimately, although Operation '*Kugelblitz*' killed a confirmed 2,280 Partisans with an estimated 2,000 more as well as taking 2,330 Partisans and 1,900 renegade Italian soldiers prisoner, it failed to achieve its aims. Tito had correctly surmised the German intention to encircle his troops and spread them wide to each flank as well as slipping through the advancing Germans to attack from the rear. By avoiding any frontal attacks, the bulk of the Partisan forces eluded their enemy and by 18 December 1943 the operation was called off. A second assault, codenamed '*Schneesturm*' ('Snowstorm') against Partisan forces in the Krivaja Valley began almost immediately but was similarly unsuccessful. Other operations continued throughout December by XV *Gebirgs* Corps in northern and western Bosnia which also inflicted casualties, but failed to trap and destroy Tito's army. The Partisan war would continue into 1944 with undiminished intensity.

On Christmas Eve, Pfuhlstein issued a customary message to his division in which he summarised the achievements of the previous year, singling out those men who had particularly distinguished themselves. The final section of his message also painted the immediate future of the division:

> What will 1944 bring us? Our ranks have been thinned by the battles at the end of this year. This will change at the start of the New Year. Beginning in January hand-picked volunteers from every branch of the armed forces will join us, who will be assigned to the front-line regiments. We will also be receiving the

first young soldiers who were carefully trained in the new training regiment under the command of *Major* Martin. I have seen these recruit companies; they are trained in all styles of fighting and have exercised in the field. The regiments will be keen to get these excellent young soldiers. Our weaponry will be improved to the maximum degree possible. NCO courses, combat school courses and other opportunities for the best possible training will be exploited to the utmost. In the preceding summary I have mentioned several officers by name. But our success would not have been possible if these officers had not had hundreds of brave NCOs and men standing at their side as part of a true fighting team. To all of them goes an equal measure of my thanks and recognition. The Brandenburg Division enters the New Year self-confident, with head held high. No one in the entire German Wehrmacht and certainly no one on the enemy side, can impress or show us Brandenburgers anything! Our motto for the year 1944 is the same as in the old year. It is: Brandenburgers Forward Everywhere![19]

CHAPTER 11

Metamorphosis, 1944–1945

'Was not a traitor. Did my duty as a German.'
Admiral Wilhelm Canaris, 8 April 1945

1944 was a tumultuous year for both the Brandenburg Division and its current commander Alexander von Pfuhlstein. Pfuhlstein had spent months visiting his individual units in the south-east region as they became embroiled in the savagery of guerrilla warfare. In May 1943, he had spent a few days with the 4th Regiment in Montenegro, time with the 1st Regiment in Greece north of Athens during autumn and would go on to visit the 2nd Regiment at Banja Luka in Bosnia during the spring of 1944. The town had become the centre for anti-Partisan operations and so-called *Bandenjägerlehrgänge* (Anti-Partisan Training Units) were formed for training German and Croat troops, mostly for *Volltarnung* missions behind enemy lines. In charge was *Hauptmann* Konopacki, who had gained partisan-hunting experience with various police regiments, while the specialist instructors were all drawn from the ranks of experienced Brandenburgers. Pfuhlstein later recounted the motives for his string of visits in post-war interrogations regarding possible Brandenburg involvement in the regular shooting of hostages by German troops in the Balkans. Since the expansion of the Brandenburgers to divisional strength, Canaris and Oster had reminded him of the likelihood of action against Hitler during the year to come and the potential role that the Brandenburgers could play:

> The reasons for these visits were to clarify the personnel and material requirements of the regiments and, above all, to seek out officers from the regiments who seemed suited to me per their political position, for the revolution which I had to prepare to act on in Berlin ... I received extensive and detailed reports, especially from the 2nd Regiment. I am not aware of the shooting of hostages by the commanders' orders.
>
> I did have in one case an officer, of whom I suspected something like this and relieved him of his position with immediate effect while requesting an investigation. This officer then reported me for defeatism, which ultimately led

to my release from the Regiment. It was *Oberleutnant* Böckl. In Böckl's case, I suspected that he harboured an innate cruelty, so I had him removed with immediate effect.¹

A letter denouncing Pfuhlstein's behaviour during his visit to '*Abteilung Böckl*' on 29 February, was received by *Oberbefehlshaber Südost* and, though crawling through official channels for several months, came at a particularly unfavourable moment for Pfuhlstein. The Abwehr as a whole had come under increasing suspicion from other security agencies and more political branches of the Third Reich for potentially treasonous activities. The presiding Judge of the Luftwaffe's Court Martial court, *Oberstkriegsgerichtstrat* (Judge Advocate) Dr Manfred Roeder, a hard and ultra-conservative legal mind, had been tasked with investigating rumours of Abwehr plans to topple the government. While Canaris may have become increasingly vague and distant from the front-line plotters against Hitler, the tenacious and highly intelligent Roeder had soon detected traces of conspiracy that swirled around Canaris and, by extension, the Abwehr.

Roeder arrested Abwehr *Sonderführer* Hans von Dohnányi on charges of breaching foreign currency regulations. The Hungarian-born Dohnányi, was a deeply committed member of the anti-Hitler conspiracy and Oster's direct subordinate and had illegally transferred funds from Germany to a Swiss bank on behalf of Jews that he had personally helped escape Germany. Papers incriminating Oster and other high-ranking Abwehr men were found and Oster was dismissed from his post on 15 April 1943, placed initially into the personnel reserve while investigations continued. Roeder's hunt for conspirators virtually paralysed all activity by Canaris and his officers and it was an ironic twist that it took the Allied invasion of Sicily to diminish the darkening shadow of suspicion over the Abwehr. Officers sympathetic to Canaris convinced Keitel at OKW that the Abwehr's full faculties were required in Italy and Roeder was quietly called off his hunt. A replacement for Oster as head of Abwehr II, *Oberst* Baron Wessel von Freytag-Loringhoven, was appointed and the immediate peril posed by investigations into alleged treason appeared to have passed.

Attempts were made to repair damaged prestige and restore some measure of effectiveness with the new blood that was subsequently brought into the Abwehr. Abwehr III's new chief, *Oberst* Theodor Heinrich, instigated measures to transform previously static counter-espionage and counterintelligence units into mobile reconnaissance units – *Frontaufklärungskommando* (FAKs) – whose operations closely resembled aspects of the Brandenburger Division's previous covert work, but who remained departmentally separate from the division.

Meanwhile, there were many of the veteran Brandenburgers who felt disgruntled by the change in the division's role and there had even been some major defections from the division. While on leave in Germany, Adrian Baron von Fölkersam, representing a delegation of eleven Brandenburg officers, arrived at SS *Sturmbannführer* Otto Skorzeny's office of the 502nd SS *Jagderverbänd* in October 1943.

> He told me that there was great dissatisfaction in the ranks of the old 'Brandenburgers'. The division was no longer employed on special service, but used as a stop-gap at various points along the front – a role which any other division could have played equally well. Its losses had always been very high and it was almost impossible to make them good, having regard to the special training they had received . . . He and ten other officers from his battalion would like to join my command, the formation of which they had only just heard . . . It was in this connection that I came into contact, for the first and last time, with the well-known Admiral Canaris, Director of German Military Intelligence.[2]

Skorzeny accompanied Walter Schellenberg and Ernst Kaltenbrunner to a meeting with Canaris superficially aimed at establishing greater cooperation between the deadly rivals of the Abwehr and the RSHA. The SS commando appears to have been impressed by Canaris, both as an enigmatic man and a skilled negotiator. Skorzeny negotiated for the transfer of Fölkersam and his comrades over the course of several hours until Canaris eventually agreed, though it took a further month before the Brandenburg volunteers were released. Fölkersam, promoted and commissioned into the Waffen SS as a *Hauptsturmführer*, became Skorzeny's chief of staff and second-in-command and went on to distinguish himself yet further as a member of the *Jagdverbände*.

Meanwhile Canaris had travelled to Venice accompanied by Lahousen and Freytag-Loringhoven and met with his Italian intelligence counterpart at the end of June 1943.[3] There he was confidentially informed of Italian efforts to achieve an armistice with the Allies, returning to Germany and engaging in wilful misdirection by advising his superiors that the likelihood of Italian surrender was highly improbable. This mistaken bid to reduce German reinforcement of Italy was to have profound consequences as Walter Schellenberg at the SD obtained solid information of exactly what Canaris had, in truth, been told. He now had the ammunition with which to assassinate his rival. However, he had not reckoned with Canaris' wiles and the elderly *Admiral* skilfully extracted his head from the noose by submitting more accurate papers on the Italian matter once he had learned of Schellenberg's imminent exposure of his ruse. The clandestine fencing for advantage resumed between the Abwehr and SD.

By January 1944, Roeder had once again taken up the unfinished Dohnányi case, causing fresh concerns for Canaris who then proceeded to use Pfuhlstein as a means of shutting the investigation down or, at the very least, deflecting attention. During an examination of a witness in court at Dohnányi's trial, Roeder was quoted on record as proferring the opinion that 'the *Sonderverbänd* Brandenburg is a shirkers' club'. Aware of his subordinate's tempestuous nature and undoubted bravery, Canaris informed Pfuhlstein of Roeder's statement in the course of a hastily convened meeting. Though Pfuhlstein initially appeared to calmly appraise his response options, Canaris applied further pressure, appearing agitated and virtually goading Pfuhlstein into action. The commander of the Brandenburg Division unfortunately rose to the bait and immediately travelled with his adjutant *Leutnant* Arnold von Gustedt to the headquarters of *Luftflotte IV* in Lviv, marched straight into Roeder's office and, receiving no mollifying response to his challenge of the Luftwaffe judge's original comments, punched him in the face.

This could not go unpunished and Keitel sentenced Pfuhlstein to seven days' confinement to quarters and, though he claimed full responsibility and even officially thanked his superiors for allowing him to defend his division's honour in person, Pfuhlstein never forgave Canaris for compelling him to act in 'violation of his official standing'.[4] Though it transpired that Roeder had actually been referring to the '*Kurfürst* Battalion' that was no longer a part of the division, it was a petty and trivial victory for Canaris against his Luftwaffe inquisitor, but ultimately achieved little. Roeder's pride may have been injured, but his desire to trace conspiracy and treason remained undiminished. Ultimately, the Abwehr did not even need such activities to destroy itself and it finally fell victim to its own inertia, after failing to identify the threat of additional Allied landings in Italy due to incontrovertible failures in the gathering and analysis of intelligence.

Friedrich Hummel, leader of the frogmen of *Meeresjäger Abteilung 'Brandenburg'*, unwittingly aided the downfall of the Abwehr by his activities in neutral Spain. He and his small group had been mounting covert sabotage missions against British freighters that lay at anchor in Spanish harbours. Following Italy's surrender, they widened their target list to include Italian merchant ships. He was always careful to use British explosives and leave no trace of Brandenburg/Abwehr involvement, and although the Spanish authorities had been investigating him for some time and were convinced of his role in the series of mysterious explosions, they had no evidence. Finally, in early January 1944, a three-man sabotage team that had been based on the German ship *Lipari* in Cartegena harbour blundered and one of its number, Carl Kampen, was killed in an explosion as he planted his charges, and the Brandenburg operation was subsequently exposed. Hummel, disguised as a diplomat of the German

Embassy, was immediately arrested and he and his men expelled from Spain. It was one more embarrassment for the Abwehr, but was swiftly followed by yet another. On 12 January, a group of intellectuals opposed to Hitler and his regime who frequently met to discuss the situation and potential solutions, was penetrated by the Gestapo and arrested en-masse. Amongst them was Otto Kiep, a Foreign Office official with close ties to many Abwehr members, including two agents stationed in Istanbul, Erich Vermehren and his wife, the former Countess Elizabeth Plettenberg. Both were summoned to Berlin by the Gestapo for interrogation regarding the Kiep case and, in fear for their lives, they contacted British intelligence and defected on 27 January.

This proved to be the final straw for the Abwehr which had been constantly under siege by the SD and Ribbentrop's Foreign Office. Hitler, incensed at the shambles that Canaris' organisation had become, signed a directive on 12 February 1944 that created a 'unified German secret intelligence service' to which he appointed the *Reichsführer SS* as commander.[5] Canaris was relieved of his command and *Oberst* Georg Hansen, head of Abwehr I, placed nominally in charge.[6] Hitler's order necessitated the Abwehr being absorbed into the SS, specifically Amt VI/RSHA, effective from 1 June. However, in practice Abwehr I (intelligence) and Abwehr II (sabotage), although nominally under Amt Mil/RSHA, remained under OKW control until 1 December 1944. Nonetheless, an independent Abwehr was no more and the Brandenburg Division was completely removed from Abwehr influence and placed solely under the authority of OKW.

In the field the machinations of power in the office corridors of Berlin had little relevance. On New Year's Eve Banja Luka, the main German and Ustaše base in western Bosnia and home to XV Corps headquarters, had been attacked by ten Partisan brigades that attempted to relieve German and Ustaše pressure on Partisan forces in eastern Bosnia. The V Bosnian Corps battled its way into the city streets as the Axis defenders were squeezed into a small area centred on the Zalužani airfield: a grass runway shared by the Luftwaffe and ZNDH (Air Force of the Independent State of Croatia). The base personnel of 310 Germans had been significantly reinforced as the Partisan attack developed and elements of the 4th Regiment 'Brandenburg' were present as the street fighting raged.

The Partisan offensive was slowly beaten back but not before Brandenburger reinforcements had been called from Kotor Varoš, 20km to the south-east. There, Brandenburgers of the small unit '*Einheit Kirchner*' had trained local militia groups which were also thrown into the fray. Brandenburger troops established a bridgehead over the Vrbas River but it was the arrival of the 92nd Motorised Brigade that eventually repulsed the Partisans. The Brandenburgers suffered one man killed and thirteen wounded before being placed in the Army Corps reserve.

Leutnant Wolfram Kirchner had been tasked by Pfuhlstein with finding Tito's headquarters and had begun his hunt for the communist leader with clandestine reconnaissance in the Banja Luka area during October 1943.[7] Towards the end of the previous summer, Kirchner had been tasked with establishing a small special unit in Vienna known as '*Einheit Kirchner*'. Its purpose had originally been envisioned as a parachute unit bound for Kurdistan, but the events on the Eastern Front nullified this plan. Instead it was to be used solely for the gathering of intelligence regarding Tito in preparation for operations to be mounted directly against the Partisan headquarters. During October, the platoon-sized '*Einheit Kirchner*' was relocated to the heavily fortified Trappist Mariastern Abbey just outside Banja Luka in northern Bosnia and commenced operations. By the successful use of local Chetniks, he narrowed the likely location of NOVJ headquarters to the town of Jajce and obtained information that Tito was present at that time, attending the second meeting of the AVNOJ (Anti-Fascist Council of the National Liberation of Yugoslavia). Kirchner immediately suggested a precise operation to target Tito and his immediate staff, presenting two options to Rendulic.

The first called for a surprise Brandenburg raid by night, supported by Chetniks, all the attackers disguised in Partisan uniforms. Their mission would be to capture Tito if possible, kill him if not. The second idea was more convoluted and comprised two corpses (probably murdered prisoners of war) to be dressed in British battledress and dropped by parachute near Jajce. With their deaths attributed to faulty parachutes, one was to be carrying a letter addressed to Tito personally, which on opening would explode and kill the Partisan leader. However, both of Kirchner's proposals were overruled by Rendulic who appears to have been piqued by the fact that Brandenburgers were operating in his combat zone but outside his control. Instead the town of Jajce was included in the list of objectives of Operation '*Kugelblitz*'. The heavy-handed attempt failed, of course.

During December *Hauptmann* Böckl arrived from Greece at the head of his own small unit of similar purpose that included approximately eighty Bosnian Muslims in its ranks. His unit and Kirchner's were subsequently merged as *Verband Wildschütz* ('Poacher'), its strength approximately 200 men, one half remaining under Kirchner's command, the other under Böckl. During February 1944, Böckl was relieved of his post at Pfuhlstein's request and replaced by *Major* Ernst Benesch who began to expand the size of the intelligence-gathering unit. Interestingly, the name of the listed commander of *Verband Wildschütz* – Benesch – was replaced by a pseudonym on 18 August 1944, in an order issued from divisional headquarters entitled 'Camouflage for *Verband Wildschütz*':

The *Verband Wildschütz* has been renamed '*Wehrwirstschaftsstab 85*' for further camouflage. Commander: *Major* Benesch, who now appears under the name *Major* Neumann.[8]

While heavily engaged in Yugoslavia, the Brandenburger order of battle for January 1944 showed a division still split between different theatres of operations.

Brandenburg Division.
Division Staff *(Berlin)*
Commander: *Generalmajor* Alexander von Pfuhlstein.
1st General Staff Officer: *Major* Frankfurth.
Ia: *Hauptmann* Wülbers (from 31 May 1943).
IIa and Division Adjutant: *Hauptmann* Helmut Pinkert.

1st Regiment Brandenburg (Temporarily *Hauptmann* Gerlach while *Major* Walther on leave) in Greece.
Regimental units: One company from Signals Battalion 'Brandenburg'. (Artillery battery attached in 1944).
1st Battalion (*Hauptmann* John).
1st, 2nd and 3rd Companies.
2nd Battalion (*Hauptmann* Pinkert).
5th, 6th, 7th Companies.
3rd Battalion (*Hauptmann* Wandrey).
9th, 10th, 11th (Heavy), 12th Companies.

2nd Regiment Brandenburg (*Oberstleutnant* Franz Pfeiffer) in Montenegro.
Regimental units: One company from Signals Battalion 'Brandenburg'.
(Light Artillery battery attached in 1944).
1st Battalion (*Hauptmann* Steidl).
1st, 2nd, 3rd Companies.
2nd Battalion (*Hauptmann* Oesterwitz).
5th, 6th, 7th Companies.
3rd Battalion (*Hauptmann* Renner).
9th, 10th, 11th Companies.

3rd Regiment Brandenburg (*Oberstleutnant* F. Jacobi) in Soviet Union/Italy/France.
Regimental units: One company from Signals Battalion 'Brandenburg'.
1st Battalion (*Hauptmann* Gerhard Pinkert).
1st, 2nd, 3rd Companies.

2nd Battalion (*Hauptmann* Bansen).
5th, 6th, 7th (Heavy), 8th Companies plus Italian 3rd 'M' Assault Battalion '9 September'.
3rd Battalion (*Hauptmann* Wasserfall).
9th, 10th, 11th, 12th Companies.

4th Regiment Brandenburg (*Oberstleutnant* von Hugo) in Yugoslavia.
1st Battalion (*Hauptmann* Hollmann, later replaced by *Hauptmann* Gerlach).
1st, 2nd, 3rd, 4th Companies.
2nd Battalion (*Oberleutnant* Lau) merged with 1st Battalion, 1 August 1944.
6th, 7th, 8th Companies plus 9th (Legionnaire) Company.
3rd Battalion (*Hauptmann* von Koenen).
11th, 12th, 13th Companies.
Verband Wildschütz.

Independent Companies
Fallschirmjäger **Company**. This latter parachute unit was later expanded into the '*Fallschirmjäger* Battalion' of four companies in March 1944, based in Stendal and commanded by *Hauptmann* Weithoener.
16th (Light) Company (*Oberleutnant* Hettinger), in Pisa, Italy, at the end of 1943 before returning to Germany.
Translator Company.

Divisional Units
Signals Battalion (*Hauptmann* Eltester) headquarters in Berlin, divided between the regiments.
Lehrregiment 'Brandenburg' (*Major* Martin).
   1st Battalion based in Brandenburg an der Havel.
   2nd *Gebirgsjäger* **Battalion** based in Baden bei Wein and later Veldes/Oberkrain.
   3rd Battalion created in 1944 in Stein.
   4th Battalion created in 1944 in Domzale.
Küstenjäger **Battalion** based at Langenargen/Bodensee (*Rittmeister* Conrad von Leipzig).
   2nd, 3rd, 4th (Heavy) Companies.
   Küstenjäger Kompanie Rhodos (*Leutnant* Bertermann).
Legionärbataillon 'Alexander' (*Hauptmann* Alexander Auch).
   1st 'White Company' and 2nd 'Black Company'.

Pfuhlstein managed to finally get his full training regiment during March 1944. His original proposal was intended to streamline the flow of replacements and reinforcements and had been for the establishment of four battalions. Instead he had been granted just two; the 1st *Lehr* Battalion in Brandenburg an der Havel, concerned with basic training and 2nd *Lehr* Battalion that focussed on *Gebirgsjäger* training. On 5 March 1944, a request was received from the Wehrmacht Operations Staff for all existing elements of the *Lehrregiment* to provide troops for the establishment of an 'Alarm Regiment' that was originally intended for despatch to Hungary as the country teetered on the brink of surrender to the Allies. It appears that this deployment never actually took place although the resultant organisation gave Pfuhlstein the full training pool that he had desired originally:

Lehrregiment 'Brandenburg' ('Alarm Regiment'): *Oberstleutnant* Martin.
Regimental Headquarters: Veldes.
18th Heavy Training Company (Veldes).
    1st Battalion: (Veldes, formerly located in Freiburg).
    2nd (*Gebirgs*) Battalion: (St Vein an der Save).
    3rd Battalion: *Hauptmann* Grawert (Stein).
    4th Battalion: *Oberleutnant* Bistrick (Domzale-Hannsburg).
    Training Battalion 'U': *Hauptmann* Auch (Hungarian *Volksdeutsche*).

The 'Alarm Regiment' was initially deployed against an expected Allied landing near Trieste and the Istrian Peninsula and they took up positions by 12 May 1944. Once the perceived threat dissipated, they returned to Germany.

In Yugoslavia, Tito's Partisans remained locked in combat with German, Chetnik and Ustaše forces. Though the Balkans region had become like a bleeding wound in the side of the Wehrmacht, it could not be relinquished as it provided nearly 50 per cent of Germany's petroleum, 100 per cent of its chrome supplies, 60 per cent of its bauxite and 21 per cent of its copper. Yugoslavia had to be held to safeguard this vital source of resources as well to maintain lines of communication with German forces in Greece. However, the Wehrmacht was not strong enough to dominate a country of such difficult terrain and limited transportation options. Correspondingly, German troops occupied major urban areas while the Partisans took greater control of much of the rugged countryside. It was an appalling situation that resulted in frequent brutal but inconclusive battles and a general sense of despondency amongst German troops stationed in the area.

Unable to kill the Partisan beast, *Generaloberst* Rendulic then attempted to cut off its head. Early plans by the SD and Skorzeny's SS *Jagdverbände* to capture Tito during January 1944 (Operation '*Theodor*') had been cancelled but still yielded valuable intelligence about the Partisan leader and the location of his headquarters. Meanwhile Kirchner of *Verband Wildschütz* was still on Tito's trail and, using his Chetnik contacts, he eventually tracked his quarry to Potoci and then onwards to Drvar. Kirchner avoided cooperation with Ustaše units as their reputation for wanton cruelty only served to alienate themselves and their allies from the general populace. He established a small camp near Bos Grahovo and finally found the area of the Drvar caves in which Tito had established his headquarters; Partisan radio broadcasts, intercepted by German signals intelligence, provided confirmation of Kirchner's reports. This combined information would later form the basis of an ambitious operation to kill or capture Tito during May 1944.

In southern Greece, the 1st Regiment was released from coastal guard duties but remained around Piraeus and Athens under LXVIII Army Corps control, on missions against the growing surge of *Andartes* activity. The German policy of taking and executing hostages as reprisal for *Andarte* action had served their enemy well and generated hordes of recruits for the guerrilla bands. The German-sponsored Security Battalions also grew in strength, but did little to placate a volatile situation in Greece while suffering an increasing rate of desertion to the enemy as the Reich's military situation continued to deteriorate. Walther's regiment began fighting communist guerrillas south-east of Athens and suffered casualties, including the 3rd Battalion adjutant, Palestinian *Oberleutnant* Walter Minzemay, killed on 3 January. They fought inconclusively against their shadowy enemy throughout January and were finally moved out of Greece during the following month to Prilep, Macedonia, and thence onward to Albania where they were subordinated to Second Army and held in operational reserve for countering an expected landing on the Dalmatian coast. *Hauptmann* Wandrey returned to Germany for training, his 3rd Battalion taken over by *Oberleutnant* Seuerblich in time for it to be moved to Šibenik, Croatia, where Walther also established his own headquarters. Seuerblich's battalion, along with the 2nd Battalion that had transferred to Benkovac, were involved in a series of anti-Partisan sweeps beginning with Operation '*Baumblüte*' on 18 March. Operations '*Bora*' and '*Denkzettel*' followed over succeeding weeks and the Brandenburgers suffered serious casualties. The 1st Battalion moved to Tirana and was also part of major drives against the Partisans that took a heavy toll in killed and wounded, including *Hauptmann* John injured on 20 May. At that point, the listed strength of all nine battalions of Walther's 1st Regiment totalled only 824 men.

There were still numerous Brandenburg personnel in Italy at the beginning of 1944. Bansen's 2nd Battalion/3rd Regiment had arrived there from the

Eastern Front during November 1943 and the regiment's remaining battalions joined them in June, finally withdrawn from months of fighting against the Red Army. While officially resting and rehabilitating, they were also engaged in anti-Partisan operations, perhaps of less intensity than those they had experienced in the swamps of the Pripet marshes, but equally deadly for the unwary.

Before the arrival of the two other battalions, Bansen's men appear to have been involved in the hunt for Allied prisoners of war that had taken the opportunity escape following the Italian surrender. Despite an appalling and misguided order issued by MI9 to British prisoners instructing them to remain where they were following the departure of Italian guards – and allowing equally surprised German troops to arrive and imprison them once again – hundreds of Allied ex-prisoners still roamed behind German lines. However, their expectations of meeting advancing friendly forces were soon dashed. Heavy winter snows had aided the stubborn German defence of the Gustav Line stretching across the narrowest part of the Italian peninsula and an Allied landing south of Rome at Anzio during January 1944 had been successfully contained. Despite Abwehr intelligence completely failing to detect the imminent landing, the timid advance of Allied commanders, who could have advanced virtually unopposed into Rome if they had moved immediately after landing, thwarted their attempt to bypass German defences. Frontal attacks on the lynchpin of the Gustav Line, Monte Cassino, during February were repulsed, the mountain being held by German troops until May. With no Allied victory in sight and unable to reach friendly troops, escaped prisoners were either in hiding in the mountainous interior or being helped by welcoming Italian civilians and guerrilla bands.

Some of the Allied escapees who were recaptured received extremely harsh treatment by German units, including elements of Bansen's 2nd Battalion. The Brandenburger unit had moved from the Avezzano area that they had occupied at the end of 1943 to Ascoli during early March, Bansen occupying the Villa Marina as his headquarters. On 10 March 1944, *Leutnant* Fischer's company, stationed at Montalto, recaptured three British prisoners of war and an Allied parachutist in civilian clothes and shot them after interrogation by Fischer and his deputy *Leutnant* Rommel. Taken to a bridge near Montalto, they were executed and their bodies dumped into the river. Two American escapees were also shot at the same time by 6th Company commanded by *Leutnant* Hossfeld. The following day a raid on the village of Pito near Norcia found three British escapees, one of whom, Warrant Officer Barker, attempted to escape through a window and was shot dead. The remainder were captured and later executed on the outskirts of the village. The Germans recaptured several other Allied prisoners dressed in civilian clothes and who were also summarily executed, believed to have been by men of Bansen's battalion though confirmation is lacking.

During April, Bansen vacated the Villa Marina, which was taken over by *Hauptmann* Otto Hettinger as the 16th (Light) Company returned to Italy and headed to Macerata where they were was billeted in a former POW camp at Sporza Costa.[9] On 8 April, the company started its move south to the Ascoli Piceno area where they deployed with Hettinger in Villa Marina. The company now had the Italian Fascist Battalion '9 September' placed under its command and became '*Kampfgruppe Hettinger*'. Unfortunately, they too carried on the hunt for Allied escapees and a number were captured and shot, frequently by Italian fascist firing squads under German command. It was an unnecessary – and illegal – part of the Brandenburgers' history. Meanwhile, Bansen's 2nd Battalion was placed on the Adriatic Coast under the command of *SS und Polizeiführer*, *Obergruppenführer* Karl Wolff, responsible for anti-partisan warfare in occupied Italy. There, Bansen was promoted and replaced as battalion commander by *Hauptmann* Helmut Pinkert.

Parts of the 4th (Heavy) Company of the *Küstenjäger Abteilung* were also deployed in Italy during this period. They and the *Linsen* explosive motorboats that they had been designing and testing on Lake Constance were finally entrained for the front line and a planned operation against the accumulated Allied shipping off Anzio beach. They departed by train on 24 March and were originally due to be used in support of a human torpedo (*Neger*) attack planned by the Kriegsmarine's *Kleinkampfverbände*.[10] However following cancellation of the *Neger* deployment, the *Küstenjäger* finally went it alone on 1 July, launching from La Spezia and heading into the Gulf of Genoa. There, the deficiencies of the little craft were fully revealed as the light spruce hulls were virtually unmanageable in rough seas as opposed to the calm lake in which they had trained. The mission was a disaster and never got anywhere near the enemy. *Vizeadmiral* Helmuth Heye, head of the *Kleinkampfverbände*, furiously demanded that naval operations be left to his Kriegsmarine and the explosive motorboats transferred to his command. Members of the 4th Company were presented with a choice: return to the *Küstenjäger* for redeployment under the command of their popular 'Conny' von Leipzig, or join the Kriegsmarine. The company divided itself, many of the men having been involved with the development of the little craft under Brandenburg *Major* Golbach and wanting to finally use them in action, even if it meant leaving the division. At any rate, by the time that they made their decision to stay or leave, the Brandenburg Division had undergone a final and dramatic metamorphosis.

One of the last major operations that Pfuhlstein took part in as commander of the Brandenburg Division was '*Margarethe*', the occupation of Hungary (the special forces part of the action codenamed Operation 'Trojan Horse'). Aware of the way the winds of war were blowing, Hungarian Prime Minister Miklós

Kállay was discussing an armistice with the Allies, with the complete approval of the Regent, Admiral Miklós Horthy. Though Hungary supported Germany's war against the Soviet Union, neither Horthy nor Kállay were particularly sympathetic to fascism and had maintained communications with the Western Allies. Since Italy's surrender, Hitler had ordered contingency plans created in the event of further Axis satellite states withdrawing from the conflict. After becoming aware of Hungary's intensifying negotiations, Hitler invited Horthy to the palace of Klessheim near Salzburg, Austria, on 15 March, to apply pressure for greater contributions to the war effort and allow increased deportation of Hungarian Jews to the camps of his 'Final Solution'. The meeting also forced Horthy's absence while German troops staged their prepared occupation of critical areas of Hungary.

Pfuhlstein and the Brandenburgers were was heavily involved as four separate *Kampfgruppen* converged on the country from all points of the compass. From Banat in the south, 1st Regiment 'Brandenburg' was attached to '*Kampfgruppe A*' alongside strong Wehrmacht and SS forces under the command of XXII *Gebirgs* Corps. The Brandenburger 'Alarm Regiment' was originally intended to support the northern advance, but was released as unnecessary before it began. *Hauptmann* Weithoener's newly expanded *Fallschirmjäger* Battalion 'Brandenburg' was tasked with capturing Budaörs Airport, on the outskirts of Budapest, which they did by air-landing from Junkers Ju 52 transport aircraft augmented by a scattering of Italian Savoia Marchettis. Meanwhile convoys of troops entered the country, one composed of Brandenburgers from the 1st, 2nd and 4th Regiments and elements of the Panzer '*Lehrdivision*', the conglomeration of Germans arriving in Budapest unhindered and on schedule. Pfuhlstein coordinated his men by use of a Brandenburg signals unit that had been covertly installed in a Budapest hotel room by 16 March.

Despite some minor skirmishes, the Hungarian military appeared paralysed as Horthy was supreme commander and without him, no orders could be issued to prevent the German takeover. Upon his return, he was presented with a fait-accompli and informed that he could remain in office and cooperate with Germany or be removed, his country fully occupied and a *Gauleiter* put in his place. Horthy remained.

Pfuhlstein had accompanied his troops into Hungary for the virtually bloodless occupation. During his later confinement by the Allies, he related a story in which he had shared a 'tricky moment' on 19 March 1944 with RSHA chief Ernst Kaltenbrunner. Faced with a large group of angry Hungarian troops that wanted to arrest the two officers, it was only Pfuhlstein's aggressive determination as he faced down the threat which avoided them being shot out of hand. Though he could not be aware of it at the time, Kaltenbrunner's apparent sense of indebtedness would later come to Pfuhlstein's rescue. In the meantime, he returned in April to Serbia where his 4th Regiment took part in Operation '*Maibaum*' against Tito's troops alongside the 7th and 13th SS *Gebirgs* Divisions.

Unfortunately, Pfuhlstein's list of transgressions against National Socialist and military orthodoxy had reached critical mass. Already denounced by one of his subordinates for defeatism, guilty of striking a Luftwaffe judge and now firmly classified as 'politically unreliable' as evidence collected by SD investigations of Abwehr plotting against Hitler and his government grew, Pfuhlstein was finally relieved of his command on 1 April 1944. The decision had been taken in Berlin nearly a month previously, on 7 March 1944, and a flurry of orders issued from Wehrmacht Operations Staff that placed the division completely under their control and insisted on the removal of Pfuhlstein as divisional commander at the beginning of April at the earliest (dependent on the outcome of Hungarian operations). Pending further investigations, Pfuhlstein was placed at the disposal of OKH and sent on a divisional commander's course at Hirschberg before being appointed commander of the 50th Infantry Division on 1 July 1944. His replacement in the Brandenburg Division was 51-year-old *Generalleutnant* Friedrich 'Fritz' Kühlwein, officially appointed on 14 April. A veteran of the First World War, Kühlwein had continued his army service throughout the interwar period and then taken command of 2nd Battalion, 55th Infantry Regiment immediately before the outbreak of war at the rank of *Oberst*. As the commander of 133rd Infantry Regiment (45th Infantry Division) he was awarded the German Cross in Gold on 19 January 1942 before being given command of the division itself and involved in bitter fighting throughout the year as part of Army Group Centre. On 13 April 1944, after nearly a year in the Führer Reserve, he arrived to take control of the Brandenburg Division, a new Chief of Staff, Romanian-born Knight's Cross holder *Major* Dr Johannes Erasmus, also being appointed by OKH in June.[11]

Plans to Kill or Capture Tito

In Yugoslavia, Kühlwein's division took part in the ambitious attempt to kill or capture Tito that at last came to fruition. The infiltrators of *Verband Wildschütz* had increased their activities: small radio-equipped reconnaissance parties operating deep within Partisan-held territory for up to a week at a time, occasionally resupplied by Luftwaffe air drops. They soon confirmed that Tito's location was in the Bosnian valley town of Drvar. The settlement had already seen the worst aspects of the Yugoslavian war. The Wehrmacht occupied it in April 1941, replaced by Italian troops shortly thereafter. During these early years of occupation brutal massacres by both Chetnik and Ustaše troops were committed before the Axis forces were pushed out of the region by mid-1942. The Wehrmacht responded by retaking Drvar in 1943 and razing large parts of the town to the ground before once again being expelled by Tito's troops.

Various German intelligence groups were involved in the hunt for Tito's location and it was partially this fact that would ironically thwart the Germans' eventual attack. The shortcomings of the intelligence used to pinpoint the target stemmed from the familiar problem of poor inter-service cooperation as at least three competing intelligence organisations were involved. First, there were conventional Wehrmacht units attached to Army Group F and Second Panzer Army, primarily supplied by Abwehr's company-sized FAK 201. Second, there were the Brandenburgers of the 1st and 4th Regiments and *Verband Wildschütz*. Lastly there was Skorzeny and his *Jagdverbände*. The ambitious *Sturmbannführer* had been ordered personally by Hitler to eliminate the Partisan leader and flew to Belgrade during mid-April where he found Abwehr intelligence reports both contradictory and inadequate. Through his *SS Jagdverbänd Südost* in Bosnia he learned that Tito was in Drvar. His initial plan was to kill or kidnap Tito with a small commando team, despatching *Hauptsturmführer* von Fölkersam to the XV *Gebirgs* Corps headquarters in Banja Luka in order to liaise with *General der Infanterie* Ernst von Leyser regarding his plan. However, Leyser was already well on the way to developing his own operation with the same objective and resented what he saw as SS interference, snubbing Fölkersam and refusing to cooperate with Skorzeny's proposal. Convinced that preparations for a large-scale operation would alert the enemy and that it was therefore doomed to fail – as it had before – Skorzeny withdrew completely from the undertaking.

However, though Kirchner's *Verband Wildschütz* had obtained much valuable information regarding Tito's presence at Drvar and the precise locations of British and American military missions (confirmed by radio intercepts), he did not know *exactly* where Tito was located. It appears that the Germans believed his headquarters to be somehow hidden around the town cemetery, which was designated Objective 'Citadel' in the attack that followed. This assumption was largely based on aerial reconnaissance photographs that showed an established line of trenches, several anti-aircraft guns and an American jeep. However, it was later found that the trenches, ironically, had been dug by Italian occupation troops months previously.

The small town of Drvar had been chosen by Tito because it was difficult to approach, entry limited to three easily defended roads as surrounding hills and the Unac River provided natural defensive barriers. Tito and his staff arrived on 22 January, initially using a house in the town as headquarters before the threat of Luftwaffe attack prompted their move to a natural cave situated in a cleft in the escarpment north of the town across the Unac River. The cave was relatively spacious internally but had a narrow entrance, a wooden hut erected before the cave mouth that served as Tito's quarters and office when no enemy activity threatened. However, an increase in Luftwaffe air raids prompted a move to a second cave at the village of Bastasi, less than 6km to the west. Tito remained here throughout each day, before travelling by jeep to the Drvar cave, where the rest of his command staff had remained and where Tito would spend each night. Skorzeny had already surmised that the Drvar cave was the likely objective, but his intelligence was not offered to Leyser or his staff and, even if it had been, it would probably have been ignored.

Rendulic accepted the final prepared mission plan which was subsequently endorsed by *Generalfeldmarschall* Maximilian von Weichs, *Oberbefehlshaber Südost* and commander of *Heeresgruppe F*. The operation was codenamed '*Rösselsprung*' ('Knight's Move') and involved elements of V SS-*Freiwilligen-Gebirgs* Corps and XV *Gebirgs* Corps. A heavy bombardment of Partisan positions in and around Drvar by aircraft of *Fliegerführer Kroatien* would precede a parachute and glider assault by *Hauptsturmführer* Kurt Rybka's 500th SS *Fallschirmjäger*. There were several specialist teams that would accompany the *Fallschirmjäger*, including a group from Abwehr Section II – *Frontaufklärungstrupp 216* – composed of former Brandenburgers commanded by *Leutnant* Walter Zawadil, who were primarily concerned with the retrieval of code material and documents. Forty men of *Einheit Benesch* (*Verband Wildschütz*) also joined the airborne attack, transported by glider into action. Commanded by *Leutnant* Gerhard Dowe, they were charged with the interrogation of prisoners taken, be they Partisans or members of the Allied military missions. Several Chetniks with local knowledge of the Drvar area and Croats who could act as interpreters were included in this team. While this vertical envelopment was taking place, elements of XV Corps would converge on Drvar from all directions, planning to link up with the SS *Fallschirmjäger* that day. It was ambitious: speed, surprise and shock would be required to carry the day.

The Brandenburgers had several roles to play in '*Rösselsprung*' alongside that of Kirchner's men. The 1st Regiment, with the addition of other elements from *Verband Wildschütz* and supporting Croatian troops, was ordered to advance overland from Knin 70km towards Drvar. Once they had pierced Partisan lines they were to deploy small mobile groups of men in Partisan *Volltarnung* to disrupt enemy movements and their expected path of retreat from the SS airborne assault. Furthermore, they were to cooperate with the SS *Gebirgsjäger* of the 'Prinz Eugen' Division advancing from the east should Tito escape the expected attack. However, the orders that he had received already exceeded Walther's abilities. His regiment had only recently arrived from Greece and had neither the interpreters nor local *Volksdeutsche* available for a successful *Volltarnung* infiltration.

Nevertheless, on 25 May, '*Rösselsprung*' began. At 0635hrs Stukas and medium bombers had begun their attack on Drvar and twenty-five minutes later the first *Fallschirmjäger* began dropping, some wounded by 'friendly' shrapnel from the last wave of bombs. By the time that the final *Fallschirmjäger* were on the ground, thirty-four gliders began landing after throwing off the tow ropes from Henschel Hs 126 reconnaissance aircraft that had acted as tugs. Despite losses, the landings were generally successful, though 'Citadel', the main objective that had been thought to be Tito's headquarters, was quickly seized and found to be just the town's cemetery after all.

Benesch's Brandenburgers had been part of a landing group designated '*Draufgänger*' and had been perfectly placed on top of their objective at the western crossroads which were thought to be adjacent to an enemy communications centre. The Brandenburgers immediately attacked the main building nearby but were repulsed by a strong force of over a hundred Partisans. After they called for reinforcements, the building was finally taken after savage fighting. Unfortunately for Benesch and his men, nothing of intelligence value was found inside. By 0900hrs Drvar was under German control with 200 Partisans taken prisoner and another 200 civilians rounded up and held in the town's cellulose factory under guard.

Frustrated, Benesch began a series of brutal interrogations, but they failed to establish the whereabouts of either Tito or his headquarters. The Germans had captured one of his uniforms from a town tailor's as well as his jeep which still carried American markings, but nothing more. Summary executions of many prisoners were also carried out, although by whom exactly is unclear from the after-action reports. While *Hauptsturmführer* Rybka established his headquarters in the cemetery, the large volume of fire continuing to the north of the town at *Fallschirmjäger* patrols led him to correctly surmise this to be the probable location of Tito's headquarters. However, with little cover and a river to cross under withering fire, attempts at assaulting the location failed. Counter-attacks were also beginning to come from the flanks and rear of the *Fallschirmjäger* positions, including a brief appearance by light tanks that were quickly driven off with grenades. Rybka ordered all forces to take up defensive positions and await reinforcements. It was during this lull in the fighting at 1115hrs that Tito escaped the cave to the town of Potoci.

The operation had failed. Tito, his headquarters and the members of the Allied military missions had all escaped. Four unfortunate Allied war correspondents were taken prisoner, but their value was purely symbolic to the Germans. A second wave of *Fallschirmjäger* were dropped shortly before noon, suffering heavy casualties from ground fire. Close combat against the Partisans continued into the afternoon, with severe losses on both sides. The fighting was particularly brutal, wounded left where they fell and some German dead later found mutilated, with ears and noses cut off, red stars carved into their foreheads or lengths of explosive cord tied around their limbs to blow them off. The *Fallschirmjäger* battalion, surrounded by five Partisan battalions, held their ground throughout a night punctuated by extremely violent attacks. Finally, at 1045hrs the following morning the advance units of SS *Aufklärungs Abteilung 373* linked up with the embattled *Fallschirmjäger* and the Partisans withdrew. Though further fighting took place over the days that followed as Partisan forces attempted to reclaim Drvar, the operation was officially ended on 4 June. Both sides claimed victory in this battle. The Germans succeeded in disrupting Tito's headquarters, scatter the Partisans in the Drvar area and capturing large amounts of weapons, equipment and supplies, but did not achieve their ultimate goal. The Partisans, on the other hand, saved Tito and decimated an SS battalion despite losing thousands of men.

The 1st Regiment 'Brandenburg' was later criticised for its slow movement towards Drvar, but it had always seemed an unlikely schedule given that the regiment was unfamiliar with the terrain and facing an enemy to whom it was home ground. The regiment (minus 3rd Battalion which guarded Skradin, Benkovac and the Lozovac aluminium factory) spearheaded a mixed *Kampfgruppe* reinforced with rifle and engineer companies from 373rd Division and a large number of Chetniks. The advance began at 0505hrs and within two hours the motorised column was strafed by six Allied aircraft bringing it to an abrupt halt. North of Strmica, near a demolished bridge, the vanguard of the column ran into two Partisan detachments and from that point onward Walther's men fought their way to Grahovo along a frequently sabotaged and mined road. The key position of Cigelj was captured by 1600hrs, but the leading vehicle had been damaged by a mine and the road itself cut in seventeen places. To compound their problems, two large bridges had been destroyed, requiring an estimated two days to repair. During the following morning, one truck ran off the road at Derala, killing two men and injuring another five. Finally, 2nd Battalion was sent on foot through undefended Jelina Polja to Grahovo where at 1600hrs they linked up with 105th SS Reconnaissance Battalion and together they fought their way through to the plateau of Livanjsko Polje. The motorised column did not arrive in Drvar until 1400hrs on 28 May after further harassing air attacks had destroyed one Flak 38 and a staff car and caused severe damage to six trucks and one motorcycle.

After the days of prolonged fighting that followed, the regiment was redirected on 5 June to head towards the Dalmatian coast where an Allied landing on

Brač was initially feared to presage a larger landing attempt. Walther planned a reconnaissance in force to launch a surprise attack on the Partisans' VII Corps headquarters near Grahovo. Heavy fighting followed in which the commander of the 2nd Company, *Oberleutnant* Waldemar Späth, suffered a painful stomach wound and *Leutnant* Karl Karolus von Wrede, battalion adjutant, was killed. Further advance over mountain peaks was impossible as Partisan reinforcements flooded into the area, and Walther retreated, his regiment suffering one officer killed, three NCOs and fourteen soldiers wounded.

Allied air power now had total control over the Yugoslavian skies and 1st Regiment frequently paid the price for the defeat of the Luftwaffe. A single air attack killed eight men and wounded twelve from the 3rd Company as they travelled towards the coast in column by daylight. Walther's regiment retreated to the Dalmatian shores of the Adriatic coast until late September when they transferred to Belgrade in time to face the advancing Red Army.

Establishing the *Streifkorps*

By the end of the battle in Belgrade, the Brandenburg Division had already reached the penultimate critical crossroads in its history. Kühlwein inherited a formation scattered and bruised by recent battles and having been on the receiving end of operational use for which they were neither intended nor equipped to handle. Morale had plummeted amongst the 'old guard', as evidenced by the defection of officers to the Waffen SS, while new recruits were joining what appeared to be a relatively standard *Jäger* unit, but one of reduced organisational strength as it still carried the shadow of an organisation suited to small-unit operations. Rather than continue the apparent inertia that had overtaken the Brandenburg command, Kühlwein made a direct written proposal to OKW on 27 May to reorganise once more.

> The division was created as a special organisation for attack operations. Since the German Wehrmacht have been fighting on the defensive, the division has adapted itself to this situation and become the *Verfügungstruppe* [disposal troops, i.e. 'fire brigade'] of the Wehrmacht for fighting bandits. The division's experience during the retreat in the East, during the battles against bandits in the Balkans, France and Italy, as well as in preparations for small unit warfare on Sardinia and in the Peloponnese, show that the division's tasks can only be carried out if they can rely on enough combatants and recruited locals/translators. To be able to cope with growing demands, it is therefore proposed to establish provincial units.

Proposals:
Split the division into
a) *Streifkorps* [Raiding Groups]
b) *Jäger* Regiments and Specialised Battalions.[12]

Kühlwein concisely laid out his plans to create specialist groups (*Streifkorps*) equipped with enough local knowledge and small-battle skills to create havoc amongst the existing paramilitary bands that his division was constantly fighting. The remainder of the division would become either a standard *Jäger*, light infantry unit, with the additional *Küstenjäger* and *Fallschirmjäger* battalions remaining untouched. The two sides of the Brandenburg Division could act in concert: the *Streifkorps* used to pinpoint enemy positions and gather intelligence whereupon the fast-moving 'orthodox' units could move in and engage the enemy in battle. He finished his communique with the following words:

> The division must be given the opportunity, after submitting framework proposals, for the use of *Streifkorps*, before orders are issued. Finally, every troop leader must be made aware of Napoleon's principle based on his experiences in Spain against the guerrillas and in Germany and Russia against the paramilitaries and partisans: Wherever there are Partisans, we must fight like Partisans. [*Partout ou il y a partisans, faut combattre en partisans*]. Or in good German: You have to hunt the Devil with Beelzebub.[13]

Evidently his idea fell on fertile ground as a reply submitted by OKW on 8 June readily agreed to his proposals. Kühlwein was to concentrate on constructing *Streifkorps* units, with an emphasis on the Balkans, Italy and France. The Baltic states, Denmark and Norway were to be ignored and Romania and Bulgaria temporarily omitted for 'political reasons'. Provided that his organisational measures had no effect on the fighting power of his troops – for example, by the removal of officers, NCOs, men or equipment – and therefore no influence on the situation at the front line, he was given the go ahead to begin and a timetable that planned completion of restructuring by 1 August.

From a total strength of 14,056 men in the Brandenburg Division, Kühlwein estimated that 900 would form the *Streifkorps*, including the bulk of the available language experts, including 210 Russian-speakers, 181 English-speakers, 185 Serbo-Croatian-speakers and 310 Italian-speakers. The reorganisation began immediately. *Hauptmann* Träger's 8th Company/2nd Battalion/3rd Regiment was detached and redesignated '*Streifkorps Südfrankreich*' on 14 July. The unit's organisation was fixed at two '*Einsatzgruppen*' ('special purpose groups', unrelated to the SS *Einsatzgruppen* responsible for murdering Jews in the East) with a separate headquarters and communications section. A small part of the 8th Company that had comprised approximately twenty Spanish volunteers (formerly of the 'Azul' ('Blue') Division fighting with the Axis forces in the East) was detached and formed *'Einsatzgruppe Pyrenäen'*, the cadre around which *Streifkorps Biskaya* would be built. Led by *Leutnant* Demetrio, they would continue operations against the Maquis along the Franco-Spanish border until the Allied invasion of southern France.

In total, Kühlwein eventually established five separate *Streifkorps* and an independent *Einsatzgruppe* under the command of Army Group North:

Streifkorps Südfrankreich (*Hauptmann* Träger).
    Two *Einsatzgruppen*.
Streifkorps Biskaya.
    Einsatzgruppe Pyrenäen (*Leutnant* Demetrio).
Streifkorps Nordfrankreich (*Leutnant* Hoven).
    Einsatzgruppe Bretagne (*Leutnant* Pawel).
    Einsatzgruppe Flandern.
(Operations of all three French *Streifkorps* to be coordinated by the enigmatic
    Major Hollmann)
Streifkorps Kroatien (*Hauptmann* Benesch).
Streifkorps Karpaten (*Oberleutnant* Müller).
    Einsatzgruppe Slowakei (*Leutnant* Pawlofsky), one officer, four NCOs, sixteen men.
    Einsatzgruppe Rumänien/Siebenbürgen (Romania/Transylvania).
Einsatzgruppe Baltikum (*Oberleutnant* Seuberlich), two officers, thirty-six men.
    Training Battalion (*Major* Auch).

To muddy the organisational waters even more, the Abwehr's FAK units were also designated *Streifkorps*, identical to covert Brandenburg units in all but their place in the hierarchical administrative tree. Kühlwein feared the instant absorption of his division into the Waffen SS as part of Skorzeny's *Jagderverbänd* following the subordination of the Abwehr under the umbrella of the RSHA. Together with his Chief of Staff, *Major* Erasmus, he repeated his calls for the elements outside of the *Streifkorps*, *Fallschirmjäger* and *Küstenjäger* to be transformed into a standard *Jäger* division, or perhaps upgraded to that of a Panzergrenadier formation. On 17 August, another milestone passed in the division history; they were authorised to wear the newly issued 'Brandenburg' cuff title.

While this reorganisation had been taking place, the division continued to suffer depletion against guerrilla forces in every theatre in which they were deployed. In Yugoslavia German casualties from disease were unusually high, chiefly typhoid, dysentery and malaria. So too were casualties inflicted by the physical exhaustion of long marches and movements over extremely inhospitable terrain. Conversely, Tito's forces continued to grow in both numbers and military sophistication with the assistance of Allied commandos and liaison missions.

Amongst the Brandenburg casualties of that time was *Major* Friedrich von Koenen, killed on 21 August 1944, 15km south-east of Višegrad, Bosnia. The man who had led the 'Tropical Company' with such success was ambushed in an open-top staff car by what appears to have been not a Partisan unit but a group of Yugoslavian bandits who opportunistically attacked him on a lonely stretch of road. Koenen's battalion adjutant was also killed and Koenen's wedding ring and Knight's Cross stolen while a briefcase carrying valuable secret documents was left untouched. Another of the 'old guard', *Hauptmann* Kriegsheim, assumed command of the 3rd Battalion.

On 17 August 1944 Tito offered an amnesty to all Axis collaborators, the Yugoslavian King in exile broadcasting a message in support from London calling upon all Serbs, Croats and Slovenes to join Tito's 'National Liberation Army'. The effect that this astute move had on Axis forces was profound as morale plummeted amongst the Chetniks and many took the opportunity to change sides and defect to the Partisan cause. In neighbouring Romania on 23 August, as the Red Army pierced the Moldavian front, King Michael I mounted a successful coup, deposing the Antonescu dictatorship and effectively taking Romania out of the Axis. Romanian authorities offered German forces an unobstructed withdrawal from their country. Hitler, however, was certain that he could repeat the success of Operation '*Margarethe*' and reverse the coup, and regional Wehrmacht and Waffen SS troops were immediately placed on alert to obstruct Soviet advances and quell Romanian 'unrest'. Amongst those troops, the Brandenburger *Fallschirmjäger* Battalion and elements of the 4th Regiment were made ready.

The Brandenburgers were tasked with relieving German forces trapped in Bucharest and began landing at the German-held Otopeni airport which was being used as a Luftwaffe night fighter base. The first wave parachuted in and were soon joined by the remainder who were flown in aboard huge six-engine Messerschmitt Me 323 *Gigant* transport aircraft. Romanian forces, justifiably, saw this as a breach of the terms offered for a peaceful withdrawal and fighting began almost immediately, Soviet troops soon joining the battle and the German forces forced to retreat to the west under heavy pressure. In the northern Carpathian foothills, the 3rd Battalion of the 4th Regiment became involved in bitter fighting against the first wave of Red Army attacks, suffering heavy casualties and being pushed back into Hungarian territory.

Meanwhile, the 2nd Regiment had remained in Prijepolje and conducted small-scale actions supported by Muslim militia against Tito's Partisans. During July, it took part in the last large-scale anti-Partisan drive in central Yugoslavia, Operation '*Rübezahl*'. Once again subordinated to 1st *Gebirgs* Division, Pfeiffer's troops acted in concert with the 7th SS *Gebirgs* Division and *Hauptmann* Weithoener's newly established Brandenburg *Fallschirmjäger* Battalion, finally brought up to strength during March. Alongside other Wehrmacht units, '*Rübezahl*' intended to seal off elements of the main Partisan main force on the plateau between the rivers Piva and Tara in Montenegro and prevent them from moving into south-western Serbia.

However, due to the collapse of Army Group South Ukraine's front in Romania, the operation was peremptorily called off and all constituent units sent to intercept Soviet forces approaching Serbia: the 2nd Regiment sent to Belgrade and Weithoener's battalion to Budapest. All three Brandenburger Regiments suffered heavy losses in the defensive fighting in Belgrade, which came under direct Soviet attack during October. *Oberstleutnant* Walther was wounded on 13 October and sent back to Germany, his place taken by *Oberst* von Brückner, previously of the 23rd Panzer Division.[14] Brückner later won the Knight's Cross while in command of the regiment on 11 March 1945. The 2nd Battalion was heavily engaged in the battle and *Hauptmann* Wandrey wounded on 16 October and evacuated with *Hauptmann* Heine taking charge, *Hauptmann* John also being forced to relinquish his command of 1st Battalion two days later as his old abdominal wound had never properly healed and incapacitated him once more. As John returned to Germany, *Oberleutnant* Kohl took his place. *Hauptmann* Hans Gerlach's 1st Battalion north of Belgrade took part in a spoiling thrust against Soviet troops west of the Morava River alongside the 1st *Gebirgs* Division but were repulsed in fierce fighting against Soviet armoured units; Gerlach was killed and *Oberleutnant* Schonherr assumed command as the Brandenburgers retreated into the chaos of Belgrade. During the *Kampfgruppe* fighting that followed in the cauldron, South African *Rittmeister* Rudolf Louis Ferdinand Mertens, commander of the 3rd Regiment, was killed near Apatin on 22 November and Heine's hard-pressed 2nd Battalion was virtually annihilated in the close-quarters street battles. As the city fell to Soviet troops on 20 October, the last twenty-four able-bodied men of the 2nd Battalion attempted to escape across the Sava River but only Heine and his runner survived.

As the Soviet advance continued into the Balkans, Army Groups F and E had both mounted operations aimed at combatting guerrillas, but both had failed. In Yugoslavia, despite inflicting grievous casualties on Tito's troops, '*Rübezahl*' failed to achieve its objective as the main Partisan force extricated itself from the German noose, partially due to the removal of 1st *Gebirgs* Division to reinforce the worsening situation in Romania. The tenuous German hold on the Balkans was crumbling and before long the evacuation of Greece began as Soviet advances threatened to completely isolate the German troops of Army Group E who held the Greek mainland. By the time that this evacuation had begun, the Brandenburg Division underwent its final transformation.

Repurposing the Brandenburg Division

On 8 September, OKW delivered an order that conclusively relieved the Brandenburg Division of all specialist roles and incorporated it into the standard Wehrmacht order of battle, *Generaloberst* Alfred Jodl issuing a proclamation to the division's troops dated 11 September, 1944:

> Soldiers of the Brandenburg Division!
> The division is being relieved of its duties as a special operations unit and reorganised as a motorised *Jäger* division. You are therefore leaving the area of my direct command.
> I thank you for the readiness for action and your willingness to sacrifice that you have demonstrated. The division has fulfilled all my expectations in infantry battles and in special operations. I recall the particularly successful strike against Tito's leadership in May of this year in which the division was decisively involved, using powerful forces.
> Nevertheless, orders for your reorganisation as a *Jäger* division have been given, only so that all forces that have proved themselves in special operations might be employed en-masse under a unified command and therefore achieve new successes. The name Brandenburg is a commitment! I am certain that in its new form the division will do its duty and continue its glorious tradition.
> *Heil* to the Führer!

The division was to be expanded and have artillery and engineer battalions attached, along with *Sturmgeschütz* and anti-tank units. Only the *Küstenjäger* and *Fallschirmjäger* were to remain outside of this new designation, continuing in independent roles, as they already had been, until the end of the war. The men of the *Streifkorps* units were presented with a different option: either they relinquished their specialist status or they could be absorbed into the Waffen SS as part of Skorzeny's longed-for expansion of his commando forces.

Where previously Skorzeny's command had comprised only *Jagdverbänd 502*, the Brandenburg *Streifkorps* would form the nuclei around which territorial *Jagdverbände* would be created. Skorzeny was given authorisation to recruit

800 Brandenburg volunteers during September 1944. In fact, 1,200 volunteered, though only 900 were accepted, virtually the entire *Streifkorps* strength.

Each *Jagdverbänd* was a separate battalion drawn from political and nationalist groups of the countries in which they would operate, much along the original lines that the Brandenburg Regiment had pursued. This was unsurprising as *Hauptsturmführer* von Fölkersam was instrumental in assisting Skorzeny with his expanded *Jagdverbände* creation along the lines of original plans dating back to June 1944. Each theatre of operations was to have a separate *Jagdverbänd* to carry out special operations and sabotage behind enemy lines. To avoid the mistakes that had been made with the Brandenburg Division, the SS *Jagdverbände* were to operate independent of each other and never go into action as a regimental or divisional unit.

Existing Brandenburg *Kampfschule* (now the domain of the *Streifkorps*) were incorporated into Skorzeny's command, with each separate *Jagdverbänd* having one or more schools allocated. The central headquarters hub (*SS Jagdverbände Führungs Stab*) was in Friedenthal. Its remit was to issue orders covering the principles of recruiting and training which it then submitted to agencies of the Reich for authorisation. Each separate *Jagdverbänd* would then assume control of implementing these actions. Likewise, the headquarters staff remained a central point of contact (generally through the SS Ic *Obersturmbannführer* Dr Graf) for military requests which were then disseminated to the relevant *Jagdverbänd*.

The structure of Skorzeny's organisation was as follows:

Commander: *Obersturmbannführer* Skorzeny.
Adjutant and Liaison Officer: *Sturmbannführer* Radl.
Chief of Staff: *Hauptsturmführer* von Fölkersam (succeeded by *Obersturmbannführer* Walther in January 1945).
Ia: *Hauptsturmführer* Hunke.
Ib: *Hauptsturmführer* Gerhardt.
Ic: *Obersturmbannführer* Dr Graf.
(plus extensive headquarters departments and personnel).
Jagdverbänd Ost: (*Hauptsturmführer* von Fölkersam) approximately 300 men including Germans, Russians, Estonians, Latvians, Lithuanians and Poles.
    Three separate subordinate units, one commanded by *Sturmbannführer* Auch, another by *Untersturmführer* Riedel, plus **Jägd Einsatz Baltikum** (*Sturmbannführer* Dr Pechau).
Jagdverbänd Südost: (*Obersturmbannführer* Benesch) approximately 800 men of *Streifkorps Kroatien, Streifkorps Slowakei, Streifkorps Rumänien* and miscellaneous Brandenburg personnel.

Subordinate units include **Jägd Einsatz Slowakei** (*Untersturmführer* Pawlofsky), **Jägd Einsatz Ungarn** (*Hauptsturmführer* Kirchner) and **Jägd Einsatz Rumänien** (*Haupsturmführer* Müller).

Jagdverbänd Südwest: (*Hauptsturmführer* Gerlach, formerly commander of Brandenburg *Kampfschule 'Döberitz'*) approximately 130 men including *Streifkorps Süd Frankreich, Streifkorps Nord Frankreich, Streifkorps Italien, Kampschule Freiburg* and miscellaneous Brandenburg personnel. Subordinate units included **Jägd Einsatz Italien** of approximately 120 Germans and 40 Italians.

Jagdverbänd Nordwest: (*Hauptsturmführer* Hover) no Brandenburg personnel. Subordinate units include **Jägd Einsatz Flandern** (*Untersturmführer* Bachot).

Jagdverbänd Mitte: predominantly made up of *Jagderverbänd 502 'Friedenthal'* personnel.

Fallschirmjäger Battalion 600: (*Hauptsturmführer* Milius) originally an SS penal unit (designated by the number 500 as all units numbered in the 500 range were penal units). After the '*Rösselsprung*' raid the criminal element was removed and the battalion passed into Skorzeny's command by Hitler's order during August 1944.

There were several operations mounted by the ex-Brandenburgers in the SS *Jagdverbände*, but they are outside the scope of this book, requiring their own separate treatment. Suffice to say that amongst the familiar names that became casualties during the final months of the war was Adrian Baron von Fölkersam, listed as killed in action after being shot in the head by Soviet troops at Hohensalza, West Prussia.[15]

Interestingly, Otto Skorzeny's reputation – which persists to this day, in no small part due to his own writings and interviews before his death in Spain in 1975 – appears to have been wildly exaggerated. While he certainly possessed bravery and charisma in equal measure, his immediate subordinate *Sturmbannführer* Karl Radl later observed to American interrogators that his 'frequent absence from his Headquarters on active operations' caused him to lose touch with administrative details. He therefore did not realise the wide gulf that existed between his plans and their execution.

In addition, his gullibility and enthusiasm led him to believe every dressed-up report submitted by his ambitious inferiors. Skorzeny's leadership was inadequate according to Radl. After the successful Mussolini rescue, Hitler and Himmler used him for all sorts of special missions at the expense of the agencies he was supposed to be organising. This scattering of his interests became absolute early in 1944 when he became chief exponent of the *Sonderkampf* (miracle weapons) idea . . . Radl is more accurate than Skorzeny on detailed information. In his opinion, Skorzeny's sabotage services were bound to fail.[16]

The Brandenburg Division that has been the focus of this history, from this point on, no longer existed. For the shattered remnants of those units caught in the battles against Tito and the Red Army there was some time to rest and regroup once they had been withdrawn from the line that was finally established by the end of 1944. In southern France, the Allies had come ashore in Operation 'Dragoon' on 15 August and Demetrio's *Einsatzgruppe Pyrenäen* retreated northward, Demetrio himself being captured by American troops on 10 September at Autun in Bourgogne as he attempted to reach German lines. Elements of *Oberstleutnant* F. Jacobi's 3rd Regiment formed part of the German 'Armee Ligurien', attached to the LXXXVIII Army Corps that mounted a fighting retreat to the north.

The division was officially reorganised as the Panzergrenadier Division 'Brandenburg', *Generalleutnant* Kühlwein departing as commander on 16 October 1944. His replacement was *Generalmajor* Hermann Schulte-Heuthaus who remained at this post until the war's end. The order of battle at the Panzergrenadier Division's inception in October 1944 was:

Jäger Regiment 1 'Brandenburg' (*Oberst* Erich von Brückner).
Jäger Regiment 2 'Brandenburg' (*Oberstleutnant* Karl-Heinz Oesterwitz).
Panzerjäger-Abteilung 'Brandenburg' (*Hauptmann* Königstein).
Nachrichten Abteilung 'Brandenburg' (*Major* Bansen).
Feld Ersatz-Bataillon 'Brandenburg' (*Hauptmann* von Einem-Josten).
Divisionseinheiten 'Brandenburg'.

The division continued to fight in the Balkans until transferred to Austria in October 1944 with elements from *Sturm Division Rhodos* attached. From there they fought as part of Panzer Corps '*Grossdeutschland*' against the Red Army, pushed back into eastern Germany where they surrendered at the war's end to Soviet and Czech forces. That brief history too, is the subject for another book.

In the shadow of the Brandenburgers, the fate of some other important names from its history need to be accounted for. Following the 20 July assassination attempt on Adolf Hitler, revenge was swift against those with even the most tenuous connection to the plot. The SS threw a wide net and many of those caught were Abwehr officers. Friedrich Heinz, Pfuhlstein's least favourite 'political officer', was implicated but escaped arrest after being tipped off that the

SS were coming for him. While he went successfully into hiding until the end of the war, papers that he had accumulated and diligently stored were ferreted out. In an almost staggering breach of security – especially when one considers the perilous nature of potential revolution against the Nazis – Oster had carefully written out full and detailed plans for the removal of Hitler and dismantling of the National Socialist regime. These were amongst the papers that Heinz had stashed with his brother-in-law and which were soon recovered by the Gestapo. There, in minute detail, the conspirators' hopes for a liberated Germany were chronicled. Oster and many others were tried and hung. Canaris himself, even though he had become somewhat removed from active participation in what culminated in the 20 July attempt to kill Hitler with a bomb, was also implicated, named by the conspirator and nominal head of the Abwehr, *Oberst* Georg Hansen under interrogation as the 'spiritual instigator of the revolutionary movement that led to 20 July'.[17] It was Walter Schellenberg who took Canaris into custody, and *Hauptsturmführer* Adrian Baron von Fölkersam that drove the car carrying them to the *Admiral*'s detention in Fürstenberg an der Havel Frontier Police College. Canaris would be found guilty of treason by a specially convened SS court and placed in Flossenbürg Concentration Camp. There he was finally hanged, only days before liberation on 8 April 1945.

Alexander von Pfuhlstein was also arrested. Wounded in the head on 18 July 1944 while commanding the 50th Infantry Division, he had been repatriated to Germany to recuperate. During August, he was suddenly appointed commandant of the fortified area of Hohenstein-Ortelsburg Wald, a role that was considered as 'light duties' by his superiors. Implicated by transcripts of interrogations of plotters from 20 July, he was arrested during the night of 31 August and taken in handcuffs to Berlin. Under intense questioning he admitted that he had been aware of the plan to remove Hitler and assigned the duty of occupying west Berlin in the event of a coup. For three months, he was kept in the cellars of SS headquarters at Prinz Albrecht Strasse, before being transferred to a newly established prison camp for officers in the fortress city of Küstrin (*Festungshaftanstalt Küstrin*). Pfuhlstein believed that he was almost certainly due for execution and later, in American captivity, offered an intriguing glimpse of his own personal theory regarding the fate of two previous subordinates:

> I know that many officers who were not immediately apprehended [following the 20 July assassination attempt], their nerves strained by mental uncertainty, sought and found death on the front or through suicide. This was the case of *Oberst* von Voss, Chief of Staff, Army Group Centre and probably of

Hauptmann von Koenen and *Hauptmann* Helmut Pinkert of the Brandenburg Division.[18]

To his surprise, Pfuhlstein was abruptly released on 5 January, something that he later attributed to Ernst Kaltenbrunner and the debt he believed he owed him after Budapest. Reduced in rank to *Major*, he was offered the chance of rehabilitation through front-line service as a battalion commander. Pfuhlstein agreed, though he never had any intention of fulfilling his obligation, his status as 'recovering from wounds' keeping him out of action until he surrendered to American troops on 2 April 1945 in his home town of Wertheim.

The two elements of the original Brandenburg Division that continued to function semi-independently were the *Fallschirmjäger* Battalion and *Küstenjäger*. The *Fallschirmjäger* do not appear to have made any more combat drops and were thrown into action as line infantry. It is unclear if any opted to join Skorzeny's *Fallschirmjäger* Battalion 600 before the battalion was attached to the Luftwaffe's 25th *Fallschirmjäger* Regiment, formed near Stettin during February 1945. The Brandenburgers made up 2nd Battalion, under the command of *Hauptmann* Skau. Part of the 9th *Fallschirmjäger* Division, they were involved in combat at the Altdamm bridgehead east of the Oder River which the 3rd Panzer Army had established between Gollnow and Greifenhagen. They held this position until 17 March 1945, at which point the regiment's entire strength was listed as only 200 able-bodied men. On 20 March 1945, they withdrew to the west side of the Oder and later took part in the battle for Berlin. There, the entire 9th *Fallschirmjäger* Division and its Brandenburger cadre was swallowed by the inferno and ceased to officially exist.

Far to the south the *Küstenjäger* had fought in the Aegean and Adriatic until the end of hostilities. The fight against Tito's Partisans had taken the form of raiding parties against Partisan-dominated islands, intercepting small convoys of arms shipments and skirmishes with increasing numbers of Royal Navy MTBs and MGBs. Following the departure of the *Küstenjäger Kompanie Rhodos* to its permanent station in the Dodecanese, a new 1st Company was created, designated 'Special Purpose Construction Training Headquarters' and stationed in Bar in Montenegro. Its members wore the brown uniform of the Organisation Todt and acted in commando missions against partisans and against the British ships that supplied them.

The *Küstenjäger Abteilung* appropriated a Greek sailing ship, the *Kajikis*, and two additional assault boats that bolstered their fire power. Frequently combining with armed MFPs of the Kriegsmarine, the Brandenburgers launched regular raids and interception missions. On 19 August, the *Küstenjäger* were ordered to reconnoitre the islands of Saria, Skarpanto, Stakida, Umia/Unja-Nisia,

Kamilioni, Zaphrani, Syrina, Kandelousia and Perigousa. Instructed to engage any enemy forces encountered, they chanced upon an unknown camouflaged vessel on 26 August and attacked it. The Germans successfully boarded what turned out to be the British *HDML 1381* with fourteen men of the Special Boat Squadron on board. This heavily armed boat was repaired and recommissioned as *KJ25*, the 'battleship' of the *Küstenjäger*.

Some days later a new commando operation was launched against the Isle of Calchi which was occupied by volunteers of the Greek 'Holy Battalion'. After a short but sharp engagement, the surviving Greeks were captured, their dead commander later buried in a ceremony accompanied by a *Küstenjäger* guard of honour. Sixty-one members of the 'Holy Battalion' with British support landed on Tilos on the night of 26 October and overwhelmed the island's German garrison made up of the penal unit 999th Regiment, consisting of personnel previously considered unworthy to serve in the Wehrmacht due to their criminal record or 'politically offensive attitude' toward the Nazi regime. *Küstenjäger* were amongst the counter-attacking force that stormed ashore at the rear of the Allied troops and, after four days' fighting in which the Greek destroyer *Navarino* provided artillery support to the enemy, the Allied forces were forced to withdraw. However, not all *Küstenjäger* operations ended in success. A small troop landed on Alinna on 14 November was captured soon after coming ashore by British commandos, as was a second troop put ashore to investigate four nights later.

Turkey declared war on Germany on 20 February 1945 and the *Küstenjäger* mounted what was probably the only attack on Turkey undertaken by the Wehrmacht. On 1 March a small heavily armed group sailed from Rhodes for the Turkish coast where they landed and stole sheep, goats, grain and general supplies as the Kriegsmarine had stopped supplying Rhodes by sea, the garrison left reliant on bomber aircraft of *Kampfgeschwader* 200 instead which frequently used captured B 17 or B 24 bombers as well as the more familiar Fw 200 or Ju 290. On 23 March, *KJ25* headed a commando action against the island of Calchi where Greek troops and several small vessels were captured. The 'battleship' *KJ25* was again used on a patrol west of Castellrosso on 13 April. Disguised as British personnel, the *Küstenjäger* captured a heavily armed vessel with nine soldiers of the Levant Schooner Flotilla, Special Boat Squadron. Finally, the last combat mission of the *Küstenjäger Kompanie Rhodos* took *KJ25* to the waters around Castellrosso on 7 May, but after only a few hours at sea the Brandenburgers were recalled. The war had ended.

On 8 May 1945, the commander of the Rhodes garrison, *Generalmajor* Otto Wagener, was brought by *KJ25* to the island of Symi to sign the island's surrender. There Wagener ratified the end of hostilities with Germany in the

Aegean in the presence of Brigadier James Moffat (British Army) and his second in command Colonel Baird, Colonel Christodoulos Tsigantes (Commander of the 'Holy Battalion') and Captain H.C. Legge (Royal Navy). The following day, the *Küstenjäger's KJ25* transported the first British troops to Rhodes and the last independent Brandenburger unit was dissolved.

APPENDIX

Major Decorations Awarded

Baulehr-Bataillon z.b.V. 800
Knight's Cross
Wilhelm Walther, 24 June 1940, *Oberleutnant*, 4th Coy.

Lehrregiment z.b.V. 800
Oak Leaves
Siegfried Grabert, 6 November 1943, *Hauptmann*, 8th Coy./Lehr.Rgt. 'Brandenburg' z.b.V. 800.

Knight's Cross
Siegfried Grabert, 10 June 1941, *Oberleutnant*, 8th Coy.
Adrian Baron von Fölkersam, 14 September 1942, *Leutnant* Adjutant, I Btn.
Ernst Prochaska, 16 September 1942, *Leutnant*, Führer 8th Coy.
Hans-Wolfram Knaak, 30 November 1942, *Oberleutnant*, Commander 8th Coy.
Werner Lau, 9 December 1942, *Leutnant*, *Zugführer*, 5th Coy.
Friedrich von Koenen, 16 September 1943, *Hauptmann*, Commander, III Btn.

German Cross in Gold
Dietrich Wolter, 12 March 1942, *Leutnant*, 6th Coy.
Karl Klein, 5 June 1942, *Leutnant*, 9th Coy.
Hans-Gerhard Bansen, 9 July 1942, *Oberleutnant*, 6th Coy.
Edgar von Hübschmann, 27 October 1942, *Unteroffizier*, 10th Coy.
Karl-Heinz Oesterwitz, 13 December 1942, *Oberleutnant*, 7th Coy.
Dr Walter Slama, 10 January 1943, *Leutnant*, 7th Coy.
Gerhard Pinkert, 9 April 1943, *Hauptmann*, 2nd Coy.

Army Honour Roll Clasp
Dr Helmut Weber, 16 October 1942, *Stabsarzt*, 8th Coy.
Hans-Erich Seuberlich, 19 November 1942, *Leutnant*, 5th Coy.

Commendation Certificate of the Commander-in-Chief of the Army
[first name unknown] Haut, 12 July 1941, *Feldwebel*, Lehr.Rgt. z.b.V. 800 'Brandenburg'.
Hans-Wolfram Knaak, 12 July 1941, *Oberleutnant*, Commander 8th Coy.

[first name not listed] Werner, 12 July 1941, *Oberfeldwebel, Lehr.Rgt. z.b.V. 800 'Brandenburg'.*
Oskar Hüller, 5 October 1942, *Leutnant, Halb Kompanieführer* 8th Coy.

Romanian Order of Michael the Brave, 3rd Class (Orden 'Michael der Tapfere' III. Klasse)
Hans Bansen, 31 March 1943, *Leutnant, Lehr.Rgt. z.b.V. 'Brandenburg'.*

Sonderverbänd Brandenburg
German Cross in Gold
Karl Renner, 14 February 1943, *Oberleutnant,* III Btn./*Verband 82.*
Werner John, 2 April 1943, *Hauptmann, Verband 81.*
Hans-Erich Seuberlich, 24 April 1943, *Leutnant, Verband 82.*

Brandenburg Division
Knight's Cross
Friedrich von Koenen, 16 September 1943, *Hauptmann,* Commander III Btn./4th Rgt. 'Brandenburg'.
Max Wandrey, 9 January 1944, *Oberleutnant,* Chef 11th Coy./1st *Jäger* Rgt. 'Brandenburg'.
Konrad Steidl, 26 January 1944, *Hauptmann,* Führer I Btn./2nd Rgt. 'Brandenburg'.

German Cross in Gold
Albert Hald, 26 December 1943, *Feldwebel,* 15th Coy./4th Rgt. 'Brandenburg'.
Gustav Froboese, 30 December 1943, *Hauptmann,* III Btn./1st Rgt. 'Brandenburg'.
Robert Breitkreiz, 2 May 1944, *Oberjäger,* 2nd Coy./2nd Rgt. 'Brandenburg'.
Conrad von Leipzig, 20 May 1944, *Rittmeister, Küstenjäger-Abt.* 'Brandenburg'.
Wolfram Kirchner, 8 July 1944, *Oberleutnant, Verband Wildschütz*/Div. 'Brandenburg'.
Erich Horsthemke, 23 September 1944, *Oberfeldwebel,* 9th Coy./1st Rgt. 'Brandenburg'.
Ernst-Eberhard Frey, 9 October 1944, *Oberleutnant,* III Btn./4th Rgt. 'Brandenburg'.
Karl Ernst Kiefer, 13 December 1944, *Oberleutnant,* I Btn./1st *Jäger* Rgt. 'Brandenburg'.
Heinz-Willi Töppner, 15 December 1944, *OberFeldwebel,* III Btn./4th Rgt. 'Brandenburg'.

Army Honour Roll Clasp
Conrad von Leipzig, 17 November 1944, *Rittmeister, Küstenjäger-Abt.* 'Brandenburg'.
Wilhelm Rowohl, 25 March 1945, *Leutnant, Wehrwirtschaftsstab 85* [cover for *Verband Wildschütz*].

Commendation Certificate of the Commander-in-Chief of the Army
Dieter Weithoener, 7 July 1944, *Oberleutnant*, Battalion Leader I Btn./2nd Rgt. 'Brandenburg'.

Commendation Certificate of the Commander-in-Chief of the Army for Shooting Down Aircraft
Anton Rauch, 27 June 1944 [Date of Action], *Feldwebel*, III Btn./4th Rgt. 'Brandenburg'.

Knight's Cross of the War Merit Cross with Swords
Reinhardt Volkmann, 12 August 1944, *Fahnenjunker-Oberwachtmeister*, Div. 'Brandenburg'.

Panzergrenadier Division 'Brandenburg'
Oak Leaves
Karl-Heinz Oesterwitz, 10 February 1945, *Oberstleutnant*, Commander 2nd *Jäger* Rgt. 'Brandenburg'.
Max Wandrey, 16 March 1945, *Major* d.R., Commander II Btn/1st *Jäger* Rgt. 'Brandenburg'.

Knight's Cross
Erich von Brückner, 11 March 1945, *Oberst*, Commander 1st *Jäger* Rgt. 'Brandenburg'.
Eckard Afheldt, 17 March 1945, *Oberleutnant*, Leader II Btn./2nd *Jäger* Rgt. 'Brandenburg'.
Erich Röseke, 14 April 1945, *Oberleutnant*, Leader 9th Coy./1st *Jäger* Rgt. 'Brandenburg'.
Hellmut von Leipzig, 28 April 1945, *Leutnant*, *Zugführer* Pz.Aufkl.Abt 'Brandenburg'.
Wilhelm Brökerhoff, 8 May 1945, *Major*, Leader Pz.Art.Rgt 'Brandenburg' (unconfirmed).
Friedrich Müller-Rochholz, 8 May 1945, *Hauptmann*, Commander Pz.Pi.Btl 'Brandenburg' (unconfirmed).
Werner Voshage, 8 May 1945, *Major*, Commander Heeres-Flak.Art.Abt 'Brandenburg' (unconfirmed).

German Cross in Gold
Konrad Steidl, 13 January 1945, *Hauptmann*, Commander I Btn./2nd *Jäger* Rgt. 'Brandenburg'.
Dr Theodor Becker, 31 January 1945, *Oberarzt*, 1st *Jäger* Rgt. 'Brandenburg'.
Erich Glaser, 22 March 1945, *Feldwebel*, 6th Coy./1st *Jäger* Rgt. 'Brandenburg'.
Erich Röseke, 22 March 1945, *Oberleutnant*, 9th Coy./1st *Jäger* Rgt. 'Brandenburg'.
Karl-Heinz Gohlke, 30 March 1945, *Leutnant*, II Btn./2nd *Jäger* Rgt. 'Brandenburg'.

Army Honour Roll Clasp
Gerhard Pinkert, 5 February 1945, *Hauptmann*, I Btn./Rgt. 'Brandenburg'.

Wolf Meschkeris, 5 March 1945, *Oberleutnant*, *Begleit Kompanie*/Pz.Gren.Div. 'Brandenburg'.
Hans-Gerhard Bansen, 25 March 1945, *Major*, Pz.Aufkl.Abt. 'Brandenburg'.
Werner Stalf, 1945 [date unconfirmed], *Leutnant*, 7th Coy/2nd *Jäger* Rgt 'Brandenburg'.

Notes

Prelude: The Concept Behind the Brandenburger Regiment
1. CIA Archives, report by General Lahousen; also National Archives, KV2/173.
2. 'The Lohmann Affair', Central Intelligence Agency. https://www.cia.gov/library/center-for-the-study-of-intelligence/kent-csi/vol4no2/html/v04i2a08p_0001.htm
3. Nuremberg Trial Proceedings, Ninth Day, Friday 30 November 1945. See: www.avalon.law.yale.edu/imt/11-30-5.asp
4. The *Höheren Offizierskurse* existed because Article 160 of the Treaty of Versailles forbade General Staff Officer training.
5. National Archives, KV2/173, Erwin von Lahousen interrogation.
6. National Archives, KV2/1736. Abshagen was later arrested by the Gestapo following the 20 July bomb plot, his name linked to the explosives procured by von Stauffenberg, which he had in fact supplied. Released through lack of evidence in November 1944, he was dismissed from the Army. In May 1945, he was arrested by the Soviet SMERSH (an acronym for the Russian phrase 'Smert Shpionam', or, 'Death to Spies' which was popularised by James Bond novels and correspondingly frequently thought of as fiction) and condemned to death for his Abwehr role. He was executed in Brest, Belarus, in August 1945.
7. These numbers quoted by author Andrzej Szefer and Major Dietrich Witzel respectively.
8. According to these biographical details, Ebbinghaus was promoted to *Major* and awarded the EK II after the conclusion of the Polish campaign. After the war he lived in the Federal Republic of Germany and died in 1958 in Lünen, Westphalia. See Grzegorza Bębnik, *Sokoły kapitana Ebbinghausa* (Libron, 2014).

1 Baptism of Fire
1. See Peter Hoffmann, *History of the German Resistance, 1933–1945* (McGill-Queen's University Press, 1996), pp. 92–6 for a detailed account of the event.
2. When the actual invasion came on 1 September, the tunnel was successfully blown up by its Polish defenders, only minutes before the arrival of German troops.
3. Seeliger would later be killed in action at the rank of *Oberstleutnant* while leading *Frontaufklärung 202* (FAK202) made up of Russians, Ukrainians and Poles during the late summer of 1944.
4. See National Archives, KV2/1736.

5   The *Füsilier-Regiment Nr. 35* and *Kürassier-Regiment Nr. 6* had maintained barracks in the town from 1880 until the First World War.
6   Jahnke served as intelligence adviser to Walter Schellenberg of the SD but later fled to Switzerland after Gestapo investigators discovered his links with British Intelligence. Returning as the war was ending, he and his wife were captured by Soviet SMERSH agents in May 1945, interrogated and executed. In November 1944 Marcus crossed Allied lines in France in uniform to surrender himself to British Intelligence, acting as a peace emissary on Jahnke's behalf with information for Allied intelligence officers.
7   Von Lahousen later described fellow Austrian Fleck, who had agitated greatly as a member of the illegal Austrian Nazi organisations prior to the Anschluss, as a 'fanatical Nazi, who was proud of his dynamiting operations in Austria. Removed by me from the Abwehr even before the French campaign.'
8   Dietrich F. Witzel, 'Kommandoverbände der Abwehr II im Zweiten Weltkrieg', *Militärgeschichtliches Beiheft zur Europäischen Wehrkunde*, no. 5 (October 1990), pp. 6–7.
9   It was no surprise that recruits were enlisted from Australia and Ireland, as both nations had large German immigrant communities. German Palatines had attempted to settle in Britain during the eighteenth century and were moved onward to either Ireland or the United States while Germans made up the largest non-British/Irish settler community to Australia during the 1800s. Such men returning to the Reich as *Volksdeutsche* would consider themselves as being patriotic; far removed from the Australians that are known to have enlisted in the SS '*Britisch Freikorps*' during the Second World War.
10 See Martom Cüppers, Klaus-Michael Mallmann and Krista Smith, *Nazi Palestine: The Plans for the Extermination of the Jews in Palestine* (Enigma Books, 2010).
11 Gartenfeld later commanded reconnaissance units and was awarded the Knight's Cross in March 1943 while part of *2./Versuchsverbänd Ob.d.L* that specialised in flying captured enemy aircraft and, in his case, landing agents successfully behind Soviet lines. He subsequently also served as commander of I./KG 200 and was employed after the war by the 'Gehlen Organisation'.
12 Dietrich F. Witzel, 'Kommandoverbände der Abwehr II im Zweiten Weltkrieg', *Militärgeschichtliches Beihef zur Europäischen Wehrkunde*, No. 5 (October 1990), pp. 6–20.

2   Operation '*Weserübung*' and 'Case Yellow': Scandinavia and the West
1   Sorgenfrey was later killed on 25 April 1941 in a training accident in Brandenburg.
2   Peter Wilkinson and Joan Astley, *Gubbins & SOE* (Pen & Sword, 2010), p. 58.
3   During January 1940 two Luftwaffe officers had made a forced landing in Belgium carrying plans for the forthcoming invasion which they failed to destroy in what is now called the 'Mechelen Incident'. Fortunately for German planners, Allied intelligence doubted the documents' veracity.
4   Ulrich von Hassell, *The Ulrich von Hassell Diaries* (Frontline Books, 2011), p. 73.

Notes 293

5 Werner Warmbrunn, *The Dutch Under German Occupation 1940–1945* (Stanford University Press, 1963), p. 7. July. See also Peter Voute, *Only a Free Man* (The Lightning Tree, 1982), p. 22.
6 Gisele de Posch, '*WW2 People's War*', article ID: A3942885, contributed on: 24 April 2005. http://www.bbc.co.uk/history/ww2peopleswar/stories/85/a3942885.shtml
7 Corporal Touw was posthumously awarded the Bronze Cross by Royal Decree during May 1946 (one of fifteen won that day), with the following citation: 'Showed exceptional courage hindering an enemy attempt at attacking the guard at the east side of the railway bridge at Buggenum on 10 May 1940, during which he was killed.'
8 Helmuth Spaeter, *Die Brandenburger* (Karl-Heinz Dissberger, 1991), pp. 59–60. *Oberfeldwebel* Stöhr later perished in the Soviet Union south of Stalingrad, wounded on 24 August 1942 and dying four days later.
9 After crossing the river and breaking through the Dutch 'Peel Line', the armoured train was derailed during its return trip to Germany after running into a barrier that had been closed.
10 Spaeter, *Die Brandenburger*, p. 61.
11 Einstmann's battlegroup was the so-called 'Grave Group' and comprised the reconnaissance battalion of the SS *Verfügungstruppe* and a Wehrmacht machine-gun battalion and artillery battalion detached from the 254th Infantry Division.
12 The four Belgian *Volksdeutsche* – Joseph Hoffmann, Nikolaus Huppertz, Henri Noel and Wilhelm Pip – had deserted from the Belgian military in early 1940 and gravitated towards the Brandenburgers, who also enlisted other Belgian deserters in the months leading up to 'Case Yellow'.
13 'The Flooding of the Yser' by Belgian Minister of Justice Carton De Wiart; an address delivered in London in June 1915. Charles F. Horne (ed.), *Source Records of the Great War, Vol. II* (National Alumni, 1923).

3 The Regiment Brandenburg
1 Franz Halder, Kriegstagebuch, Bd. I, 25–8 June, 1940. Quoted in Klaus Urner, *Let's Swallow Switzerland: Hitler's Plans Against the Swiss Confederation* (Lexington Books, 2001), p. 155.
2 National Archives, KV2/769, Haller, Dr Kurt; Extract of Special Interrogation Report 19 August 1946.
3 Central Intelligence Agency, Counter Intelligence Corps Detachment 970, US Army, APO757, German Intelligence Services, 9 February 1946.
4 Extract from a personal diary kept by Theodor von Hippel, provided by his personal estate and quoted in Spaeter, *Die Brandenburger*, pp. 78–9.
5 Von Aulock had served in Flanders as platoon leader, company commander and battalion adjutant during the First World War, subsequently joining a *Freikorps* before being discharged from the Army at the rank of Captain in 1920. Uninterested in a military career, he was, however, recalled to active duty on

the 1939 German mobilisation. After his brief tenure with the Brandenburgers he was appointed to the staff of the military commander north-west France. During the defensive fighting near Paris he commanded an ad hoc infantry unit and was captured on 2 September 1944. His brother was *Oberst* Andreas Maria Karl von Aulock who had stubbornly held St Malo until overwhelmed by US forces.

6 National Archives, KV2/173.
7 Letter from von Hippel to Hildegard von Kotze dated 17 December 1968, quoted in Heinz Höhne, *Canaris, Hitler's Master Spy* (Cooper Square Press, 1999), p. 377.
8 Rudloff worked in Spain and Portugal until June 1942 whereupon he was transferred to the Soviet Union to establish Abwehr anti-partisan and counter-espionage units and then on to North Africa in October that year. His duties were counter-intelligence by nature, based in Tripoli. During 1943 he served in France, joining the retreat into Germany during 1944 and surrendering on 8 May 1945 as Commander *Leitstelle der Front-Aufklaärungs-Kommando III, Oberbefehlshaber West*. He later served as a reserve officer in the Bundeswehr.
9 Central Intelligence Agency, Pouch 70, 2-196, reports by Generalmajor Lahousen, 'Canaris Secret Organisation Part I & II', p. 6.
10 Ibid.
11 Hitler reportedly later ordered the killing of General Giraud who had been captured in 1940 and escaped from his POW camp with Canaris' help. Canaris used the sudden death of Heydrich to complicate the issue of who had been tasked with the murders in ficticious conversations between himself and Heydrich and when they had been instructed, thereby never passing the instruction further down the chain of command.
12 Sepp De Giampietro, *Das falsche Opfer?* (Leopold Stocker Verlag, 1984), pp. 49–51.

4 Declared and Undeclared War in the Balkans

1 This was the same haul of captured documents that had revealed Switzerland's planned mutual defence pact with France.
2 Grabert remained with the Company as a *Zugführer*. According to Sepp De Giampietro (*Pioneertruppführer* in the 8th Company), the arrival of Buchler as company chief was not entirely welcomed as he 'seemed very arrogant' from the outset.
3 Bazing was a veteran of the First World War and was serving as Engineer Officer with the German Wehrmacht Mission in Romania at the time of '*Marita*'. He was later promoted and ended the war as *Generalmajor* in command of the 89th Infantry Division. He was interned in Switzerland on 2 May 1945 and released in November 1947.
4 Pinkert's brother Gerhard was also a Brandenburger.
5 Franz J. Haller, Arbeitskreis Visuelle Dokumentation Südtiroler Volkskultur e.V., Südtirol Archiv, 1936–1938, Arthur Scheler.

5 Hitler Turns East: The Invasion fothe Soviet Union

1. *Walli I* was in turn subdivided thus: IX – Intelligence on ground forces; IL (*Luft*) – Intelligence on air forces; I Wi – Economic intelligence; I G – Fabrication of false documents; I I – Ciphers, codes and transmitters.

    Walli III was subdivided thus: 1 – Command group – general administration and planning; 2 – Intelligence analysis; 3 – Military topographical preparation; 4 – Radio transmitter group (in conjunction with *Walli I*); 5 – Repairs of transport for field operatives.
2. Hinrich-Boy Christiansen, *Mit Hurra gegen die Wand* (Books on Demand GmbH, 2010), p. 11.
3. The SD – eager to challenge the dominance of the Abwehr – had then established a school for the training of prospective recruits from Ukrainian collaborators, Polish police officers and other Sipo or SD personnel, including *V-Leute*. By July 1941, the school had relocated to Bad Rabka.
4. Spaeter, *Die Brandenburger*, p. 135. Herbert Kriegsheim later wrote a novelised account of his time as a Brandenburger, accurate to his wartime experience, though, of course, we must allow for dramatic licence. This also appears in that book, *Getarnt, Getäuscht und doch Getreu; Die geheimnisvollen 'Brandenburger'* (Bernard & Graefe Verlag, 1959).
5. Spaeter, *Die Brandenburger*, pp. 160–1.
6. The five men killed were *Gefreiter* Rudolf Wieser, *Jäger* Adam Schmiedt, Sonnhofer, Taaktmann and Kurt Weiss.
7. *Gefreiter* Heinz Rösler, Anton Stauder, Karl Innerhofer and *Oberschutz* Matthias Plattner were also killed.
8. Letter written 17 July 1941.
9. http://volodymyrmuseum.com/krayeznavchi/118-pochatok-viyny-22061941r-ustyluh-lutsk
10. Bandera was released in the vain hope that he would rally Ukrainian supporters to the lost German cause. Though he survived the war, in 1959 he was murdered by the KGB in Munich, Germany.
11. Nachtigall commander and veteran Brandenburger Herzner was later shot in the back and severely wounded in 1942 and taken to the SS hospital at Hohenlychen. The hospital acted as a sanatorium but also hosted somewhat sinister experiments with sulphonamide on the treatment of battlefield injuries. Human experimentation was carried out on female inmates from Ravensbrück concentration camp and probably on wounded troops brought for treatment. The final circumstances of Herzner's death on 3 September 1942 are unknown; he was apparently last seen lying on a float in a lake on the hospital grounds and then disappeared. His body was found two hours later and he was posthumously promoted to *Hauptmann* and buried with honours in Potsdam.
12. Oberländer was captured by US forces in 1945 though the OSS fully appreciated his expertise on Eastern European matters and he passed with ease through the 'denazification' process. Somewhat ironically, he became the West German government's Federal Minister for Displaced Persons, Refugees

and War Victims between October 1953 and May 1960. In 1960, Oberländer was sentenced *in absentia* to life imprisonment by an East German court, for his alleged involvement in the Lviv massacre of 1941 and in 1996 a new case was opened against him in which he was charged with the murder of a female teacher in Kislovodsk in 1942 while he was in command of *Sonderverbänd Bergmann*. Oberländer died two years later, denying all the allegations.
13 National Archives, KV2/173, p. 17.
14 Quoted in Nuremberg Judgement: War Crimes and Crimes Against Humanity; http://avalon.law.yale.edu/imt/judwarcr.asp#prisoners
15 *Oberleutnant* Alfred Wohlgefahrt, *Oberleutnant* Dr Erich Benkelberg, *Oberleutnant der Reserve* Karl Troebs and *Leutnant* Rudolf Gluening were all killed in action that day.

6 War in the Desert
1 National Archives, HW14/122; Frank Laurence Lucas (a Fellow of King's College, Cambridge, Hut 3 Army and Luftwaffe Enigma Intelligence Section, Bletchley Park) letter to DD1 (Deputy Director 1 responsible for security and the production and distribution of intelligence), 21 February 1945.
2 Wilhelm Kohlhaas, *Hitler-Abenteuer im Irak* (Verlag Herder, 1989), p. 26.
3 National Archives, KV3/88, CICI Counter-Intelligence Summary No. 23, 13 April 1944, f 18a.
4 Matin Baraki, *Die Beziehungen zwischen Afghanistan und der Bundesrepublik Deutschland, 1945–1978* (Peter Lang GmbH, Internationaler Verlag Der Wissenschaften, 1996), p. 64.
5 A young Hindu girl had converted to Islam and married a Pashtun in the frontier province of Bannu. Accused by her family of kidnapping the girl, the Pashtun was ruled against by the British colonial court who judged her to have been a minor and, while no evidence of abduction was proven, she was ordered to live with a third party until reaching the age of majority. The Muslim community read the verdict as religious bigotry.
6 Quoted in Jeffery J. Roberts, *The Origins of Conflict in Afghanistan* (Praeger, 2003), p. 79, n. 21.
7 CIA Archives, SIME/CO.101.903, S.I.M.E Report No. 4, Interrogation Hans-Jürgen Kirchner.
8 Ibid.
9 See Glossary for *Sonderführer*.
10 Lieutenant Colonel Geoffrey Keyes was also awarded a posthumous Victoria Cross.
11 Von Tiesenhausen waited for the required length of time before continuing his patrol in which he would later sink the battleship HMS *Barham* on 25 November.
12 Desmond Young, *Rommel: The Desert Fox* (Collins Publishing, 1950), p. 134.
13 The description of the two spies is taken from the manuscript of Ritter's own memoirs, *Deckname Dr Rantzou* (p. 413), quoted in Saul Kelly, *The Hunt For*

Zerzura (John Murray, 2003), p. 176. His account differs somewhat from that supplied by the interrogation of Johann Eppler.
14 Ritter was posted to personnel reserve and then a Flak unit before briefly serving in the Supply Regiment 'Hermann Göring'. He ended the war a *Major* commanding Flak Regiment 60 in Hamburg.
15 Wilscher was a Sudeten German who had worked in West and Central Africa as a forestry engineer. After his Brandenburg service he joined Otto Skorzeny's SS *Jagdverbände* and commanded the sniper school in Zeithain (Saxony) at the rank of *Untersturmführer*. Before the war he had been a expert hunter and his skill with the rifle was notable. A bearer of the EK I, he continued to wear his Brandenburger sleeve insignia while in the SS and was remembered as 'very arrogant' by some of his fellow members in Skorzeny's unit. He survived the war and later established a big-game hunting company based in Hamburg with regular safaris to Africa. He died on 21 July 1988.
16 National Archives, WO 208/5520, 'Interrogation Reports on German Prisoners of War: S/50/1/0842-0847, Consolidated Reports on Johann Eppler and Heinrich Sandstede (known as Kondor Max and Moritz)'.
17 Hauer was later repatriated to Vienna in 1946 by the British.
18 National Archives, KV2/1468, Eppler, Hans W.
19 Timothy Mulligan, 'The German Navy Evaluates Its Cryptographic Security', October 1941', *Military Affairs*, Vol. 49, No. 2 (1985), pp. 75–9, p. 75.
20 National Archives, WO 208/5520, 'Interrogation Reports on German Prisoners of War: S/50/1/0842-0847, Consolidated Reports on Johann Eppler and Heinrich Sandstede (known as Kondor Max and Moritz)'.
21 National Archives, KV2/1467.
22 It appears that Voppel was later commissioned in the Kriegsmarine Artillery as an *Oberleutnant* where he won the German Cross in Silver.
23 Between autumn 1942 and spring 1943 an office codenamed '*Dora II*' functioned in Berlin under the direction of Luftwaffe *Major* Gericke. This both evaluated the information received from '*Dora*' and passed it on to the appropriate military authorities and kept '*Dora*' supplied with the necessary personnel and material. After the retreat from North Africa, '*Dora*' received a more extensive commission. While Haeckel moved on, Schulz-Kampfhaenkel was made *Reichsförschungsrat* (Special Commissioner of Geographical Questions) and took over the scientific leadership of '*Dora*' in the western and eastern theatres. The new tasks included determining the best methods of camouflaging defensive works by means of foliage, investigating the practicability of the Russian swamp areas for tanks, as illustrated on Russian maps, and the production of new reliable maps.
24 The details of this aircraft remain sketchy at best. It is possible that it was a captured Spitfire provided under exactly the circumstances described, but perhaps more plausibly could have been one of the Hurricane fighters captured in North Africa during 1941 and 1942.
25 Recollections of a Brandenburger named Lohse, quoted in Spaeter, *Die Brandenburger*, p. 256.
26 Spaeter, *Die Brandenburger*, pp. 258–9.

27 Yasmin Opielok, 'Rommels Fahrer in Afrika entdeckt', *Welt Am Sonntag* (February 2001), Article 609680.
28 Lazarus had been a Colonial Office surveyor in peace-time and was tasked with continuing his geographical survey work alongside intelligence gathering for the Allied forces.

7 Rebuilding

1 US Department of State, German Foreign Ministry Records, Wipert von Blücher (German ambassador to Finland) telegram to Foreign Ministry, No 1204, 28 January 1941. Quoted in William L. Langer and Everett S. Gleason, *The Undeclared War, 1940–1941* (Harper and Brothers, New York, 1953), p. 831.
2 The six Finnish SS men were *Scharführer* Kaarlo Paananen, *Unterscharführer* Lauri Tolomen, *Unterscharführer* Lauri Kuosmanen, *Unterscharführer* Paavo Pasanen, *Rottenführer* Paavo Korhonen, *Sturmann* Lauri Kuittinen.
3 Bundesarchiv, RHG21-2/709, Bericht des Chefs Abwehr II, Nr. 1509/42 gKdos v. 26.6.1942.

8 'Case Blue'/Operation '*Braunschweig*': The 1942 Summer Offensive in the Soviet Union

1 *Der Prozess gegen die Hauptkriegsverbrecher vor dem Internationalen Militargerichtshof, Nürnberg*, 14. Nov. 1945–1. Okt. 1946 (Nürnberg: Internationales Militartribunal in Nürnberg, 1947–9), 7: 290.
2 The newspaper *Die Bewegung*, of the *Nationalsozialistischen Deutschen Studentenbundes* (National Socialist German Student Union) published this account of Grabert's death in January 1944, though some names differ from official records. The account was entitled 'A heroic figure from our ranks. Witness the best of Student Life.'
3 The NKVD played a significant role in the fighting in the Caucasus during 1942. As well as their normal security duties as part of Stalin's oppressive regime, large numbers were brought in to the region to quell Chechen uprisings and safeguard vital installations such as oil refineries and pipelines.
4 Spaeter, *Die Brandenburger*, pp. 209–11. The casualties that day in Dondukovskaya were: *Leutnant* Dr Hans Pils, *Feldwebel* Hermann Schink, *Unteroffizier* Felix Graf Schaffgotsch, *Obergefreiter* Faller, *Gefreiter* Jaki Maier, *Gefreiter* Hubert Binder, *Gefreiter* Walter Perntner, *Gefreiter* Sepp Taschler, *Sanitäts Gefreiter* Rudi Wittmann.
5 Spaeter, *Die Brandenburger*, p. 197. Report from 1st Company, south of Stalingrad.
6 FSB Public Relations Group for the Republic of North Ossetia-Alania, http://osetia.info/articles/460/
7 70 летие битвы за Кавказ.Фронтовой путь Бучукури А.М. http://nsportal.ru/ap/library/drugoe/2013/05/05/neugasimoe-plamya-pamyati

9 Regeneration, 1943

1. Kriegsheim, *Getarnt, Getäuscht und doch Getreu*, pp. 303–4. The term '08/15' references the machine gun MG 08/15 that had garnered a terrible reputation for malfunction. The term became commonly used slang by German soldiers when referring to anything that was wrong with the Army in general. Kriegsheim's interesting book is split into two sections. The first is a thinly fictionalised account of his war, the second an overview of the history of the Brandenburgers.
2. Lieutenant Colonel John S. Bird Jr., *North African Campaign: A Case Study* (US Army, US Army War College, April 1991), pp. 26–9.
3. Various secondary sources state that Arab agents later reported Slouka captured by French troops and shot.
4. Letter from Willi Clormann, 1958, quoted in Spaeter, *Die Brandenburger*, p. 262.
5. Alastair Mars, *Unbroken: The Story of a Submarine* (Frederick Muller, 1953), p. 202.
6. Mallory-Falconer was later transferred to Germany and held in captivity in the Sachsenhausen and Buchenwald concentration camps before being liberated at Tyrol in May 1945.
7. Haehling von Lanzenauer was buried in Baden Baden and posthumously promoted to *Generalmajor* on 20 April 1943.
8. National Archives, KV2/173.
9. German Naval Staff (Seekriegsleitung) War Diary, 26 May 1943.
10. Spaeter, *Die Brandenburger*, p. 308.
11. Notes on the Situation Reports and Discussions at Hitler's Headquarters from 12 August 1942 to 17 March 1943, taken by Helmuth Greiner. US Army Military Institute. Historical Division, Headquarters, United States Army Europe, Foreign Military Studies Branch.
12. Spaeter, *Die Brandenburger*, p. 238, quoted from a personal letter written and received in 1960 by Steidl. Max Horlbeck emerged later as the commander of 2nd Battalion, 435th Infantry Regiment and won the Knight's Cross on 12 August 1944. He was killed in action in Gotenhafen on 26 March 1945.
13. Höhne, *Canaris*, p. 497.
14. Gestapo chief SS *Gruppenführer* Heinrich Muller's report to Bormann of his interrogation of Pfuhlstein, 8 September 1944, p. 370. Quoted in Höhne, *Canaris*, p 575.
15. Christiansen, *Mit Hurra gegen die Wand*, pp. 9–10.
16. Ibid., p. 23.
17. Ibid., p. 48.
18. CIA Archives, SCI Weekly Operations Report, Wednesday, 10 January thru Wednesday, 17 January 1945. Nebel, Ludwig, Vol. 2_0008. Schwinn later went on to join Skorzeny's SS *Jagdverbände*.
19. Neugebauer was subsequently moved on from the Hôtel Continental, being replaced there by *Leutnant* Striefler during November 1943 while he transferred to the 1st Regiment in Greece.

20 Testimony from Gerhard Blank; Karl Heidinger, *Widerstand gegen die Wehrmacht* (Books on Demand, 2004), p. 120.
21 Testimony from Demetrio; ibid., p. 123.

10 Partisan War in the Balkans
1 Hoffman, *History of the German Resistance*, p. 276.
2 Alexander von Pfuhlstein, *Bericht über meine Erlebnisse in Verbindung mit Herrn Heinz*, 10 June 1953, quoted in Höhne, *Canaris*, p 497.
3 Hoffmann, *History of the German Resistance*, p. 617, n. 74.
4 Walter Lucas, 'In Greece, "Quislings" are pro-British', *Daily Express*, 11 October 1944.
5 Konrad Steidl's personal diary, quoted by Spaeter, *Die Brandenburger*, p. 288.
6 Ibid., pp. 289–90.
7 National Archives and Records Administration, T315 roll 2112, 'Brandenburg Division', Tatigkeitsbericht fur die Zeit vom 10.8.1943–10.9.1943, 2 Regiment Brandenburg, dated 11.9.1943.
8 Internal strife in the Chetniks and lack of activity against Axis forces led to the Allies ceasing all useful support by the end of 1943 and subsequently breaking all contact by spring 1944.
9 Four German divisions (1st *Gebirgs*, 118th Infantry, 369th Infantry and 7th SS *Gebirgsjäger* 'Prinz Eugen'), three Italian divisions (Taurinenze, Ferara and Venecija), one Bulgarian-German divisional battle group (comprised of the bulk of 61st and 63rd Bulgarian), Croatian 4th *Jäger* Brigade, elements of 4th Regiment 'Brandenburg' and a German motorised pioneer battalion. Two additional German divisions (117th and 373rd) were located in the area of Sarajevo and in the Neretva River valley and four Italian divisions (Emilija, Peruđa, Murđe and Marke) in the coastal area of the Bay of Kotor to the lower course of the Neretva.
10 Bundesarchiv, BA-MA, film MFB4/56160, file 34404/2, frames 407–09. *Befehlshaber der deutschen Truppen in Kroatien*, 12 January 1943. *Befehl für die Kampfführung im kroatischen Raum*.
11 http://www.friedrich-wilhelm-heinz.de/ p. 45.
12 Bundesarchiv, BA-MA RH 31 X/1, 11 September 1943, quoted by Mark Mazower, *Inside Hitler's Greece* (Yale University Press, 2001), p. 149.
13 National Archives and Records Administration, T315 roll 2112, 'Brandenburg Division'.
14 Christiansen, *Mit Hurra gegen die Wand*, p. 26.
15 Ibid., p. 29.
16 Höhne, *Canaris*, p. 575.
17 National Archives and Records Administration, T315 roll 2112, 'Brandenburg Division', p. 131.
18 OKW War Diary, 29 November 1943.
19 National Archives and Records Administration, T315 roll 2112, *Weihnachts und Neujahrsbefehl*, December 1943. The emphasis is in the original.

11 Metamorphosis, 1944-1945

1. Institut fur Zeitgeschichte Archiv, Bf v. Pfuhlstein o.D. betr. d. dt. Militäropposition (m. Anschr. von Witzleben v. 8.3.55) Bl 34-35.
2. Otto Skorzeny, *Skorzeny's Special Missions* (Greenhill Books, 2006), p. 36.
3. Lahousen transferred to the Eastern Front in January 1944 to take command of a combat unit. He was wounded on 19 July 1944 and would subsequently be overlooked during the purges that followed von Stauffenberg's assassination attempt.
4. Record of the interrogation of *Leutnant* von Gustedt, 18 January 1944, reproduced in Höhne, *Canaris*, p. 538.
5. *Geheime Kommandosache, Der Führer, Chef OKW, Nr. 1/44*, 12 February 1944.
6. Hansen was an 'absolute foe of the system and of Hitler' according to Lahousen (CIA Archives, Arnim Lahousen documatation). He had been appointed the head of Abwehr I after the departure of *Oberst* Hans Piekenbrock who had left to take command of 208th Infantry Division in 1943.
7. Kirchner provides an example of how unsuitable the Brandenburg Division had become for any counter-revolutionary purposes; he had previously been a Hitler Youth leader and remained a devout National Socialist.
8. Division Brandenburg, Abt.Ia Nr. 351/44 gKdos, 18.8.1944.
9. A small assault unit designated *Kampfgruppe Hettinger* had also previously captured the island fortress of Maddalena where it was believed Italian partisans had incarcerated Mussolini.
10. See Lawrence Paterson, *Weapons of Desperation: German Frogmen and Midget Submarines of World War II* (Chatham Publishing, 2006).
11. Erasmus received his Knight's Cross on the day that Kühlwein took command, for his service as Chief of Staff of the XXXXVI Panzer Corps in the southern Ukraine.
12. Division Brandenburg, Abt.Ic. 23/44 g.Kdos. Anlage 3a zu WFSt IOp (H) Südost. Nr. 005734/44 g.Kdos.
13. Division Brandenburg, Abt.Ic. 23/44 g.Kdos. Anlage 3a zu WFSt IOp (H) Südost. Nr. 005734/44 g.Kdos
14. Walther, lame in one leg after his injury, later joined Skorzeny's *Jagdverbände* as an *Obersturmbannführer*. He appears to have been involved in the provisioning of so-called 'Werewolf' supply dumps that Skorzeny was organising: the 'stay behind' resistance groups that never became properly established in war-weary European countries.
15. There are conflicting accounts that he was badly wounded and taken prisoner by the Red Army, though the lack of information about this version of events leads one to believe that it is unlikely.
16. National Archives, KV2/403, Otto Skorzeny file.
17. Höhne, *Canaris*, p. 570. Hansen was executed for his role in the 20 July plot.
18. Nuremberg, Germany, International Military Tribunal, 1945-04-10, Ref No. SAIC/2, 10 April 1945, Seventh Army Interrogation Centre, US Army; 20 July Putsch, held by Cornell University Law Library, Ithaca New York.

Bibliography

Articles

Becker, Dr Peter W., 'The Role of Synthetic Fuel in World War II Germany', *Air University Review* (July/August 1981), pp. 45–53.

Haller, Franz J., 'Südtirol Archiv, 1936-1938, Arthur Scheler', Arbeitskreis Visuelle Dokumentation Südtiroler Volkskultur e.V., 2014.

Hayward, Joel, 'Too Little, Too Late: An Analysis of Hitler's Failure in August 1942 to Damage Soviet Oil Production', *Journal of Military History*, Vol. 64, No. 3 (July 2000), pp. 769–94.

Kalyvas, Stathis N., 'Armed Collaboration in Greece, 1941–1944', *European Review of History—Revue européenne d'histoire*, Vol. 15, No. 2 (April 2008), pp. 129–42.

Mulligan, Timothy, 'The German Navy Evaluates Its Cryptographic Security, October 1941', *Military Affairs*, Vol. 49, No. 2 (1985), pp. 75–9. www.jstor.org/stable/1988402.

Opielok, Yasmin, 'Rommels Fahrer in Afrika entdeckt', *Welt Am Sonntag* (February 2001), Article 609680, digital edition.

Pike, David Wingeate, 'Franco and the Axis Stigma', *Journal of Contemporary History*, Vol. 17, No. 3 (1982), pp. 369–407.

Pradier, Christian, 'Attaque de la Brigade de Gendarmerie de Sainte-Foy-la-Grande le 7 décembre 1943', *Les Amis de Saint Foy et sa Région*, Vol. 2 (1995), pp. 3–15.

Shepherd, Ben, 'With the Devil in Titoland: A Wehrmacht Anti-Partisan Division in Bosnia-Herzegovina, 1943', *War in History* (1 January 2009), pp. 77–97.

Thomas, David, 'Foreign Armies East and German Military Intelligence in Russia 1941-45', *Journal of Contemporary History*, Vol. 22, No. 2 (1987), pp. 261–301.

Thomas, David, 'The Importance of Commando Operations in Modern Warfare 1939-82', *Journal of Contemporary History*, Vol. 18, No. 4 (1983), pp. 689–717.

Witzel, Dietrich F., 'Kommandoverbände der Abwehr II im Zweiten Weltkrieg', *Militärgeschichtliches Beiheft zur Europäischen Wehrkunde*, No. 5 (October 1990), pp. 6–20.

Books

Baraki, Matin, *Die Beziehungen zwischen Afghanistan und der Bundesrepublik Deutschland, 1945-1978* (Peter Lang GmbH, Internationaler Verlag Der Wissenschaften, 1996).

Bassett, Richard, *Hitler's Spy Chief* (Cassell Publishing, 2005).

Bębnik, Grzegorza, *Sokoły kapitana Ebbinghausa* (Libron, 2014).

Bibliography

Bird Jr., Lieutenant Colonel John S., *North African Campaign: A Case Study* (US Army, US Army War College, April 1991).
Birstein, Vadim, *Smersh: Stalin's Secret Weapon* (Biteback Publishing, 2013).
Bloomenkranz, Sol, *Charles Bedaux – Deciphering an Enigma* (iUniverse, July 2012).
Buzatu, Gheorghe, *A History of Romanian Oil Vol. II* (Mica Valahie Publishing, 2012).
Christiansen, Hinrich-Boy, *Mit Hurra gegen die Wand* (Books on Demand GmbH, 2010).
Cüppers, Martin, Mallmann, Klaus-Michael and Smith, Krista, *Nazi Palestine: The Plans for the Extermination of the Jews in Palestine* (Enigma Books, 2010).
De Giampietro, Sepp, *Das falsche Opfer?* (Leopold Stocker Verlag, 1984).
Dumitran, Daniel and Moga, Valer, *Economy and Society in Central and Eastern Europe: Territory, Population, Consumption* (Lit Verlag, 2013).
Eichholtz, Dietrich, *Krieg um Öl: Ein Erdölimperium als deutsches Kriegsziel (1938–1943)* (Leipziger Universitätsverlag, 2006).
Flachowsky, Sören and Stoecker, Holger, *Vom Amazonas an die Ostfront: Der Expeditionsreisende und Geograph Otto Schulz-Kampfhenkel (1910–1989)* (Böhlau-Verlag GmbH, 2011).
Garlef, Machael, *Deutschbalten, Weimarer Republik und Drittes Reich. Band 2* (Böhlau-Verlag GmbH, 2008).
Gavard, Guy, *Histoire d'Annemasse et des communes voisines: Les relations avec Genève de l'époque romaine à l'an 2000* (La Fontaine de Siloé, 2006).
Geerken, Horst, *Hitler's Asian Adventure* (Books on Demand, 2015).
Greentree, David, *Knight's Move: The Hunt for Marshal Tito 1944* (Osprey Publishing, 2012).
Grenkevich, Leonid D., *The Soviet Partisan Movement, 1941–1944: A Critical Historiographical Analysis* (Routledge, 1999).
Guard, J.S., *Improvise and Dare* (Book Guild, 1997).
Hassell, Ulrich von, *The Ulrich von Hassell Diaries* (Frontline Books, 2011).
Heidinger, Karl, *Widerstand gegen die Wehrmacht* (Books on Demand, 2004).
Hnilicka, Kar Dr, *Das Ende Auf Dem Balkan 1944/45* (Musterschmidt Verlag, 1970).
Höhne, Heinz, *Canaris, Hitler's Master Spy* (Cooper Square Press, 1999).
Hoffmann, Peter, *History of the German Resistance, 1933–1945* (McGill-Queen's University Press, 1996).
Horne, Charles F. (ed.), *Source Records of the Great War, Vol. II* (National Alumni, 1923).
Houlihan, Thomas L., *Kriegsprache* (Maps at War, 2009).
Jung, Michael, *Sabotage Unter Wasser* (Mittler Verlag, 2004).
Kahn, David, *Hitler's Spies* (Da Capo Press, 1978).
Kaltenegger, Roland, *Oberst Franz Pfeiffer* (Flechsig Verlag, 2014).
Kelly, Saul, *The Hunt for Zerzura* (John Murray Publishers, 2003).
Kohlhaas, Wilhelm, *Hitler-Abenteuer im Irak* (Verlag Herder, 1989).
Kriegsheim, Herbert, *Getarnt, Getäuscht und doch Getrau; Die geheimnisvollen 'Brandenburger'* (Bernard & Graefe Verlag, 1959).

Kurowski, Franz, *Deutsche Kommandotrupps, Band I & II* (Motorbuch Verlag, 2003/4).
Langer, William L. and Gleason, S. Everett, *The Undeclared War, 1940–1941* (Harper and Brothers, New York, 1953).
Lefevre, Eric, *Brandenburg Division* (Histoire & Collections, 2000).
Lucas, James, *Kommando* (Cassell Publishing, 1998).
Lynch, Tim, *Silent Skies: Gliders at War 1939–1945* (Casemate Publishing, 2008).
Mars, Alastair, *Unbroken: The Story of a Submarine* (Frederick Muller, 1953).
Marshall, Alex, *The Caucasus Under Soviet Rule* (Routledge, 2010).
Mazower, Mark, *Inside Hitler's Greece* (Yale University Press, 2001).
Neitzel, Sönke, *Tapping Hitler's Generals* (Frontline Books, 2007).
O'Reilly, Terence, *Hitler's Irishmen* (The Mercier Press Ltd, 2008).
O'Sullivan, Adrian, *Nazi Secret Warfare in Occupied Persia (Iran)* (Palgrave Macmillan, 2014).
Paterson, Lawrence, *Weapons of Desperation: German Frogmen and Midget Submarines of World War II* (Chatham Publishing, 2006).
Pigoreau, Olivier, *Sanglante Randonnée* (Histoire & Collections, 2013).
Roberts, Jeffery J., *The Origins of Conflict in Afghanistan* (Praeger, 2003).
Rossolinski-Liebe, Grzegorz, *Stepan Bandera: The Life and Afterlife of a Ukrainian Nationalist: Fascism, Genocide and Cult* (Ibidem-Verlag, 2014).
Sachs, Michael, *Leben und Sterben des Dr med. Manfred Oberdörffer* (Alcorde Verlag, 2007).
Samuel, Wolfgang W.E., *The War of Our Childhood: Memories of World War II* (University Press of Mississippi, 2002).
Schulze-Holthus, Bernhardt, *Daybreak in Iran* (Staples Press, 1954).
Skorzeny, Otto, *Skorzeny's Special Missions* (Greenhill Books, 2006).
Spaeter, Helmuth, *Die Brandenburger* (Karl-Heinz Dissberger, 1991).
Stewart, Jules, *The Kaiser's Mission to Kabul: A Secret Expedition to Afghanistan in World War I* (I.B.Tauris, 2014).
Tikkanen, Pentti H., *Kanoottisissit* (Arvi A. Karisto Osakeyhtiö, 1971).
Toye, Hugh, *The Springing Tiger: A Study of the Indian National Army and Netaji Subhas Chandra Bose* (Cassell, 1959).
Trigg, Jonathan, *Hitler's Jihadis: Muslim Volunteers of the Waffen SS* (The History Press, 2012).
Urner, Klaus, *Let's Swallow Switzerland: Hitler's Plans Against the Swiss Confederation* (Lexington Books, 2001).
Verhoeyen, Etienne, *Spionnen aan de achterdeur: de Duitse Abwehr in België, 1936–1945* (Governance of Security Research report series, Vol. 4), Maklu Uitgevers; Auflage, 2011.
Voute, Dr Peter, *Only a Free Man* (The Lightning Tree, 1982).
Warmbrunn, Werner, *The Dutch Under German Occupation 1940–1945* (Stanford University Press, 1963).
Wilkinson, Peter and Astley, Joan, *Gubbins & SOE* (Pen & Sword, 2010).
Young, Desmond, *Rommel: The Desert Fox* (Collins Publishing, 1950).

Index

Brandenburger Units
1. Baulehr Kompanie z.b.V. (1939), 19

Baulehr Kompanie z.b.V.800 (1939), 1, 19, 21, 22

Baulehr-Bataillon z.b.V.800 (1940), 21, 23, 47, 31, 32, 75, 123
   1st Baulehr Kompanie z.b.V., 23, 26, 73
   2nd Baulehr Kompanie z.b.V., 23, 26, 30
   3rd Baulehr Kompanie z.b.V., 23, 27, 30, 50, 57
   4th Baulehr Kompanie z.b.V., 27, 30, 43

Lehrregiment 'Brandenburg' z.b.V. 800 (1940–2)
   1st Battalion, 56, 57, 59, 62, 68, 70, 89, 90, 103, 107, 112, 159, 179, 181
      1st Company, 62, 70, 71, 89, 90, 159, 162, 177, 178, 181
      2nd Company, 70, 89, 91, 103, 109, 110, 112, 122, 159, 161, 162, 174, 179, 181, 206
      3rd Company, 70, 89, 91, 103–5, 122, 159, 162, 166, 178, 206, 207
      4th Company, 28, 70, 71, 89, 91, 103, 105, 117, 206
      4th (Light) *Fallschirmjäger* Company, 159, 174, 181
   2nd Battalion, 56, 57, 62, 70, 75, 78, 79, 80, 84, 89, 91, 102, 160, 178, 179, 180
      5th Company, 70, 79, 80, 81, 89, 91, 134, 155, 160, 165, 171, 178, 179, 181, 207
      6th Company, 70, 79, 84, 89, 91, 102, 103, 145, 146, 147, 160
      7th Company, 70, 80, 84, 89, 91, 98, 160, 165, 170
      8th Company, 24, 54, 70, 71, 78, 80, 82, 83, 84, 89, 91, 98, 160, 163, 164, 165, 169, 170, 178, 179, 181, 207
   3rd Battalion, 57, 60, 62, 68, 70, 80, 89, 91, 96, 160, 181, 190
      9th Company, 70, 89, 145, 147, 160, 181, 190
      10th Company, 59, 60, 70, 90, 93, 160, 176, 179, 181
      11th Company, 60, 70, 90, 114, 160, 174, 181
      12th Company, 60, 71, 90, 91, 96, 97, 160, 181
   Regimental Units
      13th (Tropical) Company, 71, 90, 122, 123, 124, 126, 130, 138, 145, 160, 202, 204
      14th (Replacement) Company, 71, 80, 90
      15th (Light) Company, 90, 152, 153, 160, 205
      16th (*Jäger*) Company, 71, 90, 148, 238
      17th (Special) Company, 71, 80, 90; renamed 1st Company: 107
   Fallschirmjäger Platoon, 71, 89, 90, 91, 101, 102
   Fallschirmjäger Battalion, 130, 210, 263, 268, 275, 277, 278, 284
   Funktruppe Schildkröte, 134, 135
   Interpreter Company, 71

Lehrregiment 'Brandenburg' z.b.V. 800
(1940–2) (*continued*)
Kampfgruppe Horlbeck (1942–3), 181, 207
Kampfgruppe Walther (1942–3), 181, 206, 207
Kampfgruppe Weithoener (1943), 207
Küstenjäger Abteilung z.b.V. 800 'Brandenburg', 144, 157, 160, 196, 202, 203, 211, 234, 238–40, 242, 243, 245, 246, 248, 267, 284
Lehr und Ausbildungskompanie, 71
Light Engineer Company (*Leichte Pionierkompanie*), 143, 156, 157, 160, 174, 176, 181
Meeresjäger Abteilung 'Brandenburg', 144, 157, 259
Motorcycle Platoon, 71
Nachtigall Battalion, 88–91, 103, 105–8
North Platoon (1940), 35–7, 56
Signals Company, 71
'Trommsdorf' Company, 71, 149, 150, 160
Tropical Abteilung von Koenen, 189, 191, 200
V-Leute Company, 71, 90; renamed *V-Abteilung*, 107, 189
West Platoon (1940), 28–30, 38, 39

Sonderverbänd 800 'Brandenburg'
(1943)
Verband 801, 189, 190, 207, 213
1st Battalion, 207, 213
Verband 802, 189, 204
Verband 803, 189
Verband 804, 189, 205
14th Einheit 205
Verband 805, 189

Brandenburg Division (1943–4)
1st *Jäger* Regiment 'Brandenburg', 209, 213, 230, 239, 241, 245, 249, 251, 262, 265, 268, 270, 271, 273, 278
1st Battalion, 209, 213, 214, 239, 245, 249, 262, 265, 278
2nd Company, 274
3rd Company, 214, 274
4th (Light) Company, 214
2nd Battalion, 209, 234, 239, 249, 262, 265, 278
3rd Battalion, 209, 239, 245, 247, 251, 262, 265, 273
2nd Regiment 'Brandenburg', 209, 230, 239, 240, 241, 249, 251, 253, 262
1st Battalion, 209, 232, 233, 239, 253, 254, 262, 278
2nd Battalion, 209, 239, 262
3rd Battalion, 209, 233, 239, 254, 262
3rd Regiment 'Brandenburg', 180, 209, 213, 249–51, 262, 265, 275, 278, 282
1st Battalion, 209, 213–18, 249–51, 262
2nd Company, 213, 215
4th Company, 215
2nd Battalion, 209, 218, 219, 221, 250, 263, 265, 267, 275, 278
5th Company, 219
6th Company, 219
7th Company, 219
8th Company, 180, 209, 219, 220, 223, 275, 276
3rd Battalion, 209, 214, 216–18, 250, 263
4th Regiment 'Brandenburg', 210, 229, 234, 236, 237, 239, 249, 251, 263, 269, 270, 277
1st Battalion, 210, 230, 234, 236, 239, 249, 251, 263
2nd Battalion, 210, 230, 239, 249, 263
3rd Battalion, 210, 230, 249, 263, 277
14th Company, 210
15th (Light) *Fallschirmjäger* Company, 210, 239, 242–6, 251, 263
16th (Light) Company, 263, 267
Einheit Kirchner, 260, 261
Fallschirmjäger Battalion 'Brandenburg', 130, 210, 263, 268, 275, 277, 278, 284
Kampfgruppe Heinz (1943), 234, 237

Index

Kampfgruppe Hettinger (1944), 267
Kampfgruppe Kuhlmann, 242
Kampfgruppe Wagner (1943), 216
Küstenjäger Battalion, 210, 211, 234, 238, 239, 240, 242, 243, 245–8, 251, 263, 267, 275, 276, 279, 284–6
Küstenjäger Kompanie Rhodos, 248
Legionärbataillon 'Alexander', 210, 217, 218, 251, 263
Lehrregiment 'Brandenburg', 210, 263, 264
Lehrregiment 'Kurfürst', 208, 210
Nachrictenabteilung (Signals Battalion), 210, 263
Verbänd Wildschütz, 261–3, 265, 269–71

Brandenburg *Streifkorps* established (1944), 275, 276

Related Units
502nd SS *Jagdverbänd*, 189, 258, 264, 270, 276, 279–81
Aussenstelle 'Wido', 111, 112, 125, 131, 134, 137
Bataillon z.b.V. 100, 47–8
Deutsche Kompanie (1939), 12, 14, 17, 18, 19, 22, 23, 73
Ebbinghaus Organisation (1939), 12–14, 17–19, 24
Hercules Group (Belgian Rexists), 52, 58
Kampfgruppe Hecker, 126, 127
Kampforganisation Jablunka (1939), 16
KODAT (Kommando Deutsch-Arabischer Truppen), 65, 197–9
Roland Battalion, 88, 108
Sonderstab Hollmann, 52, 60, 61
Sonderkommando Blaich, 141
Sonderkommando Dora 137, 138
Sonderverbänd Bergmann 108, 146, 161
Sonderverbänd Felmy 90, 114, 115, 197, 198, 207
SS Fallschirmjäger Battalion 500, 271, 273

SS Fallschirmjäger Battalion 600, 281, 284
SS Sondereinsatzverbände z.b.V. 'Oranienburg', 157
SS Sonderlehrgang z.b.V. 'Friedenthal', 188
SS Sonderlehrgang z.b.V. 'Oranienburg', 187, 188
Tamara I and II, 146

Abshagen, Hans-Joachim Wolfgang, 11, 12
Almásy, Count László, 112, 129–36
Aretz (*Oberleutnant*) 70, 90, 92
Auch, Alexander, 210, 212, 217, 263, 264, 276
Aulock, Hubertus von, 65

Babuke, Fritz, 45, 71, 80, 90, 107, 159, 162, 177, 214
Bachmann, Peter, 177
Bamler, Rudolf, 7
Bandera, Stepan, 87, 88, 105, 108
Bansen, Hans-Gerhard, 145–7, 160, 209, 218, 219, 221, 222, 239, 263, 265, 266, 267, 282
Bazing, Richard, 80, 81
Benesch, Fritz, 35, 36, 90, 148, 149, 205, 238, 239, 261, 262, 271, 272, 276, 280
Berndt (*Oberleutnant*), 90
Bisping, Ferdinand, 123, 143
Brandt, Fred, 119–21
Bredow, Ferdinand von, 6, 7, 15
Brückner, Erich von, 278, 282
Brügmann, Hans, 252
Bruhn, Fritz, 244
Buchler (*Hauptmann*), 78–80, 82

Canaris, Wilhelm, 3–11, 13–15, 17, 19, 21, 24, 30, 37, 58, 60, 63, 64–70, 75, 88, 101, 107–10, 112, 116, 131, 138, 145, 155, 184–6, 197, 201, 205, 208, 229, 230, 237, 250, 251, 256–60, 283

Christiansen, Hinrich-Boy, 212, 213, 214, 218
Clissmann, Helmut, 60, 188
Clormann, Willi, 193, 194

Deininger, Friedrich, 36
Demetrio, Helmut, 221, 222, 224–6, 276, 282
Dlab (*Oberleutnant*), 27, 89, 91
Dowe, Gerhard, 271
Drenger, Gert, 100

Ebbinghaus, Ernst, 13
Eichhorn, Reinhold, 126
Eickeren, Ernst von, 189
Eltester (*Hauptmann*), 71, 210, 263
Eppler, Johann, 130–6

Fabian (*Hauptmann*), 23, 26, 70
Felmy, Hellmuth, 114, 115, 197–9, 206, 206
Fendt (*Oberleutnant*), 70, 90, 114
Fischer (*Leutnant*), 220, 221
Fölkersam, Adrian von, 159, 166–70, 241, 258, 270, 280, 281, 283
Froboese, Gustav, 209, 245, 247, 248

Gerlach, Hans, 181, 210, 249, 262, 263, 278, 281
Giampietro, Sepp De, 24, 71
Grabert, Siegfried, 12, 14, 17, 19, 20, 22–4, 30, 39–41, 51–4, 59, 70, 71, 82–4, 91, 100, 145, 160, 163–4
Grawert (*Hauptmann*), 209, 214, 216, 264
Griesheim, Witilo von, 112
Groscurth, Helmuth, 3, 7, 10

Haalen, Martin van, 44
Hardy, Peter, 49
Hartmann, Dr Wolf-Justin, 70, 89, 103, 107, 109, 110, 210, 230
Hecker, Hermann-Hans, 126
Heinz, Friedrich Wilhelm, 15, 66–8, 70, 87, 89–91, 103, 105–8, 112, 189, 201, 210, 229, 230, 232–7, 250, 251, 282, 283

Herzner, Dr Hans-Albrecht, 15–17, 64, 65, 67, 88, 89, 108
Hettinger, Otto, 81, 151, 152, 205, 210, 267
Heydrich, Reinhard, 5–8, 11, 21, 116, 186
Hippel, Theodor von, 2, 3, 10–13, 19, 20–5; 27, 28, 31, 35, 55, 57, 59, 60, 63–5, 67, 111, 199
Hoesch, Ulrich Otto, 130
Hollmann, Wilhelm, 52, 60, 61, 64, 188, 189, 210, 230, 234, 249, 263, 276
Horlbeck, Max, 143, 156, 160, 175, 176, 181, 207
Hugo, Christoph von, 237, 249, 263
Hüller, Dr Oskar, 163
Hummel, Friedrich, 143, 157, 259
Hütten (*Oberleutnant*), 22, 30, 49, 160, 174

Jacobi, Franz, 70, 89, 91, 160, 181, 189, 209, 214, 262, 282
Jacobi, Dr Paul, 70, 78, 81, 84, 89, 91, 160, 180
Janowski, Werner Alfred, 53, 54, 59
Johannes, Wilhelm, 12, 51, 52, 63, 70
John, Werner, 70, 89, 91, 104, 105, 159, 162, 207, 209, 262, 265, 278

Kaltenbrunner, Ernst, 186, 258, 268, 284
Kewisch, Hubert, 32, 35, 37, 56, 62–5
Kirchner, Hans-Jürgen, 123
Kirchner, Wolfram, 260, 261, 265, 270, 271, 281
Knaak, Hans-Wolfram, 15, 89, 91, 98–100
Kniesche, Dr Gottfried, 19, 20, 23, 26, 70, 73, 79, 80, 145, 147, 160
Kobylinski, Wolfgang von, 189, 209
Koenen, Friedrich von, 90, 122–7, 129, 130, 133, 138, 142, 144, 145, 160, 181, 189–93, 199, 200, 202, 204, 210, 211, 230, 249, 263, 277, 284
Kohlhaas, Wilhelm, 113, 116
Kohlmeyer, Karl, 92, 96, 215
König, Ernst Gerhard, 92, 93
Koudele, Franz, 168, 169
Krautzberger, Franz, 123

Index

Kriegisch, Walter, 75
Kriegsheim, Herbert, 92–6, 143, 156, 175, 185, 209, 211, 214–16, 234, 277
Kuhlmann, Armin, 143, 144, 190, 191, 203, 240, 242, 243
Kühlwein, Friedrich, 269, 274–6, 282
Kürschner, Hermann, 28–30, 38, 39, 70, 89, 159, 174, 181
Kutschke (*Oberleutnant*), 20, 23, 70, 80, 82

Lahousen, Erwin von, 3, 8–12, 31, 57, 61, 63–6, 68, 70, 87, 101, 108, 143, 146, 154, 161, 184, 185, 258
Lanzenauer, Paul Haehling von, 65, 70, 110, 201
Lau, Werner, 155, 178, 210, 249, 263
Lawicki, Manfred, 128
Leipzig, Conrad von, 123, 125, 138–42, 144, 203, 210, 211, 263, 267
Lohmann, Walter, 5, 6
Ludewig, Rudolf, 203
Lütke, Hermann, 28, 71, 89, 91, 101, 102

Mark, Wladimir, 253
Marwitz, Rolf von der, 131, 132
Meissner (*Oberleutnant*), 70, 79, 84, 89, 91, 102, 145
Mertens, Rudolf, 278
Mohler (*Leutnant*), 83, 84
Müller, Otto, 142

Neugebauer, Helmut, 179

Oberdörffer, Manfred, 119–21
Oberländer, Theodor, 88, 108, 161
Oesterwitz, Karl-Heinz, 160, 170, 209, 233, 262, 282
Operations:
  Achse (1943), 220, 221, 237–40
  Baumblüte (1944), 265
  Beowulf I (1941), 148
  Beowulf II (1941), 145, 148
  Bora (1944), 265
  Case Black (1943), 235–7, 251
  Case Blue (1942), 156, 158–9, 161, 163, 165, 167, 169, 171, 173, 175, 177, 179, 181–3, 207
  Case White (1943), 235
  Case Yellow (1940), 22, 28, 30, 31, 33, 35, 37–55
  Denkzettel (1944), 265
  Dora (1942), 138–41
  Eisbär (1943), 242
  Herkules, 128, 143, 144
  Kugelblitz (1943), 252–4, 261
  Leopard (1943), 244
  Lutto (1942), 151
  Maibaum (1944), 269
  Margarethe (1944), 267
  Morgenrot (1940), 38–50
  Neptun (1943), 206
  Rösselsprung (1944), 271–2
  Rübezahl (1944), 278
  Schneesturm (1943), 254
  Seagull (1940), 60, 188
  Sportverein Wiking (1940), 23
  Taifun (1941), 147
  Taifun (1943), 246, 248
  Trojan Horse (1944), 267
  Verrat (1943), 241
  Weserübung (1940), 34–7
  Zeppelin (1942), 187
Oschatz (*Oberleutnant*), 210, 242, 243–5
Oster, Hans, 7, 8, 15, 25, 37, 40, 58, 64, 66–8, 73, 184, 201, 229, 230, 251, 256, 257, 283

Paananen, Kaarlo, 152
Pfannenstiels (*Leutnant*), 89
Pfeiffer, Franz, 209, 230, 232, 233, 241, 249, 253, 254, 262, 278
Pfuhlstein, Alexander von, 159, 201, 202, 207–9, 211, 217, 229, 230, 237, 241, 245, 249–52, 254, 256, 257, 259, 261, 262, 264, 267–9, 282–4
Piekenbrock, Hans, 7, 69
Pils, Dr Hans, 155, 171, 172
Pinkert, Gerhard, 70, 159, 161, 162, 180, 209, 216, 234, 249, 262

Pinkert, Helmut, 56, 70, 80, 159, 170, 209, 262, 267, 284
Plitt, Hans, 190, 209, 213, 214, 234
Prochaska, Ernst, 165, 169, 170

Regenwurmlager, 56, 71, 107, 118, 189, 213, 229
Reichert, Eric, 102
Reiger, Bruno, 60, 188
Renner, Karl, 170, 181, 209, 233, 262
Ritter, Nikolaus, 129, 130
Ronte (*Oberleutnant*), 160, 176
Rudloff, Hans-Jürgen, 21–3, 27, 30, 48–50, 57–62, 68, 69, 197

Sandstede, Heinrich Gerd, 130–6
Schäder (*Oberleutnant*), 71, 90, 92, 96, 97, 160
Schatz, Oskar, 110, 174
Schellenberg, Walter, 184, 186–8, 258, 283
Schoeler (*Oberleutnant*) 70
Schweim, Ernst, 128
Schwinn, Hans, 219–21, 226, 227
Seeliger, Heinrich, 20, 87, 91
Seuberlich, Hans-Erich, 155, 276
Skorzeny, Otto, 157, 188, 189, 219, 237, 258, 264, 270, 271, 276, 279–82, 284
Sölder, Alfred, 151, 153
Sorgenfrey, Robert, 34
Späth, Waldemar, 274
Steffans, Hans von, 112, 131, 132
Steidl, Konrad, 155, 171, 180, 207, 232, 233, 253, 254, 262
Stöhr, Hermann, 30, 43
Stöhr, Leo, 75
Stolze, Erwin, 66, 63, 64, 66

Striefler (*Oberleutnant*), 220, 221
Süss, Gustl, 75

Tanzer, Johann, 49
Träger (*Hauptmann*), 220, 221, 223, 224, 226, 275, 276
Trommsdorf (*Leutnant*), 150, 151

U-200, 252
U-331, 124, 125

Vatter, Fritz, 71, 89, 90
Verbeek, Heinrich, 12, 19, 20, 75
Vinck, Fernand de, 40
Vosswinkel, Herbert, 128

Wagner, Dr Kurt, 156, 175, 202, 203
Walther, Uwe-Wilhelm, 27, 28, 30, 43–5, 56, 70, 91, 98, 159, 161, 177, 181, 189, 206, 207, 209, 230, 234, 241, 245, 248, 249, 162, 265, 271, 273, 274, 278, 280
Wandrey, Max, 209, 248, 262, 265, 278
Wasserfall (*Hauptmann*), 216, 263
Weber, Dr Helmut, 164
Weber, Waldemar, 131, 132, 134–6
Weithoener, Dieter, 105, 207, 209, 210, 233, 254, 263, 268, 278
Werner, Alfred Ernst, 99–101
Wilscher, Odo, 130
Witzel, Dietrich von, 24, 30, 46, 117, 119, 121
Wodjerek, Franz, 194
Wrede, Karl Karolus von, 274
Wülberg (*Oberleutnant*), 70

Zülch, Karl Fürchtegott, 35, 56, 70, 155, 160, 171–3